Modernism

Palgrave Sourcebooks

Series Editor: Steven Matthews

Published
Simon Bainbridge: **Romanticism**
Steven Matthews: **Modernism**

Forthcoming
Carolyn Collette and Harold Garrett-Goodyear: **Medieval Literature**
Lena Cowen Orlin: **The Renaissance**
John Plunket, Ana Vadillo, Regenia Gagnier, Angelique Richardson, Rick Rylance
    and Paul Young: **Victorian Literature**
Nigel Wood: **The 'Long' Eighteenth Century**

Palgrave Sourcebooks

ISBN 978–1–4039–4277–7 hardback
ISBN 978–1–4039–4278–4 paperback

You can receive further titles in this series as they are published by placing a standing
order. Please contact your bookseller or, in the case of difficulty, write to us at the address
below with your name and address, the title of the series, and the ISBN quoted above.

Customer Services Department, Palgave Ltd.
Houndmills, Basingstoke, Hampshire, RG21 6XS, England

Modernism

A Sourcebook

Edited by Steven Matthews

First published 2008 by
PALGRAVE MACMILLAN
Houndmills, Basingstoke, Hampshire RG21 6XS and
175 Fifth Avenue, New York, N.Y. 10010
Companies and representatives throughout the world

PALGRAVE MACMILLAN is the global academic imprint of the Palgrave
Macmillan division of St. Martin's Press, LLC and of Palgrave Macmillan Ltd.
Macmillan® is a registered trademark in the United States, United Kingdom
and other countries. Palgrave is a registered trademark in the European
Union and other countries.

ISBN-13: 978-1-4039-9829-3   hardback
ISBN-10: 1-4039-9829-9   hardback
ISBN-13: 978-1-4039-9830-9   paperback
ISBN-10: 1-4039-9830-2   paperback

This book is printed on paper suitable for recycling and made from fully
managed and sustained forest sources. Logging, pulping and manufacturing
processes are expected to conform to the environmental regulations of the
country of origin.

A catalogue record for this book is available from the British Library.

A catalog record for this book is available from the Library of Congress.

10 9 8 7 6 5 4 3 2 1
17 16 15 14 13 12 11 10 09 08

Printed and bound in China

Short Contents

For Elleke, Thomas and Sam

Detailed Contents

List of Illustrations

Acknowledgements

I am grateful to Dr Michèle Perry, who aided research (for all too brief a period) on this volume in its first few months. I am also grateful to Professor Susan McRae and Oxford Brookes University, who provided monies for Dr Perry's post, and for a subsequent sabbatical in which the project was completed. I have enjoyed and learnt much from my conversations about modernism with graduate students, including Helen Farish, Alex Goody, Matthew Feldman and Catherine Morley; I have hugely benefited from my teaching undergraduate classes in the area at the universities of York, Leeds and Oxford Brookes. This book, as always, is for Elleke, Thomas and Sam.

The editor and publisher wish to thank the following for permission to use copyright material:

The Albert Einstein Archives, for the extract from Albert Einstein, *The Meaning of Relativity* (1921), reprinted by permission of the Albert Einstein Archives, the Hebrew University of Jerusalem, Israel.

Cambridge University Press, for the extract from Émile Durkheim, *Émile Durkheim: Selected Writings*, ed. Anthony Giddens (1972), and for the extract from Arthur S. Eddington, *Space, Time and Gravitation* (1920);

The Edward Gordon Craig Estate, for the extract from Edward Gordon Craig, 'The First Dialogue';

Nicholas Deakin, for the extracts from Havelock Ellis, *The Erotic Rights of Women* and *The Objects of Marriage* (1918);

Sigmund Freud Copyrights/Paterson Marsh Ltd, for the extract from Sigmund Freud, *The Interpretation of Dreams*;

HarperCollins Publishers, for the extract from *John Dewey: The Essential Writings*, edited by David Sidorsky (1977);

Oxford University Press, for the extract from W. E. B. Du Bois, *The Souls of Black Folk*, edited by B. H. Edwards (2007), and the extract from A. N. Whitehead, *An Introduction to Mathematics* (1968);

Palgrave Macmillan, for the extract from John Maynard Keynes, *The Economic Consequences of the Peace* (1919), and the extract from J. G. Frazer, *The Golden Bough*;

Philadelphia Museum of Art, for the image of *Nude Descending a Staircase* by Marcel Duchamp (1912);

Brian Read, for extracts from Arthur Symons, *The Symbolist Movement in Literature*, and 'The Music Hall';

Russell & Volkening, Inc., as agents for the author, for extracts from 'I Am Here To-day: Charlie Chaplin' and 'Toujours Jazz' from Gilbert Seldes, *The 7 Lively Arts*, copyright © 1924 by Gilbert Seldes, copyright renewed 1952 by Gilbert Seldes;

Tate Images, for the image of *Red Stone Dancer* by Henri Gaudier-Brzeska, © Tate, London 2007;

Taylor & Francis Books UK, for the extract from Bertrand Russell, *The ABC of Relativity*, © Taylor & Francis and the Bertrand Russell Peace Foundation Ltd;

University of Arkansas Special Collections Department, for the extract from John Gould Fletcher, 'Vers Libre and Advertisements', from *The Little Review*, vol. II, no. 2 (April 1915).

Every effort has been made to trace the copyright holders, but if any have been inadvertently overlooked, the editor and publisher will be pleased to make the necessary arrangements at the first opportunity.

Series Editor's Preface

For at least twenty-five years, questions about the relation between literature and the historical period in which it was created have formed the central focus and methodology of critics. From the early 1980s, crucially, a range of literary scholars have sought to explore and define the parallels and differences between the representational language deployed in creative texts, and uses of similar rhetorical strategies in other contemporary cultural sources, such as journals, court documents, diaries and religious tracts. This kind of historicist reconsideration of literature has had far-reaching consequences in the academy and beyond, and the drive better to understand the dialogue established between texts and their originating period has brought new dynamism to ideas of context and contextualization.

The *Sourcebooks* series aims to provide a comprehensive and suggestive selection of original cultural sources for each of the major artistic moments from the medieval period onward. Edited by internationally renowned British and American experts in their chosen area, each volume presents within suitable subsections a panoply of materials relating to everything from historical background, to gender, philosophy, science and religion, which will be of use both to students and scholars seeking to contextualize creative work in any given period. It has been a particular ambition of the series to put back into circulation ephemeral original texts from magazines, newspapers, and even private sources, in order to offer a more representative sense of any one period's cultural debates and processes. Literature remains the primary focus of the volumes, but each contains documents relating to the broader artistic and cultural context which will be of interest and use to everyone working in the humanities area.

Each volume contains an informative general Introduction giving an overview of pertinent historical and cultural movements and pressures of its time. Each document is edited to a high scholarly standard through the use of headnotes and other supportive apparatus, in order to make the document accessible for further study. This apparatus is not prescriptive in determining the relation between any one literary text and these background resources, although each volume contains instances where documents directly alluded to by major writers are specifically excerpted. Generally, however, the series seeks to further historicist study and research by making available important or intriguing materials which might act to instigate further thought and reflection, so aiding to determine a more substantial picture of any literary work's moment of coming into being.

Steven Matthews

Timeline

1892 Independent Labour Party formed in UK

1895 Marconi invents 'wireless' technology; cinematograph also invented

1897 Queen Victoria's Diamond Jubilee

1899 Anglo-Boer War begins

1901 Queen Victoria dies

1902 Anglo-Boer War ends

1903 Emmeline Pankhurst founds Women's Social and Political Union

1905 Albert Einstein proposes theory of relativity

1906 British Liberal Party wins election and begins programme of social and class reform

1908 Protests for women's rights in London

1910 King Edward VII dies; George V becomes King; Union of South Africa

1911 National Insurance Act, UK. Beginning of several years of industrial unrest (miners and shipworkers) UK

1912 Sinking of the *Titanic*. Start of suffragette window-breaking campaign. First Balkan War. Woodrow Wilson elected President of US

1913 London Psychoanalytical Society founded. Second Balkan War

1914 First World War breaks out (August). Britain and France occupy German colonies in West Africa.

1915 Zeppelins attack London. Wartime coalition government formed in UK. Italy enters the war. Gallipoli

1916 Universal Conscription introduced in the UK. Battles of Verdun and the Somme. Lloyd George becomes Prime Minister. Easter Rising in Ireland (April)

1917 USA enters the war. Russian Revolution

1918 Armistice brings the end of the war (11 November). Women granted limited voting rights in UK

1919 Treaty of Versailles allocates reparations to the aggressor parties in the War. Non-cooperation protests led by Gandhi in India; Amritsar massacre. Ernest Rutherford splits the atom

1920 League of Nations created.

US Constitution amended to give women the vote.
Palestine becomes British mandate.
Prohibition of alcohol sale begins in US

1921   Irish Free State founded

1922   Mussolini comes to power in Italy

1924   Lenin, Russian revolutionary leader, dies.

First (minority) Labour government in the UK elected

1926   General Strike in UK.
John Logie Baird invents television

1928   Vote given to women over 21 in UK for the first time

1929   Wall Street Crash, New York

1930   Beginning of widespread civil disobedience in India

Chronological List of Major Literary Texts

The numbers given after some of the entries in this chronology indicate those extracts in this Sourcebook which might be particularly helpful in contextualizing a particular modernist text. The first number given in the brackets denotes the section of the Sourcebook indicated, the second number given denotes the extract (so '(2.7)' indicates Section Two, Extract 7 – the passages from John Dewey's *Reconstruction in Philosophy*).

NB: These indications are meant to be merely suggestions: the work of contextualizing a literary text is complex, and many potential sources of influence upon any one piece of text are likely to be in play at once. Extracts in this volume not included here nonetheless provide vital background context regarding ideas and issues in the period. Likewise, texts which receive no numerical indication pointing to a specific extract often partly derive from several of the ideas contained in the various sections of this Sourcebook.

1910   E. M. Forster, *Howard's End* (novel) (2.4)
       Henry James, *The Finer Grain* (stories)
       Ezra Pound, *The Spirit of Romance* (essays)
       W.B. Yeats, *The Green Helmet and other poems*

1911   Joseph Conrad, *Under Western Eyes* (novel)
       D. H. Lawrence, *The White Peacock* (novel)
       Katherine Mansfield, *In a German Pension* (stories)

1912   Joseph Conrad, *'Twixt Land and Sea* (stories)
       T. E. Hulme, *The Complete Poetical Works* (5.4)
       D. H. Lawrence, *The Trepasser* (novel) (5.1)
       Ezra Pound, *Ripostes* (poetry) (5.5)

1913   Ford Madox Ford, *Collected Poems*
       D. H. Lawrence, *Sons and Lovers* (novel) (2.4)
       Leonard Woolf, *The Village in the Jungle* (novel) (9.1, 9.2)

1914   Joseph Conrad, *Chance* (novel)
       James Joyce, *Dubliners* (stories)
       Wyndham Lewis (ed.), *Blast* (journal –1915) (6.4)

Gertrude Stein, *Tender Buttons* (stories)
W. B. Yeats, *Responsibilities* (poetry)

1915 Richard Aldington, *Images, 1910–15* (poetry) (5.4)
Joseph Conrad, *Victory* (novel)
Ford Madox Ford, *The Good Soldier* (novel)
D. H. Lawrence, *The Rainbow* (novel) (2.2, 2.4, 3.2)
Ezra Pound, *Cathay* (poetry)
Dorothy Richardson, *Pointed Roofs* (novel)
Virginia Woolf, *The Voyage Out* (novel)

1916 H.D., *Sea Garden* (poetry)
James Joyce, *A Portrait of the Artist as a Young Man* (novel)
Ezra Pound, *Lustra* (poetry) (8.1)
Ezra Pound, *Gaudier-Brzeska* (memoir)
Dorothy Richardson, *Backwater* (novel)
W. B. Yeats, *Reveries Over Childhood and Youth* (memoir)

1917 Joseph Conrad, *The Shadow-Line: A Confession* (novel)
T. S. Eliot, *Prufrock and Other Observations* (poetry)
D. H. Lawrence, *Look! We Have Come Through* (poetry)
Dorothy Richardson, *Honeycomb* (novel)
May Sinclair, *The Tree of Heaven* (novel)
W. B. Yeats, *The Wild Swans at Coole* (poetry)

1918 James Joyce, *Exiles* (drama)
Wyndham Lewis, *Tarr* (novel) (5.1, 5.2)
Katherine Mansfield, *Prelude* (story)
Rebecca West, *The Return of the Soldier* (novel) (10.4, 10.5)

1919 Joseph Conrad, *The Arrow of Gold* (novel)
T. S. Eliot, *Poems*
Ezra Pound, *Quia Pauper Amavi* (poetry)
Dorothy Richardson, *Interim* (novel)
Dorothy Richardson, *The Tunnel* (novel)
Virginia Woolf, *Night and Day* (novel) (3.2, 3.3)

1920 Joseph Conrad, *The Rescue* (novel)
T. S. Eliot, *The Sacred Wood: Essays on Poetry and Criticism*
D. H. Lawrence, *The Lost Girl* (novel)
Katherine Mansfield, *Bliss, and Other Stories*
Ezra Pound, *Hugh Selwyn Mauberley* (poetry)

1921 John Dos Passos, *Three Soldiers* (novel)

Aldous Huxley, *Chrome Yellow* (novel)
D. H. Lawrence, *Women in Love* (novel) (2.2, 2.6)
Dorothy Richardson, *Deadlock* (novel)
W. B. Yeats, *Michael Robartes and the Dancer* (poetry) (1.2, 9.7)

1922   T. S. Eliot, *The Waste Land* (poetry, published in Eliot's *The Criterion*) (4.1, 4.4)
James Joyce, *Ulysses* (novel) (1.2, 9.7)
D. H. Lawrence, *Aaron's Rod* (novel)
Katherine Mansfield, *The Garden-Party, and Other Stories*
May Sinclair, *Life and Death of Harriet Frean* (novel)
Virginia Woolf, *Jacob's Room* (novel) (4.5)
W. B. Yeats, *The Trembling of the Veil* (memoir)
W. B. Yeats, *Later Poems*

1923   Elizabeth Bowen, *Encounters* (stories)
Joseph Conrad, *The Rover* (novel)
D. H. Lawrence, *Psychoanalysis and the Unconscious; Fantasia of the Unconscious* (essays) (10.1)
D. H. Lawrence, *Kangaroo* (novel) (1.1)
Katherine Mansfield, *The Dove's Nest* (stories)
Dorothy Richardson, *Revolving Lights* (novel)
Wallace Stevens, *Harmonium* (poetry) (2.7, 4.2, 6.4)
William Carlos Williams, *Spring and All* (poetry) (2.7, 4.2)

1924   T. S. Eliot, *Homage to John Dryden* (essays) (5.5)
Ford Madox Ford, *Some Do Not* (first volume of novel sequence *Parade's End*) (1.1, 2.8)
E. M. Forster, *A Passage to India* (novel) (9.1, 9.2, 9.6)
T. E. Hulme, *Speculations* (essays) (5.4)
D. H. Lawrence, *England, My England* (stories) (1.1)
D. H. Lawrence, *Studies in Classic American Literature* (essays)
Katherine Mansfield, *Something Childish, and Other Stories*

1925   John Dos Passos, *Manhattan Transfer* (novel)
T. S. Eliot, *Poems, 1901–25* (5.5)
F. Scott Fitzgerald, *The Great Gatsby* (novel) (1.1)
Ford Madox Ford, *No More Parades* (second novel in *Parade's End*)
Ernest Hemingway, *In Our Time* (stories)
Aldous Huxley, *Those Barren Leaves* (novel)
Hugh MacDiarmid, *Sangshaw* (poetry)
Gertrude Stein, *The Making of Americans* (novel)
Virginia Woolf, *Mrs Dalloway* (novel) (4.1, 5.4, 6.4, 10.4, 10.5)
Virginia Woolf, *The Common Reader*, 1st series (essays)
W. B. Yeats, *A Vision* (essays) (5.6)

1926   Ford Madox Ford, *A Man Could Stand Up* (third volume of *Parade's End*)
Henry Green, *Blindness* (novel)
D. H. Lawrence, *The Plumed Serpent* (novel)
Hugh MacDiarmid, *A Drunk Man Looks at the Thistle* (poetry)
William Plomer, *Turbott Wolfe* (novel)
May Sinclair, *Far End* (novel)
Gertrude Stein, *Composition as Explanation* (essays)
Sylvia Townsend Warner, *Lolly Willowes* (novel)

1927   Elizabeth Bowen, *The Hotel* (novel)
E. M. Forster, *Aspects of the Novel* (essays)
Wyndham Lewis, *Time and Western Man* (essays) (5.4)
William Plomer, *I Speak of Africa* (stories)
Jean Rhys, *The Left Bank, and other stories*
Dorothy Richardson, *Oberland* (novel)
Virginia Woolf, *To the Lighthouse* (novel) (5.4)

1928   T. S. Eliot, *For Lancelot Andrewes: Essays on Style and Order* (5.5)
Ford Madox Ford, *Last Post* (final volume of *Parade's End*)
Radclyffe Hall, *The Well of Loneliness* (novel) (3.7)
Aldous Huxley, *Point Counter Point* (novel)
D. H. Lawrence, *The Woman Who Rode Away, and Other Stories*
D. H. Lawrence, *Lady Chatterley's Lover* (novel) (1.1, 2.8, 9.2)
William Carlos Williams, *The Descent of Winter* (poetry)
Virginia Woolf, *Orlando* (novel)
W. B. Yeats, *The Tower* (poetry)

1929   Richard Aldington, *Death of a Hero* (novel) (1.1)
Elizabeth Bowen, *The Last September* (novel) (1.2, 9.7)
William Faulkner, *The Sound and the Fury* (novel)
Henry Green, *Living* (novel)
Ernest Hemingway, *A Farewell to Arms* (novel)
Virginia Woolf, *A Room of One's Own* (essay) (3.1, 3.2, 3.3, 3.6, 3.7)
W. B. Yeats, *A Packet for Ezra Pound* (essay)

1930   W. H. Auden, *Poems*
Samuel Beckett, *Whoroscope* (poetry)
Hart Crane, *The Bridge* (poetry)
John Dos Passos, *The 42nd Parallel* (first of novel trilogy *USA*) (6.5)
T. S. Eliot, *Ash-Wednesday* (poetry)
William Faulkner, *As I Lay Dying* (novel) (2.6)
James Joyce, *Anna Livia Plurabelle* (fragment of a novel, *Finnegans Wake*)

Introduction

Modernisms and Modernist Studies

The field of modernist studies in literature has seen a succession of critical 'revisions', 're-mappings', and 're-thinking' across the past thirty years. Driven initially by pioneering feminist critics, critical response to literary texts from the first third of the twentieth century has gone through several phases of reassessment. During these phases, earlier critical opinion about the methods, politics, ambition, and even the key authors involved in modernism, has been comprehensively interrogated. More recently, compelling challenges have been made to the notion that there ever existed a single, monolithic, literary movement which might be called *modernism*. Critics including Peter Nicholls, Michael North, and Marjorie Perloff have instead seen *modernisms* as a more indicative term for the many competing modes and impulses which govern the diverse writings of both the more and the less well-known writers from this era of literature. In the course of this specific recent revision of the canon, early twentieth-century writing in English is deliberately set alongside, or seen in contrast to, broader movements of thought and literary experiment from Europe and beyond. Further work in the area has sought to link the *literary* 'moment' of modernism to similar 'moments' in the other arts, of sculpture, of painting, and of music.

To a large extent, this latter cross-media interest in modernist studies, as also many of the other 'revisions' of modernism across the past thirty years, have been anticipated by the modernist writers in English themselves. Think of the musical reference in T. S. Eliot's 1936–42 sequence *Four Quartets*, or in his early colleague and collaborator Ezra Pound's vast *Cantos* (poems to be sung). Think of the multiple allusions to pictorial representation and to fine art in Gertrude Stein. The openness to diverse influence from European and non-European (including African-American) sources in Stein, as in many other writers of this period, precisely anticipates the pluralism signalled by the title of Peter Nicholls's *Modernisms: A Literary Guide* (1995). Given these anticipations, then, a major part of the struggle of recent critical response to modernist literature has been the attempt to distance itself from the formulations and (self-)interests of the writers themselves.

The early twentieth century was a period in which the *creative* output of writers was accompanied by an outpouring of *critical* work from those same people, such as was not seen before in literary history in English (Sidney's 'Apology', Wordsworth's Introduction to *Lyrical Ballads*, or Matthew Arnold's to his *Poems*,

1

mark rare earlier excursions into the genre). A welter of critical essays, mani-festos, statements, and 'blasts' – which often themselves stray into the areas of art and music criticism, philosophy and psychology – appeared in these years in order to justify and explain the poems, novels and plays that the writers were themselves working on, or which they had recently published. As a result, the researcher, critic or student of writing from the modernist period can often feel as though she or he has been handed the decoding key to any one creation by its creator; or that a whole jumbled pocketful of keys has been offered to explain the general trends and ambitions of the original text. This is almost inevitably overwhelming and disabling for more recent students and researchers in the field. The self-proclaimed 'obscurity' or 'difficulty' of modernist texts – from Eliot's *The Waste Land* to James Joyce's polyglot *Finnegans Wake*, from the clas-sical allusion of the poetry of H.D., to the rebarbative and aggressive poetics of Mina Loy – all of this divergent and confrontational literary ambition can leave critics relieved at being able to 'pin' ready-made explanations on any particular (and particularly baffling) moment in these texts. Further, this process of presenting the 'ready-made' idea as a finished and comprehensive response is licensed in itself by the bric-a-brac and detritus offered as 'explanation' or 'order' or finished 'art' in the modernist period. Eliot's famous, and famously exhausted, concluding statement in *The Waste Land* that 'these fragments I have shored against my ruins' is matched in visual art by the inclusion of scraps of newspaper in the 'Cubist' canvases of Pablo Picasso or Georges Braque, and by the episodic and dissonantly fugitive suites or ballet scores of the composers Arnold Schoenberg and Igor Stravinsky.

What is shared by all recent critics of the literature in English from the early part of the twentieth century is excitement at the experimental challenge that this work offers, at the sheer variety of the ways in which poets, novelists, and playwrights themselves sought to re-envision and re-style the processes and scope of their creations. That, from the 1890s onwards, there was a shared impa-tience with, and anger at, the conventions received from the immediately preceding generation has become a critical platitude. Divergent, and positively disruptive, social and political pressures, from the rise of the women's move-ment to that of the socialist one, from horror at industrialism and rampant tech-nology, to scepticism about urbanization, social stratification, capitalism and imperialism – all of these pressures grew in the years preceding 1914 and across the First World War. These pressures inevitably spilled over into contemporary and succeeding cultural and artistic practice in ways which demanded new forms and modes of expression. The modernists were writers and artists self-consciously writing at a moment of massive cultural and social change, and their self-consciousness extends from their registering of the demands of the age upon them, to a re-examination of the literary techniques they might use to mediate their response to that pressure.

It is the ambition of this Sourcebook for modernist studies to present a full and representative range of the manifestations of these demands upon artistic production at the time; pressures and changes which operated particularly sharply across political, social, philosophical and religious ideas in the years leading up to, and during, the modernist period. The texts included here often (as the head notes to the selections indicate) bear a direct influential or dialogic relation to specific authors or writings from the time. Other selections indicate broader trends and thinking which form a crucial part of the general context out of (and sometimes against) which the literature was produced. Sometimes these texts do not belong historically to the period now conceived as the 'high point' of modernist output, roughly 1910–30. But these are offered here as representative texts from c.1890 onwards which lay the ground, in terms of their social, cultural or philosophical content, for some of the characteristic features of modernist texts.

What emerges from the materials included here is a great diversity of stance, impulse and voice in putting forward the pressing concerns and preoccupations of the time. And yet, across the range of categories sampled in this book, there are certain consistent threads, even metaphors and images, which were deployed to express similarly felt challenges, both to the immediate Victorian past, and to the bewildering present of its aftermath. It is these threads and metaphors which later sections of this Introduction will be concerned to draw out, in order to further define the nature of the radical and innovative literature generated from often similar kinds of urgency and excitement. The process of contextualization which is then continued in the Sourcebook (and in the introductions to each Section) might in this way be perceived as a part of the movement to wrest interpretation of literary texts away from the controlling terminology evolved by their authors, whilst at the same time acknowledging that the authors were their own first readers, that their attempts to 'explain' the processes and impact of the texts they were creating form an essential part of the mediation of their age's demands and counter-demands – demands with which any researcher or student of modernism must engage.

Making it New

The substantial cultural shifts brought about by the movement of general population into the urban centres from the 1880s onwards were mirrored by similar changes amongst the life experiences of key writers of this period. Many writers moved from rural districts, or areas culturally void in terms of literature or 'fine' arts – from the scenes and situations of their childhood, in other words – to the acceleratingly and exhilaratingly modern cities. They transplanted, therefore, a set of local and national traditions to a wholly new urbanized cultural situation. At the same time, of course, the cities themselves were undergoing rapid change as a result of industrial and technological progress, of imperial developments beyond the nation's borders (which saw, amongst other things, the first Pan-African Congress to discuss black rights, being held in London), and from the influx of this divergent range of writerly immigrants itself. Pound arrived in London in 1908 to sit at the feet of the older poet W. B. Yeats, who had shuttled between the capital and rural Ireland for over ten years by this point. The poet H.D. arrived there in 1910; T. S. Eliot followed in 1914; the New Zealand short-story writer Katherine Mansfield never returned home from Europe after 1908. British writers themselves were drawn to London from the provinces: D. H. Lawrence from Nottinghamshire became a school-teacher there in 1908, the novelist and story writer Mary Butts came to the capital to attend college. Other key writers, including E. M. Forster, Wyndham Lewis, and Virginia Woolf, knew the city from childhood, and had witnessed its rapid changes at first hand.

Meanwhile, Paris provided a location for other émigré artists from the early 1900s. The Irishman James Joyce settled there, to be followed in the 1920s by his fellow countryman Samuel Beckett; Gertrude Stein was in Paris from 1903 with her art-dealer brother, and had soon become friends with the leading figures of the French artistic movement, including Pablo Picasso and Henri Matisse. Pound relocated to Paris in 1920, in disgust at conservative English attitudes to culture during and after the war; Ernest Hemingway soon joined him, and F. Scott and Zelda Fitzgerald frequently passed through. The Dominican-born novelist Jean Rhys moved between the two capitals Paris and London, as did the Edwardian Ford Madox Ford, who was an important advisor of Pound, collaborator with Joseph Conrad, and sometime lover of Rhys's.

What I am describing here is something of the artistic and literary turmoil within the major capital cities of Europe, and other urban centres (including New York, as will become clear below), in the 1910s and early 1920s. English-language writers from local, provincial, and colonial backgrounds were suddenly moving through and between urban spaces, seeking the collegiality of fellow creators, but also striving for access to the major publishing outlets, the 'little' magazines and journals, and the more innovative publishing houses. To this end, there was a constantly shifting alignment and realignment of friendships, mutual sponsorships, and crucial conversations and cross-influences between these writers, which the beleaguered years of the First World War only served to exacerbate. There was also a key trend towards a fictionalized autobiography that came to characterize modernist texts, an autobiography preoccupied with the shift from early experience towards a more alienated and unsettled maturity within modernity. D. H. Lawrence's *Sons and Lovers* (1913), Katherine Mansfield's *Prelude* (1916), James Joyce's *A Portrait of the Artist as a Young Man* (1916), E. M. Forster's *A Passage to India* (1924) – all reflect upon personal experience from an estranged and estranging perspective.

What these writers met with in these capitals, in terms of 'culture' and 'ideas', was, it needs to be emphasized, and as this Sourcebook amply demonstrates, strikingly diverse. Despite the dangerous political situation between the imperial powers at the time (to be discussed later on), there had only a couple of times, in the past five hundred years, been such openness in English-language culture towards ideas from mainland Europe.[1] From the 1890s onwards, German thinkers and philosophers, including Max Nordau, Friedrich Nietzsche, Max Weber, Sigmund Freud, and (later) Otto Spengler, were readily available in translation; Émile Durkeim, Georges Sorel, Henri Bergson, from France also. In the literary field, critical work like Arthur Symons's *The Symbolist Movement in Literature* (1899) – a key text for Yeats, Pound and Eliot – introduced the English-speaking world to a range of French poets, from Baudelaire through Mallarmé to Jules Laforgue, in an accessible and compelling form. The literary journals of the day reflected this openness in lead articles and reviews, as well as the regular 'Letters' from London or Paris which appeared in *The New Age*, *The Egoist* and *The Dial*. There was a rare sense at this moment in the 1910s and 1920s that English literary culture was not resistant to European philosophy and literature; indeed that there was a mutual cross-fertilization to be had, and that it needed immediate 'news from elsewhere' in order to stimulate further discussions and developments. In the novel, modernist writers including the Americans Henry James, Edith Wharton, Ernest Hemingway and William Faulkner, the Irishman Joyce, and Woolf and Lawrence from England, show the impact of European fiction from France (Flaubert) and Russia (Turgenev, Dostoevsky).

And this particular influence of European ideas – both Nietzscheanism and Symbolism were concerned to overturn established traditions – was immediate in its impact upon literary outputs which would later be declared 'modernist'.[2] In poetry, this is evident from the work that Eliot produced before arriving in England, modelled on the poems of Jules Laforgue which he first came across in Symons's survey of French Symbolism. Another American poet, Wallace Stevens, displayed in work across his career (from 'Sunday Morning', 1915, to 'The Auroras of Autumn', 1948) a playful interest in the idea of the natural object as a symbol, and of the imagination as a force 'pressing back' against reality. European influence is evident in Ezra Pound's interest in medieval and Renaissance French and Italian poetry, present in his own poetry from the outset. Notoriously, when Pound sought to galvanize English-language poetry in association with the American poet H.D. (Hilda Doolittle) and the Englishman Richard Aldington in the summer of 1912, he did so by 'inventing' what he initially called *Imagisme* (what later became simply 'Imagism'). The original

---

1 Behind every previous revolutionary moment in English literature, there had been a similar openness. Great translations of classical and modern European works underpin many of the innovations of the Renaissance; French social, and German idealist, philosophy underwrote much of Romanticism.

2 Stan Smith has pointed out that, although the term 'modernist' is usually presumed to have been first attributed to the poetry in the period (principally in this case to Eliot's poetry) by Robert Graves and Laura Riding in their *Survey of Modernist Poetry* (1928), the term had been derived by them from its regular use for similar purposes by contributors to the magazine *Fugitive* in the southern USA – contributors who included the poets Allen Tate and John Crowe Ransom ('The Disconsolate Chimera: T. S. Eliot and the Fixation of Modernism', *Rethinking Modernism*, ed. Marianne Thormahlen (Basingstoke: Palgrave Macmillan, 2003), p. 184).

designation set the new movement in a supposed line of inheritance from French *symboliste* precursors.

Modernist Poetry

Symons had emphasized the mysteriousness and the spirituality of French symbolist poetry:

> What is Symbolism if not an establishing of the links which hold the world together, the affirmation of an eternal, minute, intricate, almost invisible life, which runs through the whole universe? . . . To get at that truth which is all but the deepest meaning of beauty, to find that symbol which is the most adequate expression, is in itself a kind of creation.[3]

In replacing the 'symbol', which had this vast scale of reference and resonance, with the 'image', Pound and his interlocutors were immediately signalling that their ambition was more modest than such French precursors, but also more focused and concentrated. Pound later recalled the principle doctrines of 'Imagism' as 'Direct treatment of the "thing", whether subjective or objective'; 'To use absolutely no word which does not contribute to the presentation'; 'As regarding rhythm: to compose in the sequence of the musical phrase, not in the sequence of the metronome'.[4]

What 'Imagism' was proposing was a significant break with past poetry; it wished to do away with the rhetoric which Pound, as principal proselytizer, felt had marred much nineteenth-century verse, the use of adjectives and adverbs for 'poetic' effect. Perhaps most radical, however, is the third Imagist 'principle', the suggestion that the new movement break with the alternately-stressed syllables so familiar a presence in English poetry from the early Renaissance onwards, and instead synaesthetically allow the 'musical phrase' – whatever shape it may assume – to dictate the sound and lineation of the verse. So, we find this as the opening stanza of H.D.'s 'Sea Violet':

> The white violet
> is scented on its stalk,
> the sea-violet
> fragile as agate,
> lies fronting all the wind
> among the torn shells
> on the sand-bank.[5]

---

3 Arthur Symons, *The Symbolist Movement in Literature* (London: Archibald Constable, 1899; 2nd, revised edn, 1908), pp. 144–5.

4 Ezra Pound, 'A Retrospect', *Literary Essays of Ezra Pound*, ed. T. S. Eliot (London: Faber, 1954), p. 3.

5 H.D., *Selected Poems*, ed. Louis L. Martz (Manchester: Carcanet, 1997), p. 8.

This poem, from H.D.'s first (wartime) collection *Sea Garden* (1916), typically sets the 'fragile' against the buffeting blows of the wind, or of history. But we are made to perform a double-take: 'fragile as agate'. Agate is a hard stone, a variety of chalcedony; the vulnerable is the strong here. 'The torn shells', of course, has topical reference to the debris of the Western Front ('fronting' a subliminal urge towards this reading); the rare and unlikely sea violet, flora but also rock, stands against the abysm, an image of the endurance of poetry, and perhaps also of women, in these circumstances. Musically, the poem is also delicate but robust, the lineation marking each sense-group in the sentence as it unfurls. The voice reading the poem is slowed, weighing and weighting each movement and change of direction of the sentence's address.

This manner and music is H.D.'s personal signature; Pound, in describing it as originally 'Imagiste', was hitching his propagandist restlessness to her practice. Although he would continue to produce beautifully wrought poetry of his own in this manner, down to that collected in his wartime book *Lustra* (1916–17), he had already become impatient with the delicacy and seemingly static qualities of the small poems written under the 'Imagist' aegis. By 1914, he had entered into another conversation, which involved him in *visual* analogies for poetry as opposed to the musical ones of his earlier 'movement'. In league now with the painter and novelist Wyndham Lewis, Pound worked on the short-lived 'Vorticist' doctrines, most fully presented in the two issues of the magazine edited by Lewis, *Blast*, in June 1914 and July 1915. *Blast 1* contained poems by Pound, stories by Rebecca West and Ford Madox Ford (a portion of his novel *The Good Soldier*), and a play, *The Enemy of the Stars*, by Lewis, amid a welter of typographical shifts and displacements designed to disorient the reader. The issue also contained manifestos for the 'movement', and illustrations from leading and lesser-known artists including Lewis himself, Edward Wadsworth, Jacob Epstein, and Gaudier-Brzeska, a Polish–French artist championed by Pound and soon to be killed at the Front.

'Vortex. Pound.', the poet's statement about the movement, spells out the implications and indebtedness of its name. 'The vortex is the point of maximum energy. // It represents, in mechanics, the greatest efficiency.' In a later section of this manifesto, called 'The Turbine', he asserts that 'All experience rushes into this vortex. All the energized past, all the past that is living and worthy to live.'[6] Pound, in other words, has moved from the largely flora-and-fauna subject-matter of his and others' 'Imagist' work, to embrace the dynamism of modern technology, the kinetic forces and energies of machinery as metaphors for the force and whirl of an essentially modern poetry. In one of the poems he contributed to the first issue of *Blast*, he imagined the Greek goddess Athene rising into the sky, 'gone up as a rocket', and spiralling there, a sense of the divine force in the universe displaying the exhilarating power of modern-day

---

6 *Blast 1*, ed. Wyndham Lewis (Santa Rosa: Black Sparrow Press, 1997), p. 153.

Henri Gaudier-Brzeska, *Red Stone Dancer*

speed and rush. 'Vortex. Pound.' shows the poet anxious to distance his ideas from those of the Futurist movement founded by the Italian poet and performance artist Filippo Marinetti, which Pound condemns as having no true force behind it; but in the admiration for the machine at this moment, before the destructiveness of the weaponry in France silenced this admiration forever, British and American art and letters at this point moved closer than ever to Marinetti's popular and *modern* version of art.[7] During the war, Pound was to shift again, seeking to display his 'energy' through building a succession of historical moments and phases into single long poems, the 'Three Cantos' of 1917, which formed initial experiments towards the epic work that would sustain him for the rest of his life.

In Pound's native United States, there was felt across the years of the war and down to the end of the decade a similar cross-fertilization between literature, music, performance, and the visual arts – one which introduced work from European movements, including Dadaism, to New York. Dada, a nihilistic

---

7 Marinetti's 1909 'Manifesto of Futurism' included: '1. We intend to sing the love of danger, the habit of energy and fearlessness. . . . 4. We affirm that the world's magnificence has been enriched by a new beauty: the beauty of speed. A racing car whose hood is adorned with great pipes, like serpents of explosive breath – a roaring car that seems to ride on grapeshot is more beautiful than the *Victory of Samothrace*' (*Selected Writings*, translated by R. W. Flint (New York: Farrar, Straus and Giroux, 1972), p. 8). Lawrence Rainey has argued that 'Imagism' was 'founded' by Pound as a reaction against Marinetti's visits to London in 1912 (*Institutions of Modernism: Literary Elites and Popular Culture* (New Haven, CT: Yale University Press, 1998), p. 12).

protest against all Western values, had been founded in Zurich in 1916 by the Romanian poet Tristan Tzara and others; it became influential in America through the work of Marcel Duchamp, who adapted everyday items as art objects (most famously, the urinal titled 'Fountain'). Duchamp attracted a salon around him which included writers such as Wallace Stevens and William Carlos Williams, alongside the photographer and painter Man Ray. Briefly in the years 1917–19, America glimpsed the experimental radicalism which had entered European work during the earlier part of the war. And yet the Euro-centric vision which fuelled Pound and Eliot's version of poetic modernism met both vocal and tacit opposition from US writers seeking to establish a modern, but also a vernacular poetry, one resistant to the mythologizing and *literary* tendencies of the Europe-based émigré poets. The poets associated with the Harlem Renaissance in New York sought to adopt the racial rhythms of jazz music, and the intonations of their own spoken English, in the discovery of a different consciousness through their writing. One of Pound's former classmates, William Carlos Williams, produced his own epic, *Paterson*, between 1946 and 1958. Williams's poem does not avoid the potential of myth – what he calls near the end of Book I of this work 'the myth / that holds up the rock, / that holds up the water thrives' – but, as this passage presumes, 'the myth' is 'holding up' a *specific* rock, *particular* water (the water of the Passaic River near the city which gives Williams's epic poem its name). Williams, in other words, and in contrast to Pound and Eliot, brought his learning to bear, a learning which included the classical languages and eastern religions as theirs did. But he brings learning to bear upon a *local* landscape and a local context, deploying the vernacular rhythms of his locale to do so:

> We sit and talk,
> quietly, with long lapses of silence
> and I am aware of the stream
> that has no language, coursing
> beneath the quiet heaven of
> your eyes[8]

This brief passage scores its line-endings carefully: 'coursing' drops neatly down to 'beneath'; 'of / your eyes' brings a nice turn, one carried by the seeming casualness of the spoken idiom, round to the intimate expression of love at this end of a verse paragraph. 'Quietly' plays off against 'quiet', but the whole is given an unassuming air by the way in which the lineation also matches itself to the sense-groups within the sentence of poetry. As with the H.D. poem quoted above, there is shared interest in scoring poetry to the speaking voice in this way

---

8 William Carlos Williams, *Paterson* (Harmondsworth: Penguin, 1983), pp. 39, 24.

by certain of the modernists, making it play off against and within the freedoms of a new, non-traditional, rhythm and metre.

A similar preoccupation with the ways in which the spoken idiom can cross with poetic technique notably underlies the work of Marianne Moore, another friend of the modernist émigré poets, who saw her version of modernity within the intonations of everyday life. Like Eliot and Pound, Moore deploys quotation throughout her work, but it does not serve to suggest a past of literary shards which must be somehow forced into a new coherence, as quotation does in their writing. Instead, quotation works to authorize, or cast strikingly different lights upon, her perception of 'reality' in the present. Moore's poetic hymn to 'New York', for instance, focuses upon the city's Native American origin, which underpins its atmosphere of 'savage's romance', against the urban sophistication for which it is familiarly known:

> . . . it is not the atmosphere of ingenuity,
> the otter, the beaver, the puma skins,
> without shooting-irons or dogs;
> it is not the plunder,
> but 'accessibility to experience.'[9]

What the city amounts to is not its veneer of cleverness, or the natural 'plunder' seemingly yet miraculously obtainable from its 'pre-civilized' past. It amounts, rather, to its openness before experience, and to the fact that experience is available there. Moore's deployment, in the final line, of a phrase from Henry James is extremely witty, suggesting, because it is a quotation, that experience may not be all that easily accessible; yet, at the same time, it reveals a means to celebrate the many currents of experience that the city denotes.

Moore's consistent concern with the issue of the relation between literary technique and the need to encapsulate contemporary reality in her work is, of course, persistent across all modernist poetry: a perception that, when previous values are in question, literature itself must be made to develop new strategies of response. The solutions which individual poets came up with in the face of this problem at this time are radically different the one from the other, however much they share a perception of the nature of the crisis – Pound's from Eliot's, Stevens's from Moore's, Williams's from H.D.'s. It is these differences which underlie the vertiginous and moving variety of modernist writing and its experimentalism.

Modernist Drama

Similar issues about the relation between aesthetics and reality, of course,

---

9 Marianne Moore, *Complete Poems* (London: Faber, 1968), p. 54.

confronted writers addressing the other literary genres at the time. Modernist drama played in Britain, as exemplified by the late plays of W. B. Yeats, the translated Japanese works of Ezra Pound, or the plays of T. S. Eliot, however, was extremely resistant to the modern vocabularies and idiom deployed elsewhere in these writers' poetry. Playing in small salons to invited audiences at the time of the First World War, Pound's and Yeats's versions of Japanese Noh drama brought to the modern stage an extremely stylized action, often including dance. It was resolutely anti-realistic, stripping the stage of much scenery and props. The actors wore masks throughout. Pound, introducing a selection of the Noh plays for a modern audience, did not hesitate to expatiate upon their implication:

> The art of allusion, or this love of allusion in art, is at the root of the Noh. These plays . . . were made only for the few; for the nobles; for those trained to catch the allusion. In the Noh we find an art built upon the god-dance, or upon some local legend of spiritual apparition . . .[10]

The sense here of working within a tradition to which a later writer could refer or allude obviously had appeal to modernist poets deeply involved with their own versions of the Western literary inheritance. The apparitions and general ghostliness of the Noh was a central feature also of these modern poets' work, deriving for Yeats from his preoccupation with Irish folklore, and partly for Pound and also Eliot from their appalled reaction to events on the Western Front. But what marks Pound's 1916 introduction to his Noh translations is the drive to move the drama away from the realism of late nineteenth-century writers like that, most famously, of Henrik Ibsen. The central impetus, here and elsewhere, is to move the form back to its perceived ancient origins when theatre was closer to religious ritual and symbolism. Hence its deliberately alienating impact, its music and masks – and its alarming sense that it might be understood only by the elect few.

Pound and Yeats's discovery of the Noh had tremendous implications for their own work and for that of modernist drama more broadly. Yeats's later plays swung even more radically towards symbolism from this moment. His 1917 play *At the Hawk's Well* discovers a nameless old man and a boy waiting by the well to drink of the waters which will soon flow, waters which confer immortality. The Old Man has been accompanied throughout his life-long vigil by a solitary girl, who at the end of the play defies expectation to become the hawk of the title, an avenging hawk which distracts the two from actually taking the waters. The whole play, in fact, seems a telling parable about the tension between the symbolic, or poetic, and the active life: the distraction of the old man and boy at the moment that the waters begin suggests Yeats's vision of an humanity

---

10 Ezra Pound, *The Translations of Ezra Pound*, ed. Hugh Kenner (London: Faber, 1953), p. 214.

unable to carry through its highest religious aspirations. Instead, and topically, given the moment of the play's creation, violence is once again unleashed at the end of the drama: 'What are those cries? . . . The clash of arms again.'[11] It is as though the work of art on the stage is offered as a momentary calm which yet warns of the failure and chaos that result once this refined world is ignored.

That combination of allusiveness with predestination marks much other modernist drama. From *The Family Reunion* (1939) onwards, Eliot retained a ritualistic element at the heart of his plays, basing his narrative each time upon ancient Greek originals, and therefore sustaining a sense of Fate and retribution which, sometimes uneasily, operates within and against the everyday world presented on the stage. In America, Eugene O'Neill's work for New York's Greenwich theatres across the 1920s and into the early 1930s carried a similar sense of menace. His stage settings are often extremely elaborately delineated in a realist sense, with the position of furniture in the represented rooms, for instance, carefully dictated in the stage directions. But within these 'real' contexts, O'Neill increasingly used expressionistic techniques to suggest the shocking contrast between the interior life of his characters and their social and public situations.

Most famously, in *The Great God Brown* (1926), the central conflict between the all-American successful businessman of the title character and the maverick creative intelligence of Dion Anthony, which is unable to accommodate itself to the conventions of smalltown America, is conveyed in this manner. Masks are put on to allow the characters to make socially acceptable utterances, and taken off when their true passions are exposed – as when Dion, wracked by his failings, for a last time shows his true self to his wife:

> DION: . . . Look at me, Mrs Anthony! It's the last chance! Tomorrow I'll be moved on to the next hell! Behold your man – the snivelling, cringing, life-defying Christian slave you have so nobly ignored in the father of your sons. Look! (*He tears the mask from his face, which is radiant with a great pure love for her and a great sympathy and tenderness*) O woman – my love . . .[12]

It is a conflict between two realities which cannot be accommodated. Once Dion has succumbed, Brown seeks to assume his genius by wearing his mask, only for his own assumption of the other persona to prove his own unreality, and he in turn dwindles before being killed by accident. The clash O'Neill describes throughout his drama is between public demands or worldly success, and private passions; the masks in this work very literally reveal these irreconcilable forces. In later work, crucially the trilogy *Mourning Becomes Electra* (1929–31), founded upon the Greek plays of the *Orestia*, the *actual* masks are not

---

11 *The Collected Plays of W. B. Yeats* (Basingstoke: Macmillan, 1982), p. 218.

12 Eugene O'Neill, *Desire under the Elms and The Great God Brown* (London: National Theatre and Nick Hern, 1995), p. 93.

used. But all the central characters in their social selves are described as having 'life-like masks' for faces. In the trilogy, that sense that the destiny of character will out, which had featured in the typology of *The Great God Brown*, assumes even greater significance, as, within the seemingly well-to-do home at the time of the Civil War, the illicit desires and incestuous passions lead to inevitable tragedy and ruin. Instead of masks, the characters across the generations in the family closely resemble one another, as O'Neill plays repeatedly upon a sense of déja-vu in order to reinforce the claustrophobic sense that the sins of the parents are visited upon their children.

Modernist Novels

The modernist novel largely differs from its immediate late nineteenth-century precursors in the way it approaches the issue of narrative, and also in the way it focuses its content. Two late nineteenth-century innovators, Joseph Conrad and Henry James, were crucial in advancing possibilities for the genre, and tremendously influential upon subsequent modernist fiction. The Polish settler in England, Conrad, was key in breaking away from the realistic emphasis of much nineteenth-century fiction. In the 'Preface' to *The Nigger of the 'Narcissus'* (1897), Conrad laid out a doctrine of literary impressionism which was to prevail in later work of the period:

> All art . . . appeals primarily to the senses, and the artistic aim when express-ing itself in written words must also make its appeal through the senses. . . . The task approached in tenderness and faith is to hold up unquestioningly, without choice and without fear, the rescued fragment before all eyes and in the light of a sincere mood. It is to show its vibration, its colour, its form: and through its movement, its form, and its colour, reveal the substance of its truth – disclose its inspiring secret: the stress and passion within the core of each convincing moment.[13]

The demand here is that there be a break from the overt morality of previous fiction; an emphasis upon the necessity to concentrate on the immediate impact of writing's effect upon its reader, whatever the subject-matter might be. To this extent, for Conrad, novels must become more like sculpture or works of music than literary/verbal constructs. Their impact must be unmediated by any guid-ing authorial voice, such as that familiar from Victorian novels. At the heart of the novel lies 'stress and passion' rather than a social or moral purpose. Whatever the nature of the content, the writer's task to is make *presentation* the

---

13 Joseph Conrad, 'Preface' to *The Nigger of the 'Narcissus'*, ed. Cedric Watts (Harmondsworth: Penguin, 1987), p. xlix.

centre of attention. What she or he must attend to is the 'moment' of the action; plot becomes a series of moments, 'fragments', or scenes in which the 'stress and passion' is most intensely displayed. Narrative description must now operate to that end, rather than providing a background against which the story is to be set.

Conrad advocates a kind of writing in which artistic media are conflated in order to produce the 'convincing moment' mediated through the senses. Once faith in earlier modes of narration as ensuring revelation of some kind of 'truth' have given way, Conrad's characters live in and through the moment. In this mode, the 'Narcissus', the ship at the centre of this particular novel, assumes an existential reality:

> the ship, a fragment detached from the earth, went on lonely and swift like a small planet. Round her the abysses of sky and sea met in an unattainable frontier. A great circular solitude moved with her, ever changing and ever the same, always monotonous and always imposing. . . . She had her own future; she was alive with the lives of those beings who trod her decks . . . (p. 21)

The ship is a paradoxical entity, both itself and not itself as it progresses through its destiny. This ship-as-planet is both inert matter, an artefact, and a living thing, since it moves and is moved by those living creatures on board. It is this which poses the central issue and problem of *The Nigger of the 'Narcissus'*: the inert figure of James Wait, the black man at the epicentre of the novel's action, refuses to perform his labour as part of the 'living' world which the ship is, and thence he threatens the ship's destiny.

Conrad's version of impressionism as a technique, in this and his other novels, would seem to represent modernity in writing as the painting of a continuous succession of moments. It seems on the surface to be unlike later modernist prose in the nature of the outcome to which this technique leads him, but shares surprising features with it. The American writer Gertrude Stein, for instance, in her essay 'Composition as Explanation' (1926), plays, as she does in all of her texts, upon the issue of monotony and repetition, like Conrad in his 'Preface', in order to establish the continuity of living in and through writing:

> The composition is the thing seen by every one living in the living they are doing, they are the composing of the composition that at the time they are living is the composition of the time in which they are living. It is that that makes living a thing they are doing.[14]

Stein's syntax, as elsewhere in her fictions, collapses composition, living, seeing and time in much more absolute ways than Conrad's late nineteenth-century

---

14 Gertrude Stein, 'Composition as Explanation', *Look at Me Now and Here I Am: Writings and Lectures, 1911–1945*, ed. Patricia Meyerowitz (London: Peter Owen, 1967), p. 21.

adherence to plot would allow for, to the point where in Stein syntax *becomes* the narrative of her writing. But her concept of writing as a way of being is not remote from his of the ship-as-book-as-world in *Narcissus*, or James Joyce's episodic deployment of his day-in-the-life-of Dublin-as-world in *Ulysses* (1922), or even Virginia Woolf's deployment of a vividly similar structuring technique in *Mrs Dalloway* (1925).

In each of these cases, as most notoriously in Conrad's *Heart of Darkness* (1899), what is being claimed as modernity for prose writing is the removal of any concept of *externality*, the presentation of narrative in a third-person mode at a remove from either a narrator or a reader. Conrad's narrator-figure, Marlow, stands between the reader and the action of the book; we only hear *his* impressions of what happens, not those of any reliable spectators. In early modernist fiction, then, the distance between reader and narrative has broadened, and a greater space for interpretation is allowed. When writing a Preface to his last completed novel *The Golden Bowl* (1905), this was also at the forefront of the American novelist Henry James's perspective. He acknowledges the 'marked inveteracy of a certain indirect and oblique view of my presented action', and that he has repeatedly in his later fiction looked for the 'help of some other conscious and confessed agent' which has *enriched* both the writing and readers' experience. The effect of this is that the prose remains extremely close in to the characters' thoughts and consciousness, unable to fully decipher the implication of any one incident until it becomes clear later. When, near the beginning of the book, Charlotte and Amerigo talk about buying the flawed golden bowl of the title, for instance, the reader is left feeling the seriousness of the moment, but grasping for its 'meaning':

> 'Then,' she asked, 'what *is* the matter?'
>
> 'Why, it has a crack.'
>
> It sounded, on his lips, so sharp, it had such an authority, that she almost started, while her colour, at the word, rose. . . . 'You answer for it without having looked?'
>
> 'I did look. I saw the object itself. It told its story. No wonder it's cheap.'
>
> 'But it's exquisite,' Charlotte, as if with an interest in it now made even tenderer and stranger, found herself moved to insist.
>
> 'Of course it's exquisite. That's the danger.'[15]

The bowl has, of course, symbolic implication; Charlotte and Amerigo have been lovers, and her presence throughout the book threatens to undermine his new marriage to the American heiress Maggie Verver. When the bowl is later smashed, it is Maggie's concern to reconstruct it from its fragments which

---

15 Henry James, *The Golden Bowl*, ed. Virginia Llewellyn Smith (Oxford: Oxford University Press, 1983), pp. xli, 89.

manifests the generosity of her sense of relationship. But, in this early passage, whilst we sense the fluster and charge in the conversation, we are not given the understanding to decode its origin. Only through the inter-play of the character's thoughts and responses across the entire work does some truth come through.

This sense of narrative-through-character is a feature of both English and American modernist novels. In his first book, *The Sun Also Rises* (1926), for example, the American Ernest Hemingway deploys a narrative through a character who is particularly anxious that he might have misunderstood, or be out of the loop of, the central action – as, to an extent, he is at various phases. The novel is about the erosion of American assurance when encountering European culture, but it is an assurance which has been eroded also in the narrative voice: 'Somehow I feel I have not shown Robert Cohn clearly.'[16] It is a technique famously deployed by F. Scott Fitzgerald in *The Great Gatsby* (1926), where the truth about the wealth of the shape-shifting and enigmatic central figure, Gatsby, and his tragic love affair, are shielded from the reader by the fact that the book is told us by the over-credulous Nick Carraway. At its limit, this mode of modernist writing reaches the poetic meditations of William Faulkner's novels, the earlier ones of which are literally carried by the emergence of different voices who speak each phase of the shared experience. In *As I Lay Dying*, the journey to take Addie Bunden's dead body to burial amongst her people is sustained via short passages of consciousness moving through named characters. The sharpest drama is formed between Cash, who has made Addie's coffin, and who represents the workmanlike qualities of American inheritance ('I made it on the bevel'), and Darl, who represents the nation's metaphysical possibility ('It is as though time, no longer running straight before us in a diminishing line, now runs parallel between us like a looping string').[17] Both Cash and Darl, to a certain extent, describe the technical properties of the novel of which they are a part: it *is* both approaching its subject-matter at a slant, *and*, through its multiple narrators, playing tricks with narrative time. But, through this looping obliquity, the central purpose of the narrative remains occluded. Faulkner allows us to see close-in the realistic expressions and perspectives of his narrators, without providing us with a summatory overview.

This implicit call from Faulkner for a greater focus upon interiority in the novel is present everywhere elsewhere in the period. Crucially, it also marks the pioneering intensity of the felt need for a reorientation of gender relations in fiction. The famous essay by Virginia Woolf which eventually appeared under the title 'Mr Bennett and Mrs Brown' (1924), responds to the older novelist Arnold Bennett's complaint that the younger generation had not produced characters that were 'real' enough, and therefore characters that would engage the contemporary reader. Woolf's response is complex; on the one hand she feels

---

16 Ernest Hemingway, *'Fiesta'/The Sun Also Rises*, *The Essential Hemingway* (London: Arrow, 1993), p. 37.
17 William Faulkner, *As I Lay Dying* (London: Penguin, 1963), pp. 66, 115.

that some of her contemporaries, including E. M. Forster and D. H. Lawrence, were, in their first novels, too eager to compromise with the doggedly realist determination of the older generation such as Bennett. She also feels that the work of Joyce and T. S. Eliot (in his earlier, society-based poems) is somewhat aestheticized and anaemic. However, she remains determined to prove that the realist novel, especially where it casually silences the responses of women, is inadequate to contemporary perceptions of reality, its 'tools' now redundant:

> [Realist writers] have laid enormous stress upon the fabric of things. They have given us a house in the hope that we may be able to deduce the human beings who live there. To give them their due, they have made that house much better worth living in. But if you hold that novels are in the first place about people, and only in the second about the houses they live in, that is the wrong way to set about it. . . . In the course of your daily life this week you have . . . overheard scraps of talk that have filled you with amazement. You have gone to bed at night bewildered by the complexity of your feelings. In one day thousands of ideas have coursed through your brains; thousands of emotions have met, collided, and disappeared in astonishing order. Nevertheless, you allow the writers to palm off on you a version of all this . . . which has no likeness to that surprising apparition whatsoever.[18]

Again, it is previous fiction's emphasis upon the external shell of the world (the 'house') which is under attack; the 'fabric' of the world it is which has taken up earlier novelists' attention rather than internal human issues. Contentiously, therefore, Woolf is claiming that the realist novel is in fact *unrealistic*, negligent of the actualities of the multitudinous but transient 'complexity' of feeling and ideas which people truly experience every day. And this is something which she clearly feels has not yet been satisfactorily addressed in her own day. The dilemma of her fellow writers is to find a way of containing that complexity in literary form, especially as it applies to the hitherto largely hidden lives of women characters.

Woolf's two novels published soon after this essay, *Mrs Dalloway* and *To the Lighthouse* (1927), compellingly confront this dilemma. They focus upon two women, the named heroine in the former, and Mrs Ramsay in the latter, who act as catalysts bringing the flow of life (and therefore the shape of each novel) to some purpose and resolution. Mrs Dalloway performs this task through her party, the lead-in to which forms the content of the novel's action, and which, when it arrives, gives the book its ending. *To the Lighthouse*, by putting the character of the painter Lily Briscoe to the fore, more openly displays the artistic

---

18 *The Essays of Virginia Woolf*, vol. 3: *1919–24*, ed. Andrew McNeillie (San Diego, CA: Harcourt Brace Jovanovich, 1988), pp. 432, 436.

issues involved in refining and balancing various strains of life, and the drive to produce a feeling of wholeness which equates (in the novel's own term) to 'reve-lation'. Lily muses, after Mrs Ramsay's death, on the gatherings of friends which the older woman had achieved at the holiday-home near the lighthouse of the title:

> Mrs Ramsay bringing them together; Mrs Ramsay saying 'Life stands still here'; Mrs Ramsay making of the moment something permanent (as in another sphere Lily herself tried to make of the moment something perma-nent) – this was in the nature of a revelation. In the midst of chaos there was shape; this eternal passing and flowing (she looked at the clouds going and the leaves shaking) was struck into stability.[19]

Within the 'shape' of Woolf's novel, the 'chaos' is readily identifiable in some senses: it is the First World War which brings the death of one of the sons of the family, and during which Mrs Ramsay passes away, as recounted in the brief 'Time Passes' central section of the book. To this extent, Lily's perception of a possible 'shape' to be given to reality, either through performing a centring role such as that Mrs Ramsay played during her life, or through composing a work of art, has a melancholy, mournful and retrospective air. Tragically, 'revelation' is not often glimpse-able at the time, as the moment passes, but is only 'struck' later, in the absence of the living subject. Like the other writers we reviewed in this section, Woolf plays complexly here and elsewhere upon the notion of time and history. It is the moments of life as they pass which the modernist writer is despairingly trying to render, given the fact that former continuities are collec-tively perceived to have 'disappeared in astonishing order'. So, the technical problem for the modernist writer conceived generically becomes one of render-ing history and the moment as it passes in the text. This dilemma, differentially approached, is symptomatic of the modernists' shared perception of the demands upon and within their art.

Modernism and History

Modernist writing, like much other writing in the early years of the twentieth century, was preoccupied by history, by its own relation to history, and by how the present differed from the past. When the poet Ezra Pound, with his own massive *Cantos* in mind, defined the ancient literary genre of epic as a 'poem containing history', he made a finely-judged ambiguous assertion. 'Containing' meant both that history would deliver the content of the epic, but also that the epic would contain, as in create, a boundary within which the

---

19 Virginia Woolf, *To the Lighthouse*, ed. Stella McNichol (Harmondsworth: Penguin, 1992), p. 176.

pattern of history might be perceived.[20] Modernist writing indeed seems inordinately preoccupied with envisaged historical pasts, with its relation to recent and immediate events, and also with its relation to *literary-historical* moments and currents. To that extent, its creative ambition is declaratively 'epic', not only a response to the immediacy of its own times, but also a seeking to comprehend those times, and to critique those times, from the perspective of a vast historical time-span. Modernist writers' view of the modern world was often of its being already and exhaustively overwritten, and dictated, by previous insights and literary formulations, formulations which it could now only uncertainly register, but which might serve to form that 'shoring up' function which Eliot envisaged for the historical voices and moments in his own mini-epic, *The Waste Land*.

In this emphasis, the modernist writers were both continuous with, and resistant to, preoccupations developed by thinkers and historians in Britain, the United States, and continental Europe, throughout the nineteenth century. The American philosopher Ralph Waldo Emerson asserted in his essay 'Self-Reliance' (1847) that 'In every work of genius we recognize our own rejected thoughts: they come back to us with a certain alienated majesty. Great works of art have no more affecting lesson for us than this.'[21] Emerson's sense of past lives and works being embodied in, but actively challenging ('alienated'), the present is echoed elsewhere, in work such as the French novelist Victor Hugo's *Notre-Dame de Paris* (1831). The fascinated and fascinatingly idealized medievalism of that work is present in much British writing of the nineteenth century, including Thomas Carlyle's *Past and Present* (1843), and the writings on social and industrial relations by John Ruskin and William Morris. The nineteenth century saw also an emerging interest in (particularly) the early Italian Renaissance, through novels such as George Eliot's *Romola* (1863), critical works by John Addington Symonds and (most pressingly) Walter Pater, and the poems of Robert Browning (staple reading of the late nineteenth and early twentieth centuries in which our modernist writers were growing up).[22]

All of these works perceive history as a place of contestation and judgement, and the writers' task as historians, as principally to weigh the merit of one historical 'period' against another, often with the purpose of envisioning a 'golden

---

20 Ezra Pound, *Guide to Kulchur* (London: Peter Owen, 1952), p. 60. T. S. Eliot made a similar point about epic in his review of James Joyce's Homer-governed *Ulysses*, whose 'method', Eliot claimed, provided a way of 'controlling, of ordering, of giving a shape and a significance to the immense panorama of futility and anarchy which is contemporary history' (*Selected Prose*, ed. Frank Kermode (London: Faber, 1975) p. 177).

21 *Ralph Waldo Emerson*, ed. Richard Poirier (Oxford: Oxford University Press, 1990), p. 131. James Longenbach has traced this existential version of history in modernism in his *Modernist Poetics of History* (Princeton, NJ: Princeton University Press, 1987).

22 J. B. Bullen, in *The Myth of the Renaissance in Nineteenth-Century Writing* (Oxford: Clarendon Press, 1994), has interesting commentary on the European context behind the tensions between conceptions of the Medieval and the Renaissance periods in the years before modernism.

age' from which the present can be viewed as a period of decadence, impropri-
ety, or cultural emptiness. This is a Victorian version of historical contestation
which will be familiar, as carried over, to any reader of a critical or creative text
from the early part of the *twentieth* century, whether it be Pound's views on early
medieval Provence, Eliot's on English Renaissance literature, Joyce's *Ulysses* or
Virginia Woolf's repetition, through the mouth of her protagonist in *Jacob's
Room*, of fantasies of the cultural, social, literary and human superiority of
Ancient Greece to the present. Such a differential weighing and weighting,
though, as becomes clear from the extracts included in this book from Oswald
Spengler and others (predominantly perhaps in the 'Society, Politics and Class'
section), was a familiar aspect of the historiography and social thought of the
era, as it was of its philosophy. Further, as the extracts included in 'Religion and
Belief' from anthropologists and classicists such as J. G. Frazer, Jane Harrison and
Jessie Weston suggest, a sense that even the 'primitive' past manifests a series of
declines and falls from a period of mythic coherence and original powerfulness
directs many of the intellectual endeavours of the late nineteenth century, and
thence the modernist, period.

History, then, is at issue in our period, more pressingly and powerfully in
writing in English than at any time since the English Renaissance. But the relation of past to present was an intensely fraught one, which had great *technical*
impact upon modernist works in all forms, although it is the poets who most
fretted about it in their essays. The idea that the modern period was (to adopt
the title of Max Nordau's book excerpted below), for good or ill, one of 'degeneration' from a perceived or imagined earlier time of unity and creativity over-
writes many of the literary works of the period. Eliot's famous despairing
assertion (or battle-cry?), when in a review-essay of 1921 he suddenly turns aside
from his task of reviewing some poets of the Renaissance in order to address their
inheritance in the present, is both symptomatic and emblematic of this
modernist situation:

> it appears likely the poets in our civilization, as it exists at present, must be
> *difficult*. Our civilization comprehends great variety and complexity, and this
> variety and complexity, playing upon a refined sensibility, must produce vari-
> ous and complex results. The poet must become more and more comprehen-
> sive, more allusive, more indirect, in order to force, to dislocate if necessary,
> language into his meaning.[23]

Eliot's writing here is as enigmatic in some ways as the kinds of poetry which
it sees as inevitable at this time. The adamant and repeated 'our civilization' is
determinedly inclusive, but at the same time raises the question of who the 'we'
is that share its values – all poets, or all people everywhere? It is a tension which

---

23 T. S. Eliot, 'The Metaphysical Poets', *Selected Essays* (London: Faber, 1972 edition), p. 289.

runs through much modernist writing in all genres.[24] Eliot displays anxiety about the history of his time in his attempt at clarification, 'as it exists at present', which acknowledges almost in spite of itself that the temporality and transience of all judgement make his assertions inevitably open to qualification. 'Comprehends' is a finely balanced term, correlative to Pound's use of 'containing' discussed above; it carries over from its French origin (Eliot was an extremely competent writer and reader in French) both the sense of 'including' and also that of 'understanding'. These are wholly different stances, one seemingly inside the historical situation being described, the other standing outside or above it, and able from that perspective to make sense of what is currently the case. Both meanings are then subtly extended by Eliot when he plays on words in the next sentence, where he suggests that such 'comprehension' demands 'comprehensiveness' from the contemporary poet, an all-inclusiveness (similar to his own in making these assertions) which is also an all-knowingness.

There is a further tension between what, in these circumstances, might seem Eliot's startling (because so resonantly 'old-fashioned', and 'aesthetic' or 'Romantic') notion that poets are marked out because of their 'refined sensibility', and his conclusion that they must commit extreme acts of violence, at this time, upon the language, in order to make it mean what they wish it to. 'To force, to dislocate if necessary' are shockingly aggressive acts: 'force' carries resonances not just of compulsion, but also of imposition, overstraining; to 'dislocate' means to disrupt normative connections, but also to wrench out of context, to displace geographically and even metaphysically.

Eliot's reading in this review-article of his ('our') historical situation in comparison with, and admiration for, that of the earlier, Renaissance, literary period, is therefore a starkly unsettled one. He moves from a stance of *passivity* to one of (sometimes) destructive and disruptive *activity*, and he combines both possibilities nicely within his puns. He is clearly attracted by the traditional 'literary' qualities of 'refinement', and even of 'civilization' as a shared conversation. Yet, at the same, he is aware that such virtues might, at any moment, be overwhelmed, washed away by the currents of other, un-containable forces of history. As a result, his conceit of poetry, and of a new modernist poetry, is that it must be both curiously passive before its historical moment, 'comprehending' its contents in the sense of merely reflecting them, and also active in containing and reflecting *upon* it.[25]

Remarkable within this unsettledness is Eliot's manifest distrust of the tools of his own and of 'our' trade; the basic, and to this point seemingly natural,

---

24 Leopold Diepeveen's opening chapter, 'Difficulty as Fashion', from his *The Difficulties of Modernism* (London: Routledge, 2003), makes some play with this tension.

25 The complaint against modernist literature that it was merely passive before contemporary events and experience was made most grandly and compellingly by the older, more formally traditional, poet W. B. Yeats, in his 1937 'A General Introduction for My Work', *Essays and Introductions* (London: Macmillan, 1989 edition).

obligation of language to make and carry meaning. It is a distrust which Eliot evidenced across his career in poetry: in 'Burnt Norton', the first work of the *Four Quartets*, he continues to contend that 'Words strain, / Crack and sometimes break, under the burden', lines which could provide a late gloss upon his complex use of 'force' when writing of the poets of the English Renaissance fifteen years before this work.[26]

Viewed as a manifesto, Eliot's remarks about variety and complexity, their reading of history and of their place in history, might be taken as a call for a new, disconnected and differently situated, modern writing – one moored to the past ('allusive' towards past texts), but also one which has broken with it. The failure of convention, in however a disenabled and wounded circumstance, provides also his and other modernist writers' exhilaration, their opportunity. It is necessary now to review the historical pressures which brought this sense of compulsion to Eliot and others at this precise moment, and which altered European and non-European writing irrevocably.

History and Modernism

> The War finished me . . . I had been walking in Westmorland . . . we came down to Barrow-in-Furness, and saw that war was declared. And we all went mad. I can remember soldiers kissing on Barrow station, and a woman shouting defiantly to her sweetheart – 'When you get at 'em, Clem, let 'em have it,' as the train drew off – and in all the tramcars, 'War'. – Messrs Vickers-Maxim call in their workmen . . . and the thousands of men streaming over the bridge. Then I went down the coast a few miles. And I think of the amazing sunsets over flat sands and the smoky sea – then of sailing in a fisherman's boat, running in the wind against a heavy sea . . . and the electric suspense everywhere – and the amazing, vivid, visionary beauty of everything, heightened up by the immense pain everywhere.[27]

D. H. Lawrence's reminiscence, in a letter to one of his patrons, of his feeling in August 1914 at the moment of the outbreak of war, fully carries, in its stark and rapid contrasts, the shock of that historical cataclysm upon a contemporary sensibility. Moving out of, then back into, a typically Romantic landscape, Lawrence remembers almost being thrown out of one century into the next, as the rush of volunteers into the army in the early days of the war in August 1914, and the rapid increase in munitions manufacture at factories such as Vickers-Maxim, led to many partings of lovers and massive shifts of population

---

26 T. S. Eliot, *Collected Poems* (London: Faber, 2002), p. 182.

27 D. H. Lawrence, letter to Cynthia Asquith, 31 January 1915, *The Letters of D. H. Lawrence*, vol. II: *June 1913–October 1916*, edited by George J. Zytaruk and James T. Boulton (Cambridge: Cambridge University Press, 1981), p. 268.

(Lawrence's sight of 'thousands' streaming over the bridge eerily looks forward to Eliot's vision of the crowd flowing over London Bridge in the post-war *The Waste Land*, the many undone by death). There is defiance in Lawrence's memory, but also the madness; it is as though traditional views of the country-side are transformed by the experience of war, 'electric', 'amazing', 'vivid'.

But also deadly: 'My heart has been as cold as a lump of dead earth, all this time, because of the War.' Lawrence, like all writers who had sought to adapt their technique to expressing modern experience in the years before the war, felt that the years of conflict, 1914–18, transformed everything, and demanded even more radical methods from artists in response. The novels he was working on at the time of the fighting in Europe, which became *The Rainbow* (1915) and *Women in Love* (1920), adopted a much more psychological and dramatic approach to the expression of their protagonists' feelings and understanding than his earlier work; in the novels he then published in the aftermath of the conflict (*The Lost Girl*, 1920, *Aaron's Rod*, 1922, and *Kangaroo*, 1923), he came close to breaking with traditional novel form altogether.

When war finally broke out in August 1914, it had seemed imminent for so long that it took everyone, including Lawrence, by surprise. For nearly forty years, the major political powers of Europe had been building an increasingly complex structure of rivalries and pressure points, largely driven by capitalist and industrial concerns, and by an imperial quest for more natural resources to fuel the factories and to provide markets for the goods produced. In 1870, Britain and its Empire produced over 32 per cent of the world's manufactured goods; by 1910, it produced only 14 per cent, as other competing national powers emerged.[28] The United States rapidly increased its industry in the last decades of the twentieth century; but in Europe, Germany, strengthened by a rapid growth in military armaments and by its alliance with the Austro-Hungarian Empire, had become a major rival, not just to Britain's manufacturing base, but also to its (and to the other European imperial power, France's) colonial possessions. Britain was increasingly overstretched in sustaining its Empire, as the Anglo-Boer War in South Africa (1899–1902) dramatically proved. This war on the other side of the world cost Britain £200 million, a massive sum at the time, and required the deployment of half a million men, before the relatively small band of Afrikaner Boers could be defeated.

These imperial conflict-points between the major European powers were tested in 1905, when the French displayed reluctance to allow the promised full independence to its colonial possession Morocco. The German Kaiser actually landed at Tangiers to make clear Germany's support. Whilst this direct challenge did not bring war (and there was a near repeat of this scenario in 1911, when

---

28 The narrative of the outbreak of the war is drawn here, and in my following pages, from 'The Origins of the War', chapter 1 of Huw Strachan's *The First World War*, vol. 1: *To Arms* (Oxford: Oxford University Press, 2001).

trouble again flared in Morocco), and whilst Germany did not intend it to do so, the Kaiser's action revealed Germany's new confidence in intervening in world politics, and particularly in the issue of relations between colonies and their European colonial masters. Meanwhile, to the east, Germany's ally Austria-Hungary was facing nationalist and anti-imperial unrest in several of its own possessions in the Balkans, including Serbia, which brought it into direct confrontation with a Russia anxious about its supply lines of food and manu-factured goods through the Black Sea, supply lines constantly threatened by the Austro-Hungarian domination of the region.

Treaties which had been forged between Britain and Russia over Britain's imperial territories in Asia, and between Britain and France to aid their mutual imperial progression, meant that an attack on any one of the so-called 'Triple-Entente' amounted to an attack on them all, and instant military mobilization to support the injured party. A similar arrangement had been forged between Germany and Austria-Hungary. All of which ensured that when, on 28 June 1914, the Archduke Franz Ferdinand, heir-apparent to the Austro-Hungarian throne, was assassinated in Sarajevo, in Serbia, by the nationalist Gavrilo Princip, the direct path to a catastrophic war was laid. The forces unleashed in the succeeding weeks meant that Serb jubilation at the Archduke's death led to Austro-Hungarian threats of reprisal; Russia, which inevitably supported Serbia's claim to freedom, confronted Austria-Hungary; Germany moved to support its ally. In the early days of August 1914, and according to a plan to forge a rapid victory for Germany in the case of such a conflict which had been drawn up many years earlier, Germany attacked France through Belgium. Britain inevitably declared war in response on Germany. The course of events outlined in the introductory materials and head notes to The First World War part of the 'Key Historical Events' section of this anthology was under way.

Whilst the impact of the four years of the Western Front and the war in the east between Russia, Austro-Hungary and Germany was fundamental to post-war literature, as also to philosophy, social thinking, psychology – in fact, to many of the documents in the Sourcebook dating from after 1918 – it is also true that the increasing unsettledness outside national borders in the pre-war era had been matched by growing social tension in both Britain and the United States. Britain had seen an immediate dramatization of later issues relating to the Empire in its wrestling with claims for Irish Home Rule from the 1880s onwards. The rise of a coherent socialist movement, also from the 1880s, led to pressure for social change. There was a new urgency, particularly, to put a greater support system in place for the financially impoverished classes, which brought about a series of reforms from the Liberal administration of 1906 onwards. While in both Britain and America, increases in industrialization were leading to acceleration in the urban population, with attendant social and political problems brought about by the rise of a relatively rootless labouring class, and by the concomi-tantly sudden modernization of outlook and expectation.

At the same time, the rise of a women's movement, seeking principally the right to the vote (a movement only temporally held in check by the First World War), on both sides of the Atlantic led to a re-examination of the balance of power, both in the home and in society at large. In America, the war saw also a new phenomenon – the migration of an increasingly vocal Black population from the South to the urban centres of New York and Chicago, in order to work in the factories and to take over work from soldiers called to the Front, after America joined the war in Europe in April 1917. This population movement, spearheaded by an educated and newly emergent professional class, was soon making its own claims to the cultural and literary centre-ground. The details of all of these movements relating to women's rights, social change, and racial shifts, are given in the introductions and head notes of the requisite sections of the Sourcebook.

Redefining Modernism

The response to such radical pressures amongst English language writers in the first thirty years of the twentieth century was, as recognized by early critics writing about them, to explore two seemingly divergent possibilities and their inter-relation. The key terms were 'realism' and 'symbolism'. In *realism*, a work's content reflects (however critically) the surface features of the modern world or individuals' response to them; in its *symbolism* or mythologizing, that content is either subsumed by, or ordered within, some other, 'higher', patterning. In modernist texts, this was a patterning which more often than not defied traditional Christian ideas. The novelist and artist Wyndham Lewis caught the fine tension between realism and myth in introductory remarks to his *Time and Western Man* (1927):

> Everyone, I am persuaded, must to-day fit themselves for thinking more clearly about the problems of everyday life, by accustoming themselves to think of the abstract things existing, more distinctly than ever before, behind such problems. Where everything is in question, and where all traditional values are repudiated, the everyday problems have become, necessarily, identical with the abstractions from which all concrete things in the first place come.[29]

Lewis's perspective here is a Platonic one, suggesting that in the modern period, where the veneer of traditional belief systems and normalizing systems in life have been comprehensively stripped away, we are returned to primal ideas and forms.[30]

---

29 Wyndham Lewis, *Time and Western Man* (New York: Harcourt Brace, 1928 edition), p. vii.
30 A similar idea had driven Sigmund Freud's desire to interpret dreams from the time of his *The Psychopathology of Everyday Life* (1901).

Exemplary of such tension between (problematic) present and ('repudiated') past, and similar trends in contemporary thinking, is James Joyce's *Ulysses* (1922). Joyce's encapsulation of one day in the life of Dublin is, on the one hand, ultra-realist, going far beyond nineteenth-century attempts to render the everyday in a literary form. Several of Joyce's famous literary experiments in the novel are in fact perhaps paradoxically aimed towards this end – as most obviously at the opening of the 'Sirens' episode, which provides a kind of musical score for the sounds which are to be heard in its succeeding pages: 'Bronze by gold heard the hoofirons, steelyringing Imperthnthnthnthnthn.'[31] What at first seems an alienating abstraction (as in 'Bronze by gold', which denotes the hair colour of the two barmaids central to the episode) is given a rhythmic base which captures more truly the sound of the horse's hooves passing in the street outside the Dublin bar. The reader is bewildered by the literary ambition and effect, but once she or he has 'caught up' with the governing idea behind Joyce's experiment here, the *realism* of the sentences, their mimetic function in capturing the glinting impressions of the everyday, is obvious. And yet at the same time, the episode (like the whole novel) is structured upon its consonance with an original episode in Homer's *Odyssey*, in which a hero is nearly lured onto the rocks by the beauty of the sirens' singing. What we have in these few phrases, as at all points in the novel, is a supreme rendition of the everyday which constantly falls away to remind us of its literary and mythological origin, its relation to ancient human urges and understanding.

In terms of the formation of modernist canons by recent literary and cultural critics, however, this tension between realism, symbolism, and mythology has very real consequences. Principally this has led (and often so in the United States) to the exclusion of those England-based Edwardian novelists such as Conrad, Lawrence, and Forster, who were clearly less formally experimental in many respects than those modernist writers always favoured by the critical establishment, including Joyce. These Edwardians continued a version of realism inherited from the nineteenth-century novel in order to offer critical perspectives upon the social, imperial and industrial realities of their time. On the other hand, by exploring the psyche of those entrapped by these modern realities, the Edwardian novelists displayed a focus that they held in common with many more technically-experimental modernist writers and, as this volume illustrates, with many modern thinkers. Several telling collections of essays in the past decade have sought to overcome this tension within canon-formation for the period, and to forge accommodations between modernism and Edwardian literature; several critics have sought to untangle the complex origins of modernism from the conservative and traditional contemporary literary trends out of which, and against which, it emerged.[32]

---

31 James Joyce, *Ulysses. The 1922 Text*, ed. Jeri Johnson (Oxford: Oxford University Press, 1993), p. 245.
32 On modernism and Edwardianism see, for instance, *Seeing Double: Revisioning Edwardian and*

Yet such accommodations, and important contextualizing work around them, whilst they perform valuable service in establishing the shared literary and social perceptions amongst a diverse range of artists at the beginning of the twentieth century, only serve ultimately to weaken the definition of *modernism* further. They leach out the distinctiveness of modernism as a phenomenon, as a set of shared hopes and ambitions which could be read across a definite social and literary grouping of writers at one point in literary history. The critical *impasse* around modernism continues, while the 'canon' of the period expands ever wider to accommodate issues raised by attention to gender and race amongst others, and the time-scale of the period extends and extends. What has not happened at the moment critically is any comprehensive attempt to trace the everyday life of modernism itself, the kind of palaeography which has underlain critical explorations of earlier literary groupings, such as popular recent work on the Renaissance.[33] Furthermore, the modernists, as has now been broadly recognized, undertook a conscious campaign (one largely orchestrated by the American poet Ezra Pound) to promote their work as the true product of modernity in a number of so-called 'little' magazines. And yet, although the gender and marketing aspects of this phenomenon have been well discussed,[34] not much detailed attention has been given to the content of these magazines as a whole, and to their implicit commentary upon the divergent trends and tensions within the literature of the time.[35] It is in this area that a further-developed understanding of modernism perhaps lies.

Take, for example, a number of the magazine *Poetry* for August 1914, the month in which the First World War broke out. 'A Magazine of Verse' edited in monthly parts by Harriet Monroe, *Poetry* sought to capture for its genre the modernity evident in the cityscapes of its place of origin, Chicago. Monroe's ambition for the journal is evident in the subscription form printed towards the back of the journal, as one of 'forwarding the recognition of those younger poets

---

Modernist Literature, ed. Carola M. Kaplan and Anne B. Simpson (New York: St Martin's, 1996), and *Outside Modernism: In Pursuit of the English Novel, 1900–1930*, ed. Lynne Hapgood and Nancy L. Paxton (Basingstoke: Macmillan, 2000). For modernism, and its interwoven history with modest English literary ambitions, in the period, see 'Modernism and the Georgians' by Marianne Thormahlen, in her collection *Rethinking Modernism* (Basingstoke: Palgrave Macmillan, 2003), and *British Poetry in the Age of Modernism* by Peter Howarth (Cambridge: Cambridge University Press, 2005).

33 See, for example, James Shapiro, *1599: A Year in the Life of Shakespeare* (London: Faber, 2005).

34 See Mark S. Morrison, *The Public Face of Modernism: Little Magazines, Audiences and Reception, 1905-1920* (Madison: University of Wisconsin Press, 2001); Jayne E. Marek, *Women Editing Modernism: 'Little' Magazines and Literary History* (Lexington: University of Kentucky Press, 1995); and *Marketing Modernisms: Self-Promotion, Canonization, Rereading*, ed. Kevin J. H. Dettmar and Stephen Watt (Ann Arbor: University of Michigan Press, 1996). The 'Literary Production and Reception' section of this anthology selects some key statements about the ambition of these magazines.

35 The Modernist Journals Project at Brown University, which is currently engaged in putting the full content of *The New Age* online, is performing extremely valuable work to which I am indebted in this volume. The editorial apparatus for the Project is, however, still in the process of formation.

whose work belongs to this generation, but whose acceptance might otherwise be retarded by a lack of adventurous application'. The contemporary nature of the magazine's content is immediately associated, for a would-be subscriber, with the relative youth of the writers printed there; Monroe's ambition is, like that of many of the co-editors of these 'little' magazines, to win broader acceptance for those writers who most reflect upon the present, and whose work will be therefore most challenging to established views.

It is clear from her 'Editorial Comment' to this number of *Poetry* that, for Monroe, 'acceptance' includes financial reward for good poetry. Challenging an article in a newspaper which had claimed that poets should not be provided with financial support or write in expectation of reward, Monroe launches her own attack on Romantic notions that poetic genius is displayed by those who live in conditions of extreme hunger and poverty, in the garrets of major European cities:

> A masterpiece of art is not a miracle of individual genius so much as the expression of a reciprocal relation between the artist and his public. He who must butt his head against a stone wall of apathy cannot long get out of it his best work.[36]

Monroe's challenge here runs intriguingly against that trend, which many have seen within modernism, for the work of art to sustain a hieratic and intransigent relation towards its audience, one in which the obscurities of the work serve to mark a coterie elitism that runs right across the novels and poems of the time. Her call for a 'reciprocal relation' between writer and public, one which will guarantee proper financial rewards for decent work, suggests rather that modern poetry might be conceived as a dialogue between writer and audience; or that, at least, journals such as her own seek to foster such reciprocation. To this end, later in this edition of her journal, she objects to the (of course, highly topical) martial poems in a new collection by the American writer Louis Untermeyer, because of their deployment of subject-matter in order to bully and brutalize the reader's response: 'Muscle is not magic, and art may not be achieved by brawn alone' (p. 204).

Monroe's editorial comment anticipates many of the dilemmas faced by poets once the war fully broke out, and its brazen destructiveness became fully realized. As the Anglo-Irishman W. B. Yeats, the senior poet of the time, put it rather grandly in 'On Being Asked for a War Poem', it is better that poets be silent at such times, since 'We have no gift to set a statesman right,' and the poets' audience must be other than politicians or soldiers.[37] But Ezra Pound, through his

---

36 Harriet Monroe, 'Editorial Comment', *Poetry: A Magazine of Verse*, vol. IV, no. V (August 1914), pp. 197–8. Subsequent references to this number are included in the text.

37 W. B. Yeats, *Collected Poems* (London: Macmillan, 1979), p. 175.

version of a Roman poet's works, would wrestle with dilemmas about the relation between brutal war experience and aesthetics in his 'Homage to Sextus Propertius' (1917). It is Pound's work which obviously met Monroe's criteria for poetic 'reciprocity' in what would be the first month of war, and in this issue of *Poetry*, which opens with a selection of his new poems. These poems are in Pound's sarcastic and satiric (also misogynistic) mode for the most part, although they notably raise also the issue of aesthetics in the midst of a busy and distracting everyday life. 'The Study in Aesthetics' recalls an incident in the life of the medieval Italian poet Dante when he paused (according to the poem) in a noisy fish-market, and murmured 'for his own satisfaction' *'Ch'e be'a'* ('How beautiful she is') – presumably remembering his epical love, Beatrice. Other Pound poems included by Monroe here rage at the fakeness of the upper-class rich ('The Bellaires') and (hatefully) at the shallowness of contemporary female aesthetes ('Ladies'). 'Salvationists' is rather more interesting, suggesting archly and sardonically that anything smacking of 'perfection' at the time was certain to be 'rather disliked' (p. 172). Extraordinary is the final poem in this small selection from Pound – 'Abu Salammamm – A Song of Empire', which unsurprisingly, given its content, he did not include in a book-length collection of his poetry until 1949.[38] *'Being the sort of poem I would write should George the Fifth have me chained to the fountain before Buckingham Palace'*, as the poem is introduced, its theme questions the bravado of the imperial project so crucial to the run-up to the First World War (see this Introduction's 'History and Modernism', above) in ways which again anticipate Pound's own sequence on Propertius:

> Great is King George the Fifth;
> For his army is legion,
> His army is a thousand and forty-eight soldiers
>   with red cloths about their buttocks
> And they have red faces like bricks.
>
>   (p. 177)

Presuming that he will soon be usurped as court jester, the speaker of this Song's anti-monarchism, and anti-imperialism, is given fuller vent.

The other poems in this edition of *Poetry* form a 'study' similar to that of Pound into the relation of art to the contemporary, of aesthetics to the mundane. Amy Lowell's 'The Coal Picker' shows an ordinary, suffering worker, who gleans small reward from his toil, but who imagines an almost medieval splendour arising from the light and heat which his coal will raise ('an enduring goal! / He sighs and grubs another coal') (p. 179). Allan Updegraff's 'The Dance before the Arch' imagines an outbreak of revelry and pageantry from Roman

---

38 *Pound: Poems and Translations*, ed. Richard Sieburth (New York: The Library of America, 2003), p. 610.

times breaking out in the modern city streets, revealing a consonance of classical tropes, between what we associate as 'high' modernist poetics and the work
of lesser-known poets from the period. The most intriguing work in the issue is,
though, James Stephens's 'The Waste Places I–II', which in its manner and some
of its ideas anticipates Eliot's *The Waste Land* by eight years. A poem in traditional quatrains, Stephens's work shows its speaker confronted with the void of
desert places 'As a naked man', losing his identity, his singleness, and his gender.
Coming upon a 'couching lion', he reveals 'the terrors of a maid', and suffers
Christ-like pain of mind and body. Imagining (or imagining an hallucination of)
the ravishing of a maiden by a demon, he becomes wholly split from himself:

> I am the maiden and the fear;
>   I am the sunless shade, the strife;
> I am the demon lips, the sneer
>   Showing under every life.
>
>   (p. 191)

Here, the satiric intention of contemporary work, such as Pound's 'Song of
Empire' early in the number of the journal, is given a terrible and haunting quality, a sense that humanity is truly and pointlessly stricken when confronted by
the primal realities underlying all events.

Taken as a brief, but coherent, snapshot of modernist writing at the outbreak
of the war, then, this issue of *Poetry* suggests several trends: a shared urge by this
'young' generation to 'see through' the surface qualities and values of the
contemporary world, in order to 'sneer', as Pound does in this mode, or in order
to suggest the continuance of imaginative possibilities even within its mundane-
ness and hardship. At this level, the selection of work presented offers a continuation, on different ground, of the kinds of Romantic vision and sublimity being
written a hundred years before, if one with a hard contemporary, and often city-
situated, edge which is newly open to ancient world-views as part of its imaginative reach.[39] However, that relation between 'aesthetics' and the 'everyday'
continues to form a central issue and source of anxiety, as it had before the war,
and as it would in subsequent work in all genres. But there is also the sense that
in this extreme self-consciousness, there is a shared perspective between poet
and audience, an understanding being built which will license writing in a range
of genres, from Pound's satires to Updegraff's Bacchic reverie. In Stephens's
contribution there is a darker urge, a sense that nothing can remain stable when
confronted by the terrors of the imagination itself.

What might arise from such a study of the early publishing contexts of writ-

---

39 For discussion of the continuation of Romantic methodologies into modernism, see George
   Bornstein, *Transformations of Romanticism in Yeats, Eliot, and Stevens* (Chicago: University of Chicago
   Press, 1976).

ing from this period, barely hinted at by this brief diversion into one number of a key journal of the time, is not a further expansion of the modernist canon (as driven by laudable political or textual initiatives elsewhere in criticism of the last thirty years), but a fuller sense of the pressing concerns and shared resonances of writing at this moment, one in which the sense of a loss of value, but also a lasting set of literary strategies and techniques in response to that loss, were emerging. These are a set of strategies and techniques which continue to echo in writing to this day. Part of these techniques, and a result of them, was a shared questioning of the value of literary writing, its significance for the early twentieth century in comparison with earlier eras, which the other sections of the Introduction explore.

Crucial for that deeper comprehension of the shared anxieties and compensatory techniques between literary communities, and of the literary reciprocities – real or imagined – in the first three decades of the twentieth century, is a full realization of the interdisciplinary contexts out of which the texts emerged at the end of the previous century, and which they in turn speak to. This context is in part (and largely uncharted to date) the everyday history of the era; its newspapers, films, shows, as well as its intellectual and cultural publications – the normal life, in other words, of an ambitious artistic class living for the most part in metropolitan centres, at any period in history. Another, large part of establishing a deeper comprehension of the period, is achievement of a greater knowledge of the multiple shifts in ideas across the intellectual disciplines at the time, in philosophy or science, politics or theology. Most immediately as examples, the sections in this Sourcebook on 'Empire . . . ' and 'Society . . .', as on 'Religion and Belief' and 'Philosophy and Ideas', help more broadly to understand the poems by Pound, Updegraff and Stephens selected by Harriet Monroe for *Poetry* in August 1914; the selections on 'Literary Production and Reception' help to locate the ambition she had for her journal amidst that of other modernist outlets. This Sourcebook, in other words, offers preliminary footsteps towards a greater shared understanding and clarification of the instigations for writing, as for the other arts, at the time.

Conclusion: Modernism and/as the Local

When in 1953, T. S. Eliot, the by now fantastically successful elder statesman of letters, lectured at the University of Washington – one of several re-encounters he made with his native land later in life – he made a surprising assertion about his preference amongst the American writers whom he had read and admired when young:

> Twain, at least in *Huckleberry Finn*, reveals himself to be one of those writers, of whom there are not many in any literature, who have discovered a new way of writing, valid not only for themselves but for others. . . .[t]he

Mississippi of Mark Twain is not only the river known to those who voyage
on it or live beside it, but the universal river of human life – more universal,
indeed, than the Congo of Joseph Conrad.[40]

Eliot was himself brought up in St Louis, beside the River Mississippi: as he says
of this 'strong brown god' at the opening of 'The Dry Salvages', 'his rhythm was
present in the nursery bedroom'.[41] The revelation being made at the University
of Washington is, therefore, about a return to roots and beginnings, to a sound
which was familiar to Eliot in the earliest days, and to a rhythm that he feels is
captured in the stories of boyhood by Mark Twain. There are other self-catch-
ings-up by Eliot in this lecture also; Joseph Conrad's story set on the River
Congo, *Heart of Darkness* (1899), had, earlier in his life, seemed to present Eliot
with the most compelling diagnosis available of that modern condition which
he was himself trying to render in poetry. He had wanted to append a quotation
from it to *The Waste Land*, but dropped it on Pound's advice, before finally using
it as epigraph to 'The Hollow Men' (1925). Now, towards the end of his own life,
Eliot sees Conrad's statement as somehow still 'universal', but also less comprehensively so than the voice of his local river, Twain's 'river of life', the comings
and goings of the barge-men and river-men, with their dialect and technical
vocabularies. It is summatory placing by Eliot of local, idiomatic, and comedic,
continuities over and above the alien, foreign encounter, and loss of self before
indescribable immensities ('The horror! The horror!') in Conrad's tale.

Eliot's self-reversal here seems indicative of the various tensions within
modernist writing. In the first decades of the twentieth century, a group of writers were drawn, from personal ambition, into the burgeoning metropolises, and
sought to make sense of their new situation out of the experiences and resources
they carried with them. The local and the international meet head on within
modernism, and the unresolved tensions between the two forces make for much
of its excitement for later readers. As a result of these tensions, the feelings of
rootlessness and alienation which are keynotes of modernist art sound again and
again. Writing of the music of the Austrian composer Gustav Mahler, the critic
and theorist Theodor W. Adorno declared that

The inauthenticity of the language of music becomes its tonal substance.
Mahler's tonal chords, plain and unadorned, are the explosive expressions of
the pain felt by the individual subject imprisoned in an alienated society.
They are the cryptograms of modernism, guardians of the absolute dissonance which after him became the very language of music.[42]

---

40 T. S. Eliot, 'American Literature and the American Language', *To Criticize the Critic and Other Writings*
     (London: Faber, 1978), p. 54.
41 Eliot, *Collected Poems*, p. 192.
42 Theodor W. Adorno, 'Mahler', *Quasi una Fantasia: Essays on Modern Music*, translated by Rodney
     Livingstone (London: Verso, 1998), pp. 85–6.

In modernist literature in English, that 'inauthenticity' everywhere resounds alongside the feeling that when these writers began their careers, there were no available literary models upon which they could base their own renditions of their experiences. In 'Mr Bennett and Mrs Brown', Woolf bemoans the fact that, in 1910, at the beginning of the modern age from her point of view, the most likely models were Joseph Conrad, whose Polish-ness set him aside from being 'helpful', and Thomas Hardy, who had not written a novel for fifteen years. (These were also, to state the obvious, male writers, to whom, in Woolf's quest to render women's experience, she would largely turn in vain.) T. S. Eliot, when responding to Woolf about her essay, agreed, lamenting 'the absence of any masters of the previous generation whose work one could carry on' and the correlative 'amount of waste' that is incurred in trying to establish a new way of writing adequate to modern experience.[43]

Modernism, and modernist technique, is to that extent improvisation and adaptation, a making shift with the materials which were available to the individual writer, and therefore an attempt to bring into some consonance the materials from their background with their experience of modern life in the cities and foreign contexts to which they each in their way translated themselves. Into this melting-pot went, therefore, a vivid range of regional, colonial, and translingual, experiences and familial memories, which cross with alien historical and modern matter. This trend underscores the diversity of modernist writing, from Ezra Pound's reminiscence of his ancestors' frontiersman past at the opening of 'Canto XXII', to Katherine Mansfield's stories such as 'The Garden Party'. In each case, the immediate and local experience or lore rests uneasily within and against the swirl of cosmopolitan thoughts and feelings, the multiple other voices which also enter the poetry or prose of each. In each case, the local material registers the fractures and accommodations of the modernist text, as is evidenced particularly in the many-voiced novels of the American South by William Faulkner.

It is this sense of compromise and rootlessness, self-alienation, which modernism would seem to have bequeathed, and which would seem to have endured in the much more fractured modern world that has succeeded it. As the Anglo-Welsh poet David Jones – himself an admirer of the work of Joyce and Eliot – remarked in the Preface to his epic on classical, Catholic, and Welsh themes, *The Anathemata* (1952): 'The poet is born into a given situation and it follows that his problems . . . will be . . . what might be called "situational problems".'[44] As a soldier who had fought at the Western Front, and whose previous work *In Parenthesis* (1937) had sought to convey that traumatic and fracturing experience, Jones was alert to the ways in which 'situation' now included both

---

43 Quoted in T. S. Eliot, *Inventions of the March Hare: Poems, 1909–1917*, ed. Christopher Ricks (London: Faber, 1996), p. 387.

44 David Jones, *The Anathemata* (London: Faber, 1952), p. 22.

the failure of local inheritance and international catastrophe. The 'situational problems' which result from that dual perspective, both towards personal experience, and towards the outer limits of modern communication, have continued as a preoccupation of *all* writing to this day. Arguably therefore, all twentieth and twenty-first-century writing is to that extent modernist writing. The late Russian poet Joseph Brodsky claimed that

> Because civilizations are finite, in the life of each of them comes a moment when centers cease to hold. . . . The job of holding at such times is done by [those] from the provinces, from the outskirts. Contrary to popular belief, the outskirts are not where the world ends – they are precisely where it unravels.[45]

Brodsky's silent citation here, 'when centers cease to hold', is, of course, a reference to W. B. Yeats's apocalyptic vision in the immediate aftermath of the First World War, as it is conceived in 'The Second Coming':

> Things fall apart; the centre cannot hold;
> Mere anarchy is loosed upon the world,
> The blood-dimmed tide is loosed, and everywhere
> The ceremony of innocence is drowned. . . .[46]

To the extent that Yeats's historical diagnosis has proved correct – as also to the extent that it is writers working with their local experience who have had to 'hold' 'things' together in their texts – it is inevitably the writers from the 'provinces' (whether literally, or in terms of their need to give voice to experience never before expressed) who, in their modernism, have been, and continue to be, the most dynamic and at the same time stabilizing writers of the twentieth century and up to the present day.

Note on the Texts Selected

Where possible the earliest published editions of each of the works excerpted has been used, as those most contemporaneous with the period, even where differences occur between original and later versions of any one text. I have also always sought out original or early translations of foreign works, in order again to allow readers of the Sourcebook to experience those works as modernist writers themselves probably would have done. Where it is the case, as with Max

---

45 Joseph Brodsky, 'The Sound of the Tide', on the West Indian poet Derek Walcott, *Less Than One* (Harmondsworth: Penguin, 1987), p. 164.
46 W. B. Yeats, *Collected Poems*, p. 211. Although the poem was published in *Michael Robartes and the Dancer* in 1921, it was written in 1919.

Weber's work, for example, that the first English translation did not appear until the 1930s, although his ideas were known in popular versions in the little magazines during the modernist period, I have again excerpted the earliest translation possible.

Where three dots appear in an extract ('. . .'), it is signifying that there is a silent break made in the given text, and that some material from the original has been omitted. In some parts of the Sourcebook, I have taken the editorial decision to include longer extracts from key texts, where it is important to see the development of an argument or set of ideas which have had a significant impact upon modernist literature. This has meant that some of the sections below contain a smaller number of extracts than others.

1

Key Historical Events

1.1 The First World War

The military conflict which devastated Europe for four years from 1914 to 1918 began as a local war between Austria-Hungary and Serbia in July 1914, spread with a series of declarations of war by the major European imperial powers in early August, and soon sucked in 32 nations. The immediate cause of the war was the assassination of the heir-presumptive to the Austro-Hungarian throne by Gavrilo Princip, a Serb nationalist. But the near-immediate involvement of so much of Europe and the wider world in the conflict revealed the delicate and doomed balance which had been sustained for some time between competitive nationalisms, imperial ambitions, and economic competition between a range of states. All of these forces built a paranoia between nations resulting in a vast military and naval build-up from 1900, which eventually saw major countries drawn up into two opposing groups in Europe: the Triple Entente powers of Britain, Russia and France, and the Triple Alliance of Germany, Austria-Hungary and Italy. After wars in the Balkans in 1912–13, Serb determination to bring back areas of Austria-Hungary which had traditionally formed part of the Slav peoples grew. But with Russia determined to support Serbia in any conflict with the Austro-Hungarians, and with all the powers in each of the triple configurations of nations committed to mobilize their armies to support any of the others if threatened, any spark such as that caused by the assassination of Franz Ferdinand would inevitably and rapidly draw all the major powers into battle with one another. This duly happened in the first four days of August 1914, although Italy remained neutral until May the next year. The Germans advanced rapidly through Belgium, defeating a British Expeditionary Force and the French once they arrived in northern France. But the German advance was too rapid; one army, under General von Kluck, became isolated ahead of the others, and was defeated at the First Battle of the Marne. Despite their best efforts, the Germans could advance no further after another battle at Flanders in late 1914, and both sides 'dug in' to begin the awful attrition of the trench warfare that lasted almost without let up until 1918. By the end of 1914, more than 500 miles of trenches had been constructed by each side, stretching from the Swiss border, across northern France, to the North Sea. Many attempts were made on each side to break through, and technologies were rapidly developed which sought to bring maximum devastation upon the enemy. Poisonous chlorine gas was first used by the Germans in April 1915; tanks were first deployed on a large scale by the British at the Battle of Cambrai in November 1917. Shells and weaponry became more and more sophisticated and appalling in terms of destructive power, across the years of conflict. The United States entered the war in April 1917; Russia was defeated by Germany in early 1918; a last German offensive at Arras was halted eventually, and with the arrival of the American troops, the tide turned. The conflict was finally drawn to a close with the unconditional surrender of the Triple Alliance Central Powers on 11 November 1918. In terms of resources, there had never been a war remotely on this scale: total costs of the conflict have been estimated at $186 billion. Casualties amongst the troops fighting on the ground have been put as high as 37 million. Over 70% of those mobilized in Russia or France were either killed, wounded, taken prisoner, or listed as missing; over 35% of those from the British Empire (many from the Crown Colonies, including India, Canada, Australia and Ireland, fought in the trenches). In addition, it has been estimated that 10 million civilians were killed as a result of the conflict.

In many ways the war changed perceptions and beliefs, and many of these changes are reflected in the literature written both during and after the conflict; the extracts offered here are intended to signal a range of broader issues from the vast welter of information and opinion from these years. The extracts should be read alongside several more included in Section 10 of this book, which review the psychological impact on those caught up in the warfare; and several in Section 3, which outline some women's response to the conflict.

1.1(a) The Military Service Bill, which brought universal conscription to the UK

*Editorial, Daily News and Leader, **Thursday, 6 January 1916***

The patriotic surge which greeted the final onset of war, after what seemed like a period of several years in which the war had been about to break out, brought over 300,000 volunteers into the Recruitment Offices in Britain. But by 1916, news had reached home of the mechanized devastation on the Western Front in northern France, and the high level of casualties, both killed and wounded, was evident to everyone. In addition, it was unclear when the war would be over; some estimates from politicians ran to as long as a decade of conflict before any armistice could be concluded. These factors had great impact on the willingness of men of military age to volunteer. Others felt that by bringing many more soldiers into the army immediately, it might be possible to overwhelm the Germans by sheer force of numbers. General Kitchener, in command of the British forces, sought 1.5 million extra men by the end of the year. Herbert Asquith, the Prime Minister of the Coalition government formed in May 1915, sought to introduce measures which would eventually lead to compulsory conscription of all able-bodied men to the services. But there were tremendous disagreements amongst his ruling administration; the Liberal Party, for instance, adamantly opposed the measures on ethical and moral lines, seeing them as an infringement of civil liberties. Asquith sought to delay as long as possible, realizing that the crisis was raising many issues embedded in the national psyche which might distract from the effort to win the conflict itself. In October he accepted a notion proposed by his Director-General of Recruiting, Lord Derby, that a semi-compulsory scheme be put in place, whereby men had to 'attest' to their willingness to serve, on the understanding that unmarried men would be called up for service first. This led to a predictable result; a rush to get married was on amongst the single male population. When it became clear that this was happening, and that over a million single men had avoided the voluntary attestation, Asquith was forced to allow the Military Service Bill to be introduced in January 1916. It enforced service upon those other than priests, conscientious objectors, and those deemed to be working in essential industries. A second Bill had to be introduced as early as April, to include married men in the draft; now, all males between the ages of eighteen and forty-one were eligible to serve. The crisis over the Bill, which eventually led to Asquith's replacement by David Lloyd George as Prime Minister, impacted upon a number of issues; individual freedoms, masculinity, the balance of society. Arguably, those who opposed the idea of the Bill were proved right in the long term. The slaughter in France continued, and the extra numbers recruited did nothing to shift the balance of power between the enemies. This extract from an editorial in the popular newspaper The Daily News *outlines the case for that opposition.*

THE CRISIS

The debate which followed the introduction of the Military Service Bill made it clear that we are on the brink of a grave internal disaster. Mr. Asquith based his case for the Bill not on the fact that the voluntary system had failed. On the contrary, the voluntary appeal had succeeded beyond all expectation, and the scandalous effort of the Conscriptionist Press to magnify the element of the 'shirker' is a flagrant falsehood as well as an insult to the nation. Out of the fewer than eight million men of military age nearly six million are already either enlisted or have offered themselves for enlistment. In the face of that immense fact the suggestion that the principle of voluntary service has failed is too grotesque to bear consideration. But, while the Derby appeal has produced all the men called for, it has produced them on conditions which, in the opinion of Mr. Asquith, made compulsion in the case of the single man necessary. His justification of the pledge is that without it the men would not have been forthcoming – that the threat of compulsion brought in the single men on the one hand, and the assurance it gave brought in the married on the other. That may be the case. No-one can say that it was absolutely the case, for it was not until a month after the pledge was given that the great rush came, and no-one is in a position to say what was the true psychology of that impulse. But Mr. Asquith, bound by his pledge and assured by Lord Derby that the failure of the single men was not negligible, considers that he has no alternative to the course embodied in the Bill he introduced yesterday. That Bill is limited enough in its scope and provides for ample exemptions. But it introduces into this country a principle which is alien to our spirit and which once introduced will remain as a permanent menace to our conceptions of liberty. It can only be admitted on evidence that cannot be disputed, and by what Mr. Asquith himself has described as 'general consent'.

The general consent is wanting. It is wanting for the reason that the Derby report has not made out the case, and that the attempt to introduce compulsion before the case is made out cannot be defended. Mr. Asquith protested against too nice a scrutiny of the figures. But the whole question is a question of figures, and it is the simple fact to say that when Sir John Simon[1] sat down the case on which the Bill rests had been torn to fragments. The 650,000 single men unaccounted for, which had been reduced by Lord Derby's own deductions to 316,000, shrank to exiguous proportions under the searching analysis to which Sir John Simon subjected the figures. It is not necessary here to traverse the ground he covered. But the conclusion to which the analysis brought him goes to the heart of the matter. It is that the government are asking for a verdict before they have heard their evidence. Mr. Asquith, in giving the pledge, undertook that before compulsion was resorted to there should be a thorough sifting of the figures and that the men who have failed to come forward should have the opportunity of giving their reasons. That condition has not been fulfilled. The figures on which the case rests are shown to be mere rough calculations which ignore whole classes of the community who under no circumstances can be regarded as available men. In a word, we do not know whether the failure of the single men represents a substantial total or a negligible total. All we know is that the net estimate of 315,000 is certainly extravagant. The true figure may be only 100,000. It is clearly not 200,000.

It is deplorable that on so grave an issue as the introduction of Conscription there should be the appearance of unwarranted haste to secure a judgement before the evidence is presented. The reason for that course goes to the root of this subject. There has been for months past a determined campaign for imposing Conscription on this country. That campaign has been motivated, not by regard for the military needs of the country, but by political aims. Compulsion has been sought as an end in itself. Now in the last resort the nation would accept compulsion if only by that means the war could be won. But it will not pay that price for the gratification of those who aim at compulsion as an instrument of government. And it is because the attempt to force this issue before the weapon of a General Election has ceased to be operative has revealed the mean-

---

1 Simon was the Liberal Party member of the Coalition Cabinet, who made the most eloquent case against conscription through his speeches in the House of Commons.

ing of the eagerness to snatch the verdict – it is because of this that we are faced with a crisis of the most serious character. . . . Is this the sort of issue that we can raise in the midst of the tremendous struggle in which we are engaged? And all for what? For 100,000, at most 200,000 men whose lack of patriotism would in any case indicate their worthlessness as soldiers. There is a possibility that the Government may fall, and that the country may be plunged into a General Election. But will that clear the path for us? The compulsionists will carry the country no doubt, but they will come back with the real problem unresolved. They will come back to face a situation intensified by the bitterness of a fierce controversy. The nation will be rent in twain, and while we ought to be using every ounce of our power to overcome the enemy we should be wasting it in profitless struggle between ourselves. Every patriotic consideration should determine us that that disastrous possibility should be avoided.

1.1(b) Documents relating to the first day of the Battle of the Somme

One immediate proof seized upon by the anti-conscriptionists in the British Parliament that the Military Service Bill was ineffective in ending the war, as its supporters sometimes claimed, was the massive carnage brought about at the Battle of the Somme in July 1916. The documents extracted here, drawn from contemporary reports of the battle, are intended to be representative of the response to the many other battles of the war. The first Somme conflict is unique in the war itself, though, since the British Generals, who had become worried about a loss of heart and hope amongst the civilian population at home, allowed newspapers access for the first time to the battle as it unfolded. As is evident from the optimistic and patriotic note frequently sounded in the reports below – and particularly at the end of each report – the news relating to the Front Line was heavily censored. But the story of the opening days of the battle was very different from the one relayed here. Seeking to relieve pressure on their lines brought about by a German attack at Verdun, the British and French forces under the British General Haig were to attack along the River Somme with nineteen divisions of British troops and two of French. The plan was to ensure a breakthrough of the German trench system by first destroying the enemy barbed wire and defensive artillery by unleashing the most momentous barrage of shelling ever witnessed. Three million shells were launched from nearly 1,500 heavy guns and howitzers in the run-up to the advance from the trenches planned for 1 July. In this plan, though, Haig was totally deluded. The shelling caused minimal damage, as the German trenches were carefully constructed to resist any barrage, and the barbed wire could not be destroyed by shells, which only detonated when they hit the ground. When the Allied ground troops climbed out of their trenches carrying their sixty pounds of equipment per man at 7.30, therefore, they expected to walk across no-man's land meeting little

German resistance. Actually they were mowed down in vast numbers; of 100,000 men deployed from their trenches, on the first day alone some 20,000 were killed and 40,000 wounded. Whole regiments were wiped out in the worst day in British military history. Only in November 1916, five months later, did reserve troops eventually make a small incursion into the German lines. What the extracts show, though, is how, faced by official censorship, the British press sought to bring their readers fuller information about the conflict through the deployment of 'eye-witness' special correspondents, who could deliver an experiential account more telling than the bulletins disseminated via the War Office. These accounts, such was the sophistication of the communications system established to transfer the reports back to London rapidly, could be updated as the battle unfolded, to make them as close as possible to a 'real time' unfolding of the narrative. These special reports were, of course, also censored. But what comes across are glimmerings of a reality such as that captured both in World War One literary writing subsequently, and also in some of the major modernist texts. There is a sense of the vast impersonality of the bombardment, the lack of concern for individual life, an impressionistic technique which surveys the pastoral glories of the landscape about to be destroyed, a sense of the hell-like transformation which the battle and preparations for it brought to humans, and a glimpsed ghostliness brought to humanity itself.

Front-pages report from the Daily Chronicle, *'FIRST ACCOUNT OF THE GREAT ATTACK ON THE BRITISH LINES', Monday, 3 July 1916*

BRITISH HEADQUARTERS, Sunday, 5.5 p.m.
(received in London 7.40 p.m.)

Substantial progress has been made in the vicinity of Fricourt (2 1/2 miles E. of Albert), which was captured by our troops at 2 p.m. today.

Up to noon to-day some 800 more prisoners have been taken in the operations between the Ancre and the Somme, bringing the total up to 3,500, including those captured on other parts of the front last night.

Above we give the latest official communiqué on our great offensive in France, which was launched, in conjunction with the French, at 7.30 a.m. on Saturday morning, and is still proceeding. . . .

The first description of the fighting, from our Special Correspondent with the British Forces, Mr. Philip Gibbs, appears on this page . . .

So far the results are satisfactory. Our troops have penetrated into the German front system of defences, along a frontage of about 19 miles from the Somme valley northwards. At points the German line has been entered to a depth of a mile to a mile and a half. The latest British communiqué says the general situation is favourable. . . .

THE HISTORIC FIRST OF JULY
From *The Daily Chronicle* Special Correspondent Philip Gibbs

WITH THE BRITISH ARMIES IN THE FIELD, July 1, 1916

The attack which was launched to-day against the German lines on a 20-mile front began satisfactorily. It is not yet a victory, for victory comes at the end of a battle and this is only a beginning. But our troops, fighting with very splendid valour, have swept across the enemy's front trenches along a great part of the line of attack, and have captured villages and strongholds which the Germans have long held against us. They are fighting their way forward not easily but doggedly. Many hundreds of the enemy are prisoners in our hands. His dead lie thick in the track of our regiments.

And so, after the first day of the battle, we may say with thankfulness All goes well. It is a good day for England and France. It is a day of promise in this war, in which the blood of brave men is poured out in the sodden fields of France.

For nearly a week now we have been bombarding the enemy's lines from the Yser to the Somme. Those of us who have watched this bombardment know the meaning of it. We knew that it was a preparation for this attack. All those raids of the week which I have recorded from day to day were but leading to a greater raid when not hundreds of men but thousands would leave their trenches and go forward in the great assault.

KEEPING THE SECRET

We had to keep the secret, to close our lips tight, to write vague words lest the enemy should get a hint too soon, and the strain was great upon us and the suspense an ordeal for the nerves, because as the hours went by they drew nearer to the time when great masses of our men, those splendid young men who have gone marching along the roads of France, would be sent into the open out of the ditches where they got cover from the German fire.

This secret was foreshadowed by many signs. Travelling along the roads we saw new guns arriving – heavy guns and field guns, week after week. We were massing a great weight of metal. . . .

THE FIRST WHISPER

A week or two ago a whisper passed, 'We're going to attack.' But no more than that, except behind closed doors of the mess-room. Somehow by the look on men's faces, by their silences and thoughtfulness, one could guess that something was to happen.

There was a thrill in the air, a thrill from the pulse of men who know the meaning of attack. Would it be June or July? . . . The fields of France were very beautiful this June. There were roses in the gardens of old French chateaux.

Poppies put a flame of colour in the fields, close up to the trenches, and there were long stretches of gold across the countryside. A pity that all this should be spoilt by the pest of war.

So some of us thought, but not many soldiers. After the misery of a wet winter and the expectations of the spring they were keen to get out of the trenches again. The spirit of the men was for an assault across the open, and they were confident in the new power of our guns.

The guns spoke one morning last week with a louder noise than has yet been heard upon the front, and as they crashed out we knew that it was the signal for the new attack. Their fire increased in intensity, covering raids at many points in the line, until at last all things were ready for the biggest raid.

The scene of the battlefields at night was of terrible beauty. I motored out to it from a town behind the lines, where through their darkened windows French civilians watched the illumination of this sky, throbbing and flashing to distant shell-fire. Behind the lines the villages were asleep, without the twinkle of a lamp in any window. The shadows of sentries paced up and down outside the stone archways of the old French houses.

Here and there on the roads a lantern waved to and fro, and its rays gleamed upon the long bayonet and steel casque of a French Territorial and upon the bronzed face of an English soldier, who came forward to stare closely at a piece of paper which allowed a man to go into the fires of hell up there. It was an English voice that gave the first challenge, and then called out 'Good-night!' with a strange and unofficial friendliness as a greeting to men who were going towards the guns.

RIDGE OF FIRE

And once again the infernal fires began, flashing, flickering, running along a ridge with a swift tongue of flame, tossing burning feathers above rosy storm-clouds, concentrating into one bonfire of bursting shells over Fricourt and Thiépval upon which our batteries always concentrated.

There was one curious phenomenon. It was the silence of all the artillery. By some atmospheric condition of moisture or wind (though the night was calm) or by the configuration of the ground, which made pockets into which the sound fell, there was no great uproar, such as I have heard scores of times in smaller bombardments than this.

It was all muffled. Even our own batteries did not crash out with any startling thunder, though I could hear the rush of big shells, like great birds in flight. Now and then there was a series of loud strokes, an urgent knocking at the doors of night. And now and then there was a dull, heavy thunder-clap, followed by a long rumble, which made me think their mines were being blown further up the line.

But for the most part it was curiously quiet and low-toned, and somehow this muffled artillery gave one a greater sense of awfulness and of deadly work.

Along all this stretch of the battle-front there was no sign of men. It was all inhuman, the work of impersonal powers, and man himself was in hiding from these great forces of destruction. So I thought, peering through the darkness over the beetroots and the wheat.

But a little later I heard the steady tramp of many feet and the thud of horses' hoofs walking slowly, and the grinding of wheels in the ruts. Shadow forms came up out of the dark tunnel under the trees, the black figures of mounted officers, followed by a battalion marching with their transport.

I could not see the faces of the men, but by the shape of their forms could see that they wore their steel helmets and their fighting kit. They were heavily laden with packs, but they were marching at a swinging pace, and as they came along were singing cheerily.

A MUSIC HALL TUNE

They were singing some music-hall tune, with a lilt in it, as they marched towards the light of all the shells up there in the places of death. Some of them were blowing mouth-organs and others were whistling. I watched them pass – all these tall boys of a North Country regiment, and something of their spirit seemed to come out of the dark mass of their moving bodies and thrill the air. They were going up to those places without faltering, without a backward look – and singing, dear, splendid men. . . .

THE DRUMS OF DEATH

For a time I could see nothing through the low-lying mist and heavy smoke-clouds which mingled with the mist, and stood like a blind-man, only listening. It was a wonderful thing which came to my ears. Shells were rushing through the air as though all the trains in the world had leapt their rails and were driving at express speed through endless tunnels in which they met each other with frightful collisions.

Some of these shells fired from batteries not far from where I stood ripped the sky with a high, tearing note. Other shells whistled with that strange, gobbling, sibilant cry which makes one's bowels turn cold. Through the mist and the smoke there came sharp, loud, incessant knocks, as separate batteries fired salvoes, and great clangorous strokes, as of iron doors banged suddenly, and the tattoo of light field guns playing the drums of death.

The mist was shifting and dissolving. The tall tower of Albert Cathedral appeared suddenly through the veil, and the sun shone full for a few seconds on the Golden Virgin and Babe which she held head-downwards above all this tumult as a peace-offering to men.[2]

At a minute after 7.30 there came through the rolling smoke-clouds a rushing sound. It was the noise of rifle-fire and machine-guns. The men were out of their trenches, and the attack had begun. The enemy was barraging our lines.

---

2 The statue on top of the tower in the Basilica in Albert gained an almost mythic significance at the time. Struck by the artillery fire which ruined the church itself, the Virgin hung at a right angle from the tower. Her impending fall seemed to spell disaster to both sides. The statue was not in fact knocked down until April 1918, six months from the end of the conflict.

THE LINE OF OUR ATTACK

The country chosen for our main attack to-day stretches from the Somme for some 20 miles northwards. The French were to operate on our immediate right. It is very different country from Flanders, with its swamps and flats, and from the Loos battlefields with their dreary plain pimpled by slack heaps.

It is a sweet and pleasant country, with wooded hills and little valleys along the riverbeds of the Ancre and the Somme, and fertile meadow-lands and stretches of woodland, where soldiers and guns may get good cover. 'A clean country' said one of our Generals, when he first went to it from the northern war zone.

It seemed very queer to go there first, after a knowledge of war in the Ypres salient, where there is seldom a view of the enemy's lines from any rising ground . . . and where certainly one cannot walk on the skyline in full view of German earthworks 2,000 yards away.

. . . I saw a German sentry pacing the village street of Curlu, and went within 20 paces of his outposts. Occasionally one could stare through one's glasses at German working parties just beyond sniping range round Beaumont and Fricourt, and to the left of Fricourt the Crucifix between its seven trees seemed very near as one looked at it in the German lines.

Before this Calvary was the Tambour and the Bois Français, where not a week passed without a mine being blown on one side or the other, so that the ground was a great upheaval of mingling mine-craters and tumbled earth, which but half-covered the dead bodies of men.

It was difficult ground in front of us. The enemy was strong in his defences. In the clumps of woodland beside the ruined villages he hid many machine-guns and trench mortars, and each ruined house in each village was part of a fortified stronghold difficult to capture by direct assault.

It was here, however, and with good hopes of success that our men attacked to-day, working westwards across the Ancre and northwards up from the Somme.

At the end of this day's fighting it is still too soon to give a clear narrative of the battle. Behind the veil of smoke which hides our men there were many different actions taking place, and the messages that come back at the peril of mens' lives and by the great gallantry of our signallers and runners give but glimpses of the progress of our men and of their hard fighting.

I have seen the wounded who have come out of the battle, and the prisoners brought down in batches, but even they can give only confused accounts of fighting in some single sector of the line which comes within their own experience.

At first, it is certain, there was not much difficulty in taking the enemy's first line trenches along the greater part of the country attacked. Our bombardment had done great damage, and had smashed down the enemy's wire and had flattened his parapets. When our men left their assembly trenches and swept forward, cheering, they encountered no great resistance from German soldiers, who had been in hiding in their dug-outs under our storm of shells.

Many of these dug-outs were blown in and filled with dead, but out of others which had not been flung to pieces by high explosives crept dazed and deafened men who held their hands up and bowed their heads. Some of them in one part of the line came out of their shelters as soon as our guns lifted, and met our soldiers half-way, with signs of surrender.

They were collected and sent back under guard, while the attacking columns passed on to the second and third lines in the network of trenches, and then if they could get through them to the fortified ruins behind.

STOICAL WOUNDED

Men were coming back from the fields of fire glad to be back behind the line. They were our wounded, who came in very quickly after the first attack to the casualty clearing stations close to the lines, but beyond the reach of shell-fire. Many of them were lightly wounded in the hands and feet, and sometimes 50 or more were on one lorry, which had taken up ammunition and was now bringing back casualties.

They were wonderful men. So wonderful in their gaiety and courage that one's heart melted at the sight of them. They were all grinning as though they had come from a 'jolly' in which they had been bumped a little. There was a look of pride in their eyes as they came driving down like wounded knights from a tourney.

They had gone through the job with honour, and have come out with their lives, and the world was good and beautiful again, in this warm sun, in these snug French villages, where peasant men and women waved hands to them, and in these fields of scarlet and gold and green.

The men who were going up to the battle grinned back at those who were coming out. One could not see the faces of the lying-down cases, only the soles of their boots as they passed; but the laughing men on the lorries – some of them stripped to the waist and bandaged roughly – seemed to rob war of some of its horror, and the spirit of our British soldiers shows very bright along the roads of France, so that the very sun seems to get some of its gold from these mens' hearts.

Tonight the guns are at work again and the sky flashes as the shells burst, over there where our men are fighting.

PHILIP GIBBS

'Our Eye-Witness's Account', by W. Beach Thomas, The Times, 3 July 1916

THE BATTLE AS I SAW IT

May I now give some pictures of the battle as I saw it; and treat it as a mere spectacle in which all that is real and cruel and human and pitiable disappears into a dramatic situation?

At midnight on the last day of June I knew that the long tension was to be over in a few hours. The raids and pettish shelling over Flanders down to the Somme and across it were to be over and done with. They were in some sort a battle and a preparation for battle; but in essentials a mere flurry and flourish, a caracole before the charge.

All was now to condense in the passion of personal contest within the compass of a narrower span. At a point within that span I stood with a few others, watches in hand, at the dawn of a perfect summer morning. The birds began to feed and chirp in the charlock by the trench's edge. The low rays of the sun ricocheting off the surface of the valley mist baffled all endeavours to penetrate the mystery of the battle field, which spread before us and, indeed, around us in a spacious arc.

THE HOUR

No more than a modicum of sullen, capricious sounds betokened the crisis. Little was to be seen anywhere. There were neither night fireworks nor day tumult. For myself, I was watching the ugly bulk of one of the huge sausage balloons rise ponderously over the trees behind me, in very poor imitation of the larks, when the hour long and nervously waited struck as suddenly as if it were unexpected.

A year of anticipation would not have prevented or lessened the surprise. The mist was burst by a shock that I will make no attempt to describe. All I know about my sensations is that I had none left after five minutes. The monster of war had no features. A Niagara of sound poured ceaselessly, in volume incomprehensible, without distinctions. The orchestra was making not music but noise in harmony; and no one was musician enough to distinguish the parts.

A GREAT GUN'S THUNDER

In this blur I had only one friend to cling by. A giant gun far away to my right was at work enfilading a German trench to my left; and as its comet projectile churned through the air I could hear distinctly the whistling note of its passage, the one individual, separate, palpable thing in an ocean, an atmosphere of dull, shapeless thunder-noise. It was neither painful nor glorious, this part of the battle as I saw it, or rather heard it; but just a dull, local, opiate, killing sensation, though leaving consciousness.

After a while the mind recovered and the senses became acclimatised. By a quite steady progression the mist thinned and rose. I could pick out batteries that I knew and watch their stabs of flame and puffs of smoke. By 7 o'clock I could be quite sure that the flashes were not, as for a moment I had feared, the bursting explosion from the enemy's howitzers; for the flame from the gun-muzzle is horizontal, from the high-explosive shell vertical.

At 7.15, so clear were the batteries, flashing here, there, and everywhere, almost as numerous and thick as tents in a camp, that you were amazed the enemy had not marked out every pit for instant destruction; but as yet not a shell came near them. The German gunners could not spare time, it seemed, for the batteries, when infantry were massing in the trenches. Nor could they see as our army could see.

OUR GREAT LINE OF BALLOONS

One after another our balloons had risen to the full height of their tether in a long line stretching quite out of sight. Their kite-tails streamed to the eastward, advertising the arrival of a good, steady west wind about to blow Heaven knows what fumes and smoke and dust and ashes from the front to the back trenches of the enemy's first line. But as yet the observers could look clear into the cockpit of battle: into the village of Fricourt, into Serée, into Beaumont-Hamel, where every leaf had been blown from the shattered trees by our fire, and every shelter and dug-out was a mangled mess.

The highest thing I saw in the place was one ten-foot wall or so; and the trenches running into it looked like the first shale-tips of a deserted mine. And our Army had yet better eyes than the balloons. Right over my head, against the clearer background of a fleecy layer of cloud, a whole squadron of our aeroplanes, almost cloud-high, but pencilled in marvellous distinctness against the cirrus flakes, flew as the crow flies, direct for their target. Argus-eyed and with more than a Cyclops voice[3] they saw and shouted back the news of the guns' precision, untouched by the monstrous tumult below. They left the dappled puffs of shrapnel in beaded ropes behind them, as a fish leaves bubbles, till soon I could not tell which was cloud and which was smoke.

At 7.30 the sights of the upper air were forgotten and quite obscured by such an earth-born cloud as might accompany the conflagration of a forest. Column after column of thick smoke rose and spread and floated forward from our trenches toward the enemy. Bullets of all sorts. That inhuman, oscillating bullet of the German rifle and machine gun and the round bullets of the shrapnel, some of them sprinkled with phosphorous, threaded the woof of the cloud; but it was blind shooting. The cloud played its part, and many a man who left his trench behind its cover owes his life to the beneficent obscurity. Nevertheless I believe many of the men would have liked to charge in full day for sheer pride of manhood and zest of clean sight. The 'Up-and-at-'em' spirit was strong in our Army this summer morning.

The scene at night had been stranger. Then, unexpected as it may sound, you saw more and heard less. Instead of the misty monotone you watched continuously the flash of guns and blaze of explosions over 20 or 30 miles of country, and the star shells stippled out the line of the trenches. . . .

NIGHT TURNED INTO DAY

No half-hour of the night was allowed to sink into its native gloom. No minute while I watched was lit by less than some one hundred flashes, not reckoning the

---

3 Argus was the figure of rumour in Classical myth, traditionally figured as wearing a cloak of many eyes; the reference to Cyclops is presumably referring to him being a giant, rather than one-eyed.

graceful and abiding star shells, which had all the semblance of a cosmic or celestial calm among the impish snap and flicker of bomb and shrapnel bursts or the thrust of the flash from the gun muzzle. One spot in front of me seemed especially selected as the scene for a spiritual conflict between the two. Every time that the star, pure white and splendid, soared to its summit, alongside its apex, now this side, now that, glinted a trio of red shrapnel sparks, like the wink of a wicked eye; and the festoon of the falling star lit a column of cloud that might have escaped from a mouth of hell.

Away on the right the flicker was so continuous and jerky as to hurt the eyes. It gave the impression of a bad kinematograph film. Farther away all the lights, good and bad, were toned to the harmless expansion of what we call summer lightning, illumining wide stretches of sky and etching the patterns of the clouds.

The great preponderance of trench mortars, at least on our side, during this night fighting dwarfed the noise of battle, and for a part of the time happened to stand in what the French call a pool of silence, one of those mysterious regions, or perhaps zones, over which the sound passes almost unheard to strike loudly the drums of the ears, it may be, ten miles or so in the rear.

MERRY HEARTS GO FORWARD

Gorgeous as the scene was in itself, it was a pitiful thing beside the immediate human interest. Moving forward, we overtook some battalions on the march to the trenches. First I heard the rhythmic tramp and muffled noises as of a ghostly army. Then I distinguished the sway and swing of a brown and lifeless pattern. Then, when the figures grew clearer, I could count the double company and even detect the English quality in the men. I still could not shake off the sense of marching with an army of ghosts in the limbo of some other world, for ever seeking to reach that unknown region of stars and thunder.

The lorries rubbing past us in the gloom were like extinct megatheria, colossal and shapeless, but half-alive. Noisier beasts, with long snouts and strange modes of progression, moved the other way or were passed as they slept, or was it grazed? under the trees. They, too, were on their way to populate this strange country beyond the gloom.

But one did not march far with the men before recovering the sense of human things and proper reality. Gallant fellows, they whistled homelike airs, and on the way to the trench kept a merry heart. A little farther and even the subdued whistle would be unwise.

'The Great Battle. Special Account from our Special Correspondent',
The Times, Monday 3 July 1916

OUR MEN MARCHING UP

As we stood, in the shadow of some trees, 20 yards from a road which led directly down to the trenches, detachments of our troops could be seen swinging across country in half-companies, companies, and battalions. Long before they came close one heard the steady roar of their feet, tramp-*tramp!*, tramp-*tramp!* And always as they passed they whistled softly in unison. Some whistled 'Tipperary,' some 'Come back, my Bonny, to me,' and some best of all in the place and surroundings, 'La Marseillaise.'

As we came back along that road, far behind the front, we saw more companies, more battalions. On the tree-shaded road it was too dark to see them, save only as vague, dark masses against the light background of the highway. One felt their presence, and heard more than one saw them; always the steady tramp-*tramp*, tramp-*tramp* as they shouldered by; and they were always whistling. Now and again a laugh broke out at some unheard joke, a completely careless laugh, as of a holiday-maker. And, knowing what it was that they were going into, for the fiftieth time one marvelled at the way in which British manhood has proved itself in this most terrible of all wars.

In the early hours of the morning I turned in and, as I lay, still watched the flare and flicker in the heavens – 'the lightning of thy footsteps in the sky.' Here, where other things interposed to hide the actual bursting of the shells, it was more than ever the ceaseless lifting and paling of the Northern Lights; and as long as I lay awake, until it was near to dawn, it went on.

It must be understood that so far, in all the fighting of the last few days, no attempt has been made to gain ground. There has been no offensive in the proper sense of the word. But in the innumerable minor attacks – notably in the astonishingly successful raid by the Highland Light Infantry and in similar raids by the Irish troops, Munsters and Leinsters – we have been inflicting heavy casualties upon the enemy, quite apart from the effects of the bombardment, which, while invisible, must have been considerable.

BEGINNING OF THE ATTACK
APPALLING GUN-FIRE

I had just finished my dispatch of yesterday when information reached me of the hour at which the great attack would begin this morning. It was necessary to be up very early, and while the night mists still hung heavy and the herbage was soaking with dew I was on the edge of a ridge by Albert overlooking the front on which the attack was to be delivered.

The plans, as we know, contemplated an advance on a front of about 25 miles immediately to the north of, and on both banks of, the Somme. At the southern end of the line, that is, on both sides of the river, the French cooperated with us. From where I stood, even after the sun had dispelled the mists, this part of the line was beyond the range of vision, the heights above the Somme, by Suzanne and Vaux, being only dimly visible on the far horizon. . . .

A SUMMER MORNING

It was a lovely morning; the sun, still low, shining directly in our faces from behind the German lines, so that where we stood it was necessary to be careful in the use of field-glasses, which flash like a heliograph when the sun falls on them, and not to display white maps too ostentatiously. Albert was almost hidden in the mist, except that the church tower, with the wonderful spectacle of the leaning figure of the Virgin, stood clear above the white bank below and gleamed in the sun.

The advance was set for 7.30. For an hour or so before that time the bombardment was perhaps more furious than ever. It was difficult to say if it really was, for it had been terrible enough when I had watched it from a similar position 24 hours before, as it had been terrible now for days. What was curious was that, while I was no nearer now than the point where I had seen the firing at night, the noise now was almost overwhelming.

Against the sunlight the bursting of shells no longer made sudden flashes of light. One heard the roar and saw the spurts of earth and *debris* as the great projectiles plunged to earth and the slowly unfolding columns of smoke from high explosives and the fleecy white of shrapnel up above. The only flashes were those of our guns.

At Thiepval on our left, at La Boiselle in front of us, and from Fricourt to Mametz on our right the concentration of our gun-fire was truly appalling. We do not know yet to what extent the Germans have been able to hold their positions and live within this awful zone. That some were there we know, for as I write (it is not yet noon) news comes in that prisoners have been taken in considerable numbers, and some of them say that no food supplies have been able to get up to them in the front line for four days past. It may or may not be true, but certainly along all the German lines, and for some distance in the rear, life for some days past must have been one hideous nightmare.

THE DEVIL'S CAULDRON OF THIEPVAL
CONCEALED GERMANS WITH MACHINE-GUNS

LATER, 7p.m.

This afternoon I have spent watching from as near as it is permissible to go. It still rages with unabated fury along the whole front. At some places the struggle is of the most desperate character. One of these points is Thiepval, where it has been fierce beyond description.

As far as can be gathered at present, our men, at the first onset, swept through the little town of Thiepval, driving the enemy whom they met before them. It appears that a very large number of Germans had concealed themselves in dugouts where they had machine guns . . . and they endeavoured to hold the place, when our artillery opened on it the most intense of fire it is possible to conceive. High explosive and lyddite simply poured into the little town, while the air above was thick with exploding shrapnel, and the trench mortars played incessantly, the projectiles of the last-named being clearly visible in the air, travelling, as they do, at a low velocity. In the sunshine each mortar shell in its slow fall gleamed amid the smoke like a great fiery spark – much as a large brass plate might look if tossed up into the sunshine.

The place was a veritable devil's cauldron, a mere bowl of seething fumes, black and green and white. Nothing is yet known of what the issue was; but it seemed incredible that anything, friend or foe, could live there through the half an hour – from about 3.45 to 4.15 – during which the struggle was at its fiercest. To us, looking on, it was a sight of pure horror.

A TRIUMPHANT BEGINNING

. . . It would be unjust yet to mention any individual regiments, which, according to the present reports, have done conspicuously well. No overseas troops are, it is believed, engaged. Only by degrees will it be possible to see the whole in anything like a true light. What at present is certain is that we have gained ground all along the line, in some places having pushed even beyond the high water-mark of our expectation.

1.1(c)   The US enters the War

President Woodrow Wilson resisted bringing about US mobilization in support of Britain, France, and Russia for as long as he could. However, the Germans were waging a war to disrupt the shipping in the Atlantic which was essential to British food supply lines, and there were several attacks also on civilian ships, which stirred American public opinion – the most notorious being the attack on the Lusitania off the coast of Ireland in May 1915. Still Wilson, who had been raised with experience of warfare through the American Civil War, sought to avoid joining the conflict. The Germans suspended their submarine campaign, and in 1916 Wilson put much effort into securing a peace in the European conflict; on 18 December he even set about reconciliation by seeking to establish the war aims of each party to the conflict. But German impatience, and their determination to starve Britain into submission, brought about the resurrection of the war at sea. As more and more ships went to the bottom of the Atlantic with American citizens, goods and property inside, Wilson found it impossible to resist any longer, and in April 1917 declared war upon Germany and began recruiting troops. These extracts reflect the national mood at that moment, but also engage the values of civilization and democracy which the US felt it was fighting on behalf of at that moment.

'For Freedom and Civilisation', The New York Times, 3 April 1917

No Government of a great people has ever been subjected to such a terrific indictment as that which President Wilson, with the full sanction and support of the American people, brings against the Imperial Government of Germany in asking Congress to declare that we are at war with that country and to authorize him to exert all the power and employ all the resources of this nation to 'bring the conflict to a successful termination.' The high crimes against humanity and civilization of which Germany has been guilty have been committed in cold blood, with purpose and calculation, and in circumstances of atrocity that have horrified the world. It is a tale often told, of which the President recites only so much as is necessary to the completeness of a document which is perhaps the most convincing justification of war that any nation has ever put forth in declaring it. We know only too well the horrors wrought in Belgium,[4] we know that vessels have been sent to the bottom 'without warning and without thought of help or mercy for those on board': we know that relief ships bearing safe conduct and declaring their character by unmistakable marks of identity 'have been sunk with the same reckless lack of compassion or principle.' It is not a civilized Government. It is a monster of autocracy beyond the order of nature, that we are called upon to fight.

But however stern our denunciation of these crimes against law and humanity, they are but the evil flower of the poisonous tree which we now unite with other great democracies to hew down and cast into the fire. Our battle is with the German autocracy, of which President WILSON'S address is the doom. It was not upon the 'impulse of the German people' that their Government acted in entering this war. They had no previous knowledge, their approval was not asked. The autocratic Government of Germany is the great criminal, there is the enemy of mankind. An end must be made of it, as the President says, 'a steadfast concert for peace can never be maintained except for a partnership of democratic nations. No autocratic Government can be trusted to keep faith within it or observe its covenants. It must be a league of honor, a partnership of opinion. Intrigue would eat out its vitals, the plottings of inner circles who could plan what they would and render account to no one would be a corruption seated at its very heart.' If spared, the autocracy would carry on its plottings and its intrigues as it has in the past. Against so dangerous a Government the nations are compelled to take the only possible measure of safety, its destruction. 'Self-governed nations do not fill their neighbour States with spies,' as Germany has filled this land with its spies, as it has sent its spies and plotters over all the world. Like CASSIUS,[5] Germany 'thinks too much' of its dastardly plans of assault upon the public peace, of conquest, of domination. There must be an end of it. 'The world must be made safe for democracy.'

---

4 Propagandist stories, which soon acquired mythic status, about the atrocities enacted by German troops as they marched through Belgium in the early days of the war, abounded in the English-speaking world. These included the stories retailing the rape of nuns, the slaughter of babies and children, and the melting-down of human flesh to make candles. None of these incidents happened. The *Times*'s reviving of these stories, with the implication that they are somehow allied to the actual attacks on shipping, forms part of the case for America's entry into the war. The process is partly self-serving, but partly also about a perceived rationale in the country at that moment that the war represented a battle for humanity and 'civilization' over barbarism.

5 In Shakespeare's *Julius Caesar*, Caesar says to Mark Antony, about one of his own future betrayers, 'Yond Cassius has a lean and hungry look; he thinks too much; such men are dangerous' (I.ii.195).

The President now knows, or is forced to admit what he must long have known, that Germany under the present dynasty, with its insatiable ambitions and its depravities of mind and heart, has never been our friend. We are now about to enter the battle against this 'natural foe to liberty,' and the President invokes the authority to 'spend the whole force of the nation to check and nullify its pretension and its power.' There is no other path of safety. We serve no selfish ends, we intend no conquest, no dominion. But we shall fight for our rights and for the deliverance of mankind from the German peril with the full determination to destroy its source. We cherish no rancor against the German people; they have been but the instruments of the Imperial power they have served too long, too obediently, because they have been bred to the tradition of obedience. Upon the allies of Germany we do not now declare war. It will depend upon them whether we shall declare it.

The measures the President recommends to Congress give proof of his earnestness and of ours. He would at once add to the present authorized strength of our army in war time a new army of 500,000 men 'chosen upon the principle of universal liability to service'; and he asks authorization to add to this force of nearly a million 'increments of equal force so soon as they may be needed and can be handled in training.' . . .

It is the President's view that, so far as is practicable, the great costs of the war should be defrayed by equitable taxation rather than by borrowing. Undoubtedly the immediate purposes of the nation may be served by taxation, but should the war be continued beyond a few months it is certain that resort would be had to the credit of the Government. Whatever may be the burdens imposed upon the American people, they will be sustained to bear them by the consciousness that we fight in the noblest of causes, not merely for our own defense and in our own interest, but for democracy, for liberty, for right, for the freedom of all nations.

'The Nation Speaks', The New York Times, Friday, 6 April 1917

Nothing in its life will more become the sixty-fifth Congress than the beginning of it – the high plane on which the discussion of yesterday and Wednesday was conducted, the dignity and gravity of its manner, and the sober simplicity, without truculence or bombast, of its speech as it made its forty-eight hours' way to the momentous decision. The American people have cause to feel pride in it; it made a picture for all the world to see of democracy rising to an occasion. It kept the note struck by the President. Its foreordained and inevitable task was performed without cheap violence or strutting defiance; the tone it held throughout was that of a pacific nation taking up, without fear or boasting, the sword that was forced upon them.

Nor did it fail to set the issue clearly forth, to show that we are going to war, not merely to avenge injuries nor even to prevent future ones, but to answer the question Shall the world be democratic or autocratic? The progress of two years and a half of war has shown that, in LINCOLN'S phrase, 'It must become all one or all the other.' Either democracy must be worldwide or democracy must perish, and in that contest, the greatest ever forced upon the world, and forced upon it, not by democracy, but by autocracy, the first of the democracies is now called upon to bear her part.

All true Americans must be proud and grateful at the manner in which their Government, in both its war-making departments, the executive and legislative, have presented their country before the world. . . . The American Government has moved at last, and moved with a resistless majesty, and never before has a nation moved so fully so as to realize JOHN MILTON'S vision:

> Methinks I see in my mind a noble and puissant nation rousing herself like a strong man after sleep, and shaking her invincible locks; methinks I see her as an eagle mewing her mighty youth, and kindling her undazzled eyes at the full midday beam.[6]

'On Not Going to War', The Masses, no. 73 (July 1917)

Like Britain, America had a number of people refusing to join the services on account of their conscientious objection to violence of any kind (in England, these included an influential group of artists and writers associated with the Bloomsbury group, including Lytton Strachey). In America, objections to war found expression in the radical periodical The Masses, edited by Max Eastman. The journal was eventually suppressed by the US Government in 1918 because of its views. See also Section 3, 'Gender and Sexuality', for several extracts from British women expressing dissent from the militaristic rhetoric of the time.

So far as has come to their notice, the American people, with the exception of a few hyphenates, cowards and traitors, are a unit in demanding war. It is our duty to inform them that this optimistic view does not represent the true state of affairs. Not only, they will regret to learn, do the American people appear generally reluctant, cynical or indifferent in the matter of this war, to a degree that it has seemed necessary to institute conscription to raise a large army, but a certain proportion of them are actually determined, as will be shown presently, not to go to war even if they are drafted. These facts create a problem which it is the patriotic duty of the newspapers to discuss, so that the best solution of it may be discovered, and we are glad to assist them by furnishing the materials for such a discussion.

---

6 Milton wrote this in his speech calling for unlicensed printing, *Areopagitica*.

It is, we are aware, the official and proper view that the present war is necessary and hence good. Citizens of New York have been sent to prison, and to the observation ward of our insane hospital, for expressing a disagreement with this view, and it might seem to the enthused observer of our newspapers that such cases of disagreement with the popular view must be rare. But that is not quite the fact. It is possible to meet scores of people daily who express unqualified disapproval of the war and, moreover, the most uncompromising resolution to take no part in it. These people report the existence of numbers of other such people, and altogether it would appear that they form at least an embarrassing minority.

In order to deal with the problem created by the existence of this minority, it will be necessary to understand its psychology. To being with, it is not, as might be presumed, pro-German. It does not wish any harm to America. It simply does not believe in war, and all the publicity given to the merits of the present war has failed to shake its conviction. The passage of the Conscription bill, which might be expected to make this minority realize the necessity of helping the war along does nothing of the kind. They cannot conceive of the possibility of submitting to the law against their judgement and their conscience. They regard it as a commonplace that they should abide by their convictions, regardless of the consequences.

Those consequences should now be considered. The penalty for failing to register in either the state or the federal military census appears to be a term of imprisonment. The anti-militarist students of Columbia and of Hunter College voted unanimously to refuse to register. It is their opinion that the best time to resist the draft is at the very beginning. This is not the universal opinion amongst those who intend to resist the draft, however. The alternate view is held that since it is really the draft to which they object, their resistance should be confined to that. It may be expected that a considerable number, but not by any means all of them, will feel obliged to refuse to register in the preliminary census, and will incur cheerfully the specified punishment.

The punishment for resisting the draft will doubtless be more serious. It is well known to these people that a batch of Conscientious Objectors in England were taken to France, and sentenced to be shot; and that it was only because Parliament learned of this sentence in time, and felt that it would give the cause of liberty a black eye that it was changed in the nick of time, to ten years hard labor. It is generally felt among the Conscientious Objectors here in America that it is at least unlikely that there will be executions on any large scale for resisting the draft – when the claim to exemption on the grounds of conscientious objection has been disallowed – jail, an occasional beating-up to test the sincerity of the objector, frequent opportunities to decide to obey orders and go, perhaps an alternate offer of ambulance service or other war-work; and, if these persuasions fail, a term in prison at hard labor. The possibility of simply being shot against a wall, instead of the longer process, is not left out of sight. To complete this psychological description it should be added that the attitude of the conscientious objector toward the prospect of being shot or sent to prison is one of mingled relief and regret: regret, that there is no happier alternative to going to war, relief that *that* alternative does actually exist. Its existence, more-over, for their point of view, constitutes a break-down of the theory of conscrip-tion. When a conscientious objector is shot or imprisoned, it merely means the whole organized might of a militarized government has shown itself powerless to break the will of a single unarmed individual.

This stubbornness is not without a certain dignity. And it would be suffi-ciently ironic if a nation going to war for liberty's sake should find it necessary to kill or imprison all those whose conception of liberty differed from its own. It is not to be expected, perhaps, of a government which appears to have been unwilling to rely for the armed prosecution of its cause upon those anxious or willing to undertake it, that there would be any excessive tolerance of conscien-tious objectors to war. But it might be urged in their behalf that most of them have been, in times of peace, useful citizens, and are likely to be so in times of peace to come. So, unless the government expects this war to last forever, it might be saner public policy to admit the existence of a kind of person who cannot be coerced for military purposes, and deal with him as a temporarily rather than totally objectionable person. And, unless the newspapers wish the word 'treason' to lose all its ancient terrors, it might be well to find a different term to describe his behavior.

1.2   Irish Rising, Easter 1916

The Rising which took place during April 1916 in the Irish capital city, Dublin, provides an early example of a direct confrontation to British Imperial rule. Along with the issue of women's suffrage, Ireland had provided perhaps the most destabilizing influence in British political life since the turn of the century. By the outbreak of the First World War, the issue of establishing so-called Home Rule for a partly or wholly liberated Ireland was still not resolved. The third Bill to this end had finally been passed through the British Parliament after a two-year struggle, 1912–14. But the outbreak of the war saw little chance of it being enacted. The war itself saw upwards of 150,000 Irish troops joining the Allied cause. But Nationalist resentments were also running high; the Home Rule Bill crisis in 1912 had led to a hardening of attitude amongst those in Ireland wish-ing to remain in union with Britain, and Sir Edward Carson had drawn up the famous Ulster Covenant, which hundreds of thousands signed in Belfast. As a result, political parties in other parts of the island, and particularly in Dublin, argued all the more strenuously for freedom. The Irish Parliamentary Party at this time was led by John Redmond, who had succeeded in using the fact of his holding the balance of power in the British Parliament to secure the Third Home Rule Bill. But more radical groups like Sinn Féin now renewed their call for instant cessation of British rule, and an end to local recruitment to the British military. Armed groups like the Irish Republican Brotherhood (IRB) and the Irish Volunteers, as well as the 'Citizen's Army' formed a few years earlier after trades disputes, began to apply pressure. All of these forces found leadership under Patrick Pearse (1879–1916), a teacher and poet, as well as a leader in the Volunteers and the IRB. Many attempts were made to recruit German support for an armed uprising in Ireland, and eventually a shipload of weapons was promised to land on the west coast of Ireland during Easter 1916. In the end, misinformation and leaks led to the scuttling of the ship and the arrest of Sir Roger Casement, a rebel who had been involved in arranging the shipment. Pearse and others planned to strike at this moment, while Britain was preoccupied by the struggle on the Western Front (no artillery remained in Ireland to fight the rebels – it had to be shipped back urgently), and while, over the Easter weekend, many were relaxing. The occupation force of British soldiers were, in fact, largely enjoying a day out at Fairyhouse Races.

The narrative of events is briefly sketched out in the first extract given here; the rebels were able rapidly to take over the symbolic centres of British rule, except the Castle in Dublin, the real seat of British power. In the succeeding few days, however, the British troops reasserted themselves, threw a circle round the city, and gradually moved inwards with navy support to destroy the rebel strongholds. Pearse and fourteen others were summarily shot at Kilmainham Jail in early May. The brutality of the British response to a short-lived revolt caused consternation around the world, and temporarily led to the suspension of American support for their war effort. As later in the massacre at Amritsar, India, in 1919, when British soldiers killed 400 protesters, this brutality in Dublin by the British only served to fuel the anti-imperial cause and started a wave of protest which eventually saw the break-up of British rule across the world.

The texts extracted in this Section come from a loyalist perspective on the rebellion; those collected around Easter 1916 in Section 9, 'Empire, Race and Postcolonialism', give the rebels' ambitions. Regret around the Rising found most immediate and resonant expression in the poems about it by the poet W. B. Yeats, most famously 'Easter 1916'. More broadly, the issues which the Rising brought to the forefront of contemporary consciousness, about the relation between war, imperialism, and everyday life, disturb subsequent modernist writing, including Ezra Pound's 'Homage to Sextus Propertius' (1917), Virginia Woolf's *Mrs Dalloway* (1925) and *The Years* (1937), and D. H. Lawrence's later novels, from *Kangaroo* (1923) to *Lady Chatterley's Lover* (1928), in which the gamekeeper Mellors's experiences as an imperial soldier are contrasted with the events on the Western Front experienced by Clifford Chatterley.

'The Alpha and Omega of a Short-lived Republic', Dublin and the Sinn Féin Rising *(1916)*

These extracts come from one of the several souvenir albums produced almost immediately after the Rising ended. These contained narratives of events, alongside glossy photographs and biographies of the main protagonists.

THE FIRST BLOOD SPILT AT THE CASTLE GATES

Shortly after the mid-day Angelus a small body of Volunteers marched up Cork Hill straight to the gates of the Upper Castle Yard, where stood a policeman and a sentry. The policeman raised his hand as a signal to the approaching body to halt. The only response of the insurgents was a volley, in the midst of which the unfortunate man fell dead. The scene of this sad happening is tragic ground. To this gate the daughter of the Lord Chief Justice, Viscount Kilwarden, dragged herself. She had accompanied her father to town, and at the outbreak of Robert Emmet's rebellion in 1803 the mob pulled him from his carriage in Thomas Street and had there done him to death.[7] The horrified girl escaped and fled to the gate of the Upper Castle Yard, there told her terrible tale to the sentry, and fell at his feet insensible. The alert sentry on last Easter Monday escaped unharmed and effectually barred the way to the seizure of the Castle by a sudden snapping-to of the iron gates. Thus foiled the handful of resolute men at once took possession of the City Hall, the *Daily Express* office, and Messrs. Henry and James's ready-made clothes store, with a view to dominating the Castle and its approaches. The deadly reign of the sniper had begun.

SEIZURE OF THE GENERAL POST OFFICE

Meanwhile the well-conceived strategy of the Insurrection was elsewhere insidiously pursuing its course. The main body of the insurgents, under the Commandant General P. H. Pearse, the avowed Commandant-in-Chief of the Army of the Republic and President of the abortive Provisional Government, and Commandant General James Connolly, who was in control of the Dublin districts, took bloodless possession of the General Post Office in Sackville Street, and proceeded to break and barricade all the lower windows. Before half-past twelve the English and Scottish cables had been severed, thus cutting off all cross-Channel telegraphic communication. This materially delayed the arrival of military reinforcements, and gave full time for the proper ensconcement of the insurgents in their various positions. For a poor forty-eight hours they were monarchs of all they surveyed. But a grave oversight was committed in not seizing the Telephone Exchange before its occupation by the forces of the Crown, a strategical blunder turned to material advantage by the military, whose command of the wires shortened the struggle by several days.

THE RAILWAYS SEIZED. TELEGRAPH AND TELEPHONE WIRES CUT

In keeping with the Insurgent policy of geographical isolation, most of the railway termini were taken temporary possession of about noon, the approaches

---

7 Emmet had sought to exploit the Napoleonic War, as the current rebels were the First World War, in order to throw off colonial rule while Britain's attention was elsewhere. His attempt to secure French support in that instance was as unsuccessful as the later rebels' attempts to secure German. The allusion here to history shows, however, the immediacy with which the Easter 1916 Rising was read by contemporaries, including poets such as W. B. Yeats, as part of a bloody tradition.

barricaded, and the telegraphic and telephone wires cut. For days on end Dublin was a trainless, tramless, policeless, postless, theatreless and almost newspaperless city. Civilisation disappeared and primitive man emerged. . . . The Broadstone Terminus was also seized, and a number of Military officers on returning from Fairyhouse Races in the evening were captured by the Rebels and detained in the station till next day, when the forces of the Crown dislodged the insurgents and released the prisoners. The race-goers who returned by motor had their cars seized and used to build barricades in the streets.

Meanwhile there were stirring doings in the neighbourhood of the General Post Office. The ill-fated 'Irish Republic' had been again proclaimed from the foot of Nelson's Pillar by a steady-voiced insurgent before a mob of puzzled curiosity-mongers. Here and there was posted up a pronunciamento signed by the members of the new Provisional Government setting forth their aims and ends. . . . So far from proving the life-warrant of the Irish Republic this declaration came to be the death-warrant of its signatories. All were eventually shot by order of Courtmartial.

BARBED WIRE ENTANGLEMENTS stretched across Sackville Street and barricades closed the entrances to many of the side streets. A formidable barricade was erected at the entrance to Lower Abbey Street, and this obstacle was largely constructed of reels of newspaper web taken from the emergency office of the *Irish Times*. The highly combustible character of this material caused a shocking disaster, for when the military shell fire directed against the General Post Office set the paper alight the fire was carried across the barricade and devastated Lower Abbey Street, destroying the Royal Hibernian Academy, where was in progress the annual exhibition of pictures, valued at £10,000.

MARTIAL LAW PROCLAIMED

One man in Dublin was fully alive to the seriousness of the position – his Excellency Lord Wimborne. His first act was to summon the troops from the Curragh on Monday, and Martial Law was quickly proclaimed. . . .

THE MILITARY GET TO WORK

Owing to their initial strategic precautions the advantage had lain on the side of the insurgents, but with the steady arrival of strong military reinforcements from England, beginning on Wednesday afternoon, and more particularly a formidable array of field artillery – of which the depleted military garrison of Ireland had little and the insurgents none – affairs began to assume a different aspect. Little by little military cordons were drawn round the disturbed areas to the ultimate strangulation of the rising.

THE SHELLING OF LIBERTY HALL

On Wednesday morning for the first time in her history Dublin heard the booming of naval guns in the heart of the city. The 'Helga', formerly the

Department of Agriculture's fishery patrol, came up the Liffey, and moored opposite Gandon's fine Custom House, then in the possession of the military, and set to work to rout out the 'Citizen Army' from the dingy stronghold of Liberty Hall. The ship's guns, seconded by two formidable eighteen pounders worked from Tara Street, soon accomplished their object, and, although the combined fire left the shell of James Larkin's notorious headquarters standing, the interior was literally pulverised. The proximity of the railway viaduct rendered the control of fire difficult, and Northumberland House, next to Liberty Hall, unfortunately suffered much from several accidental hits.

THE HOLOCAUST OF SACKVILLE STREET
But before the long-drawn out, awe-inspiring pyrotechnical display which began in Sackville Street on Easter Wednesday and ceased not till it left that queen of Irish thoroughfares and many adjacent streets in ruins, even the nerve-racking terrors of Lower Mount Street or any experiences of South Dublin pale their ineffectual fires. For three days and nights no living being passed from the Rotunda to O'Connell Bridge, so constant was the deadly hail of fire from rifle and battery and machine gun. Only on one occasion was there a desperate dash across the street, when from the burning bank at Lower Abbey Street corner eight desperate insurgents sprinted through the showers of singing lead and safely reached the General Post Office. A man fell dead on O'Connell Bridge and lay there untouched until Sunday. No one dared approach the body lying stark in the central link between the North and South City. . . .

ARRIVAL OF THE NEW COMMANDER-IN-CHIEF
With the arrival of General Sir John Maxwell on Thursday evening to take supreme command of His Majesty's Forces in Ireland came the beginning of the end. Drastic measures were elaborated and put into action, and after a fierce combat the end was in sight, when a terrible loss of life and property had been caused. To the conduct of the insurgents the Prime Minister in the House of Commons bore this testimony: 'So far as the great body of the insurgents are concerned I have no hesitation in saying in public they conducted themselves with a humanity which contrasted very much to their advantage with some of the so-called civilised enemies which we are fighting in Europe.'

THE DESTRUCTION OF THE 'REPUBLIC'S' HEADQUARTERS
Although severely wounded in the leg on the previous day Commandant-General J. Connolly issued a manifesto to the insurgents on Friday morning, reporting progress. 'Courage, boys, we are winning,' was the gist of his message. Further, there was a determined message from P. H. Pearse. Delusive hopes! That very night the military trained artillery on the General Post Office, and by vigorous shelling soon set fire to the structure. The surrender of the main body of insurgents and their leaders became only a question of hours. The prisoners were allowed to escape into Moore Lane by Henry Street, and in attempting to follow

them The O'Rahilly was shot down. Desperate as was their position in this living hell, the chief insurgents fought on and on against Fate.

THE SURRENDER

But there is a limit to human endurance, even under the exultations of fanaticism, and about midday Saturday P. H. Pearse, James Connolly, Thomas Clarke, and their adherents, numbering some two hundred and fifty men, rang down the curtain on Ireland's bitterest tragedy. Pearse in his final manifesto declared that, actuated by a desire to prevent further slaughter of unarmed people and to save the lives of the followers, 'now surrounded and hopelessly outnumbered,' members of the Provisional Government at headquarters had agreed to surrender unconditionally.

As to the outnumbering there can be no question. Including the comparatively small number of the Irish Volunteers who had risen, and allowing for a fairly full muster of the syndicalist 'Citizen Army', the insurgents probably did not number two thousand men. When Bulwer Lytton wrote that 'in the bright lexicon of youth there is no such word as "fail"' he was not thinking of youth armed with rifles, and a few shot guns, facing modern artillery and opposed to a largely superior and perfectly equipped force.

THE EXECUTION OF THE LEADERS

Then came the pitiful aftermath. On Wednesday morning, 3rd May P. H. Pearse, Thomas MacDonagh, and T. J. Clarke, the first of the signatories to pay the dread penalty, were shot by order of Field General Courtmartial. . . .

The total executions numbered fifteen, eight were sentenced to penal servitude for life, and shorter sentences, ranging from twenty years' penal servitude to six months' imprisonment with hard labour numbered considerably over one hundred. The deportations were very numerous.

'The Insurrection', The Irish Times, *28 and 29 April and 1 May; and 'The Government's Duty'*, The Irish Times, *2 May 1916*

In *the aftermath of the Rising, the press loyal to the union with Britain called for severe measures to be taken against the rebel leaders. These extracts sum up the local feeling in Ireland's leading newspaper after the revolt, and the shared establishment view at the time, that it was a disaster for all Irish aspirations.*

The 'Sinn Féin' Insurrection, which began on Easter Monday, is virtually at an end. Desultory fighting continues in suburban districts. The severity of martial law is maintained indeed, it is increased. . . . Many streets and roads are still dangerous for the careless wayfarer. But the back of the insurrection is broken. Strong military forces, skilfully directed by a strong hand, have decided the issue sooner than most of us had dared to hope. The cordon of troops which was flung around the city narrowed its relentless circle until further resistance became impossible. On Saturday, P. H. Pearse, one of the seven ring-leaders, surrendered unconditionally with the main body of the rebels. Yesterday other bodies came in dejectedly under the white flag. Of the buildings which were seized a week ago not one remains in rebel hands. The General Post Office, save for its noble portico, is a ruin. . . . St. Stephen's Green was cleared on Thursday. Liberty Hall is no more than a sinister and hateful memory. It is believed that most of the ring-leaders are dead or captured. The outlaws who still 'snipe' from roofs may give a little more trouble, but their fate is certain. So ends the criminal adventure of the men who declared that they were 'striking in the full confidence of victory', and told their dupes that they would be 'supported by gallant allies in Europe'. The gallant ally's only gift to them was an Irish renegade whom it wanted to lose. Ireland has been saved from shame and ruin, and the whole of Europe from a serious danger. Where our politicians failed – and worse than failed – the British army has filled the breach and won the day. The Dublin Insurrection of 1916 will pass into history with the equally unsuccessful insurrections of the past. It will have only this distinction – that it was more daringly and systematically planned than any of its predecessors.

The story of the last week in Dublin is a record of crime, horror, and destruction, shot with many gleams of the highest valour and devotion. We do not deny a certain desperate courage to many of the wretched men who to-day are in their graves or awaiting the sentence of their country's laws. The real valour, however, and the real sacrifices, were offered on the altar of Ireland's safety and honour.

In the House of Commons last week Sir Edward Carson and Mr. Redmond were at one in their desire that, so long as the country remains in the present urgent danger, nobody should try to make political capital of the old, narrow kind out of these tragic events in Dublin. Until the danger is definitely at an end, we shall only say – and we are expressing the opinion of the whole world – that this outbreak and all its deplorable consequences could have been averted. For the last year all Irishmen have known that the danger existed, and that it was coming surely and steadily to a head. Urgent and repeated warnings were given to the government. The men who neglected them have accepted one of the gravest responsibilities in history. . . . At the moment, however, it is more important to avoid possible mistakes than to call the inevitable to judgement. The crime has been committed, the explosion has occurred; and we have gained at least one advantage. We know now, yea or nay, the extent, the power, and the motives, and the methods, of the seditious element in Ireland.

In the provinces the few sporadic attempts at insurrection have been suppressed. Nothing remains of this act of criminal lunacy except its track of sorrow, misery and destruction. The huge loss of property in Dublin will involve unemployment on a large scale, and it may involve heavy additions to the rates. The fantastic inducements of Messrs. Pearse, Connolly, and their colleagues have deprived hundreds of decent women and children of their bread-winners. It is not impossible, we fear, that some business houses which have been destroyed will not be re-established in Dublin. This distress, added to the decline which, for a time at least, must follow the war, cannot fail to bring acute hardship and poverty to Dublin. We may survive such misfortunes, for our country's natural resources are very great; but the recovery of Dublin's prosperity depends upon one all-important condition. For many years Ireland, with all her fertility, geographical advantages, and endowments of character and intellect, laboured under a curse of insecurity. Land agitation interfered with the steady development of agriculture. Capital fought shy of a restlessness that was fatal to dividends, and we begged in vain for the creation of new Irish industries. Of late conditions have improved. The land question was settled; capital began to come in, slowly, but with ever-increasing confidence; we seemed to be reaching the goal of economic and commercial security, and to be within sight of its national blessings. This tragic insurrection threatens to kill all our hopes. . . . That feeling can be dispelled in only one way. The British Government must take such measures as will satisfy the world that the spirit of sedition and anarchy in Ireland will be crushed, not merely for a time, but for all time.

2

Society, Politics and Class

Introduction

Politicians, economists, philosophers and social theorists who published their views on society and the inter-relationships between the social classes in the early part of the twentieth century, found it of necessity to engage with ideas which had been put forward in the nineteenth century. In Britain and America, this meant reassessing the work of, amongst others, John Stuart Mill, Herbert Spencer, Ralph Waldo Emerson, John Ruskin and William Morris. Mill had held in his *On Liberty* (1859) that the individual is sovereign, and that governments should only have power to prevent an individual exercising his will where it might lead to the harm of others. Spencer, a tremendously popular writer in the later nineteenth century in America and the UK, rejected the tenets of orthodox Christianity, and applied the evolutionary theories most cogently addressed by Charles Darwin both to individual psychology and to society as a whole. Both Mill and Spencer were crucial to liberal ideas on both sides of the Atlantic, including those formulated by William James and John Dewey (included here) in the US, and by L. T. Hobhouse and others, in Britain. Such ideas underpinned the range of social issues confronted by, and the reforms introduced by, the British Liberal Party, from its election in 1906 to the beginning of the First World War in 1914. These included protection of the poor through welfare relief, and through state benefits and pensions. Often against the Liberal Party's own inclinations, this trend in social thought also meant engaging with the campaign for votes for women (Mill had been an early advocate of women's rights), and with the issue of independence for Ireland. In the US, as in Britain, liberal thought also led to much debate about the necessity for state intervention in education.

The late nineteenth century saw a rise in preoccupation with the division of labour, and with labour relations in an increasingly industrialized and technologically advanced world of production. The inheritance of Ruskin and Morris was key to these debates in Britain; the increasing prominence of socialism, embodied in the rise of the Independent Labour Party from the 1890s, also led to a renewed focus upon the issue of poverty, and upon the relationship between the managerial class and the workforce. From the turn of the century until beyond the First World War, the socialist press was exercised by the idea of workers' 'guilds', an idea advocated initially by Ruskin – guilds in which individuals created their own products under a trade association. Such thought is represented here by the extracts from C. H. Douglas, whose articles appeared in the significant socialist (and also literary) 'little magazine' *The New Age*, edited across our period by A. H. Orage. As in every other area relating to this period, the thinking on society debated in Orage's journal, as in all newspapers and books, was in active dialogue with that developed at the turn of the century and beyond in Europe, and particularly that from France (Durkheim and Sorel are extracted here) and Germany (Weber).

As will become clear from all the extracts, the over-riding metaphor deployed in ideas about society at this time is an evolutionary and organic one derived from Darwin. Society is seen as a progressively changing entity, in which the task of the sociologist, economist, or philosopher, is to determine the relation of each part of the social realm to the whole. Herbert Spencer's view of society as an unfolding flower is echoed again and again, by thinkers who held up an ideal of the dynamic interaction of classes and social forces which brought about further development across history and into the future.

This organic model, then, provides the basis for a critique of current conditions either from the political left or right, as the powerful forces of industrialization and mechanization are taken to be threatening social cohesion. Out of this ideal model – as with the work of the period focused upon religion and belief extracted in Section 4 – arises a shared concern amongst writers on society to better understand its processes, through an attempt to retrace the primitive origins from which civilization might be said to have arisen. Close attention is paid to some version of an aboriginal situation concerning social relationship, or of elementary early relations between the various members of the workforce. Further, theoreticians such as Weber (and subsequent writers in English) argued for attention to an historical specificity of approach, in which each era of history is read both as part of a process of dynamic development, and as something to be considered in its own right, in order to better understand the causes for that development from stage to stage. For some, as for John Dewey in America, such attention to specificity led to a call for a 'scientific method' in thinking about society, thinking correlative to that deployed by Darwin when he had considered the origin of species. This was a 'scientific method' (as the final section of this anthology makes clear) also favoured as a recourse delivering an impetus and sense of purpose to various modernist writers at this time.

To this extent, the writing on society at the turn of the century and beyond perceives it as a series of historical phases marked by key moments of alteration and change, as does much literature considered now to be modernist. The concern to 'map' the past, and to project myths of social origin, runs through literature from writers politically to the left and to the right. Further, the ideal organic model of political and social interaction provided a foundation for the critique of the social world which gives energy to so many modernist texts. Whatever the allure of an aggressive and threatening technology for modernist writing, particularly around the time of the First World War, it is its alternative, the organic vision, and its consequent historicist and primitivist drives, which marks the work of writers from Ezra Pound to Wyndham Lewis, from D. H. Lawrence to E. M. Forster, from Virginia Woolf to Mary Butts. This vision was easily translated to literary culture and to notions of cultural tradition at the time. As T. S. Eliot contentiously put it, in an article dismissing the notion that there could be such a thing as Scottish literature: 'when we assume that a literature exists we assume a great deal: we assume that *there* is one of the five or six (at most) great organic foundations of history'.[1]

2.1   Émile Durkheim, *The Division of Labour* (1893)

Although this work was not translated into English until 1933, Durkheim's thinking, as a founding figure in the academic field of sociology, was widely influential in the early part of the twentieth century. Durkheim (1858–1917) felt that the modern world was in a transitional phase. For him, society was always more than, or different from, individuals' behaviours or desires. What bound peoples together into societies were their shared interests or beliefs, including their morality and religion. In ancient times, individuals had been bound together by a mechanical group solidarity, whereas in the contemporary world society was moving towards a more organic inter-relationship. But, because that 'organic solidarity' was not yet fully realized, there still existed divisions within society – both between the various occupations in which individuals are engaged, which could lead to industrial disputes and class conflict, but also between the individual's interests and those of society (what he famously called anomie). Durkheim's later Suicide: A Sociological Study *(1897) pursued the idea that this anomic condition of conflict between individual and society was at the root of the increased number of suicides in the modern world, where the traditional markers of social consensus, including Christianity, were fading. Durkheim pioneered the application of a 'scientific' approach to the study of society, and was much influenced, as these extracts which lay out the key terms of his inquiry show, by the contemporary interest in anthropology.*

It is an historical law that mechanical solidarity, which first stands alone, or nearly so, progressively loses ground, and that organic solidarity gradually becomes preponderant. But when the mode of solidarity becomes changed, the structure of societies cannot but change. The form of a body is necessarily transformed when the molecular relationships are no longer the same. Consequently, if the preceding proposition is correct, there must be two social types which correspond to these two types of solidarity.

If we try to construct hypothetically the ideal type of a society whose cohesion is exclusively the result of resemblance, we should have to conceive it as an

---

1 T. S. Eliot, 'Was there a Scottish Literature?', *The Athenaeum*, no. 4657 (1 August 1919), p. 680.

absolutely homogeneous mass whose parts were not distinguished from one another, and which consequently had no structure. In short, it would be devoid of all definite form and all organisation. It would be the actual social proto-plasm, the germ out of which all social types would develop. We propose to call the aggregate thus characterised, a *horde*.

It is true that we have not yet, in any completely authenticated fashion, observed societies which complied in all respects with this definition. What gives us the right to postulate their existence, however, is that the lower soci-eties, those which are closest to this primitive stage, are formed by a simple repe-tition of aggregates of this kind. We find an almost perfectly pure example of this social organisation amongst the Indians of North America. Each Iroquois tribe, for example, is composed of a certain number of partial societies (the largest ones comprise eight) which present all the characteristics we have just mentioned. The adults of both sexes are equal to each other. The *sachems* and chiefs, who are at the head of each of these groups and by whose council the common affairs of the tribe are administered, do not enjoy any superiority. Kinship itself is not recognised, for we cannot give this name to the distribution of the population in layers of generation. . . .

We give the name *clan* to the horde which has ceased to be independent by becoming an element in a more extensive group. . . . It is a family in the sense that all the members who compose it consider themselves relatives, and they are, in fact, for the most part consanguineous. The affinities that are thus created by these blood-ties are those which principally keep them united. In addition, they sustain relationships which we can term domestic, since we also find them in societies whose familial character is indisputable: I am referring to collective punishment, collective responsibility, and, as soon as private property makes its appearance, common inheritance. But, on the other hand, it is not a family in the proper sense of the word, for in order to belong to it, it is not necessary to have any definite relations of consanguinity with other members of the clan. It is enough to possess an external quality, which generally consists in having the same name. Although this sign is thought to denote a common origin, such a civil status really constitutes very inconclusive proof, and is very easy to copy. Thus, the clan contains a great many strangers, and this permits it to attain dimensions such as a family, properly speaking, never has. It often comprises several thousand persons. Moreover, it is the fundamental political unit; the heads of clans are the only social authorities. . . .

The structure of society where organic solidarity is preponderant is quite different.

These are formed, not by the repetition of similar, homogeneous segments, but by a system of different organs each of which has a special role, and which are themselves formed of differentiated parts. Not only are social elements not of the same nature, but they are not distributed in the same way. They are not juxtaposed in a linear fashion as the rings of an earthworm, nor entwined one with another, but co-ordinated and subordinated one to another around the same central organ which exercises a moderating action over the rest of the organism. This organ itself no longer has the same character as in the preceding case, for, if the others depend upon it, it, in its turn, depends upon them. No doubt, it still enjoys a special situation, a privileged position, but that is due to the nature of the role that it fills and not to some cause foreign to its functions, to some force communicated to it externally. Thus, there is no longer anything about it that is not temporal and human; between it and other organs, there is no longer anything but differences in degree. This is comparable to the way in which, in the animal, the dominance of the nervous system over other systems is reduced to the right, if one may speak thus, of obtaining the best food and having its fill before the others. But it needs them, just as they need it.

This social type rests on principles so different from the preceding that it can develop only in proportion to the effacement of that type. In this type, individuals are no longer grouped according to their relations of lineage, but according to the particular nature of the social activity to which they devote themselves. Their natural and necessary milieu is no longer that given by birth, but that given by occupation. It is no longer real or fictitious blood-ties which mark the place of each one, but the function which he fills. No doubt, when this new form of organisation begins to appear, it tries to utilise and to take over the existing one.

2.2 Max Weber, *The Protestant Ethic and the Spirit of Capitalism* (1904–5)

Like Durkheim's work, Weber's key book was widely discussed in the English-speaking world before it was translated, which eventually happened in 1930. Weber (1864–1920) was a major influence upon the development of sociological study in Germany, acting as editor and contributor to several pioneering magazines in the field; The Protestant Ethic *initially appeared as a series of articles in one such journal. Responding to Marxist philosophy's deterministic sense that history was dictated by economic causes, Weber sought to establish that there was instead a religious drive to the development of capitalism. He felt that the Protestant – and more particularly the Calvinist – belief in the salvation of the individual, and in the need to increase God's glory in the world through 'good works', was key to the capitalist impulse, and to the asceticism which often accompanied it. But, against the absolute determinism of the Marxist approach, Weber maintained that his definition of capitalism was specific to Western history; to what he called, in a clarifying introduction to a 1920 edition of the book, capitalism as 'not only . . . the technical means of production, but . . . a calculable legal system and . . . administration in terms of formal rules'. Furthermore, he maintained that such systems and rules demonstrably change across the course of history. In this book at least (he slightly inflected the argument elsewhere), he takes the view that 'historical concepts' must not be taken to 'grasp historical reality in abstract general formulae'. Rather, he claims, sociology must focus upon 'concrete genetic sets of*

relations which are inevitably of a specifically unique and individual character'. The
extract here comes from the end of the essay, in which Weber famously takes his argu-
ment about the historical development of capitalism, and focuses it upon the contem-
porary world.

One of the fundamental elements of the spirit of modern capitalism, and not
only that but of all modern culture: rational conduct on the basis of the idea of
the calling, was born – that was what this discussion has sought to demonstrate
– from the spirit of Christian asceticism. . . . The idea that modern labour has an
ascetic character is of course not new. Limitation to specialized work, with the
renunciation of the Faustian universality of man which it involves, is a condition of any valuable work in the modern world; hence deeds and renunciation
inevitably condition each other to-day. The fundamentally ascetic trait of
middle-class life, if it attempts to be a way of life at all, and not simply the
absence of any, was what Goethe wanted to teach, at the height of his wisdom,
in the *Wanderjahren*, and in the end which he gave to the life of his *Faust*.[2] For
him the realisation meant a renunciation, a departure from an age of full and
beautiful humanity, which can no more be repeated in the course of our cultural
development than can a flower of the Athenian culture of antiquity.

The Puritan wanted to work in a calling; we are forced to do so. For when
asceticism was carried out of monastic cells into everyday life, and began to
dominate world morality, it did its part in building the tremendous cosmos of
the modern economic order. This order is now bound to the technical and
economic conditions of machine production which to-day determine the lives
of all the individuals who are born into this mechanism, not only those directly
concerned with economic acquisition, with irresistible force. Perhaps it will so
determine them until the last ton of fossilized coal is burnt. . . .

Since asceticism undertook to remodel the world and to work out its ideals in
the world, material goods have gained an increasing and finally an inexorable
power over the lives of men as at no previous period in history. To-day the spirit
of religious asceticism – whether finally, who knows? – has escaped from the
cage. But victorious capitalism, since it rests on mechanical foundations, needs
its support no longer. The rosy blush of its laughing heir, the Enlightenment,
seems also to be irretrievably fading, and the idea of duty in one's calling prowls
about in our lives like the ghost of dead religious beliefs. Where the fulfilment
of the calling cannot directly be related to the highest spiritual and cultural
values, or when, on the other hand, it need not be felt simply as economic
compulsion, the individual generally abandons the attempt to justify it at all. In

---

2 In Goethe's two-part *Faust*, which appeared in 1808 and 1831, the hero is made into a symbol of
man's striving for the infinite. His attempt at the attainment of universal truth is sustained, however,
upon the inevitability of his own damnation.

the field of its highest development, in the United States, the pursuit of wealth, stripped of its religious and ethical meaning, tends to become associated with purely mundane passions, which often actually give it the character of sport.

No one knows who will live in this cage in the future, or whether at the end of this tremendous development entirely new prophets will arise, or there will be a great rebirth of old ideas and ideals, or, if neither, mechanized petrification, embellished with a sort of convulsive self-importance. For of the last stage of this cultural development, it may well truly be said: 'Specialists without spirit, sensualists without heart; this nullity imagines that it has attained a level of civilization never before achieved.'

But this brings us to the world of judgements of value and of faith, with which this purely historical discussion need not be burdened. The next task would be rather to show the significance of ascetic rationalism, which has only been touched on in the foregoing sketch, for the content of practical social ethics, thus for the types of organization and the functions of social groups from the conventicle[3] to the State. Then its relations to humanistic rationalism, its ideals of life and cultural influence; further to the development of philosophical and scientific empiricism, to technical development and to spiritual ideals would have to be analysed. Then its historical development from the medieval beginnings of worldly asceticism to its dissolution into pure utilitarianism would have to be traced out through all areas of ascetic religion. Only then could the cultural significance of ascetic Protestantism in its relation to the other plastic elements of modern culture be estimated.

Here we have only attempted to trace the fact and the direction of its influence to their motives in one, though a very important point. But it would also further be necessary to investigate how Protestant Asceticism was in turn influenced in its development and its character by the totality of social conditions, especially economic. The modern man is in general, even with the best will, unable to give religious ideas a significance for culture and national character which they deserve. But it is, of course, not my aim to substitute for a one-sided materialistic an equally one-sided spiritualistic causal interpretation of culture and of history. Each is equally possible, but each, if it does not serve as the preparation, but as the conclusion of an investigation, accomplishes equally little in the interest of historical truth.

2.3   A. R. Orage, 'Towards Socialism, V: the Meaning of Civilisation', *The New Age*, 31 October 1907

Alfred Richard Orage (1873–1934) was initially a teacher in Leeds, England, who was interested in the principles of theosophy; in 1900 he helped to found the influential

---

3 This was a clandestine meeting of early Nonconformists, protesting against established religion.

Leeds Art Club. He was an early enthusiast for Nietzsche's work once it became known outside Germany, and sought to bring a larger audience to the philosopher's ideas in two works: Nietzsche in Outline and Aphorism *(1907), and* Friedrich Nietzsche: The Dionysian Spirit of the Age *(1911). Orage was the editor of the arts and politics magazine* The New Age *from 1909 to 1922. Whilst, under his editorship, the magazine was later to become a highly significant site for the promotion of modernist writing and criticism, in his early series of articles called 'Towards Socialism' we find Orage seeking to lay out his beliefs on the sociological and cultural origins and implications of socialism. In the extract given here from this series, Orage seeks to define the place of the imagination within his socialist vision, hinting towards his ready welcoming into the journal of writers and artists who shared his view of the need for the imagination, five or so years later.*

A friend of mine once saw two little slum children sitting on a doorstep playing at dolls. The doll of one of them consisted of a ginger-beer bottle wrapped up in an old stocking; the other doll was a brick wound about with the remains of a flannel shirt. Goodness knows what the children saw in these objects, but it is certain that they did not see a ginger-beer bottle or a brick. Their creative imagination transformed and englamoured the vision with something entirely beautiful; and I have no doubt that if a germ of life had existed in the bottle or the brick, that same transforming imagination would have played miracles with its growth. For at the bottom of all the metaphysics that touches life is this solid fact: that imagination alone creates, imagination alone is the demiurgos of the universe.

Nothing appears to me more obvious than the fact that man himself is an imaginative creation, lives in and by and for the imagination. It always amuses one part of ourselves to remember that man is an animal after all. There are, I admit, few signs to the contrary if we except the faculty of which I am speaking. Most writers, indeed, do except this faculty, either because they are in mortal terror of their own minds or because they have no wings. The result is an admirable geologist, a lucid economist, a grave cynic or what not – something, in short, that is laughably human, but altogether without inspiration; something, in a word, dull. I can conceive such people endeavouring to disillusionise these two children about their dolls, and advocating realism not only for children, who are too wise to listen, but for adults, who are generally scoundrelly enough to believe the worst, even about themselves. I can also conceive that such iconoclasts are very useful people, but only as initiators into new illusions; for the man without illusions is no longer human; he is either a beast or a god; and the chances in these days are that he is – not a god! No, it is not being illusioned that matters, but the being illusioned by mean and paltry things. There is a hierarchy of illusion as of everything else; and the measure of the individual is not his freedom from illusion, but his susceptibility to noble illusion.

I should like to remark here the tyranny of all the masters of the imagination. The bearing of the fact on all sociology, including Socialism, is extraordinarily close. To be quite frank, we must admit that men differ enormously in the range of their imagination. Some, for instance, are as little impressionable, educable, or responsive, as alligators; others are as easily moved as gold leaf. There remain a few, a very few, who possess the power of not only being moved, but of moving, and they are really dangerous people. For ninety-nine times in every hundred, people of great creative imagination have no notion of what it is like to be without imagination . . . and by virtue of their power they often impose on the unimaginative the burden of pretence. All our institutions, without exception, are the work primarily of imaginative people, who invented the State, the Nation, Religion, Love, Art, Business, and all the rest. Left to ourselves, which of us, I ask, would ever have thought of worshipping a god? . . . Similarly, as I have often had occasion to observe, the majority of people have no inborn respect, admiration, or natural attraction for anything we call civilised. For the majority of people, civilisation is a disgusting, laborious, and useless state of affairs. . . . Where the majority of people are inwardly wretched and ill at ease, and yet unrebellious, we may be pretty sure that an influence of some kind is being exercised over them; and if it is not physical force (and only very green minds believe that civilisation really exists on physical force), it must be some power of mind which, in effect, is an imaginative power. Such, in fact, it is; and civilisation at this very moment subsists in the minds on the one hand that are possessed with the ideas of Religion, the State, etc., and, on the other hand, in minds that are obsessed by them.

As I have said, however, it is not so much the being open to ideas that distinguishes the civilised man from the barbarian. To be open to ideas is indeed the definition of humanity. What distinguishes one individual from another, one class from another, one nation or race from another nation or race, is the kind of idea to which they are severally open. It is demonstrable, I believe, that every race and every nation, every class and every individual, has at any given moment the potentiality of all ideas; but the particular ideas to which they are most easily accessible differ enormously.

The possession of wealth in the form of commodities does not make a nation great, but the possession of individuals, as many as possible, capable of entertaining or communicating great ideas. This, however, is not to disparage the plain man, even in the form of the multitudinous man in the street; nor, on the other hand, to exalt culture. . . . The man in the street, nine times out of ten, is the most readily moved of all men. In our day, as in every day, he is almost neurotic in his susceptibility to impressions. We need not complain that melodrama should stir him so much, but take a hint and stir him with real drama. But scholastic culture is often a deadly enemy to the culture of civilisation – that is, of imagination. I like well enough the habit of knowing the best that has been said about a given subject; but it is infinitely better to feel the best that has been felt. Much modern culture really incapacitates the sympathetic imagination. . . .

The end of it all is that imagination and insight exalt a people, as they also make men; that civilisation is no more than the possession by a people of individuals, on the one hand, capable of inspiring great enthusiasms and of individuals, on the other, capable of being inspired.

2.4   L. T. Hobhouse, *Liberalism* (1911)

Leonard Trelawny Hobhouse (1864-1929) held the first Professorship in Sociology in Britain, at the University of London from 1907 to 1929. He was editor of the first issues of the Sociological Review *in 1907. Influenced by the evolutionary theories of society expressed by Herbert Spencer, Hobhouse sought in this book to present a popular statement of the Liberal position in politics – the book from which these extracts are derived appeared in the Home University Library of Modern Knowledge series. The book was published just after the controversial so-called 'People's Budget' presented to the House of Commons by the then Chancellor of the Exchequer Lloyd George. This Budget, whilst it furthered the welfare aspirations of the Liberal government and its plans for a nation-wide system of labour exchanges and unemployment insurance, also introduced heavy taxes and death duties, as well as a tax on land transactions, which negatively affected the more wealthy members of society. In* Liberalism, *we find Hobhouse seeking to explain how a political theory which had historically been associated with the struggle for an individual's rights could be used to authorize a system of state intervention which actively strove to alter the class structure in the country. To this end, Hobhouse cast the modern state as 'authoritarian', and any opposition to the state on religious, political, or economic grounds as being inherently sympathetic to the Liberal cause. But, as Hobhouse recognizes in this book, this historical principle of opposition and criticism now raises a further range of complex questions such as 'Is Liberalism doing as much for the reconstruction that will be necessary when the demolition is complete? Is Liberalism at bottom a conservative or only a destructive principle?' Such questions, which had of course featured throughout Victorian writing also, about the relationship of the individual to the state, resonate across modern writing in the 1910s and beyond, including the work of D. H. Lawrence (whose novel* The Rainbow *enters into its own debate with Spencer's philosophy) and Virginia Woolf. The extracts here give Hobhouse's classic statement, in a chapter characteristically called 'The Heart of Liberalism', of the ideal relationship between the nation and the individual.*

The term organic is so much used and abused that it is best to state simply what it means. A thing is called organic when it is made up of parts which are quite distinct from one another, but which are destroyed or vitally altered when they are removed from the whole. Thus, the human body is organic because its life depends on the functions performed by many organs, while each of these organs depends in turn on the life of the body, perishing and decomposing if removed therefrom. Now, the organic view of society is equally simple. It means that, while the life of society is nothing but the life of individuals as they act one upon another, the life of the individual in turn would be something utterly different if he could be separated from society. A great deal of him would not exist at all. Even if he could maintain physical existence by the luck and skill of a Robinson Crusoe, his mental and moral being would, if it existed at all, be something quite different from anything that we know. By language, by training, by simply living with others, each of us absorbs into his system the social atmosphere that surrounds us. In particular, in the matter of rights and duties which is cardinal for Liberal theory, the relation of the individual to the community is everything. His rights and his duties are alike defined by the common good. What, for example, is my right? On the face of it, it is something that I claim. But a mere claim is nothing. I might claim anything and everything. If my claim is of right it is because it is sound, well grounded, in the judgement of an impartial observer. But an impartial observer will not consider me alone. He will equally weigh the opposed claims of others. He will take us in relation to one another, that is to say, as individuals involved in a social relationship. Further, if his decision is in any sense a rational one, it must rest on a principle of some kind; and again, as a rational man, any principle which he asserts he must found on some good result which it serves or embodies, and as an impartial man he must take the good of every one affected into account. That is to say, he must found his judgement on the common good. An individual right, then, cannot conflict with the common good, nor could any right exist apart from the common good.

The argument might seem to make the individual too subservient to society. But this is to forget the other side of the original supposition. Society consists wholly of persons. It has no distinct personality separate from and superior to those of its members. It has, indeed, a certain collective life and character. The British nation is a unity with a life of its own. But the unity is constituted by certain ties that bind together all British subjects, which ties are in the last resort feelings and ideas, sentiments of patriotism, of kinship, a common pride, and a thousand more subtle sentiments that bind together men who speak a common language, have behind them a common history, and understand one another as they can understand no one else. The British nation is not a mysterious entity over and above the forty odd millions of living souls who dwell together under a common law. Its life is their life, its well-being or ill-fortune their well-being or ill-fortune. Thus, the common good to which each man's rights are subordinate is a good in which each man has a share. This share consists in realizing his capacities of feeling, of loving, of mental and physical energy, and in realizing these he plays his part in the social life, or, in Green's phrase,[4] he finds his own good in the common good.

---

4 T. H. Green was latterly a Professor of Philosophy at Oxford, whose work was actively in dialogue with the ideas of John Stuart Mill and Herbert Spencer.

Now this phrase, it must be admitted, involves a certain assumption, which may be regarded as the fundamental postulate of the organic view of society. It implies that such a fulfilment or full development of personality is practically possible not for one man only but for all members of a community. There must be a line of development open along which each can move in harmony with others. Harmony in the full sense would involve not merely absence of conflict but actual support. There must be for each, then, possibilities of development such as not merely to permit but actively to further the development of others. Now, the older economists conceived a natural harmony, such that the interest of each would, if properly understood and unchecked by outside interference, inevitably lead him in courses profitable to others and to society at large. We saw that this assumption was too optimistic. The conception which we have now reached does not assume so much. It postulates, not that there is an actually existing harmony requiring nothing but prudence and coolness of judgement for its effective operation, but only that there is a possible ethical harmony, to which, partly by discipline, partly by the improvement of the conditions of life, men might attain, and that in such attainment lies the social ideal.

Thus in the organic conception of society each of the leading ideas of historic Liberalism has its part to play. The ideal society is conceived as a whole which lives and flourishes by the harmonious growth of its parts, each of which in developing on its own lines in accordance with its own nature tends on the whole to further the development of others. There is some elementary trace of such harmony in every form of social life that can maintain itself, for if the conflicting impulses predominated society would break up, and when they do predominate society does break up. At the other extreme, true harmony is an ideal which is perhaps beyond the power of man to realize, but which serves to indicate the line of advance. But to admit this is to admit that the lines of possible development for each individual or, to use a more general phrase, for each constituent of the social order are not limited and fixed. There are many possibilities, and the course that will in the end make for social harmony is only one among them, while the possibilities of disharmony and conflict are many. The progress of society like that of the individual depends, then, ultimately on choice. It is not 'natural', in the sense in which a physical law is natural, that is, in the sense of going forward automatically from stage to stage without backward turnings, deflections to the left, or fallings away on the right. It is natural only in this sense, that it is the expression of deep-seated forces of human nature which come to their own only by an infinitely slow and cumbersome process of mutual adjustment. Every constructive social doctrine rests on the conception of human progress. The heart of Liberalism is the understanding that progress is not a matter of mechanical contrivance, but of the liberation of the living spiritual energy. Good mechanism is that which provides the channels wherein such energy can flow unimpeded, unobstructed by its own exuberance of output, vivifying the social structure, expanding and ennobling the life of mind.

2.5   Georges Sorel, *Reflections on Violence* (1908; 1916 translation)

Sorel (1847–1922) was a French engineer until, at 45, he decided to earn his living through his social and philosophical writing – his prolific output includes work on the Bible, Plato and the contemporary philosopher Henri Bergson. He became the principal advocate of a movement in France which developed in the 1870s called Syndicalism, a movement which accepted Marx's dream of rule by the proletariat, but which refuted the state centralization inherent in Marxist principle. Instead, Syndicalism envisaged a revolutionary and violent overthrow of the state system through a general workers' strike, and its replacement by a confederation of trade unions working in the interest of the working classes. Reflections on Violence was a massively debated work from the time of its publication, being translated into Russian, Italian, Spanish, Japanese, German and Spanish; it became an important text influencing Benito Mussolini's vision of Italian Fascism. The most extended engagement of it in English came in 1926 with Wyndham Lewis's The Art of Being Ruled. *But Sorel's work had become known earlier when, during the First World War, it had appeared in a translation by T. E. Hulme (this is the version from which these extracts are taken). Hulme had been crucially involved in debates concerning the development of a distinctively modern poetry in the first decade of the twentieth century, and was a key influence over the Imagist poetics promoted by Ezra Pound before the First World War, as well as upon modern movements in the visual arts in Britain. He wrote an important and much-discussed preface to his translation. There, Hulme draws attention to the antagonism that Sorel's ideas have provoked through their seemingly contradictory combination of a radical and anarchic socialism with a profound anti-democratic stance. Deploying some of the reasoning most comprehensively argued in earlier essays like 'Romanticism and Classicism' (see Section 5), Hulme points out the delusions of the progressive and democratic strain of liberal socialism, its faith that conditions will be improved without radical action. Instead, Hulme sees Sorel as the most significant Socialist since Marx, because of his 'classical' awareness that violence is essential in order to alter an intransigent status quo. The extracts here come from two parts of the book: the section in which Sorel outlines the significance of a general strike, and his thoughts at the end of the book on the analogies to be found between the artist and the workers of the future.*

To estimate, then, the significance of the idea of the general strike, all the methods of discussion which are current among politicians, sociologists, or people with pretensions to political science, must be abandoned. Everything which its opponents endeavour to establish may be conceded to them, without reducing in any way the value of the theory which they think they have refuted. The question whether the general strike is a partial reality, or only a product of popular imagination, is of little importance. All that is necessary to know is, whether the general strike contains everything that the Socialist doctrine expects of the revolutionary proletariat.

To solve this question we are no longer compelled to argue learnedly about the future; we are not obliged to indulge in lofty reflections about philosophy, history, or economics; we are not on the plane of theories, and we can remain on the level of observable facts. We have to question men who take a very active part in the real revolutionary movement amidst the proletariat, men who do not aspire to climb into the middle class and whose mind is not dominated by corporative prejudices. These men may be deceived about an infinite number of political, economical or moral questions; but their testimony is decisive, sovereign, and irrefutable when it is a question of knowing what are the ideas which most powerfully move them and their comrades, which most appeal to them as being identical with their socialistic conceptions, and thanks to which their reason, their hopes, and their way of looking at particular facts seem to make but one indivisible unity.

Thanks to these men, we know that the general strike is indeed what I have said: the *myth* in which Socialism is wholly comprised, i.e. a body of images capable of evoking instinctively all the sentiments which correspond to the different manifestations of the war undertaken by Socialism against modern society. Strikes have engendered in the proletariat the noblest, deepest, and most moving sentiments that they possess; the general strike groups them all in a co-ordinated picture, and, by bringing them together, gives to each one of them its maximum of intensity; appealing to their painful memories of particular conflicts, it colours with an intense life all the details of the composition presented to consciousness. We thus obtain that intuition of Socialism which language cannot give us with perfect clearness – and we obtain it as a whole, perceived instantaneously.[5]

I want now to point out some analogies which show how revolutionary syndicalism is the greatest educative force that contemporary society has at its disposal for the preparation of the system of production, which the workman will adopt, in a society organised in accordance with the new conceptions. . . .

The free producer in a progressive and inventive workshop must never evaluate his own efforts by any external understanding; he ought to consider the models given him as inferior, and desire to surpass everything that has been done before. Constant improvement in quality and quantity will be thus assured to production; the idea of continual progress will be realised in a workshop of this kind.

---

5 As a succession of brief footnotes in Hulme's translation indicate, Sorel is in these ideas displaying his indebtedness to the contemporary French philosopher Henri Bergson. Bergson held a similar notion of the division between the conscious mind, which only conceives of experience in 'snapshots', and the 'durée' or duration of experience, which operates upon the consciousness absolutely and immediately, establishing, as he saw it in *Creative Evolution* (1907), 'something that is immanent and essential in the evolutionary movement' of all life.

Early Socialists had had an intuition of this law, when they demanded that each should produce according to his faculties;[6] but they did not know how to explain this principle, which in their Utopias seemed made for a convent or for a family rather than for modern industrial life. Sometimes, however, they pictured their workers as possessed by an enthusiasm similar to that which we find in the lives of certain great artists; this last point of view is by no means negligible, although the early Socialists hardly understood the value of the comparison.

Whenever we consider questions relative to industrial progress, we are led to consider art as an *anticipation* of the highest and technically most perfect forms of production, although the artist, with his caprices, often seems to be at the antipodes of the modern worker. This analogy is justified by the fact that the artist dislikes reproducing accepted types; the inexhaustibly inventive turn of his mind distinguishes him from the ordinary artisan, who is mainly successful in the unending reproduction of models which are not his own. The inventor is an artist who wears himself out in pursuing the realisation of ends which practical people generally declare absurd; and who, if he has made any important discovery is often supposed to be mad; practical people thus resemble artisans. One could cite in every industry important improvements which originated in small changes made by workmen endowed with the artist's taste for innovation.

This state of mind is, moreover, exactly that which is found in the first armies which carried on the wars of Liberty and that possessed by the propagandists of the general strike. This passionate individualism is entirely wanting in the working classes who have been educated by politicians; all they are fit for is to change their masters.

2.6　John Maynard Keynes, *The Economic Consequences of the Peace* (1919)

Keynes (1883–1946) had strong links to Virginia Woolf and the Bloomsbury group of writers. He attended, amongst many other gatherings of the group, the 'Memoir Club' established in 1920, which enabled the group to establish its history on its own terms. Keynes was a Cambridge economist who attended the Peace Conference at the end of the First World War as Chief Treasury representative for Britain. He resigned from his negotiating role, however, when it became clear that the terms of the Peace Treaty, which exacted, as he considered, extremely unrealistic and punitive sanctions upon Germany as aggressor in the war, could not be significantly renegotiated. These

---

6　This idea would have been familiar to a British audience through the debates about 'guild socialism' which were current at the time, debates partly fuelled by late nineteenth-century models of society promoted by John Ruskin and William Morris. These debates, running up to and during the First World War, found one centre in the journal *The New Age*, which had published a slightly different version of Hulme's preface to Sorel's book in October 1915.

passages are selected from the book in which Keynes sought to justify his resignation. The book argues that the 'psychic' links which were shared between the countries of Europe meant that for one country to be singled out for punishment resulted in suffering for all. He concluded that the major events of history, such as the war itself, are often caused by secular, unseen economic and social forces rather than, as the negotiators of the Treaty seemed to maintain, any 'evil' intention on the part of individuals and national groups. For Keynes, therefore, the resolution to the question of how to ensure lasting peace lay in the rectifying of economic inequalities, which the Treaty actually exacerbated. Keynes's vision here of a 'nightmare' of ruins and suffering in Europe, and of a war and peace overseen by inadequate old men, was shared by many, including T. S. Eliot in The Waste Land, *and Ezra Pound in the early Cantos. These extracts come from the early part of the book, as Keynes reflects upon the scene in Paris at the negotiations and offers a (somewhat jaundiced) view of the pre-war world which had disappeared; and later, where he outlines his sense of a potential European ideal both economically and culturally – a vision shared by many at the time, including Eliot in his attempts to delineate a European 'tradition' and 'civilization' in the aftermath of the conflict.*

In Paris . . . at the nerve centre of the European system, British preoccupations must largely fall away and [an Englishman] must be haunted by other and more dreadful spectres. Paris was a nightmare, and every one there was morbid. A sense of impending catastrophe overhung the frivolous scene . . . all the elements of ancient tragedy were there. Seated indeed amid the theatrical trappings of the French Saloons of State, one could wonder if the extraordinary visages of Wilson and Clemenceau,[7] with their fixed hue and unchanging characterisation, were really faces at all and not the tragic–comic masks of some strange drama or puppet-show.

The proceedings of Paris all had this air of extraordinary importance and unimportance at the same time. The decisions seemed charged with consequences to the future of human society; yet the air whispered that the word was not flesh,[8] that it was futile, insignificant, of no effect, dissociated[9] from events; and one felt most strongly the impression, described by Tolstoy in *War and Peace* or by Hardy in *The Dynasts*, of events marching on to their fated conclusion uninfluenced and unaffected by the circumstances of the Supreme Council. . . .

---

7 Woodrow Wilson was President of the United States, who succeeded in having his proposal for the establishment of a League of Nations added to the peace treaty; Georges Clemenceau had become French Prime Minister for the second time towards the end of the war.

8 A reversal of the Biblical conception of divine revelation in St John, I: 'And the Word was made flesh'.

9 A key word also for Eliot in his thinking about history at around this time; in his essay 'The Metaphysical Poets' (1921), Eliot maintained that a 'dissociation of sensibility' had entered English history at the time of the Civil War.

In Paris, where those connected with the Supreme Economic Council received almost hourly the reports of the misery, disorder, and decaying organisation of all Central and Eastern Europe, allied and enemy alike, and learnt from the lips of the financial representatives of Germany and Austria unanswerable evidence of the terrible exhaustion of their countries, an occasional visit to the hot, dry room in the President's house, where the Four[10] fulfilled their destinies in empty and arid intrigue, only added to the sense of nightmare. Yet there in Paris the problems of Europe were terrible and clamant, and an occasional return to the vast unconcern of London a little disconcerting.

What an extraordinary episode in the economic progress of man that age was which came to an end in August 1914. The greater part of the population [in Britain], it is true, worked hard and lived at a low standard of comfort, yet were, to all appearances, reasonably contented with his lot. But escape was possible, for any man of capacity or character at all exceeding the average, into the middle and upper classes, for whom life offered, at a low cost and with the least trouble, conveniences, comforts, and amenities beyond the compass of the richest and most powerful monarchs of other ages. The inhabitant of London could order by telephone, sipping his morning tea in his bed, the various products of the whole earth, in such quantity as he might see fit, and reasonably expect their early delivery upon his doorstep. . . . He could secure forthwith, if he wished it, cheap and comfortable means of transit to any country or climate without passport or other formality, could dispatch his servant to the neighbouring office of a bank for such supply of the precious metals as might seem convenient, and could then proceed abroad to foreign quarters, without knowledge of their religion, language, or customs, bearing coined wealth upon his person. . . . But, most of all, he regarded this state of affairs as normal, certain, and permanent, except in the direction of further improvement, and any deviation from it as aberrant, scandalous, and avoidable. The project and politics of militarism and imperialism, of racial and cultural rivalries, of monopolies, restrictions, and exclusion, which were to play the serpent to this paradise, were little more than the amusements of his daily newspaper, and appeared to exercise almost no influence at all on the ordinary course of social and economic life, the internationalisation of which was nearly complete in practice.

Apart from other aspects of the transaction, I believe that the campaign for securing out of Germany the general costs of the war was one of the most serious acts of political unwisdom for which our statesmen have ever been responsible. To what a different future Europe might have looked forward if either Mr. Lloyd George[11] or Mr. Wilson had apprehended that the most serious of the

---

10 These were the countries involved in negotiating the Treaty: Britain, France, the USA and the defeated powers, Germany and Austria.

11 David Lloyd George had been Prime Minister of a coalition British government since December 1916.

problems which claimed their attention were not political or territorial but financial and economic, and that the perils of the future lay not in frontiers or sovereignties but in food, coal, and transport.

We in Great Britain had not based our financial arrangements on any expectation of an indemnity [from Germany]. Receipts from such a source would have been more or less in the nature of a windfall; and in spite of subsequent developments,[12] there was an expectation at that time of balancing our budget by normal methods. But this was not the case with France or Italy. Their peace budgets made no pretence of balancing. . . . These countries were heading for national bankruptcy. This fact could only be concealed by holding out the expectation of vast receipts from the enemy.

2.7   John Dewey, *Reconstruction in Philosophy* (1920)

The American philosopher, psychologist, and educationalist John Dewey (1859–1952) was the pragmatist thinker who took the most interest in applying his ideas to issues involving the state and society. Influenced by earlier pragmatists, C. S. Pierce and William James, to consider the everyday world as the ground for his philosophy, Dewey saw his task as that of offering a critique of contemporary social terminology, which tended to look to the state mechanism over the needs of the individual. In the field of education, Dewey's thought and practical involvement were vital to a shift towards student-centred, if still guided, learning, over the imposition of a formal curriculum. As someone who saw his whole project as striving against metaphysics, in whatever realm of life they be found, religious, artistic, or social, Dewey sought to derive a rigorously scientific method to 'critically examine the general beliefs and methods of inquiry of the society in which they have practised their discipline'. He was well aware that such an approach would involve a drastic change in the nature of all American institutions, and established the Dewey School at the University of Chicago in 1896 in order to conduct the famous Laboratory Experiment, in which he applied his educational ideas in controlled conditions. For Dewey, as for other pragmatists, thought always issues in practical action; divergent ideas or opinions were simply obstacles which needed to be overcome before action could take place. Dewey, therefore, saw truth as inherently contingent, open to change (he was another social thinker consciously working in the wake of Darwin) and responsive to historical and social circumstance. In the field of literature, such ideas – grounded in the everyday, yet changing and open to metaphysical readings – are entertained by American writers including the poets Marianne Moore, William Carlos Williams and Wallace Stevens, and the novelist William Faulkner. As these extracts from his key work in this area illustrate, however, Dewey's

---

12 Keynes felt that Lloyd George had fallen in with the plan to seek massive reparations from Germany in order to engineer the economic boom in Britain which ensured his re-election in late 1918.

emphasis upon a 'laboratory' approach to such change meant that he was more focused upon specific historical moments of importance, and also critical of what he saw as the 'idle luxury' of much contemporary social theory, which failed to act to provide a 'guiding method of inquiry and planning'.

In the question of methods concerned with the reconstruction of special situations, rather than in any refinements in the general concepts of institution, individuality, state, freedom, law, order, progress, etc., lies the true impact of philosophical reconstruction.

Consider the conception of the individual self. The individualistic school of England and France in the eighteenth and nineteenth centuries was empirical in intent. It based its individualism, philosophically speaking, upon the belief that individuals are alone real, that classes and organizations are secondary and derived. They are artificial, while individuals are natural. . . . To say the defect was that this school overlooked those connections with other persons which are a part of the constitution of every individual is true as far as it goes; but unfortunately it rarely goes beyond the point of just that wholesale justification of institutions which has been criticized.

The real difficulty is that the individual is regarded as something *given*, something already there. Consequently, he can only be something to be catered to, something whose pleasures are to be magnified and possessions multiplied. When the individual is taken as something given already, anything that can be done to him or for him can only be by way of external impressions and belongings: sensations of pleasure and pain, comforts, securities. Now it is true that social arrangements, laws, institutions are made for man, rather than that man is made for them; that they are means and agencies of human welfare and progress. But they are not means of obtaining something for individuals, not even happiness. They are means of *creating* individuals. Only in the physical sense of physical bodies that to the senses are separate is individuality an original datum. Individuality in a social and moral sense is something to be wrought out. It means initiative, inventiveness, varied resourcefulness, assumption of responsibility in choice of belief and conduct. These are not gifts, but achievements. As achievements, they are not absolute but relative to the use that is to be made of them. And this use varies with the environment.

When the self is regarded as something complete within itself, then it is readily argued that only internal moralistic changes are of importance in general reform. Institutional changes are said to be merely external. They may add conveniences and comforts to life, but they cannot effect moral improvements. The result is to throw the burden for social improvement upon free-will in its most impossible form. Moreover, social and economic passivity are encouraged. Individuals are led to concentrate on moral introspection upon their own vices and virtues, and to neglect the character of the environment. Morals withdraw from active concern with detailed economic and political conditions. Let us perfect ourselves within, and in due season changes in society will come of themselves is the teaching. And while saints are engaged in introspection, burly sinners run the world. But when self-hood is perceived to be an active process it is also seen that social modifications are the only means of the creation of changed personalities. Institutions are viewed in their educative effect – with reference to the types of individuals they foster. The interest in individual moral improvement and the social interest in objective reform of economic and political conditions are identified. And inquiry into the meaning of social arrangement gets definite point and direction. We are led to ask what the specific stimulating, fostering and nurturing power of each specific social arrangement may be. The old-time separation between politics and morals is abolished at its root.

Consequently we cannot be satisfied with the general statement that society and the state is organic to the individual. The question is one of specific causations. Just what response does *this* social arrangement, political or economic, evoke, and what effect does it have upon the disposition of those who engage in it? If so, how widely? Among a few, with a corresponding depression in others, or in an extensive and equitable way?

Just as 'individual' is not one thing, but is a blanket term for the immense variety of specific reactions, habits, dispositions and powers of human nature that are evoked, and confirmed under the influences of associated life, so with the term 'social'. Society is one word, but infinitely many things. It covers all the ways in which by associating together men share their experiences, and build up common interests and aims: street gangs, schools for burglary, clans, social cliques, trades unions, joint stock corporations, villages and international alliances. The new method takes effect in substituting inquiry into these specific, changing and relative facts (relative to problems and purposes, not metaphysically relative) for solemn manipulation of general notions.

Pluralism is well ordained in present political practice and demands a modification of hierarchical practice and monistic theory. Every combination of human forces that adds its own contribution of value to life has for that reason its own unique and ultimate worth. It cannot be degraded into a means to glorify the State. One reason for the increased demoralization of war is that it forces the State into an abnormally supreme position.

The other concrete fact is the opposition between the claim of independent sovereignty in behalf of the territorial national state and the growth of international and what have well been called trans-national interests. The weal and woe of any modern state is bound up with that of others. Weakness, disorder, false principles on the part of any state are not confined within its boundaries. They spread and infect other states. The same is true of economic, artistic and scientific advances . . . In such ways as these, internationalism is not an aspiration but a fact, not a sentimental ideal but a force. Yet these interests are cut across

and thrown out of gear by the traditional doctrine of exclusive national sovereignty. It is the vogue of this doctrine, or dogma, that represents the strongest
barrier to the effective formation of an international mind which alone agrees
with the moving forces of present-day labor, commerce, science, art and religion.

2.8   Charles F. G. Masterman, *England After War* (1922)

*Masterman (1874–1927) studied natural and moral sciences at the University of
Cambridge. He was a sometime editor of the newspaper the* Daily News. *He was also a
cabinet minister in the Home Office and Treasury in the Liberal government during
1909–15, and had special responsibility for enabling the National Insurance legislation
which brought sickness benefits to poorer workers into practice. He had produced a report
on the 'state of England' in 1908, and, in this later book* England After War, *was seeking to provide a sequel which registered the changes wrought by the recent war in Europe.
As the first of these extracts shows, Masterman, like many, saw the war as having
destroyed a system of social, political and class relations which had held since medieval
times. From the late nineteenth century through to the start of the war, the issue of class
had emerged as a key determinant in Britain, as initiatives around welfare, health and
schooling were added to the traditional separation between aristocrats and peasants
through land ownership, to enforce a greater stratification of British society. The rise of the
socialist and labour movements across these years drew further attention to the economic
gap between rich and poor in the post-industrialized world. Masterman's earlier work on
the state of the nation had been preoccupied with tracking these layerings; now, after the
war, he returned to his earlier concerns to find the world radically and irrevocably altered
by the conflict. In the process, as one extract here makes clear, he sees the subject-matter
of the modern (Edwardian) novel under threat. Masterman's conclusions chime with many
tensions to be found in English modernist writing also. The loss of family land is reflected
at the end of Ford Madox Ford's* Parade's End *sequence of novels, for example; D. H.
Lawrence's* Lady Chatterley's Lover *maps the intimate crossing of former class boundaries. The selections here are derived from three chapters in Masterman's study: 'The
Passing of Feudalism', 'The Plight of the Middle Class' and 'Labour'.*

There is taking place the greatest change which has ever occurred in the history
of the land of England since the days of the Norman Conquest: with the possible exception of the gigantic robberies of the Reformation. It is being effected,
not by direct confiscation, but by enormous taxation,[13] which is destroying the

---

13 Taxation had risen steadily during the war in order to pay for armaments; afterwards, and under
   pressure from the trade unions, in 1919–20, the government moved to relieve many from the working class from the tax net. In addition, the extension of the National Insurance scheme, which had
   been effected in 1911, to a more-or-less universal tax, meant that after the war a much larger proportion of national taxation fell upon the middle classes than before.

whole Feudal system as it extended practically but little changed from 1066 to 1914. Until now the land-owning class has always been able to absorb the intruders which came in with great wealth to obtain the prestige and amenities which belonged to ownership of great estates. Thus, in the eighteenth century, England saw the 'nabobs', who had plundered India, purchase or build great country houses, with acres which gave them possession of the tenants, the labourers, and of many seats in Parliament. Later came the wealth of the Sugar Islands. And then the big manufacturers and traders commenced to see how they could obtain enjoyment, bought titles, and renovated bankrupt estates, and passed from allegiance to Nonconformity in to the broad bosom of the Church of England. A courageous attempt to shore up the old system was made by the American marriages, in which the daughters of transatlantic millionaires were married to the heirs or owners of historic titles; and the marriage *dots* provided for the maintenance of unproductive estates. . . .

Yet this tough old English landed system swallowed them all up, and compelled them to conform to its demands. . . . The system might have continued until the last aged labourer had been borne to his rest, and no one was left to till and dig and harvest the produce. But, with the most patriotic support to the Government in the great challenge of 1914, the Feudal system vanished in blood and fire, and the landed classes were consumed.

It is interesting and a little pathetic to trace the influence of war and a rise in prices in the slow disintegration and decay of this whole standard of civilisation of Middle-Class England. That civilisation has been built up in the belief that a sudden doubling of prices was as unlikely to occur during its lifetime as the opening of a volcano in the middle of its streets. Before the war it was living a little beyond its income, in that stretching forward to more elaborate social life which, according to the orthodox economists, is the motive power of all 'progress'. It was enabled to this largely because it had taken the control of its birth-rate in its own hands,[14] and, despite the warnings and admonitions of high dignitaries of orthodox faiths, was rigorously limiting the number of its children. . . . Now it finds itself, like a shipwrecked voyager, tossed about on unfathomable seas. It is true that in most cases its income has been increased, and in many others 'our trade' and 'our business' cheers it up with a substantial Christmas bonus. But in no case do these at all adequately compensate for the rise in cost of living. . . .

The efforts of those who still maintain the civilised standard of pre-war times are tremendous, and yet the general impression is that of a whole body of decent

---

14 The average of five surviving children per marriage in the 1850s had declined to three by the early 1900s, and was falling further for the first two decades of the twentieth century. Various reasons have been ascribed to this: the decline in real terms of wages across these years; later marriages; but also, from the 1890s onwards, a greater knowledge about birth control techniques, and, from the 1890s, the postal availability of preventatives, at least for the educated classes.

citizens slipping down by inexorable God-made or man-made or devil-made laws into the Abyss. . . .

In general examination I find that the first thing which goes is the nurse or general servant, and the mother becomes the drudge of the family. Next the small savings have vanished. Then the villa takes in a gentleman lodger: the breadwinner spends less on food: farinaceous foods – cereals, lentils and the like – replace meat and more palatable diets. The bulwark against food collapse is, in a large number of cases, the garden or allotment, tilled with assiduity, in the hope of the Archbishop of Canterbury's continued approval, even extending to post-war days, in the hours normally devoted to the worship of God. Then comes the abandonment of all 'paying pleasures' – the cinema, the theatre and the like – the abandonment of holidays, and the scraping together of oddments, etc., into clothes, with the willing acceptance (in contrast to previous proud rejection) of gifts of second-hand apparel from relations and friends. Finally comes (and only the soul of the suburbs can conceive what that means) 'the abandonment of all effort to keep up appearances'. . . .

But entirely outside Suburbia lies an additional Middle Class – the *bourgeoisie*. . . . It includes at its kernel the 'professional' classes – the doctors, ministers of religion, men and women whose lives are devoted to teaching and research and scientific discovery. It includes also the Civil Servant. . . . It includes all those who have saved a little, and are living on their savings: whose 'safe' gilt-edged securities, owing to the war borrowings, have depreciated far below their former value, the missing portion having gone to pay for the war. In fact it is these, and not the big capitalists, who have really paid for the war. It includes the writers of books and the journalists . . . the shopkeepers, managers of other men's shops, and all that litter of curious life which clings about the processes of the retail trade. Everywhere in Europe it is perishing – in Vienna, Berlin, Moscow, even amongst the victors in Paris and Rome. It is the class which maintains any intellectual life, although intellectual interests do not absorb the energies of most of it. It is the class in which the old Puritan religion still dominates. Of our best novelists the late Henry James may go for subjects to the family of indefinite wealth, of American origin, and Mr Hardy can find the heights and depths of human life among his Dorsetshire peasants. But the most influential of contemporary writers, Mr Bennett, for example, and Mr H. G. Wells, never go far outside the realm of this large and spacious company of the Middle Class. . . .

The Governments of Europe are 'run by' professors and journalists. The Governments of England have long been run by lawyers and a few wealthy families, who are influenced by and modify their policy in accordance with the wishes of a small group of newspaper proprietors, who hire the journalists to represent the views they wish from day to day to present to the public. . . . The lawyers and nobles with their later additions of as yet unennobled profiteers, have never seen much value in the assistance of an *intelligenzia*, or any reason to waste money on its support. So the *intelligenzia* which is interested in public life now largely goes to Labour and identifies itself passionately with Labour ideals: to be received, however, with far more distrust and much less welcome than if it retained its position 'in its own class', or found some other outlets for its energy.

And the result to-day is that, through the combination of smashing taxation more inimical to their standard of life than that imposed on any other class, with a rise in prices which has more than doubled their expenses, and a fall in securities which has nearly halved their capital, they are probably more bitterly deserted in this unseen combat of economic standard than any other class of the community.

The masses of the people . . . know nothing and care nothing about Guild or any other Socialism. . . . They vote Labour; but they vote Labour not from aspirations for the overthrow of the Capitalistic regime, or the nationalisation of anything or everything. They vote Labour because they see that the rich have certain of the desirable things in life, and they have not got them. They want to get them. They wanted to get them before the war. They want a good deal more to get them after the war, since they believe (and rightly) that they did as much for the winning of the war as the rich themselves.

I doubt if there would be any appreciable Social discontent (I am sure that it would be little vocal) if the wealthy, and the men who made wealth during the war, either concealed that wealth in fresh investments of capital, or led the austere life of the ascetic of riches.

2.9   C. H. Douglas, *Social Credit* (1924)

Major Clifford Hugh Douglas (1879–1952) was a British civil engineer and economic theorist, who in this work and in the earlier Credit-Power and Democracy *(1920) developed a theory that the ills of post-war society derived from the fact that the goods made by industry were priced above the cost of their production, because industrial corporations needed to achieve high profitability in order to satisfy their shareholders. Douglas maintained instead that companies should offer their goods at less than the cost of production, that the kinds of goods to be offered be controlled to stem rampant consumerism, and that the gap created in a corporation's accounts be filled by a 'social credit', backed by the government's production of new money to sustain it. Douglas's ideas were discredited by most economists of the time (although a Social Credit Party based upon his ideas survived in Canada until 1935). But his work held strong appeal for thinkers and writers disillusioned by the economic divisions which were taken to have formed the real causes of the First World War. The strongest of Douglas's literary advocates was Ezra Pound, while, for over a decade, Douglas's ideas received discussion in the journal* The New Age *edited by A. R. Orage, which eventually became almost taken over by its advocacy of social credit theories.*

When we say that the objective of modern business is to obtain a maximum total price for a minimum total cost, we are implying in the case of a given undertaking that the receipts shall be at least equal to the disbursements, and in addition that the surplus of receipts shall be as large as possible. This is the same thing as saying that all the costs of an article shall be included in the price of it to the public.

. . . As no government can carry on for a month without money, it is not necessary to labour the point that the visible government of a country is obliged to take its orders and to shape its policy, and particularly its financial policy, in accordance with the instructions of dealers in this indispensable implement, so long as they hold a practical monopoly of it. . . .

The early Victorian political economists agreed in ascribing all 'values' to three essentials: land, labour, and capital. . . . But it is rapidly receiving recognition that, while there may be a rough truth in this argument during the centuries prior to the industrial revolution . . . there is now a fourth factor in wealth production, the multiplying power of which far exceeds that of the other three, and which may be expressed . . . as the 'progress of the industrial arts.' Quite clearly, no one person can be said to have a monopoly share in this; it is the legacy of countless numbers of men and women, many of whose names are forgotten and the majority of whom are dead. And since it is a cultural legacy, it seems difficult to deny that the community, as a whole, and not by any qualification of land, labour, or capital, are the proper legatees. But if . . . the owners of the legacy of the industrial arts are the general community, it seems equally difficult to deny that the chief owners, and rightful beneficiaries of the modern productive system, can be shown to be the individuals composing the community, as such.

Whether society as a whole can be imagined to have an individuality of its own or not, it may be repeated that Society's individuality is not a prime interest of the human individual. It is an auxiliary interest, and may even be a pervasive interest. It is most probably true that there can be no divergence between true Public Interest and any true private interest; if it were so, words would have lost their meaning; but it is certain that no crushing of individuality by Society can ever conduce to the well-being of other individuals. The human individual, under the same conception, contains either in a latent or active form, every function and attribute, although on a minute scale, which can be imagined to reside in a world society.

Any attempt, by current financial methods, to reduce prices (or even to stabilize them, as the phrase goes) is a mathematical absurdity unless the cost of this stabilization, or lowering of prices, is met from some extraneous source. Or to put the matter another way, the margin of profit which makes it possible for a producer to go on producing, disappears unless the financial cost, and consequently the price of production, is allowed to rise steadily in relation to direct labour cost. As a result of this, if prices are forced down production stops, and stocks are sold only at prices which mean loss, and ultimately bankruptcy, to the manufacturer and distributor.

To put the matter in a form of words which will be useful in our further consideration of the subject, *the consumer cannot possibly obtain the advantage of improved process in the form of correspondingly lower prices, nor can he expect stable prices under stationary processes of production, nor can he obtain any control over the programme of production, unless he is provided with a supply of purchasing-power which is not included in the price of the goods produced. If the producer or distributor sells at a loss, this loss forms such a supply of purchasing-power to the consumer; but if the producer and distributor are not to sell at a loss, this supply of purchasing-power must be derived from some other source. There is only one source from which it can be derived, and that is the same source which enables a bank to lend more money than it originally received. That is to say, the general credit.* In spite of the immense strides made in the direction of improved process since 1914, prices are still nearly double those obtaining at that date, while industrial profits are much less.

It may now be possible to see with some degree of clearness the difficulties in which those institutions and organizations which control the general credit at the present time find themselves.

If we imagine a country to be organized in such a way that the whole of its natural born inhabitants are interested in it in their capacity as shareholders, holding the ordinary stock, which is inalienable and unsaleable, and such ordinary stock carries with it a dividend which collectively will purchase the whole of its products in excess of those required for the maintenance of the 'producing' population, and whose appreciation in capital value (or dividend-earning capacity) is a direct function of the appreciation in the real credit of the community, we have a model, though not necessarily a very detailed model, of the relationships outlined. Under such conditions every individual would be possessed of purchasing-power which would be the reflection of his position as a 'tenant-for-life' of the benefits of the cultural heritage handed down from generation to generation. Every individual would be vitally interested in that heritage, and his clear interest would be to preserve and to enhance it. Contemporaneously with this, he might also be a 'producer', and although it is very probable that the money incentive in the form of wages could be made small in comparison with the dividends he would receive as a shareholder, the relation between these two forms of effective demand offers a perfectly flexible method of transition from the existing arrangements. It will be obvious that such a set of relationships does not impinge on what is commonly called the rights of property at all, so long as these rights are 'consumers'' rights. It renders each individual immune from economic penalization for his personal views, and thus forms the only effective bulwark against tyranny, and it places the underlying facts of co-operative production in a light in which they can be seen and grasped by the most modest intelligence.

3

Gender and Sexuality

Introduction

Issues of gender and sexuality had very much been a part of the literature of the *fin-de-siècle*. The 1890s had seen the emergence of the so-called 'New Woman' phenomenon, in which intelligent, liberated feminists were seen operating in strong roles in the public world. In contemporary novels, women were no longer the objects of the gaze in work by male authors, and female characters now explored the world through their own eyes. Elsewhere, the trial of Oscar Wilde in 1895 had focused attention upon homosexuality, and the perceived decadence of this alternative way of living was associated by conservative critics at the time with the sudden liberation of women. 'Decadence' was, of course, a key word at the time, and was often linked in the popular literate mind to 'degeneration', the term made current by Max Nordau's notorious book of that title, which was first published in German in the year of the Wilde trial (see extract in Section 5).

One of the issues which the 1890s had unleashed, in other words, was uncertainty about masculinity, and about the proper role of the male in society. Both British and American men were facing an increasingly organized, visible, and vocal movement of women determined to secure the vote, and to win equal rights in all other aspects of life. As the documents below reveal, women were also strongly involved in social projects aiming to alleviate poor health and living conditions in the larger cities – an involvement which sometimes brought imprisonment when it touched upon broader issues of 'decency' and morality.

Several of the key areas addressed by women campaigners at this period crossed over between aspects of gender rights and socialism, or social–political concerns. Birth control was something of which many in the lower classes in America and Britain were unaware. The dissemination of information about it formed a feature of the campaign to liberate women from their enslavement to men's desires, but also, in the eyes of pioneers like Margaret Sanger and Marie Stopes, performed an equally important task of seeking to limit the booming and overstrained population of the urban poor. Issues of social division emerge again and again in these documents, with the counter-feeling that, were women allowed a more prominent part in the political apparatus, the broader social problems would be those that they would immediately address.

But there was extensive questioning at the time about mens' ability to sustain their traditional status in the workplace and the home. As Section 2 of this Sourcebook demonstrated, the increasingly technologized processes of industrial manufacture were rendering the individual worker an anonymous part of a force over which he had little control. Whilst the First World War enabled men to display some of the older virtues of courage and honour on a large scale, again (and in this case to massively deadly effect), technology rendered such virtues virtually irrelevant as men were slaughtered in the trenches by heavy weaponry. On the Home Front, the mobilization of women to undertake many of the tasks formerly performed by men, again challenged gender expectations.

In Britain, some of these issues over masculinity had coalesced over ten years earlier, when the imperial army was out-thought and out-manoeuvred for a long period by a much smaller force largely of farmers, during the South African (or Boer) War, 1899–1902. After that war, a series of public inquiries were launched into the seemingly poor state of health of both the soldiery and the potential recruits. The 1904 Interdepartmental Committee on Physical Deterioration discovered widespread malnutrition and poverty, as well as industrial pollution, as major debilitating factors in the larger cities – the natural recruiting ground for soldiers in the ranks. A Royal Commission was immediately launched into the mechanisms for providing poor relief and raising general standards of health, an agenda which dictated the policies of the socially reforming Liberal government which came into power in 1906.

Amongst the educated classes, sex and sexuality were being placed at the heart of individual identity by the work of Sigmund Freud, which was becoming known in English through translations from the early 1910s onwards, known even when his work had not been read closely by those discussing it. Freud's association of the unconscious and of repression with sexuality, and especially with the traumatized sexuality of infants, formed part of the challenge to concentrate upon the inner life, and to dismiss the world of the everyday, which so marked the first two decades of the twentieth century. As part of this new interest in the psychology (or more often the psychopathology) of sexuality, there was discussion of the foundations and implications of same-sex desire, particularly, as several of these extracts demonstrate, as a response to the perceived inhospitality of the contemporary world to the emotional and individual physical or sexual life.

It has been a preoccupation of the critical writing on modernism in the past thirty years to establish the frequent misogyny of its male promulgators. And this has had a liberating effect upon discussion not just of this period, but of sexuality and politics in the later part of the twentieth century. Viewed in another light, the male writers can seem as traumatized (to use the word of the time) or uncertain about many of the issues of sexuality and relationships which were the typical responses of other writers in other fields at the time. Yet the effects of the new confidence amongst women writers such as Woolf and Dorothy Richardson, concerned to write out the *terra incognita*, in literary terms, of the female consciousness, are amongst the qualities that are truly 'new' in the literature of the period, as are the pared-down poetry of H.D. and Mina Loy, or the playful prosiness of Marianne Moore – all, in themselves, not-so-implicit rejections of the dominant and domineering claims of their male counterparts.

In other parts of the writing of the period, there is an attempt to explore some of the same-sex desires which fascinated the psychologists at this time. The trial of Radclyffe Hall, and the banning of her 1928 novel *The Well of Loneliness* about the lesbian 'invert' Stephen (despite the protestations of Woolf amongst others), forms a counterpart at the end of our period to the Wilde trial near its beginning. But Woolf's writing and non-fiction, from *Mrs Dalloway* to *A Room of One's Own*, had tried, however tentatively, to write about the same desires – as Gertrude Stein and Djuna Barnes did more openly at this time. E. M. Forster, however implicitly at the time, wrote about homosexuality. Debates about gender, sex and sexuality in the early part of the twentieth century, therefore, operating as they did in a newly-charged climate of ideas, 'science', and opinion, often engaged in a difficult, anxious and contradictory struggle for articulation, a struggle which marks the radical uncertainties of many modernist texts.

3.1   Otto Weininger, *Sex and Character* (1903; translated 1906)

Weininger was born in 1880, and committed suicide in 1903. Despite his short life, however, his one book was extremely influential upon modernist ideas of sexuality, and of the relative inherited characteristics of males and females. Although Weininger's book is deeply misogynistic throughout, it did exert some influence upon feminist debates, and upon debates about homosexuality, in the first twenty or so years of the twentieth century. Weininger's central argument was that any radical distinction between the two sexes, with absolute masculine and feminine characteristics implanted in the collective psyche, was false, and that an 'intermediate' condition was preferable. In this, though, from our perspective, he seems as prejudiced towards homosexuals as he is towards women. However, he even claimed that homosexuality is 'a higher form' of heterosexuality. As such, Weininger's ideas were deeply influential upon Edward Carpenter, the English advocate of 'homogenic love', who published his The Intermediate Sex: A Study of Some Transitional Types of Men and Women *in 1907. When treating what he called the 'woman question', however, Weininger's argument takes on a distinctly hysterical slant, and the 'intermediate' nature of most feminists, as he sees them, is displayed in their thinking and acting in opposition to their 'real female element'.*

The law of Sexual Attraction gives the long-sought-for explanation of sexual inversion, of sexual inclination towards members of the same sex, whether or not that be accompanied by aversion from members of the opposite sex. Without reference to a distinction which I shall deal with later on, I may say at once that it is exceedingly probable that, in all cases of sexual inversion, there will be found indications of the anatomical characters of the other sex. There is no such thing as a genuine 'psycho-sexual hermaphroditism'; the men who are sexually attracted by men have outward marks of effeminacy, just as women of a similar disposition to those of their own sex exhibit male characters. That this should be so is quite intelligible if we admit the close parallelism between body and mind, and further light is thrown upon it by the facts . . . as to the male or female principle not being uniformly present all over the same body, but distributed in different amounts in different organs. In all cases of sexual inversion, there is invariably an anatomical approximation to the opposite sex.

Such a view is directly opposed to that of those who would maintain that sexual inversion is an acquired character . . . the result of abstinence from normal intercourse and particularly induced by example. But what about the first offender? Did the god Hermaphroditos teach him? It might equally be sought to prove that the sexual inclination of a normal man for a normal woman was an unnatural, acquired habit – a habit, as some ancient writers have suggested, that arose from some accidental discovery of its agreeable nature. Just as a normal man discovers for himself what a woman is, so also, in the case of a sexual 'invert' the attraction exercised on him by a person of his own sex is a normal product of his development from his birth. Naturally the opportunity must come in which the individual may put in practice his desire for inverted sexuality, but the opportunity will be taken only when his natural constitution has made the individual ready for it. That sexual abstinence (to take the second supposed cause of inversion) should result in anything more than masturbation may be explained by the supposition that inversion is acquired, but that it should be coveted and eagerly sought can only happen when the demand for it is rooted in the constitution. In the same fashion normal sexual attraction might be said to be an acquired character, if only it could be proved definitely that, to fall in love, a normal man must first see a woman or a picture of a woman. Those who assert that sexual inversion is an acquired character, are making a merely incidental or accessory factor responsible for the whole constitution of an organism.

There is little reason for saying that sexual inversion is acquired, and there is just as little for regarding it as inherited from parents or grandparents. Such an assertion, it is true, has not been made, and seems contrary to all experience; but it has been suggested that it is due to a neuropathic diathesis, and that general constitutional weakness is to be found in the descendants of those who have displayed sexual inversion. In fact sexual inversion has usually been regarded as psycho-pathological, as a symptom of degeneration, and those who exhibit it have been considered as physically unfit. . . . It is not generally recognised that sexual inverts may otherwise be perfectly healthy, and with regard to other social matters quite normal. When they have been asked if they would have wished matters to be different with them in this respect, almost invariably they answer in the negative.

There are no inverts who are completely sexually inverted. In all of them there is from the beginning an inclination to both sexes; they are, in fact, bisexual. It may be that later on they may actively encourage a slight leaning towards one sex or the other, and so become practically unisexual either in the normal or in the inverted sense, or surrounding influence may bring about this result for them. But in such processes the fundamental bisexuality is never obliterated and may at any time give evidence of its suppressed presence.

Reference has often been made, and in recent years has increasingly been made, to the relation between homosexuality and the presence of bisexual rudiments in the embryonic stages of animals and plants. What is new in my view is that according to it, homo-sexuality cannot be regarded as an atavism or as due to arrested embryonic development, or incomplete differentiation of sex; it cannot be regarded as an anomaly of a rare occurrence interpolating itself in customary complete separation of the sexes. Homosexuality is merely the sexual condition of those intermediate sexual forms that stretch from one ideally sexual condition to the other sexual condition. In my view all actual organisms have both homosexuality and heterosexuality.

That the rudiment of homosexuality, in however weak a form, in every human being, corresponding to the greater or smaller development of the characters of the opposite sex, is proved conclusively from the fact that in the adolescent stage, while there is still a considerable amount of undifferentiated sexuality, and before the internal secretions have exerted their stimulating force, passionate attachments with a sensual side are the rule amongst boys as well as amongst girls.

A person who retains from that age onwards a marked tendency to 'friendship' with a person of his own sex must have a strong taint of the other sex in him. Those, however, are still more obviously intermediate sexual forms, who, after association with both sexes, fail to have aroused in them the normal passion for the opposite sex, but still endeavour to maintain confidential, devoted affection with those of their own sex.

There is no friendship between men that has not an element of sexuality in it, however little accentuated it may be in the nature of the friendship, and however painful the idea of the sexual element would be. But it is enough to remember that there can be no friendship unless there has been some attraction to draw the men together. Much of the affection, protection, and nepotism between men is due to the presence of unsuspected sexual compatibility.

If a cure for sexual inversion must be sought because it cannot be left to its own extinction, then this theory offers the following solution. Sexual inverts must be brought to sexual inverts, from homo-sexualists to Sapphists, each in their grades. Knowledge of such a solution should lead to repeal of the ridiculous laws of England, Germany and Austria directed against homo-sexuality, so far at least as to make the punishments the lightest possible. . . .

In spite of all the present-day clamour about the existence of different rights for different individualities, there is only one law that governs mankind, just as there is only one logic and not several logics. It is in opposition to that law, as well as to the theory of punishment according to which the legal offence, not the moral offence, is punished, that we forbid the homo-sexualist to carry on his practices whilst we allow the hetero-sexualist full play, so long as both avoid open scandal. Speaking from the standpoint of a purer state of humanity and of a criminal law untainted by the pedagogic idea of punishment as a deterrent, the only logical and rational method of treatment for sexual inverts would be to allow them to seek and obtain what they require where they can, that is to say, amongst other inverts.

3.2 Two articles from the leading Suffrage newspaper in Britain

(a) Christabel Pankhurst, 'The Women's Insurrection', The Suffragette, 28 February 1913

Christabel Pankhurst (1880–1958) worked alongside her mother, Emmeline, to further the cause of women's rights, and to demand the vote for women. After July 1912, when the Liberal government in Britain was widely perceived to have betrayed the women's cause for short-term political ends of its own, the women's movement, headed by the Pankhursts' Women's Social and Political Union, became more radical. They organized a series of attacks on public buildings, and sought to disrupt the mail, as well as founding publishing ventures to advertise their cause. The Suffragette was a weekly newspaper of the women's movement which ran from October 1912 to October 1915 (it continued across the war years under the more charged title of Britannia). The newspaper carried weekly editorials by Christabel Pankhurst alongside reports of speeches, local campaigns, reports of outrages and sabotage, as well as philosophical articles (often in translation), and arts and book reviews. Pankhurst's speech on 'The Women's Insurrection', given at the Town Hall, Chelsea, London, the week before, was given a verbatim rendition in the newspaper.

I am very glad to have this one more opportunity of explaining to an audience in London the meaning of the women's revolution, because it is as much a revolution that is going on in Great Britain as is that series of events taking place in Mexico – a revolution.[1] We here in Chelsea are too far away from Mexico to be able to judge of the merits of the case over there, but one thing we do know, and it is this; that rightly or wrongly a large proportion of the population of Mexico have come to the conclusion that life under the form of government there was

---

1 At this time, there was in Mexico an uprising and a seizing of power by the head of the army, Victoriano Huerta, in protest at a government slow to introduce land reform.

intolerable for them, and therefore they have done what men in all the history of the world have thought themselves justified in doing; they have revolted against their government, and they have adopted the usual methods employed by men. They have taken to methods of insurrection.

Now when the treatment of the Franchise Bill and the Women's Suffrage[2] amendments were under discussion in the House of Commons, Lord Robert Cecil said that had men in this country been treated as women had been in that matter, there would have been insurrection. There was no doubt about it. Well, I think we have convinced the British public that when women are treated in that way they also take to insurrection. Now if you get the right point of view about what we are doing, you will realise that our insurrection is characterised by very much greater self-restraint than are men's insurrections. I read that in Mexico thousands of non-combatants have not merely had their letters destroyed, but they have had their lives taken, and so terrible were the circumstances there that these human bodies had paraffin poured over them and were set alight and burned, in order to put a stop to the danger of pestilence. That is how men conduct civil wars.

Well, you know perfectly well that in spite of the alarmist accounts that you see in the Press, so far in our agitation no human being has suffered except the women who are fighting for the liberty of women. As far as we can secure it, even at tremendous risk to ourselves, that self-restraint on the part of women, and that safeguarding of human life will be maintained until we have won, but short of that we mean to do everything and all things that become necessary in order to settle this question of the status of women in this country once and for all.

'I AM A LAW-ABIDING WOMAN'

Now, when people take to methods of insurrection, when they proclaim a civil war, they take upon themselves a serious responsibility. No one recognizes that more than the women who are fighting in this women's civil war. I am by nature (and so are all women) a law-abiding woman. Nothing but extreme provocation leads women to break the law. Nothing but extreme provocation would lead women to interfere with the life of another human being, but I maintain, without fear of contradiction, that never in any civil war in this country, or any other country, have men had greater provocation, greater grievances, than women have at the present time. I accept any challenge to prove that the condition of women, that the dangers to which women are exposed, the grievances of women, are so great – no, are greater – than have been the grievances of any section of any population in any country when civil war has been thought justifiable.

---

2 There were a series of Bills introduced by the British Liberal Party government between 1907 and 1912 aimed at bringing the suffrage to women, as lobbied for by the Women's Social and Political Union, headed by the Pankhursts and Emmeline and Frederick Pethick-Lawrence. All ran into insurmountable difficulties as the conservative forces in Parliament found ways of vetoing them.

I have with me here tonight a report of women, and men too, who are engaged in dealing with those most unfortunate members of the community who are not safeguarded by law, or the administration of the law, as they ought to be, and who never will be until women possess political power and have a better control over the law. I say to women in this meeting: listen to what I am going to read you in a few words, and then tell me if you are not satisfied that this sort of thing can only be stopped by a revolution such as ours. I ask you whether we are not justified in everything that we have done in our attempt to wake up the public conscience of this country, and force the Government of the day to do something to remove these grievances. It is from a report presented at the last annual conference of that highly respectable and constitutional body, the National Union of Women Workers. These facts are given by a woman who read the paper. Early this year a girl of fourteen and a half years, expecting confinement,[3] appeared at the Central Criminal Court against a man of forty five years old. He pleaded guilty. The judge heard no evidence, gave the police no opportunity of showing there was much against the man besides. The sentence was six months' hard labour, and only this morning women who from the highest motives have broken the law because they have been driven to it by the insult to them, these women were sentenced to the same term of imprisonment as this man. But this is worse: at the September Sessions this year, a girl of thirteen and a half, and expecting confinement, appeared against a middle-aged man who was proved guilty, and the sentence pronounced was three months in prison. That is only a month more than I got on the last occasion when I was sentenced for breaking a window valued at 3s. At every assizes and at every sessions there are cases like this, and worse.

In addition to these facts, reference was made at that conference on the need that existed for rescue homes, not for women of full age, but for little children under twelve years of age. Facts were given there, and that was at a meeting where only women were present, because it was considered that these facts were not fit for discussion at ordinary public meetings. They are fit, ladies and gentlemen, so long as these things are permitted to go on. When we read of babies of two and a half years being brought into these private Lock Hospitals suffering from unnameable diseases because of the awful conditions of our so-called civilization in great cities, I say, Are women not justified in trying to get some political power to put a stop to them?

'Fight the right way,' says someone. Well, I was speaking the other night in a hall which is named after a great man who fought in this country against absolute monarchy. Cromwell and his army fought against the divine right of kings. Charles I believed sincerely – and many agreed with him – that kings, because they were kings, had a divine right to rule; they had a divine right to tax the people of this country and spend their money as they pleased without being

---

3 About to give birth.

responsible in any way. Well, you have abolished the divine right of kings, but you have got the divine right of the man voter substituted for it, and we women to-day are fighting against that divine right. You admire the courage of men like Cromwell. Well, so do we; but it takes a great deal more courage, ladies and gentlemen, to fight against eight million divine rulers than it did to fight against one.

RULERS BY DIVINE RIGHT

I know perfectly well that these rulers by divine right of ours are not against women really. I know perfectly well that the average man is fair-minded and reasonable, and I know, speaking of the average voter, he is quite ready to admit that if a woman qualifies for a vote like a man, if she pays her own rent and rates and taxes like a man, she has as much right to vote as he has. All the public opinion worth having is on the side of justice and fair-play to women, but unfortunately the average man, the average voter, wants to be allowed to go on with his own business. He does not put himself very much out of the way about any grievances except the grievances that come right home to himself. Well, we have been trying to rouse him by argument, we have been trying to rouse him by persuasion. You rouse him sufficiently at a meeting to vote for the resolution of Women's Suffrage, but he goes home after he has heard a good speech, and gone to sleep after saying what a good meeting it was, and then forgets all about it until he is roused up again. Well, now you are all moved about it. You are all excited about it. You are all interested in it.

Many of you condemn us, especially if you play golf, or if you sent a very important business letter which did not reach its destination, or if you are a shopkeeper and your windows have been broken. I expect the Chancellor of the Exchequer is coming home post haste to see what has happened to his building. You are all roused and you are all stirred up. Well, you say, 'What do you hope to get by that? What is the use of making people angry?' Life-long supporters come to me and say, 'You are completely alienating my sympathy.' I reply to them: 'What did your sympathy do for us, my good friend, when we had it? What use has your sympathy or your life-long support been to us? It is better to have you angry than to have you pleased, because sooner or later you will come to the conclusion that this intolerable nuisance must be put an end to.'

Some of you are writing letters to the papers suggesting all sorts of punishments. That won't stop us. You see, in the way of punishment you cannot go beyond a certain point without reversing the whole progress of civilization for the last hundred years. You know they thought that when they adopted forcible feeding, which is really a torture worthy of the Middle Ages, that they would put down the agitation, but it has not done so, because you see when you take to torture as punishment you can go as far as life will let you, but your victim will escape you into another life, and then your power over that human being ends, and women in this movement have so made up their minds that there is no other way but the way we have adopted, that we shall go on, and if one falls down by the way a hundred will arise to take her place.

How else than by giving votes to women are you going to govern the women of England? You cannot govern us if we refuse to be governed. If we withdraw our consent from government no power on earth can govern us. Your police force, your police magistrates, your judges, your army, the navy if you like, all the forces of civilization, cannot govern one woman if she refuses to be governed. Government rests upon force, you say. Not at all: it rests upon consent, ladies and gentlemen, and women are withdrawing their consent. Well, now that is a very serious situation; it is a very paralysing situation, and I would like our friends who think that they can govern us by punishment and by restriction, to ask themselves seriously how it is to be done. You are two women walking along the street. How are you to know which of these women is a Suffragette? How are you to know which of them has destroyed letters in pillar-boxes, or broken windows, or fired the orchid houses, or blown up Mr Lloyd George's[4] house? If you read your papers they say 'Clues to the perpetrators of the outrage to Mr Lloyd George's house!' A golosh! Two hatpins without heads! Two hairpins! And they are still searching, and I who have accepted responsibility several times, why have they not taken me? I suppose they know their own business best. I suppose they think it would be more difficult to manage things with me in Holloway than with me outside Holloway.[5] . . .

This situation will have to be ended, and how are sensible men going to end it? You can only end it in one way, and that is by seeing that political justice is done to women. This Government will have to give Women Suffrage or this Government will have to go. My advice to you men who have got the vote – and you know one voter means more in the minds of politicians than any number of voteless people – make them do it when the session opens, or make them resign office and clear out and make way for people who will.

(b) Sylvia Pankhurst, 'They Tortured Me', The Suffragette, 28 March 1913

Sylvia Pankhurst (1882–1963) had aspirations to become an artist, and studied in Manchester and London. In 1906, however, she gave up this ambition to work full-time for the suffrage movement. She was jailed many times, and protested at her treatment in being arrested, and later in being imprisoned, by going on hunger-strike, as many of the women arrested for their beliefs did. Under laws brought in by the authorities to counter this action, the women were force-fed through feeding tubes. In 1913, under the new Temporary Discharge for Ill-Health Act (popularly called the 'Cat and Mouse' Act, because of the way it encouraged the prison governors and women to play games with the truth and each other), hunger-striking prisoners could be temporarily released home

---

4 David Lloyd George was a social reformer and eventual Prime Minister of the cross-party government in the First World War, but he was also a doubter of the women's cause.

5 Holloway was the women's prison in London to which many of the Suffragettes were sent.

in order to regain their strength, before being re-imprisoned to complete their sentences. Pankhurst's treatment in this year, whereby she was force-fed for a month in Holloway prison, led to an immediate and extreme effect upon her health. Her weight dropped from over 8 stone to 6 stone 13lb in a month. Her eyes were bloodshot, and her condition deteriorated so badly that she was released three weeks early from her imprisonment for fear that she might die. This account gives vivid rendition of that appalling treatment.

I was sentenced on February 18 to two months' imprisonment for breaking a window valued at £3. On entering prison I at once refused to eat. On the third day the two doctors came into my cell and told me that they had no alternative but to feed me by force. They sounded my heart and felt my pulse, and went away.

I was in a state of great agitation – feverish with fear and horror, and determined to fight with all my strength, and to prevent by some means this outrage of forcible feeding. I did not know what to do. Ideas flashed quickly through my mind, but none seemed any use. I gathered together my walking shoes, the prison brush and comb, and other things in a little clothes basket and put them beside me where I stood at the back of the cell under my window. I thought that I would throw these things at the doctors if they dared to enter my cell to torture me. But when the door opened six women officers appeared, and I had not the heart to throw things at them, though I struck one of them slightly as they all seized me. I struggled as hard as I could, but they were six, and each one bigger and stronger than I. They soon had me on my back on the bed, firmly held down by the shoulders, the arms, the knees, and the ankles.

JAWS FORCED APART

Then the doctors came stealing in behind. Someone seized me by the head and thrust a sheet under my chin. I felt a man's hand trying to press open my mouth. I set my teeth and tightened my lips over them with all my strength. My breath was coming so fast I felt as though I should suffocate. I felt his fingers trying to press my lips apart – getting inside – and I felt them and a steel gag running round my gums and feeling for gaps in my teeth. I was tugging at my head trying to get it free. There were two of them holding it. I think there were two of them wrenching at my mouth. My breath was coming so quick and with a sort of low scream that was getting louder. I heard one say, 'Here is a gap,' and the other reply, 'No, here is a better one; this long gap here.' Then I felt a steel instrument pressing against my gums, cutting into the flesh, forcing its way in. Then it gradually forced my jaws apart as they turned a screw. It felt like having my teeth drawn. Soon they were trying to get the India-rubber tube down my throat. I was struggling madly and trying to tighten my muscles and keep my mouth closed up. They got it down, I suppose, though I was unconscious of anything except a mad revolt of struggling, for at last I heard them say, 'That's all,' and I vomited as the tube came up. They left me on the bed exhausted, gasping for breath, and sobbing convulsively.

The same thing happened in the evening, but I was too tired to struggle for so long. Day after day came the same struggle. My mouth got more and more hurt. Sometimes they gagged it open on both sides with a steel gag, sometimes with one, and the gums where they prised my mouth open were always bleeding, and other parts of my mouth sometimes got bruised or pinched in the struggle. Often I had a wild longing to scream, and after it was over I used to cry terribly with uncontrollably noisy sobs, and hear myself, as though it were someone else, saying things in a strange high voice. Sometimes these things were not true. For instance I heard myself saying, 'Now they are coming again; it is all beginning again,' over and over.

3.3 Two articles from *The Woman's Dreadnought* about the beginning of the First World War

The Woman's Dreadnought was a weekly newspaper edited by Sylvia Pankhurst from March 1914 until December 1920. Sylvia Pankhurst had always – unlike her sister and mother – conceived of the women's struggle as part of a broader socialist campaign for greater freedoms for the poor, an opinion reflected in her practical work to found a suffragette club in the impoverished East End of London in 1913. In 1914, this difference of opinion with her family led to her leaving the Women's Social and Political Union altogether, and seeking new means to voice her views, of which The Women's Dreadnought *soon became the key one. The newspaper contained the same range of articles and reports on activism as* The Suffragette, *but interestingly it took a pacifist line during the war compared with its sister newspaper's support for the conflict. Later in the war, Sylvia Pankhurst's paper became* The Worker's Dreadnought, *reflecting her interest in radical socialist solutions, not just to gender issues but also within broader society. From that point onward, the featured articles (and particularly those contemporaneous with the 1917 Russian Revolution) were more Bolshevist in their approach.*

(a) Ennis Richmond, 'What the War Means to Us', *The Woman's Dreadnought*, **12 September 1914**

We are calling for our readers to do a very difficult thing just now, and it will take us all our time to do it. It is hard enough to keep sane in peace time: it is infinitely more difficult in time of war.

At one swoop our sense of judgment and our sense of proportion seem to be swept away, the rules we have used for our ordinary conduct, the judgment we have brought to bear in ordinary cases, seem to fail us. What we have learnt to think of as wicked and horrible, we are now called upon to admire: what we *know* to be wrong we find we are trying to persuade ourselves is right.

It takes all our moral strength to pull ourselves together. We must keep on reminding ourselves that our cultivated judgment, the common sense that had served us in the past, is what we must turn to now in this crisis: we must not try to create a new standard by which to measure this sudden upheaval.

We must keep perfectly clear in our minds that this war is wicked. It is wicked because murder is wicked, and murder is wicked because hatred is of the devil. That we know: this is our normal judgment, and we must hold to it now, when our whole nation is crying out, trying to believe that there is such a thing as a righteous war, and that this is one. It is not: there is no such thing.

We must keep perfectly clear in our minds also the knowledge that the interests of war demand a certain type of enthusiasm which is kept up to simmering point by horrible stories of what our enemies do. These may or may not be true, that is not the point. The point is that we should not allow ourselves to be moved one hair's breadth from the judgment that belongs to our normal higher selves by any of these stories. A good thing cannot rest on a bad foundation, and the patriotism born of a whipped-up enthusiasm, based on stories of the enemy, is not worth the name. Love of what is best in our own nation: a determination to foster and encourage this: loyalty to those we love and a resolution to protect them: these are surely enough to make us ready to give in this hour of the country's need.

We are in for this war for good and for evil; we have got to see it through. But we shall not bring out of it the lesson it can give us, if we let ourselves slip down into sloppy emotionalism.

I do not see how it is possible for us Suffragettes to offer any judgment on the merits of England's call to arms: we have nothing to judge by, for we know only too well what governments and principalities can say and do when they are put to it. But that part of the matter has little or nothing to do with the main point at issue. The war is not the soldiers' doing, the nation is not responsible. As Suffragettes we know this: we have gone down to the depths both of the absurdity of so-called representative government as regards the present electorate, and the injustice of the position of those outside citizenship.

No, what we have to face is our responsibility *now*, plunged into this cataclysm blindfold; we have got to wrench out of it a lesson which will bring peace in the future, the only lesson of any worth that war could bring.

There is such a lesson: there must be; I have said that we are in for this war for good and for evil. The Evil is easy enough to see, in itself it is a hellish business, devils have been abroad and have been invited into men's and women's hearts or it could never have been. The devils of greed, brutality, selfishness, apathy, stupidity, and the greatest of these is stupidity; can we any of us plead innocence?

Good has got to come out of this: just as good has come before out of hideous wrong; not such good as would have been ours had the evil not come: were such a war impossible to us we should be years ahead in spiritual progress of where we stand to-day; but still a great good if it brings us of the East End[6] into closer sympathy, into some sense of a true and living fellowship which will give us, when the tyranny of war is overpast, a greater strength to fight for that which we, as a Suffrage Union, stand.

(b) Sylvia Pankhurst, 'The War Cure', The Woman's Dreadnought, 3 October 1914

It is said that the only hope of securing the peace of Europe is to go on making war until the spirit of militarism, or in other words, the war-making ideal has been exterminated. This advice to war-stricken Europe is not exactly the equivalent of prescribing the hair of the dog that bit you to cure the wound made by his teeth, the prescription is rather to cure the dog's wish to bite by advising him to go on biting more.

Many British people say that to put an end to war it is necessary that Great Britain shall have a supremely gigantic Army and Navy, in order that we British, who are always perfectly just and righteous, and 'Who do not want to fight (but by jingo if we do)' may be in a position to beat any other nation that may dare to attack us or our friends.

Numbers of British people say that, and believe it with all their hearts. Many of these people in the past have urgently demanded Home Rule for Ireland, and have been bitterly opposed to our government of India, a government which has altered little in spite of political changes in successive Cabinets. Many of these people have declared that British rule, or any other rule, is oppressive, if it is built upon the principle of brute force, and the submission of the weak to the strong. They have insistently proclaimed the need of votes for women, on the ground that even men of the same race and the same social class, will trample on the rights of women whose political power is not co-equal with their own.

These people are now casting aside the maxims they have lived by. The Government, that until August last, they hated and feared because it was only partially representative of its own people, they now assume to be capable of dealing with absolute justice towards alien peoples.

But just as do our own Insular-Patriots, so multitudes of those alien peoples view the Governments of their own countries now in this fearful war time, and whilst, to some, England is for the time being an ally, to others, she is 'Perfidious Albion' as of yore.

What is to end European strife? What is the final solution of the knotty problem towards which we all must bend our aims? Can any of us who have been fighters here for freedom believe in our inmost hearts that justice can be built on force? Can we believe that we are fitted to dominate all other peoples, we, with

---

6 A particularly impoverished part of the city of London.

those serious social and economic failings towards our own people, especially towards women and towards children, which we share with all the so-called civilized nations, but in which, in some respects, we are the greatest sinner? Can we believe that *any* group of nations should dominate the rest? Can we believe that the domination by brutal force can possibly be for the ultimate good, either of the nations who dominate or of those who are dominated by the rest?

Surely we cannot, for were we to do so the very bedrock of our faith in the representative Government for which we have been fighting would be overthrown.

Our British Law Courts often fail to give justice, because the laws which they administer have hitherto been made in the main by well-off men, and because men of the privileged classes have acted as judges and magistrates. Women have had no voice in the making or the administration of the legal system. Poor men also for long were denied a voice in the making of laws, and these facts have left their marks deeply engraven upon our legal code. To injure the health and happiness of a child is held as a lesser crime than to forge a cheque or to steal a few pennies from a gas meter under stress of hunger. He who breaks the law by taking his employer's money is sent to prison. He who breaks the law by underpaying his workers is lightly fined.

Fairer and more humane ideals must be brought into the making and administration of our national laws and law courts. Equal representation must be given to both sexes. Privileges of class must be swept away.

So, too, in the realm of law, as between men and nation, the countries with the big armies and navies and long purses must not be allowed to dominate and crush those that are smaller.

Wars are fought, as a rule, for commercial objects, for the acquisition of valuable markets and territory, but when wars are being declared, and whilst they are being fought, these material objects are kept as far as possible from public notice, and, as a rule, it is only in after years that they are fully understood. The most altruistic and disinterested motives that can be found, or invented, for going to war alone are placed in evidence, and there are widely trumpeted forth. Only for honour and justice and pity for the oppressed can the mass of the people of this or any country be aroused to enthusiasm for war.

And this fact shows us that always when great issues rise it is safe and wise to trust people, and 'the people' means women as well as men!

3.4 Alice Stone Blackwell, 'Jane Addams Testifies', *Boston Women's Journal* (1915)

Jane Addams (1860–1935) was a leading social reformer, suffragist, and peace campaigner, who eventually won a Nobel Prize for Peace. With Ellen Starr she founded the Hull House project in Chicago, the first settlement house in America. By the time of the war, she had also been active in founding the National Progressive Party, and the

Women's Peace Party, of which she became chairperson in 1915. In this same year she was elected President of the International Congress for Women, in the Hague. Blackwell's article excerpted here essentially provides a verbatim report on a speech Addams had given to the Boston Equal Suffrage Association the previous September. By 1914, several of the US States, including Illinois, had introduced the vote for women, but they were in a great minority, and the national suffrage campaign continued. The extracts are selected because they give a view of the preoccupations which fuelled American womens' anger, and also their sense of hope, as to the practical changes that would be effected were the suffrage to become universal. The US Constitution was not to be altered to enforce nationwide women's suffrage until 1920, the war years having brought some delay, as they did in Britain.

Chicago is the largest city in the world where women vote, and we have had an opportunity of trying out the advantages and disadvantages.

Several gratifying things happened as soon as women were given the vote. It made an enormous difference in the attitude of public officials. We had long sought to have policewomen appointed. Chicago has a large number of small parks which are used for dancing, as well as many dance halls. On dance evenings 86,000 young people in our city go to dances. We wanted some police-women for municipal chaperons, to safeguard young girls against the dangers that beset them on such occasions. The city government would not listen to us and the Chicago journals for years had a happy time making fun of our project. We got the right to vote on July 1, and on July 15 the Mayor appointed ten policewomen. Before Sept. 1 we had forty and we are promised that before long there shall be a hundred. We had done nothing: but the Mayor was coming up for re-election. We have found that, while it may not be necessary to vote, it is very important to be able to vote.

We have some aldermen who are called 'gray wolves,' because they have been on the board long enough to be gray, and they come there for the same purpose that wolves make their raids. The worst two were from the First Ward. It is a ward where there are few voters, and where all sorts of bad things congregate. The aldermen gave favors of various kinds, and so kept their hold on the voters of the ward. Everybody said it was very bad; but it was hard to get anybody to stand as an opposition candidate, because people hate to be beaten. Women are more willing than men to go in and fail, if they can do any good by it. An admirable woman said she was willing to make the race. Some of the men objected. They said it would stir up trouble, that things went on in the First Ward which young people ought not to know, and they would get into the papers, etc. etc. But she went in against 'Bathhouse John.' Of course, she was defeated; she never expected to win; but the whole situation which had existed for years in that ward cleared up. The processes which went on there were held up to the light, and to public scorn. 'Bathhouse John' lost his prestige, and the party which he had nominally represented repudiated him.

Those ignoble methods had spread to other wards. Now they will never be allowed again in Chicago. Letting in the light upon the First Ward was more than a local service. You cannot have a ward of which the whole city is ashamed without its affecting all the other wards.

Our great poorhouse shelters hundreds of people, and for a long time it was run very stupidly. Husbands and wives were separated. An old couple who had lived together for fifty years in honourable wedlock, and who had nothing left but their mutual affection and a bundle of common memories, were parted, and were not allowed to see each other except at long intervals, and then only through a grating, unless the guard was kind and opened the grating, and let them sit together for a while on a bench in a public hall. When we protested, we were told that it could not be helped, because 'the poorhouse was built that way'; and so human nature must be tortured and twisted to fit the building. Now, through the women's efforts, this has been changed.

[With women's suffrage] in the first place, it would be a much more democratic government. Then it would give women more power to bring about humanitarian ends. Humanitarian measures are now to the fore everywhere. One thing after another which used to be left to private individuals is being taken over by the State: so that, where they are excluded from suffrage, women today are more 'out of it' than any class since the Greek slaves.

3.5   Margaret H. Sanger, *Family Limitation* (revised 5th edition, 1916)

Both in America and in Britain there was a considerable shift downward in birth rates across the years 1870 to 1914 and beyond. The anxious state authorities, foreseeing such decline as leading to insufficient numbers in the workforce, and an insufficient supply of troops for the armed forces, made swingeing claims that this fall was due to a vague concept of 'degeneration', but also to 'deliberate restriction of child-bearing'. The Registrar General in the UK blamed 79 per cent of the fall on this last restriction in a report in 1908. Recent historians have doubted this, however, saying that evidence suggests that knowledge about birth control was actually sketchy in this period, and that the more likely reasons for the fall in birth rates were economic – later marriages as women entered the labour market, and a real decline (at least in the UK) in the standard of living in the years before the war. Middle-class women tended to be better informed about prevention, as it was then called, than the lower class. The spreading of knowledge about birth control was therefore at the centre of the women's liberation movements on both sides of the Atlantic, the encouragement to women to both control and enjoy their sexual lives without fear of pregnancy, one of the more difficult issues the conservative forces confronted at this time. These extracts come from the key work by the American birth-control pioneer Margaret Sanger (1883–1966), whose nursing experience in the slums of New York led her to believe that birth-control information, expressed in language that all could understand, was essential to social progress. Sanger founded the first birth-control clinic in Brooklyn in 1916, for which she was imprisoned, and later the American Birth Control League.

INTRODUCTION

There is no need to for any one to explain to the working men and women in America what this pamphlet is written for or why it is necessary that they should have this information. They know better than I could tell them, so I shall not try.

I have tried to give the knowledge of the best French and Dutch physicians translated into the simplest English, that all may easily understand.

There are various and numerous mechanical means of prevention which I have not mentioned here, mainly because I have not come into personal contact with those who have used them or could recommend them as entirely satisfactory.

I feel there is sufficient information given here, which, if followed, will prevent a woman from becoming pregnant unless she desires to do so.

If a woman is too indolent to wash and cleanse herself, and the man too selfish to consider the consequences of the act, then it would be difficult to find a preventative to keep the woman from becoming pregnant.

Of course, it is troublesome to get up to douche, it is also a nuisance to have to trouble about the date of the menstrual period. It seems inartistic and sordid to insert a pessary or a suppository in anticipation of the sexual act. But it is far more sordid to find yourself several years later burdened down with half a dozen unwanted children, helpless, starved, shoddily clothed, dragging at your skirt, yourself a dragged out shadow of the woman you once were.

Don't be over sentimental in this important phase of hygiene. The inevitable fact is that unless you prevent the male sperm from entering the womb, you are going to become pregnant. Women of the working class, especially wage workers, should not have more than two children at most. The average working man can support no more and the average working woman can support no more in decent fashion. It has been my experience that more children are not really wanted, but that the women are compelled to have them either from lack of foresight or through ignorance of the hygiene of preventing conception.

It is only the workers who are ignorant of the knowledge of how to prevent bringing children in the world to fill jails and hospitals, factories and mills, insane asylums and premature graves.

The working women can use direct action by refusing to supply the market with children to be exploited, by refusing to populate the earth with slaves.

It is also the one most direct method for you working women to help yourself *today*.

Pass on this information to your neighbour and comrade workers. Write out any of the following information which you are sure will help her, and pass it along where it is needed. Spread this important knowledge!

A NURSE'S ADVICE TO WOMEN

. . . Women of intelligence who refuse to have children until they are ready for them, keep definite track of the date of their menstrual periods. A calendar should be kept, on which can be marked the date of the last menstruation, as well as the date when the next should occur.

Women must learn to know their own bodies, and watch and know definitely how regular or irregular they are: if the period comes regularly every twenty eight days (normal) or every thirty days as is the case with young girls.

Mark it accordingly on your private calendar; do not leave it to memory or guess work.

Only ignorance and indifference will cause one to be careless in this most important matter.

A very good laxative (though it is a patent medicine) is Beechams Pills. Two of these taken night and morning, four days before menstruation, will give a good cleansing of the bowels, and assist with the menstrual flow. Castor oil is also a good laxative.

The American physicians may object to this advice because Beechams Pills are a patent medicine. But until they are willing to give open advice on this subject, we must resort to such as the least harmful, until such time as they do.

If a woman will give herself attention BEFORE the menstrual period arrives, she will almost never have any trouble, but if she neglects herself and waits to see if she 'comes around', she is likely to have difficulty.

If the action of quinine has not expelled the semen from the uterus, and a week has elapsed with no signs of the menstrual flow, then it is safe to assume conception has taken place.

Any attempt to interfere with the development of the fertilized ovum is called an abortion.

No one can doubt that there are times where an abortion is justifiable but they will become *unnecessary when care is taken to prevent conception*.

This is the *only* cure for abortion. . . .

Perhaps the commonest preventative excepting the use of the condom is 'coitus interruptus', or withdrawal of the penis from the vagina shortly before the action of the semen. No one can doubt that this is a perfectly safe method; and it is not considered so dangerous to the man as some authorities have formerly viewed it, but it requires a man of the strongest will-power to be certain that he has withdrawn before any semen has been deposited in the vagina. It is very difficult to determine exactly whether this has been done. The greatest objection to this is the evil effect upon the woman's nervous condition. If she has not completed her desire, she is under a highly nervous tension, her whole being is perhaps on the verge of satisfaction. She is then left in this dissatisfied state. This does her injury. A mutual and satisfied sexual act is of great benefit to the average woman, the magnetism of it is health-giving. When it is not desired on the part of the woman and she has no response, *it should not take place*. This is an act of prostitution and is degrading to the woman's finer sensibility, all the marriage certificates on the earth to the contrary notwithstanding. Withdrawal on the part of the man should be substituted by some other means that does not injure the woman.

3.6 Havelock Ellis, *The Erotic Rights of Women* and *The Objects of Marriage* (1918)

(Henry) Havelock Ellis (1859–1939) was an English psychologist who was an early birth-control advocate and a pioneer researcher into the psychology and sociology of sex. His seven-volume Studies in the Psychology of Sex *(1897–1928) formed the most comprehensive inquiry into the field to date, and all subsequent work was influenced by it. Yet the first volume was greeted with a lawsuit for its allegedly obscene content, and Ellis published much of his subsequent findings first in America. The two essays excerpted here, however, were first published in London by the British Society for the Study of Sex Psychology. They offer a succinct delineation of Ellis's views on women's rights towards their sexuality, and also upon the relation between sex and marriage.*

The Erotic Rights of Women

What is the part of woman, one is sometimes asked, in the sex act? Must it be the wife's concern in the marital embrace to sacrifice her own wishes from a sense of love and duty towards her husband? Or is the wife entitled to an equal mutual interest and joy in this act with her husband? It seems a simple problem. In so fundamental a relationship, which goes back to the beginning of sex in the dawn of life, it might appear that we could leave Nature to decide. Yet it is not so. Throughout the history of civilization, wherever we can trace the feelings and ideas which have prevailed on this matter and the resultant conduct, the problem has existed, often to produce discord, conflict, and misery. The problem still exists to-day and with as important results as in the past.

Courtship is a fundamental natural fact. There is a sound physiological reason for this courtship, for in the act of wooing and being wooed the psychic excitement gradually generated in the brains of the two partners acts as a stimulant to arouse into full activity the mechanism which ensures sexual union and aids ultimate impregnation.

It is as a natural fact that we still find it in full development among a large number of peoples of the lower races whom we are accustomed to regard as more primitive than ourselves. New conditions, it is true, soon enter to complicate the picture presented by savage courtship. The economic element of bargaining, destined to prove so important, comes in at an early stage. And among peoples leading a violent life, and constantly fighting, it has sometimes happened, though not always, that courtship also has been violent. This is not so frequent as was once supposed. With better knowledge it was found that the seeming brutality once thought to take the place of courtship among various peoples in a low state of culture was really itself courtship, a rough kind of play agreeable to both parties and not depriving the feminine partner of her freedom of choice.

The evolution of society, however, tended to overlay and sometimes even to suppress these fundamental natural tendencies. The position of the man as the sole and uncontested head of the family, the insistence on paternity and male descent, the accompanying economic developments and the tendency to view a woman less as a self-disposing individual than as an object of barter belonging to her father, the consequent rigidity of the marriage bond and the stern insistence on wifely fidelity – all these condition of developing civilization, while still leaving courtship possible, diminished its significance and even abolished its necessity. Moreover, on the basis of social, economic, and legal development thus established, new moral, spiritual, and religious forces were slowly generated, which worked on these rules of merely exterior order, and interiorized them, thus giving them power over the souls as well as over the bodies of women.

The result was that, directly and indirectly, the legal, economic, and love rights of women were all diminished . . . it had an unnatural and repressive influence on the erotic aspect of women's sexual life. It fostered the reproductive side of women's sexual life, but it rendered difficult for her the satisfaction of the instinct for that courtship which is the natural preliminary of reproductive activity. . . .

In the erotic sphere a woman asks nothing better of a man than to be lifted . . . to the higher plane where there is reciprocal interest and mutual joy in the act of love. Therein her silent demand is one with Nature's. For the biological order of the world involves those claims which, in the human range, are the love rights of women.

The social claims of women, their economic claims, their political claims, have long been before the world. Women themselves have actively asserted them, and they are all in the process of realization. The love claims of women, which are at least as fundamental, are not publicly voiced, and women themselves would be the last to assert them. It is easy to understand why that should be so. The natural and acquired qualities of women, even the qualities developed in the art of courtship, have all been utilized in building up the masculine ideal of sexual morality; it is on feminine characteristics that this masculine ideal has been based, so that women have been helpless to protest against it. Moreover, even if that were not so, to formulate such rights is to raise the question whether there so much as exists anything that can be called 'love rights'. The right to joy cannot be claimed in the same way as one claims the right to put a voting paper in a ballot box. A human being's love aptitudes can only be developed where the right atmosphere for them exists, and where the attitudes of both persons concerned are in harmonious sympathy. That is why the erotic rights of women have been the last of all to be attained.

Yet to-day we see a change here. The change required is, it has been said, a change of attitude and a resultant change in the atmosphere in which the sexual impulses are manifested. It involves no necessary change in the external order of our marriage system; for, as has already been pointed out, it was a coincident, and not designed, part of that order. Various recent lines of tendency have converged to produce this change of attitude and of atmosphere.

In part, the men of to-day are far more ready than the men of former days to look upon women as their comrades in the every-day work of the world, instead of as beings who are ideally on a level above themselves and practically on a level considerably below themselves. In part, there is the growing recognition that women have conquered many elementary human rights of which before they were deprived, and are more and more taking the position of citizens, with the same kinds of duties, privileges, and responsibilities as men. In part, also, it may be added, there is a growing diffusion among educated people of a knowledge of the primary facts of life in the two sexes, slowly dissipating and dissolving many foolish and often mischievous superstitions.

The result is that, as many competent observers have noted, the young men of to-day show a new attitude of simplicity and frankness, a desire for mutual confidence, a readiness to discuss difficulties, an appeal to understand and to be understood. Such an attitude, which had hitherto been hard to attain, at once creates the atmosphere in which alone the free spontaneous erotic activities of women can breathe and live.

The Objects of Marriage

The primary end of marriage is to beget and bear offspring, and to rear them until they are able to take care of themselves. On that basis Man is at one with all the mammals and most of the birds. If, indeed, we disregard the originally less essential part of this end – that is to say, the care and tending of the young – this end of marriage is not only the primary but usually the sole end of intercourse in the whole mammal world. As a natural instinct, its achievement involves gratification and well-being, but this bait of gratification is merely a device of Nature's and not in itself an end having any useful function at the periods when conception is not possible. This is clearly indicated by the fact that among animals the female only experiences sexual desire at the season of impregnation, and that desire ceases as soon as impregnation takes place, though this is only in a few specimens true of the male, obviously because, if his sexual desire and aptitude were confined to so brief a period, the chances of the female meeting the right male at the right moment would be too seriously diminished; so that the attentive and inquisitive attitude towards the female by the male animal – which we may often think we see still traceable in the human species – is not the outcome of lustfulness for personal gratification ('wantonly to satisfy carnal lusts and appetites like brute beasts,' as the Anglican Prayer Book incorrectly puts it) but implanted by Nature for the benefit of the female and the attainment of the primary object of procreation. This primary object we may term the animal end of marriage.

This object remains not only primary but even the sole end of marriage among the lower races of mankind generally. The erotic idea, in its deeper sense, that is to say the element of love, arose very slowly in mankind. It is found, it is true, among some lower races, and it appears that some tribes possess a word for the joy of love in a purely psychic sense. But even among European races the evolution was late. . . .

Yet, from an early period in human history, a secondary function of sexual intercourse had been slowly growing up to become one of the great objects of marriage. Among animals, it may be said, and even sometimes in man, the sexual impulse, when once aroused, makes but a short and swift circuit through the brain to reach its consummation. But as the brain and its faculties develop, powerfully aided indeed by the very difficulties of the sexual life, the impulse for sexual union has to traverse ever longer, slower, more painful paths, before it reaches – and sometimes it never reaches – its ultimate object. This means that sex gradually becomes intertwined with all the highest and subtlest human emotions and activities, with the refinements of social intercourse, with high adventure in every sphere, with art, with religion. The primitive animal instinct, having the sole end of procreation, becomes on its way to that end the inspiring stimulus to all those psychic energies which in civilization we count most precious. This function is thus, we see, a by-product. But, as we know, even in our human factories, the by-product is sometimes more valuable than the product. That is so as regards the functional products of human evolution. . . . It is, however, only in rare and gifted natures that transformed sexual energy becomes of supreme value for its own sake without ever attaining the normal physical outlet. For the most part the by-product accompanies the product, throughout, thus adding a secondary, yet peculiarly sacred and specially human, object of marriage to its primary animal object. This may be termed the spiritual object of marriage.

3.7   F. Stella Browne, 'Studies in Feminine Inversion', *Journal of Sexology and Psychoanalysis* (1923)

Stella Browne was a feminist, an activist against abortion laws and in favour of contraception, and a supporter of lesbian sexuality. Her book The Sexual Variety and Variability Amongst Women *(1917) argued that women have strong sexual impulses, defended female masturbation, and advocated the pursuit of sexual pleasure independently of conception. What is telling about this extract is that it takes Browne's interest in the psychology of women's sexuality into different areas, suggesting instead that lesbianism is partly a symptom of the current social conditions. Nevertheless, the extract is also striking for the limits even a sympathetic advocate of same-sex relations put at the time on their full expression. Like Edward Carpenter in his pioneering work on same-sex relationship, therefore, Browne creates a distinction between 'innate' 'inversion', as all same-sex desire was called even by its advocates at the time, and 'artificial' inversion created by circumstance.*

What I have to put before you to-day are only very fragmentary data, and suggestions on a peculiarly obscure subject. They have, however, the validity; that they are the result of close and careful observation, conducted so far as I am consciously aware, without any prejudice, though they would probably be much more illuminating had they been recorded by an observer who was herself entirely or predominantly homo-sexual.

The cases which I will now briefly describe to you are all well-known to me; they are all innate, and very pronounced and deeply rooted – not episodical. At the same time – though I am sure there has been, in some of them at least, no definite and conscious physical expression – they are absolutely distinguishable from affectionate friendship. They have all of them, in varying degrees, the element of passion. . . .

Case A. Member of a small family, but numerous cousins on both sides. The mother's family is nervous, with a decided streak of eccentricity of varying kinds, and some of its members much above average in intelligence. The father's family more commonplace, but robust. She is of small-boned frame, but childish rather than feminine in appearance, certainly not in the least masculine. (Throughout this paper, I use the adjectives masculine and feminine, only as referring to the pitch of the voice and outline of the body as modified by greater or less development of the secondary sexual characteristics; *not* to mental or emotional qualities.) Quick and deft in movement, neat and rather dainty about her appearance. Much manual dexterity and indefatigable motor energy and activity. Never happy unless occupied in some fairly strenuous way, though she will not, of course, admit this, and derives great moral satisfaction from the consciousness of her own industry. Unfortunately many of these activities seem, to an unprejudiced observer, to be petty and irrelevant, and a subconscious way of finding a vent for frustrated emotional force. A good organizer, but with too little sense of proportion or breadth of view for a position of supreme control. Strong sense of responsibility and capacity for detail. Methodical. Mentally very positive, emotionally shy, reserved, proud and extremely jealous. Some musical talent and keen appreciation of music. Can be extremely generous and devoted where her affections are stirred. Is virtually an agnostic, without having at all thought out the implications of that position. An absorbing devotion to a woman relative; a devotion of an unmistakably, though I believe unconsciously, passionate kind completely dominates her life; it has almost all the manifestations of a really great love; intense interest, idealization, unremitting care, joy in service, and unsparing sacrifice of her own comfort and of the happiness of third parties. Has had some very long and close friendships with other women, into which the same element entered, to a much slighter extent; notably one with a cousin, a smart, shrewd, worldly little person, who did not lose by it. She is fond of children and has a gift of dealing with them, and very sympathetic and tender to animals. . . . Has an instinctive horror of men . . . and also quite a definite antagonism to them socially. . . . As a rule, criticizes even the most harmless and upright and well-intentioned men, unsparingly.

I consider that this woman's unconsciousness of the real nature of the mainspring of her life, and the deprivation of the liberating and illuminating effect of some definite and direct physical sex-expression, have had, and still have, a disastrous effect on a nature which has much inherent force and many fine qualities. Her whole outlook on life is subtly distorted and dislocated, moral values are confused and a false standard of values is set up. The hardening and narrowing effect of her way of life is shown in a tremendous array of prejudices on every conceivable topic: caste-prejudices, race-prejudices, down to prejudices founded on the slightest eccentricity of dress or unconventionality of behaviour; also in an immense intolerance of normal passion, even in its most legally sanctioned and certificated forms. As to unlegalized sex-relationships, they are of course considered the very depth alike of depravity and of crass folly. And all the while, her life revolves round a deep and ardent sex-passion, frustrated and exasperated through functional repression, but entirely justified in her own opinion as purely family affection and duty! Though the orthodox and conventional point of view she takes on sex-questions, generally, would logically condemn just *that* form of sex-passion, as peculiarly reprehensible.

This problem of feminine inversion is very pressing and immediate, taking into consideration the fact that in the near future, for at least a generation, the circumstances of women's lives and work will tend, even more than at present, to favour the frigid, and next to the frigid, the inverted types. Even at present, the social and affectional side of the invert's nature has often fuller opportunity of satisfaction than the heterosexual woman's, but often at the cost of adequate and definite physical expression. And how decisive for vigor, sanity and serenity of body and mind, for efficiency, for happiness, for the mastery of life, and the understanding of one's fellow-creatures – just this definite physical expression is! The lack of it, 'normal' and 'abnormal', is at the root of most of what is most trivial and unsatisfactory in women's intellectual output, as well as of their besetting vice of cruelty. How can anyone be finely or greatly creative, if one's supreme moral law is a negation! Not to *live*, not to *do*, not even to try to understand. . . .

I think it is perhaps not wholly uncalled-for, to underline very strongly my opinion that the homo-sexual impulse is *not in any way superior* to the normal; it has a fully equal right to existence and expression, it is no worse, no lower; *but no better.*

By all means let the invert – let all of us – have as many and varied 'channels of sublimation' as possible; and far more than are at present available. But, to be honest, are we not too much inclined to make 'sublimation' an excuse for refusing to tackle fundamentals? The tragedy of the repressed invert is apt to be not only one of emotional frustration, but complete dislocation of mental values.

Moreover, our present social arrangements, founded as they are on the repression and degradation of the normal erotic impulse, artificially stimulate inversion and have thus forfeited all right to condemn it. There is a huge, persistent, indirect pressure on women of strong passions and fine brains to find an emotional outlet with other women. A woman who is unwilling to accept either marriage – under present laws – or prostitution, and at the same time refuses to limit her sexual life to auto-erotic manifestations, will find she has to struggle against the whole social order for what is nevertheless her most precious personal right. The right sort of woman faces the struggle and counts the cost well worth while; but it is impossible to avoid seeing that she risks the most painful experiences, and spends an incalculable amount of time and energy on things that should be matters of course. Under these conditions, some women who *are not innately* or *predominantly homosexual* do form more or less explicitly erotic relations with other women, yet these are makeshifts and essentially substitutes, which cannot replace the vital contact, mental and bodily, with congenial men.

4

Religion and Belief

Introduction

Despite the cheerful proclamation voiced by a madman in Friedrich Nietzsche's *The Gay Science* (1882), a proclamation reiterated by others elsewhere in his work, that 'God is dead', the evidence for the *particular* breakdown of religious belief at the beginning of the twentieth century is clouded. Nietzsche's target in this proclamation uttered through his personae was, of course, Christianity, but more particularly the whole moral and ethical system which Christianity entailed, in his view. Yet there is little truth to the claim, in terms of there having been an actual retreat from visibility amongst the various established churches of Britain and America in the first decades of the twentieth century. In the US, there seems to have been no fall in the numbers in church attendance across our period; in Britain in 1910 numbers attending Protestant denominational churches were actually 3 per cent higher than they had been in the 1860s, and membership of the Roman Catholic Church had doubled across the intervening time. The Christian church was a very visible part of everyday life, through its social clubs and work to alleviate poverty and deprivation in the big cities. During the First World War, inevitably, church attendance rose even further, and there was a huge growth in 'alternative' practices, such as spiritualism, as the bereaved sought to contact the lost soldiers.

Nevertheless, there had been in intellectual and literary circles for fifty years and more a questioning of Christian faith and doctrine. Anxiety about the perceived loss of Christian faith and its implications had been most famously voiced by Matthew Arnold in his poem 'Dover Beach' in the middle of the nineteenth century. One possibility raised by Arnold, in his thinking about culture, was that the retreat of the 'Sea of Faith' might imply its replacement by poetry and literature itself, as containers of 'higher' forms of meaning. Such a view received added impetus near the start of our period through the publication of such books as Arthur Symons's *The Symbolist Movement in Literature*, which found in the work of recent French poets a near equivalent to religious power, as is evident in the excerpts included below. Symons's book was greatly influential, seeming as it did to validate the kinds of poetic being practised by W. B. Yeats at the time, and opening for the younger generation including T. S. Eliot and Ezra Pound a window onto a poetry of self-consciousness and self-irony, but also of coherence and refined beauty. Such a poetics probably receives its greatest exploration in English in the work of the American Wallace Stevens, yet Pound sought a symbolic integration of seemingly intransigent content in his work right to the end, in the last *Cantos*. Eliot had transposed the symbolic force of his earlier work by the late 1920s into a poetry of Christian reverence, in sequences from *Ash-Wednesday* onwards (he accepted communion in the Anglican Church in 1927).

Notions of the religious informed modernist writings – including those of Pound and Eliot – in other ways, however. Indeed, the very term 'modernism' in this period described a division in religious scholarship, rather than a literary issue. Within the Roman Catholic Church, 'modernism' denoted a belief in the value of modern science and historical research in elucidating biblical events. From 1907, the Pope declared, priests had to swear an oath repudiating modernism. These splits in the Church were registered in the 'little magazines' of the time alongside their publication of work by writers we now consider in literary circles as 'modernist' (that term was first used by critics in America in relation to Eliot's work in the early 1920s, and was introduced into Britain via the title of Robert Graves's and Laura Riding's 1927 book *A Survey of Modernist Poetry*).

But, for American poets who had studied comparative religion at college, there was also a religious possibility included in their awareness of other world religions: witness Eliot's citation from the Sanskrit Hindu *Upanishads* in the final section of *The Waste Land*, or his and Pound's interest in the early 1910s in the work of the Indian poet Rabanindrinath Tagore (Yeats, through his occult and esoteric religious interests, was also interested in Tagore and, later, in Hinduism – see Section 9 on 'Empire, Race and Postcolonialism'). One of the hallmarks of modernism in literature is, then, its sense of a shared ambition towards that equivalent of religious 'meaning' and coherence which might be achieved through a comparison or synthesizing of various religious traditions.

The works extracted in this Section bear upon a further inquiry into the history of religion in this period: the use of anthropological and archaeological evidence to establish the early or 'primitive' origins of religious belief *per se*. The sense of an inter-layering, or evolution, of religious meaning across the millennia registered strongly at this time, and seems in many ways to have superseded faith in – or even interest in – the established church amongst academics and intellectuals. That inter-layering of different histories, religious texts and stories, in many ways prefigures the *poetic* practice of Pound and Eliot in particular. But it also marked many other facets of the context to the period being explored in this Sourcebook: the discussion of early societies in Section 2, for instance, as a way of better understanding the strengths or ills of present-day civilization, or the interest in 'primitivism' in the visual art and music of the era discussed in Section 6, ' "High" Culture'. It is through the work of such as James G. Frazer and Émile Durkheim that the religious 'charge' of such work is developed, but also historicized.

4.1   J. G. Frazer, *The Golden Bough* (1890–1915; one-volume abridged edition, 1922)

Frazer (1854–1941) was a Scot educated at the universities of Glasgow and Cambridge; he spent his academic career at Cambridge and then, from 1907, as Professor of Social Anthropology at the University of Liverpool. Although his research covered a wide area of anthropology (he published a work on Totemism in 1910), he worked essentially on mythology and the origins of religion. This work made him extremely influential in his day: he is cited by Freud in his Totemism and Taboo *(1913), for example, and his thought resonates across all of the European work on religion extracted here, as well as across other disciplines, including sociology and philosophy. Notably, his work has significant impact upon the literary and artistic interest in primitivism which is one marker of modernist art. In 'How to Read' (1928), Pound called the eventual 13-volume* The Golden Bough *'essential to clear contemporary thinking'; Eliot, in his* Notes to The Waste Land, *singles it out as a work 'which has influenced our generation profoundly'. Across the vast expanse of these volumes, Frazer maps a cyclic pattern within many mythologies and religions, one which goes through periods of purgation, purification, and regeneration. He sees these cycles as intimately related to purgation by fire, purification by water, and fertility rituals associated with the soil and also with human sexual intercourse. He also sees such cycles as underpinning the course both of history and societies, and of individual psychology. Frazer firmly held the belief that something of these primitive rites existed beneath the surface of modern individuals and social structures; in this he was followed by a range of early twentieth-century authors, from Lawrence to Woolf to Mary Butts. Eliot's* Notes *point to the two volumes of* The Golden Bough *relating to Adonis, Attis, Osiris[1] as being particularly relevant to his understanding, and these extracts have followed his cue. In them we see the essence of Frazer's methodology throughout this massive work, which might be described as the inter-layering or paralleling of narratives which seem to his understanding to display some inner similarities, whatever their difference of historical, geographical, or cultural origin.*

The story that Adonis spent half, or according to others a third, of the year in the lower world and the rest of it in the upper world, is explained most simply and naturally by supposing that he represented vegetation, especially the corn,

---

1 Attis was a Phrygian god, loved by the Great Mother goddess, Cybele, who was driven mad by her as a punishment for his infidelity. In his madness, he castrated himself and bled to death. In Phrygia, as later when this cult was introduced into Greek and Roman religion, his worshippers castrated themselves as a proof of their belief. Adonis was a beautiful youth adored by the goddess of love, Venus. Out hunting, he was gored to death by a wild boar; an anemone sprung where his blood fell. He was able to return from the underworld to his mistress for some portion of the year. Osiris was an ancient Egyptian god associated with the power of good; he was the enemy as such of the god of evil, Set. Slain by Set, he was avenged by his son Horus, and went to rule over the underworld.

which lies buried in the earth half the year and reappears above the ground the other half. Certainly of the annual phenomena of nature there is none which suggests so obviously the idea of death and resurrection as the disappearance and reappearance of vegetation in autumn and spring. Adonis has been taken for the sun; but there is nothing in the sun's annual course within the temperate and tropical zones to suggest that he is dead for half or a third of the year and alive for the other half or two-thirds. . . . On the other hand, the annual death and revival of vegetation is a conception which readily presents itself to men in every stage of savagery and civilisation; and the vastness of the scale on which this ever-recurring decay and regeneration takes place, together with man's intimate dependence on it for subsistence, combine to render it the most impressive annual occurrence in nature, at least within the temperate zones. It is no wonder that a phenomenon so important, so striking, and so universal should, by suggesting similar ideas, have given rise to similar rites in many lands. We may, therefore, accept as probable an explanation of the Adonis worship which accords so well with the facts of nature and with the analogy of similar rites in other lands. Moreover, the explanation is countenanced by a considerable body of opinion amongst the ancients themselves, who again and again interpreted the dying and reviving god as the reaped and sprouting corn.

The character of Tammuz or Adonis as a corn-spirit comes out plainly in an account of his festival given by an Arabic writer of the tenth century. In describing the rites and sacrifices observed at the different seasons of the year by the heathen Syrians of Harran he says 'Tammuz (July). In the middle of this month is the festival of el-Bugat, that is, of the weeping women, and this is the Ta-uz festival, which is celebrated in honour of the god Ta-uz. The women bewail him, because his lord slew him so cruelly, ground his bones in a mill, and then scattered them to the wind. The women (during this festival) eat nothing which has been ground in a mill, but limit their diet to steeped wheat, sweet vetches, dates, raisins, and the like.' Ta-uz, who is none other than Tammuz, is here like Burns's John Barleycorn:

> 'They wasted o'er a scorching flame
> The marrow of his bones;
> But the miller us'd him worst of all
> For he crush'd him between two stones.'

This concentration, so to say, of the nature of Adonis upon the cereal crops is characteristic of the stage of culture reached by his worshippers in historical times. They had left the nomadic life of the wandering hunter and herdsman far behind them; for ages they had been settled on the land, and had depended for their subsistence mainly on the products of tillage. The berries and roots of the wilderness, the grass of the pastures, which had been matters of vital importance to their ruder forefathers, were now of little moment to them: more and more their thoughts and energies were engrossed by the staple of their life, the corn;

more and more accordingly the propitiation of the deities of fertility in general and of the corn-spirit in particular tended to become the central feature of their religion.

In Sicily gardens of Adonis are still sown in spring as well as in summer, from which we may perhaps infer that Sicily as well as Syria celebrated of old a vernal festival of the dead and risen god. At the approach of Easter, Sicilian women sow wheat, lentils, and canary-seed in plates, which they keep in the dark and water every two days. The plants soon shoot up; the stalks are tied together with red ribbons, and the plates containing them are placed on the sepulchres which, with the effigies of the dead Christ, are made up in Catholic and Greek churches on Good Friday, just as the gardens of Adonis were placed on the grave of the dead Adonis. The practice is not confined to Sicily, for it is observed also at Cosenza in Calabria, and perhaps in other places. The whole custom – sepulchres as well as plates of sprouting grain – may be nothing but a continuation, under a different name, of the worship of Adonis.

Nor are these Sicilian and Calabrian customs the only Easter ceremonies which resemble the rites of Adonis. 'During the whole of Good Friday a waxen effigy of the dead Christ is exposed to view in the middle of the Greek churches and is covered with fervent kisses by the thronging crowd, while the whole church rings with melancholy, monotonous dirges. Late in the evening when it has grown quite dark, this waxen image is carried by the priests into the street on a bier adorned with lemons, roses, jessamine, and other flowers, and there begins a grand procession of the multitude, who move in serried ranks, with slow and solemn step, through the whole town. Every man carries his taper and breaks out in doleful lamentation. At all the houses which the procession passes there are seated women with censers to fumigate the marching host. Thus the community solemnly buries its Christ as if he has just died. At the last the waxen image is again deposited in the church, and the same lugubrious chants echo anew. These lamentations, accompanied by a strict fast, continue till midnight on Saturday. As the clock strikes twelve, the bishop appears and announces the glad tidings that 'Christ is risen,' to which the crowd replies, 'He is risen indeed,' and at once the whole city bursts into an uproar of joy, which finds vent in shrieks and shouts, in the endless discharge of carronades and muskets, and the explosion of fire-works of every sort. In the very same hour people plunge from the extremity of the fast into the enjoyment of the Easter lamb and neat wine.'

In like manner the Catholic Church has been accustomed to bring before its followers in a visible form the death and resurrection of the Redeemer. Such sacred dramas are well fitted to impress the lively imagination and to stir the warm feelings of a susceptible southern race, to whom the pomp and pageantry of Catholicism are more congenial than to the colder temperament of the Teutonic peoples.

When we reflect how often the Church has skilfully contrived to plant the seeds of the new faith on the old stock of paganism, we may surmise that the

Easter celebration of the dead and risen Christ was grafted upon a similar celebration of the dead and risen Adonis, which, as we have seen reason to believe,
was celebrated in Syria at the same season. The type, created by Greek artists, of
the sorrowful goddess with her dying lover in her arms, resembles and may have
been the model of the *Pietà* of Christian art, the Virgin with the dead body of
her divine Son in her lap, of which the most celebrated example is the one by
Michael Angelo in St. Peter's. That noble group, in which the living sorrow of
the mother contrasts so wonderfully with the languor of death in the son, is one
of the finest compositions in marble. Ancient Greek art has bequeathed to us few
works so beautiful, and none so pathetic.

4.2   Arthur Symons, *The Symbolist Movement in Literature* (1899; revised 2nd edition, 1908)

*Symons's book, essentially an introduction of French poets and poetry from the second
half of the nineteenth century to an English-speaking audience, was hugely influential
in the early phases of modernism. Recalling his first experience of reading this book –
which he did in December 1908 – T. S. Eliot described it as 'an introduction to wholly
new feelings . . . a revelation'; in a letter of 1928, Ezra Pound described the Symbolist
nexus introduced into England by Symons as crucial to his formulation of his Imagist
project.[2] Symons (1865–1945) was the son of a Welsh Methodist minister. He was a
poet, translator, and essayist, who was influenced from early on by the poetry of Robert
Browning, about whom he wrote his first book, and Walter Pater. By the 1890s,
Symons was an established leader of the 'art for art's sake' movement, and friend of the
Anglo-Irishman W. B. Yeats, to whom* The Symbolist Movement *is dedicated, as the
greatest practitioner in English of the symbolist principles outlined within it. From
1895, Symons edited the journal* The Savoy, *and published important new work by
Yeats, Conrad, the 1890s poets, and the French writer Paul Verlaine, with whom
Symons also enjoyed a long friendship. Across this period, Symons published reviews of
popular drama and Music Hall, an extract from one of which appears in the ' "Popular"
Culture' section of the Sourcebook below. Symons suffered a severe mental breakdown
in 1908, and was impaired thereafter, increasingly seeking isolation in a small cottage
with his wife in Kent. His views in* The Symbolist Movement in Literature *reflect his
developed belief that, in the absence of traditional Christian faith in the face of modern
science and technology, the arts were under an increasing burden to compensate and to
bring coherence and understanding to the world. In the French Symbolist poets, Symons
discovers, and presents with passionate advocacy, a concerted attempt to mediate, in a
wholly new language, between the innermost workings of the human psyche and the
world of magic and mystery, where the ugliness of the everyday is swept away.*

2 T. S. Eliot, 'The Perfect Critic', *Selected Prose of T. S. Eliot*, ed. Frank Kermode (London: Faber, 1975),
   p. 52; *Selected Letters of Ezra Pound, 1907–1941*, ed. D. D. Paige (London: Faber, 1950), p. 218.

*Symbolism, for Symons, and for his modernist successors, takes poetry away from exter-
nal description of the 'real' world, and into a realm where the seeming reference of
words to that 'real' world is translated into a more emotional, and at the same time
spiritual, possibility. The extracts here are from the second edition of the book; they
begin with some general remarks made by Symons in his introductory pages, then take
in some of his commentary on the major French poets of the late nineteenth century.*

The great epoch in French literature which preceded this Symbolist epoch . . .
was the age of Science, the age of material things; and words, with that facile
elasticity which there is in them, did miracles in the exact representation of
everything that visibly existed, exactly as it existed.

Symbolism is all an attempt to spiritualise literature, to evade the old bondage
of rhetoric, the old bondage of exteriority. Description is banished that beautiful things may be evoked, magically; the regular beat of verse is broken in order
that words may fly, upon subtler wings. Mystery is no longer feared, as the great
mystery in whose midst we are islanded was feared by those to whom that
unknown sea was only a great void. We are coming closer to nature, as we seem
to shrink from it with something of horror, disdaining to catalogue the trees of
the forest. And as we brush aside the accidents of daily life, in which men and
women imagine that they alone are touching reality, we come closer to humanity, to everything in humanity that may have begun before the world and may
outlast it.

In speaking to us so intimately, so solemnly, as only religion had hitherto
spoken to us, literature becomes itself a kind of religion, with all the duties and
responsibilities of the sacred ritual.

ARTHUR RIMBAUD[3]

He is a dreamer in whom the dream is swift, hard in outline, coming suddenly
and going suddenly, a real thing, but seen only in passing. Visions rush past
him, he cannot arrest them; they rush forth from him, he cannot restrain
their haste to be gone, as he creates them in the mere indiscriminate idleness
of energy. And so this seeker after the absolute leaves but a broken medley of
fragments, into each of which he has put a little of his personality, which
he is for ever dramatising, but multiplying one facet, so to speak, after
another.

---

3 Rimbaud (1854–91) was a close friend of Paul Verlaine, who, in later life, wandered Europe, the East
   Indies and Abyssinia. He has been extremely influential on twentieth-century poetry, especially
   through his collection *Illuminations* (1886).

JULES LAFORGUE[4]

The prose and verse of Laforgue, scrupulously correct but with a new manner of correctness, owe more than any one has realised to the half-unconscious prose and verse of Rimbaud. Verse and prose alike are a kind of travesty, making subtle use of colloquialism, slang, neologism, technical terms, for their allusive, their factitious, their reflected meanings, with which they can can play, very seriously. The verse is alert, troubled, swaying, deliberately uncertain, hating rhetoric so piously that it prefers, and finds its piquancy in, the ridiculously obvious. It is really *vers libre*, but at the same time correct verse, before *vers libre* had been invented.[5] And it carries, as far as that theory has ever been carried, the theory which demands an instantaneous notation (Whistler, let us say[6]) of the figure or landscape which one has been accustomed to define with such rigorous exactitude. . . . Here, if ever, is modern verse, verse which dispenses with so many of the privileges of poetry, for an ideal quite its own. It is, after all, a very self-conscious ideal, becoming artificial through its extreme naturalness; for in poetry it is not 'natural' to say things quite so much in the manner of the moment, with however ironical an intention.

It is an art of the nerves, and it is what all art would tend towards if we followed our nerves on all their journeys. There is in it all the restlessness of modern life, the haste to escape from whatever weighs too heavily on the liberty of the moment, that capricious liberty which demands only room enough to hurry itself weary. It is distressingly conscious of the unhappiness of mortality, but it plays, somewhat uneasily, at a disdainful indifference. . . .

His laughter is the laughter of Pierrot . . . he is a metaphysical Pierrot, *Pierrot lunaire*,[7] and it is of abstract notions, the whole science of the unconscious, that he makes his showman's patter . . . it is part of his manner not to distinguish between irony and pity.

---

4 Laforgue (1860–87) was the most self-consciously modern of the poets associated by Symons with the Symbolist movement. His *Les Complaintes* and *L'Imitation de Notre-Dame la Lune* (1885, 1886), with their multiple use of allusion, irony, and pierrots (puppet-like representations of humanity), were massively influential on Eliot's early work, including 'The Love Song of J. Alfred Prufrock', and 'Portrait of a Lady'. These and other, later, Eliot works also reveal the influence of Laforgue's verse technique, which broke from traditional rhythm. Eliot ordered Laforgue's collected works from France immediately upon reading Symons's chapter on him, such was the excitement he felt at coming upon this new possibility in poetry.

5 Laforgue's deployment of this technical innovation, *vers libre* ('free verse'), which seemed to break with the standard poetic line whilst also retaining the ghost of its former standard rhythm, was particularly valued by Eliot and Pound: Eliot wrote an important essay, 'Reflections on *vers libre*', as early as 1917.

6 James McNeill Whistler (1843–1903) was a hugely influential presence in the Symbolist and impressionist art scene at this time, through his works such as 'Nocturnes' and 'Symphony in White'.

7 Symons's reference here is not to Arnold Schoenberg's song-cycle of this title, which was not premièred in Berlin until 1912 (with a translated text from the poetry of another French poet, Arthur Giraud, not Laforgue), but to a popular myth of the moon-maddened Pierrot clown.

STÉPHANE MALLARMÉ[8]

It is the distinction of Mallarmé to have aspired after an impossible liberation of the soul of literature from what is fretting and constraining in 'the body of that death', which is the mere literature of words. Words, he has realised, are of value only as a notation of the free breath of the spirit; words, therefore, must be employed with an extreme care, in their choice and adjustment, in setting them to reflect and chime upon one another; yet least of all for their own sake, for what they can never, except by suggestion, express. . . . The word, treated indeed with a kind of 'adoration', as he says, is so regarded in a magnificent sense, in which it is apprehended as a living thing, itself the vision rather than the reality; at least the philtre of the evocation. The word, chosen as he chooses it is for him a liberating principle, by which the spirit is extracted from matter; takes form, perhaps assumes immortality. Thus an artificiality, even, in the use of words, that seeming artificiality which comes from using words as if they had never been used before, that chimerical search after the virginity of language, is but the paradoxical outward sign of an extreme discontent with even the best of their service.

Symbolism, implicit in all literature from the beginning, as it is implicit in the very words we use, comes to us now, at last quite conscious of itself, offering us the only escape from our many imprisonments. We find a new, an older, sense in the so worn out forms of things; the world, which we can no longer believe in as the satisfying material object it was to our grandparents, becomes transfigured with a new light; words, which long usage had darkened almost out of recognition, take fresh lustre. And it is on the lines of that spiritualising of the word, that perfecting of form in its capacity for allusion and suggestion, that confidence in the eternal correspondences between the visible and the invisible universe, which Mallarmé taught, and too intermittently practised, that literature must now move, if it is in any sense to move forward.

4.3 William James, *The Varieties of Religious Experience* (1902)

James (1842–1910) carried his early ideas about psychology, gathered into the extensive work Principles of Psychology *in 1890, into new territory across the next decade or so. The pragmatism which he derived from C. S. Peirce, and which he would concentrate upon in the latter part of his career, was added to this psychological interest when he investigated the origins of ideas of God, free will, and the ethical and moral values which are traditionally associated with religious faith. He had already published two*

---

8 Mallarmé (1842–98) was in many ways the purist of the Symbolists, the movement he founded with Verlaine. His work is sometimes extremely abstract, but also dreamily evocative, as in *L'Après-Midi d'un faune* (1876), which inspired the sensuous music of that title by the contemporary French composer Claude Debussy.

books in this area, The Will to Believe and Other Essays in Popular Philosophy *(1897) and* Human Immortality *(1898), before the summation of his work in this area which arrived with* The Varieties of Religious Experience. *The book runs through a range of topics derived from Christianity, including 'Conversion', 'The Sick Soul', and 'Saintliness', as well as other areas associated with religious experience, including 'Mysticism'. James felt that freedom and chance could enter into fate or history, on the model of Charles Darwin's principles of natural variation and selection. Religious experience consisted for him of specific forces of consciousness-like energy which we tap into at moments of personal or psychological crisis or trouble, when the accepted order of things gives way and some other understanding enters the mind. The extract here derives from James's 'Conclusions', in which he both reviews and sums up his argument, when thinking about the 'more' as he calls it, or the quality outside the self with which, in its religious moments, the self seeks some kind of harmony.*

The 'more,' as we called it, and the meaning of our 'union' with it, form the nucleus of our inquiry. Into what definite description can these words be translated, and for what definite facts do they stand? It would never do for us to place ourselves offhand at the position of a particular theology, the Christian theology, for example, and proceed immediately to define the 'more' as Jehovah, and the 'union' as his imputation to us of the righteousness of Christ. That would be unfair to other religions, and, from our present standpoint at least, would be an over-belief.[9]

We must begin by using less particularized terms; and, since one of the duties of the science of religions is to keep religion in connection with the rest of science, we shall do well to seek first of all a way of describing the 'more', which psychologists may also recognize as real. *The subconscious self* is nowadays a well-accredited psychological entity; and I believe that in it we have exactly the mediating term required. Apart from all religious considerations, there is actually and literally more life in our total soul than we are at any time aware of. The exploration of the transmarginal field has hardly been seriously undertaken, but what Mr. Myers said in 1892 in his essay on the Subliminal Consciousness is as true as when it was first written: 'Each of us is in reality an abiding psychical entity far more extensive than he knows – an individuality which can never express itself completely through any corporeal manifestation. The Self manifests through the organism; but there is always some part of the Self unmanifested; and always, as it seems, some power of organic expression in abeyance or reserve.' Much of the content of this larger background against which our conscious being stands out in relief is insignificant. Imperfect memories, silly jingles, inhibitive timidities, 'dissolutive' phenomena of various sorts, as Myers

---

9 This term, used several times by James below, applies to any leap of faith or belief beyond the self, and beyond that which is verifiable from experience in the material world.

calls them, enter into it for a large part. But in it many of the performances of genius seem also to have their origin; and in our study of conversion, of mystical experiences, and of prayer, we have seen how striking a part invasions from this region play in the religious life.

Let me then propose, as an hypothesis, that whatever it may be on its *further* side, the 'more' with which in religious experience we feel ourselves connected is on its *hither* side the subconscious continuation of our conscious life. Starting thus with a recognized psychological fact as our basis, we seem to preserve a contact with 'science' which the ordinary theologian lacks. At the same time the theologian's contention that the religious man is moved by an external power is vindicated, for it is one of the peculiarities of invasions from the subconscious region to take on objective appearances, and to suggest to the Subject an external control. In the religious life the control is felt as 'higher'; but since on our hypothesis it is primarily the higher faculties of our own hidden mind which are controlling, the sense of union with the power beyond us is a sense of something, not merely apparently, but literally true.

This doorway into the subject seems to me the best one for a science of religions, for it mediates between a number of different points of view. Yet it is only a doorway, and difficulties present themselves as soon as we step through it, and ask how far our transmarginal consciousness carries us if we follow on its remoter side. Here the over-beliefs begin: here mysticism and the conversion-rapture and Vedantism[10] and transcendental idealism bring in their monistic interpretations and tell us that the infinite self rejoins the absolute self, for it was always one with God and identical with the soul of the world. Here the prophets of all the different religions come with their visions, voices, raptures, and other openings, supposed by each to authenticate his own particular faith.

Those of us who are not personally favored with such specific revelations must stand outside of them altogether and, for the present at least, decide that, since they corroborate incompatible theological doctrines, they neutralize one another and leave no fixed result. If we follow any one of them, or if we follow philosophical theory and embrace monistic pantheism on non-mystical grounds, we do so in the exercise of our individual freedom, and build out our religion in the way most congruous with our personal susceptibilities. Among those susceptibilities intellectual ones play a decisive part. Although the religious question is primarily a question of life, of living or not living in the higher union which opens itself to us as a gift, yet the spiritual excitement in which the gift appears a real one will often fail to be aroused in an individual until certain particular intellectual beliefs or ideas which, as we say, come home to him, are touched. These ideas will thus be essential to that individual's religion; – which

---

10 Vedanta is one of the six orthodox philosophies of Hinduism, concerned with Brahman, the universal, supreme and pure being. Vedantism is discussed by James in this book, along with other Hindu religions, in his chapter on 'Mysticism'.

is as much as to say that over-beliefs in various directions are absolutely indispensable, and that we should treat them with tenderness and tolerance so long as they are not intolerant themselves. . . .

Disregarding the over-beliefs, and confining ourselves to what is common and generic, we have in *the fact that the conscious person is continuous with a wider self through which saving experiences come*, a positive content of religious experience which, it seems to me, *is literally and objectively true as far as it goes*. If I now proceed to state my own hypothesis about the farther limits of this extension of our personality, I shall be offering my own over-belief – though I know it will appear a sorry under-belief to some of you – for which I can only bespeak the same indulgence which in a converse case I should accord to yours.

The further limits of our being plunge, it seems to me, into an altogether other dimension of existence from the sensible and merely 'understandable' world. Name it the mystical region, or the supernatural region, whichever you choose. So far as our ideal impulses originate in this region (and most of them do originate in it, for we find them possessing us in a way for which we cannot articulately account), we belong to it in a more intimate sense than that in which we belong to the visible world, for we belong in the most intimate sense wherever the ideals belong. Yet the unseen region in question is not merely ideal, for it produces effects in this world. When we commune with it, work is actually done upon our finite personality, for we are turned into new men, and consequences in the way of conduct follow in the natural world upon our regenerative change. But that which produces effects within another reality must be termed a reality itself, so that I feel as if we had no philosophic excuse for calling the unseen or mystical world unreal.

God is the natural appellation, for us Christians at least, for the supreme reality, so I will call this higher part of the universe by the name of God. We and God have business with each other; and in opening ourselves our deepest destiny is fulfilled. . . .

The real effects in question, so far as I have yet admitted them, are exerted on the personal centres of energy of the various subjects, but the spontaneous faith of most of the subjects is that they embrace a wider sphere than this. Most religious men believe (or 'know', if they be mystical) that not only they themselves, but the whole universe of beings to whom the God is present are secure in his parental hands. . . . Only when this further step is taken, and remote objective consequences are predicted, does religion, it seems to me, get wholly free from the first immediate subjective experience, and bring a *real hypothesis* into play. A good hypothesis in science must have other properties than those of the phenomenon it is immediately invoked to explain, otherwise it is not prolific enough. God, meaning only what enters into the religious man's experience of union, falls short of being an hypothesis of this more useful order. He needs to enter into wider cosmic relations in order to justify the subject's absolute confidence and peace.

I believe that the pragmatic way of taking religion to be the deeper way. It gives it body as well as soul, it makes it claim, as everything real must claim, some characteristic realm of fact as its very own. What the more characteristically divine facts are, apart from the natural in-flow of energy in the faith-state and the prayer-state, I know not. But the over-belief on which I am ready to make my personal venture is that they exist. . . . By keeping faithful in my poor measure to this over-belief, I seem to keep myself more sane and true.

4.4   Émile Durkheim, *The Elementary Forms of Religious Life* (translated by Joseph Ward Swain, 1915)

Durkheim's founding work in the field of sociology, as excerpted in Section 2, always led him to consider the historical development, and primitive origins, of the social groups under his review. In The Elementary Forms, *which appeared in France in 1912, he turned that attention to early communities as they were brought together through their response to perceived numinous forces in the natural world, and therefore to some conception of divinity. Durkheim's ambition in this particular inquiry, as his Introduction makes clear, is similar to that which had underwritten his earlier work on sociology and labour division. Through a comparative methodology which surveyed religious beginnings as known principally through the writings of earlier anthropologists about the Australian aborigines, he sought to discover those 'permanent elements' which he felt must underlie religion per se, and thence to discover central truths about our humanity: 'At the foundation of all systems of beliefs and of all cults there ought necessarily to be a certain number of fundamental representations or conceptions and of ritual attitudes which, in spite of the diversity of forms which they have taken, have the same objective significance and fulfil the same function everywhere.' The principal focus of Durkheim's account of early religious practices is the totem, a symbol often derived from the natural world, but also imbued with the power to suggest wider forces separate from it. This totem served as a unifying force within the clan, something which forged their distinctive identity. As a collective force, the totem is therefore something external to the individual member of the clan, something to be revered, but also something which ensures the individual's adherence to communal life through the rituals associated with it. The extracts here are drawn principally from those parts of the work in which Durkheim draws his broad conclusions from the welter of anthropological material which he processes. They come from the Introduction, in which Durkheim outlines his methodology for his study; later passages where he talks in detail about the totem and the clan; and a passage from the chapter on 'The Principal Ritual Attitudes', in which he describes the role of art amongst these 'forms'.*

We cannot arrive at an understanding of the most recent religions except by following the manner in which they have been progressively composed in history. In fact, historical analysis is the only means of explanation which it is possible to apply to them. It alone enables us to resolve an institution into its constituent elements, for it shows them to us as they are born in time, one after another. On the other hand, by placing every one of them in the condition where it was born, it puts into our hands the only means we have of determining the causes which gave rise to it. Every time that we undertake to explain something human, taken at a given moment in history – be it a religious belief, a moral precept, a legal principle, an aesthetic style or an economic system – it is necessary to commence by going back to its most primitive and simple form, to try to account for the characteristics by which it was marked at that time, and then to show how it developed and became complicated little by little, and how it became that which it is at the moment in question. One readily understands the importance which the determinism of the point of departure has for this series of progressive explanations, for all the others are attached to it. It was one of Descartes's principles that the first ring has a predominating place in the chain of scientific truths.[11] But there is no question of placing at the foundation of the science of religions an idea elaborated after the cartesian manner, that is to say, a logical concept, a pure possibility, constructed simply by force of thought. What we must find is a concrete reality, and historical and ethnological observation alone can reveal that to us. But even if this cardinal conception is obtained by a different process than that of Descartes, it remains true that it is destined to have a considerable influence on the whole series of propositions which the science establishes. Biological evolution has been conceived quite differently ever since it has been known that monocellular beings do exist. In the same way, the arrangement of religious facts is explained quite differently, according as we put naturism, animism[12] or some other religious form at the beginning of the evolution.

For a long time it has been known that the first systems of representations with which men have pictured to themselves the world and themselves were of religious origin. There is no religion that is not a cosmology at the same time that it is a speculation upon divine things. If philosophy and the sciences were born of religion, it is because religion began by taking the place of the sciences and philosophy. But it has been less frequently noticed that religion has not confined itself to enriching human intellect, formed beforehand, with a certain number of ideas; it has contributed to forming the intellect itself. Men owe to it not only a good part of the substance of their knowledge, but also the form in which this knowledge has been elaborated.

At the roots of all our judgements there are a certain number of essential ideas which dominate all our intellectual life; they are what philosophers since

---

11 This idea underpins much of Descartes's philosophy, but is given broad discussion in his late and retrospective *Principles of Philosophy*, Part II (1644).

12 Naturism in this case is the worship of anything in the natural world; animism, the attribution of living souls to plants, inanimate objects, or natural phenomena.

Aristotle have called the categories of the understanding: ideas of time, space, class, number, cause, substance, personality, etc. They correspond to the most universal properties of things. They are like the solid frame which encloses all thought; this does not seem to be able to liberate itself from them without destroying itself, for it seems that we cannot think of objects that are not in time and space, which have no number, etc. Other ideas are contingent and unsteady; we can conceive of their being unknown to a man, a society, or an epoch; but these others appear to be nearly inseparable from the normal working of the intellect. They are like the framework of the intelligence. Now when primitive religious beliefs are systematically analysed, the principal categories are naturally found. They are born in religion and of religion; they are a product of religious thought. This is a statement that we are going to have occasion to make many times in the course of this work.

This remark has some interest of itself already; but here is what gives it its real importance.

The general conclusion of the book which the reader has before him is that religion is something eminently social. Religious representations are collective representations which express collective realities; the rites are a manner of acting which take rise in the midst of the assembled groups and which are destined to excite, maintain, or recreate certain mental states in these groups. So if the categories are of religious origin, they ought to participate in this nature common to all religious facts; they too should be social affairs and the product of collective thought. At least – for in the actual condition of our knowledge in these matters, one should be careful to avoid all radical and exclusive elements – it is allowable to suppose that they are rich in social elements.

In order to say that certain things are supernatural, it is necessary to have the sentiment that a *natural order of things* exists, that is to say, that the phenomena of the universe are bound together by necessary relations, called laws. When this principle has once been admitted, all that is contrary to these laws must necessarily appear to be outside of nature, and consequently, of reason; for what is natural in this sense of the word, is also rational, these necessary relations only expressing the manner in which things are logically related. But this idea of universal determinism is of recent origin; even the greatest thinkers of classical antiquity never succeeded in becoming fully conscious of it. . . . So long as men did not know the immutability and inflexibility of the order of things, and so long as they saw there the work of contingent wills, they found it natural that either these wills or others could modify them arbitrarily. That is why the miraculous interventions which the ancients attributed to their gods were not to their eyes miracles in the modern acceptation of the term. For them, they were beautiful, rare or terrible spectacles, or causes of surprise and marvel . . . ; but they never saw in them glimpses of a mysterious world into which the reason cannot penetrate.

The men of the clan and the things which are classified in it form by their union a solid system, all of whose parts are united and vibrate sympathetically. This organization, which at first may have appeared to us as purely logical, is at the same time moral. A single principle animates it and makes its unity: this is the totem. Just as a man who belongs to the Crow clan has within him something of this animal, so the rain, since it is of the same clan and belongs to the same totem, is also necessarily considered as being 'the same thing as a crow'; for the same reason, the moon is a black cockatoo, the sun a white cockatoo, every black-nut tree a pelican, etc. All the beings arranged in a single clan, whether men, animals, plants or inanimate objects, are merely forms of the totemic being. This is the meaning of the formula which we have just cited and this is what makes the two really of the same species: all are really of the same flesh in the sense that all partake of the nature of the totemic animal. Also, the qualifiers given them are those given to the totem. . . . It is true that among the Arunta, where visible traces of classification still exist, as we shall see, different words designate the totem and the other beings placed with it; however, the name given to these latter bears witness to the close relations which unite them to the totemic animal. It is said that they are its *intimates*, its *associates*, its *friends*; it is believed that they are inseparable from it. So there is a feeling that these are very closely related things.

But we also know that the totemic animal is a sacred being. All the things that are classified in the clan of which it is the emblem have this same character, because in one sense, they are animals of the same species, just as the man is. They, too, are sacred . . .

[On the soul] Although closely bound to the body, it is believed to be profoundly distinct from it and to enjoy, in relation to it, a large degree of independence. During life, it may leave it temporarily, and it definitely withdraws at death. Far from being dependent upon the body, it dominates it from the higher dignity which is in it. It may well take from the body the outward form in which it individualizes itself, but it owes nothing essential to it. Nor is the autonomy which all peoples have attributed to the soul a pure illusion; we know now what its objective foundation is. It is quite true that the elements which serve to form the idea of the soul and those which enter into the representation of the body come from two different sources that are independent of one another. One sort are made up of the images and impressions coming from all parts of the organism; the others consist in the ideas and sentiments which come from and express society. So the former are not derived from the latter. There really is a part of ourselves which is not placed in immediate dependence upon the organic factor: this is all that represents society in us. The general ideas which religion or science fix in our minds, the mental operations which these ideas suppose, the beliefs and sentiments which are at the basis of our moral life, and all these superior forms of psychical activity which society awakens in us, these do not follow in the trail of our bodily states, as our sensations and our general bodily consciousness do. As we have already shown, this is because the world of representations in which social life passes is superimposed upon its material substratum, far from arising from it; the determinism which reigns there is much more supple than the one whose roots are in the constitution of our tissues and it leaves with the actor a justified impression of the greatest liberty. The medium in which we thus move is less opaque and less resistant: we feel ourselves to be, and we are, more at our ease there. In a word, the only way we have of freeing ourselves from physical forces is to oppose them with collective forces.

It is a well-known fact that games and the principal forms of art seem to have been born of religion and that for a long time they have retained a religious character. We now see what the reasons for this are: it is because the cult, though aimed primarily at other ends, has also been a sort of recreation for men. Religion has not played this role by hazard or owing to a happy chance, but through a necessity of its nature. Though, as we have established, religious thought is something very different from a system of fictions, still the realities to which it corresponds express themselves religiously only when religion transfigures them. Between society as it is objectively and the sacred things which express it symbolically, the distance is considerable. It has been necessary that the impressions really felt by men, which served as the original matter of this construction, should be interpreted, elaborated and transformed until they become unrecognizable. So the world of religious things is a partially imaginary world, though only in its outward form, and one which therefore lends itself more readily to the free creations of the mind. Also, since the intellectual forces which serve to make it are intense and tumultuous, the unique task of expressing the real with the aid of appropriate symbols is not enough to occupy them. A surplus generally remains available which seeks to employ itself in supplementary and superfluous works of luxury, that is to say, in works of art. There are practices as well as beliefs of this sort. The state of effervescence in which the assembled worshippers find themselves must be translated outwardly by exuberant movements which are not easily subjected to too carefully defined ends. In part, they escape aimlessly, they spread themselves for the mere pleasure of doing so, and they take delight in all sorts of games. Besides, in so far as the beings to whom the cult is addressed are imaginary, they are not able to contain and regulate this exuberance; the pressure of tangible and resisting realities is required to confine activities to exact and economical forms. Therefore one exposes oneself to grave misunderstandings if, in explaining rites, he believes that each gesture has a precise object and a definite reason for its existence. There are some which serve nothing; they merely answer the need felt by worshippers for action, motion, gesticulation. They are to be seen jumping, whirling, dancing, crying and singing, though it may not always be possible to give a meaning to all this agitation.

Therefore religion would not be itself if it did not give some place to the free combinations of thought and activity, to play, to art, to all that recreates the spirit that has been fatigued by the too great slavishness of daily work: the very same causes which called it into existence make it a necessity. Art is not merely an external ornament with which the cult has adorned itself in order to dissimulate certain of its features which may be too austere and too rude; but rather, in itself, the cult is something aesthetic. Owing to the well-known connection which mythology has with poetry, some have wished to exclude the former from religion; the truth is that there is a poetry inherent in all religion. . . .

One would certainly commit the gravest error if he only saw this one aspect of religion, or if he even exaggerated its importance. When a rite serves only to distract, it is no longer a rite. The moral forces expressed by religious symbols are real forces with which we must reckon and with which we cannot do what we will. . . . A rite is something different from a game; it is a part of the serious life. But if its unreal and imaginary element is not essential, nevertheless it plays a part which is by no means negligible. It has its share in the feeling of comfort which the worshipper draws from the rite performed; for recreation is one of the forms of the moral remaking which is the principal object of the positive rite. After we have acquitted ourselves of our ritual duties, we enter into the profane life with increased courage and ardour, not only because we come into relations with a superior source of energy, but also because our forces have been reinvigorated by living, for a few moments, in a life that is less strained, and freer and easier. Hence religion acquires a charm which is not among the slightest of its attractions.

4.5 Jessie L. Weston, *From Ritual to Romance* (1920)

Weston (1850–1928) was a poet and translator, initially, who also studied music in Germany. She was a scholar of texts relating to the ancient English King Arthur, maintaining from the time of her early book The Legend of Sir Gawain *(1897) that this material was based upon survivals of ancient rituals which had later become occult practices. The book extracted below is now best known through T. S. Eliot's citation of it as a source for* The Waste Land. *But the work was recognized at the time for its continuation of J. G. Frazer's methodology and for carrying that methodology into new historical territory – here, in a discussion about the origins of the myths and literary romances associated with the quest for the Holy Grail in Christianity. As with Frazer's way of interweaving many stories from various sources together, in order to untangle the essential and original myth behind them all, Weston insists that her method will run counter to a 'modern tendency' to concentrate on isolated instances, in order to build her theory. Rather, she insists, she will perceive the symbols relating to the legend as a whole, and in their connection to the whole story. For Weston, as arguably for Eliot's poem, the figure of the Fisher King is central to the issue. She sees the recurrence of the Fisher King in various versions of the Grail legend as 'incomprehensible' as part of a Christian interpretation, but as a 'deeply symbolic . . . semi-divine, semi-human' presence if considered as part of an older, pre-Christian cult related to the renewal of fertility with the year's turning to Spring. She argues that the Fisher King relates to the ancient Greek god Attis, and that the Grail legends form proof of the continuation of such eastern religious forces in later mythologies. Most importantly, she sees all of these legends as being centred upon the Celtic fringes of Europe, probably within Britain. The extracts here are derived from the earlier part of the book, which displays Weston's own juxtaposition of various contexts and materials in order to understand the central force of the Fisher King; and a passage in which she brings all the elements of her argument together, along with her feeling of the obscurity of the truth of the Grail myth and its continuation, from the chapter called 'The Perilous Chapel'.*

The Shilluk, an African tribe, inhabit the banks of the White Nile, their territory extending on the west bank from Kaka in the north, to Lake No in the south, on the east bank from Fashoda to Taufikia, and some 35 miles up the Sohat river. Numbering some 40,000 in all, they are a pastoral people, their wealth consisting in flocks and herds, grain and millet. The King resides at Fashoda, and is regarded with extreme reverence, as being a re-incarnation of Nyakang, the semi-divine hero who settled the tribe in their present territory. Nyakang is the rain-giver, on whom their life and prosperity depend; there are several shrines in which sacred Spears, now kept for sacrificial purposes, are preserved, the originals, which were the property of Nyakang, having disappeared.

The King, though regarded with reverence, must not be allowed to become old or feeble, lest, with the diminishing vigour of the ruler, the cattle should sicken, and fail to bear increase, the crops should rot in the field and men die in ever growing numbers. One of the signs of failing energy is the King's inability to fulfil the desires of his wives, of whom he has a large number. When this occurs the wives report the fact to the chiefs, who condemn the King to death forthwith, communicating the sentence to him by spreading a white cloth over his face and knees during his mid-day slumber. . . .

This survival is of extraordinary interest; it presents us with a curiously close parallel to the situation which, on the evidence of the texts, we have postulated as forming the basic idea of the Grail tradition – the position of a people whose prosperity, and the fertility of their land, are closely bound up with the life and virility of their King, who is not a mere man, but a Divine re-incarnation. If he 'falls into languishment,' as does the Fisher-King in *Perlesvaus*, the land and its inhabitants will suffer correspondingly; not only will the country suffer from drought . . . but the men will die in numbers.

The Grail romances repose eventually, not upon a poet's imagination, but upon the ruins of an august and ancient ritual, a ritual which once claimed to be the accredited guardian of the deepest secrets of Life. Driven from its high estate by the relentless force of religious evolution – for after all Adonis, Attis, and their congeners, were but the 'half-gods' who must needs yield place when 'the Gods' themselves arrive – it yet lingered on; openly, in Folk practice, in Fast and Feast, whereby the well-being of the land may be assured; secretly, in cave or moun-tain-fastness, or island isolation, where those who craved for a more sensible (not necessarily sensuous) contact with the unseen Spiritual forces of Life than the orthodox development of Christianity afforded, might, and did, find satis-faction.

Were the Templars such?[13] . . . It seems exceedingly probable. If it were so we could understand at once the puzzling connection of the Order with the Knights of the Grail, and the doom which fell upon them. That they were held to be Heretics is very generally admitted, but in what their Heresy consisted no one really knows; little credence can be attached to the stories of idol worship often repeated. If their Heresy, however, were such as indicated above, a Creed which struck at the very root and vitals of Christianity, we can understand at once the reason for punishment, and the necessity for secrecy. In the same way we can now understand why the Church knows nothing of the Grail; why that Vessel, surrounded as it is with an atmosphere of reverence and awe, equated with the central Sacrament of the Christian Faith, yet appears in no Legendary, is figured in no picture, comes on the scene in no Passion Play. The Church of the eleventh and twelfth centuries knew well what the Grail was, and we, when we realize its genesis and true lineage, need no longer wonder why a theme, for some short space so famous and fruitful a source of literary inspiration, vanished utterly and completely from the world of literature.

Were Grail romances forbidden? Or were they merely discouraged? Probably we shall never know, but of this one thing we may be sure, the Grail is a living force, it will never die; it may indeed sink out of sight, and, for centuries even, disappear from the field of literature, but it will rise to the surface again, and become once more a theme of vital inspiration even as, after slumbering from the days of Malory, it woke to new life in the nineteenth century, making its fresh appeal through the genius of Tennyson and Wagner.

4.6   Jane Harrison, *Epilogomena to the Study of Greek Religion* (1921)

Harrison (1850–1928) was a cultural anthropologist and classicist based at Cambridge University from 1898 onwards – she is possibly 'glimpsed' there in a mythologized college garden by the speaker in Virginia Woolf's A Room of One's Own. Woolf was a great admirer of Harrison and of her work, both as a scholar and as a pioneer of women's university education – one subject of Woolf's own essay. Harrison's approach to the study of Greek religion, which preoccupied much of her scholarship and writing, is heavily influenced, in its mature phases, by the work of Durkheim on the collective

---

13 The Order of the Knights Templar, formed in Jerusalem during the Crusades, when in the East were supposed to have adopted immoral behaviour and religious practices alien to Christianity, for which they were disbanded by Pope Clement V in 1312.

nature of religion (in Themis, *1912, she claims he had changed her entire outlook on her subject), and by the contemporary philosophy of Henri Bergson. In the Preface to* Epilogomena, *which, as the title indicates, she saw as something of a concluding statement of her position, she adds to these influences the names of Freud and Jung, as well as that of 'the greatest of Russian philosophers, Vladimir Soloviov'.*[14] *As* Prolegomena *(1903), the first of the interlinked series of books on the Greeks to which the book now extracted forms the finale, had made clear, for all her emphasis upon myth and its relation to social origins, the true 'goal' of all Harrison's work is a better understanding of literature. When* Prologomena *appeared in its third edition in 1922, Harrison added an Introduction in which she claimed 'I have tried to understand primitive rites, not from love of their archaism, nor yet wholly from a single-minded devotion to science, but with a definite hope that I might come to a better understanding of some forms of Greek poetry.' The extracts selected here have been chosen to reflect the way in which the mythic, the social, and the psychological are all reflected in her study of early religion.*

The object of this discussion is to show the constantly shifting nature of the notion of religion which, being, if my contention be right, a function of our human nature, grows and shifts with human growth. . . . Is there no distinction between religion and magic? There is, and it is a distinction very simple but all important; religion is social, magic is or may be individual, religion is of the group however small, magic of the single unit.

The discovery of its social origin is perhaps the greatest advance yet made in the scientific study of religion. The notion of social origin upsets so many modern individualistic convictions and prejudices that it is sure to meet with some hostility. The discovery has been a long slow process and was only made possible by recent scientific examination of religious phenomena among primitive peoples. The new and unexpected facts disclosed by this examination – facts which have bit by bit revolutionized our whole outlook – may conveniently be grouped under four heads:

(1) Totem, Tabu and Exogamy.[15]
(2) Initiation ceremonies.
(3) The Medicine-Man and King-God.
(4) The Fertility Play or Year-Drama.

---

14 Solovyov attempted to draw together scientific understanding and a religious or mystical awareness; the idea that man approached closer to God through the evolution of human history.

15 Taboo, the ambiguous sense that someone or something might be sacred or cursed (or sacred *and* cursed), and exogamy, the requirement that marriages and sexual relations be conducted between individuals from different tribal groups, provided a central theme of anthropological discussion at this time, focused upon by Frazer, Durkheim and Freud amongst others.

By a brief examination of these groups of facts it will become clear (1) that religion is a social factor and can only properly be studied in relation to social structure; (2) that the idea of a god is a bye-product arising out of rites and sanctities, a bye-product of high importance but non-essential; (3) that the function of religion is to conserve the common life physical and spiritual, this function being sometimes aided sometimes hindered by the idea of a god.

Of recent years research over the most widespread areas has brought to light in a very singular and convincing fashion the tenacity and vitality of the Folk-Play or Fertility Drama. It survives not only in children's games and peasant festivals but in the forms or moulds that it has lent to literature. Among the Rig-Veda hymns[16] for example it has been shown that certain dialogue poems go back undoubtedly to a primitive form of ritual drama, the intent here, as elsewhere, being purely magical: the stimulation of powers of fertility in man and cattle, or the letting loose for the like purpose of the powers of rain and moisture of springs and rivers. Behind the literary hymn lie the fertility dances of the armed daimons, the Salii, the Maruts of ancient India.

More familiar and perhaps to us more convincing is the fact that Greek Tragedy owes to this Fertility Drama not indeed its material but the form in which that material is cast. After a detailed examination of the plays and fragments Professor Murray has come to the conclusion – and few now gainsay him – that while the contents of the plots come from the heroic saga the ritual forms in which that content is cast derive straight from the *dromena*, the doings of the Year-Daimon. Such forms are the Prologue, the Agon, the Pathos, the Messenger's Speech, the Threnos or Lamentation, the Anagnorisis or Recognition and the final Theophany. Certain of these forms, notably the Agon, survive in the Sacred Games of the Greeks, but here for the most part in shadowy fashion since they are well nigh submerged by a growing athleticism. Tragedy which took its plots, its content from the heroic saga, from the lives and struggles of the individual heroes, ended in death, because in this world the human individual knows no resurrection. Comedy is nearer to the original Folk-Play and finds its consummation in a revel and a marriage.

Still more strange is it to find the ritual mould surviving even in the plays of Shakespeare. The Hamlet-saga like the Orestes-saga has behind it the ancient and world-wide battle of Summer and Winter, of the Old King and the New, of Life and Death, of Fertility and Barrenness; behind the tragic fooling, as behind the Old King Oedipus is the figure of the scapegoat, the whole tragic katharsis rests on the expulsion of evil in the ritual of the spring.

We recognise now-a-days two types of thinking. The first which Jung calls

---

16 They form one of the four sacred ancient books of Hinduism, composed in an early version of Sanskrit; the books as known today probably date from the third century BC.

'directed thinking' is what we normally mean by thinking. It 'imitates reality and seeks to direct it.' It is exhausting and is the sort of thinking employed in all scientific research; it looks for adaptations and creates innovations. With that type of thought, which is comparatively late in development, though in embryo it may have existed from the outset, we have little to do in religion.

The second kind of thought is what is called 'dream or phantasy-thinking.' It turns away from reality and sets free subjective wishes. In regard to adaptation, because of its neglect of reality, it is wholly unproductive. Giving free rein to impulse as it does, it is not exhausting. Freud calls this sort of mind-functioning the 'pleasure and pain principle,' it is ontogenetically older than directed thinking, it is typified by the mental operations of children and savages and by those of adults in their dreams, reveries and mental disorders.

It is from this early infantile type of dream or phantasy-thinking engendered by the fertility rite that primitive theology and mythology spring. They do not seek adaptation to fact, they turn away from reality and utter unfulfilled desire. . . . We imagine what we lack, the 'dying resurrected gods and heroes are but the projected hopes and fears of humanity.' The older mind still buried in all of us, the mind of dream-fantasies is, and always has been, incessantly weaving dream-images of imaginary wish-fulfilment.

. . . In like manner arises the myth. The myth is not an attempted explanation of either facts or rites. Its origin is not in 'directed thinking', it is not in rationalization. The myth is a fragment of the soul-life, the dream-thinking of the people, as the dream is the myth of the individual. As Freud says, 'it is probable that myths correspond to the distorted residue of the wish phantasies of whole nations, the secularized dreams of young humanity.' Mythical tradition it would seem does not set forth any actual account of old events – that is the function of legend – but rather myth acts in such a way that it always reveals a wish-thought common to humanity and constantly rejuvenated.

5

Philosophy and Ideas

Introduction

It would be difficult to underestimate the significance of European philosophy for literary and intellectual circles at the beginning of the twentieth century. Many of the magazines and journals of the time carried articles discussing the importance of the ideas of the German philosopher Friedrich Nietzsche, or of the contemporary Frenchman Henri Bergson, alongside the latest episode from a novel we would now consider 'modernist', or the latest poems from H.D. or other Imagists. The English-speaking world was, it would be possible to say, transfixed by the challenge which continental philosophy, or historiography, often mounted to traditional and received ideas. These European thinkers were readily available by the 1910s in translation for those who had not already read their work in the original languages; they were often, as Nietzsche and Bergson were, available in popular form through cheap editions of their aphoristic sayings or most telling passages.

Crudely put, the shift that these continental philosophers were making was towards a view of the world which placed the *individual* at the centre of things, rather than assuming a perspective which looking for 'meaning' in broader systems, including the social and the religious. With the rise of other intellectual disciplines reflected in this Sourcebook, such as the sociology of Max Weber and Émile Durkheim, or with the left-wing politics reflected in the rise of the British Labour Party and the Labor movements in the US, there was a broad questioning of society's tendency to disempower the individual. With the rise of the women's movements on both sides of the Atlantic, the *status quo* was being further questioned. Amongst intellectual circles everywhere the former ready acceptance of Christian belief was treated sceptically.

What all of these broader pressures and trends seemed to indicate was the necessity for the revaluation of established structures of meaning, and a belated Romantic faith that the individual might achieve an understanding where these structures failed. Nietzsche's philosophy seeks to empower the individual to challenge the everyday understanding of the world; literally to rise above it and to achieve a better communion with the self, in order to better bring the outside world into some kind of system of understanding. Bergson takes snapshots of the individual consciousness, and asks how it relates to time, how it might

141

escape from time in order to achieve a unique perception of the deeper order of things. On a 'scientific' level, of course, Sigmund Freud was seeking to establish the conscious and unconscious mind of the individual as the key to unlocking more primal patterns in the human psyche. He was exploring the ways in which the continuous history of individual consciousness could be disrupted and re-written through various forms of repression. This idea that the individual self, whilst being the site of all understanding, could also be bafflingly split and divided against itself, finds its reflection in various earlier philosophical ideas, including that reading of the conflict between religious possibilities delineated by Nietzsche himself in *The Birth of Tragedy* (1872): Apollo, god of order and reason, is pitched against Dionysus, god of frenzy but also of primal poetries.

Such vivid post-Romantic energies, of course, met with great resistance from the 1890s onwards, as conceived by excerpted writers here such as Max Nordau, who perceived a pathological basis in such ideas, and the critic vital to modernist poetics, T. E. Hulme, who argued for a return to artistic and political order. But the philosophical thrust of the age was very much towards perceiving *relativism* in perception and understanding, where once there had been absolute knowledge and certainty. These ideas in Europe were at this time finding an echo in America, which had developed its relativist ideas from a very different set of post-Romantic co-ordinates, in the nineteenth-century tradition which included Emerson and Thoreau. The Harvard philosopher William James had been concluding since the 1880s, when he was considering the relation between biological and environmental circumstance and everyday life, that the individual consciousness (which operated for him as a 'stream') formed the basis of meaning. His application of this idea through the American pragmatic tradition is reflected in the extract from a later work of his given below.

What these various ideas, reinforced by the various other revolutionary impulses in the period reflected elsewhere in this book, impelled in modernist writing is a sense that traditional literary form needed questioning in order to accommodate the new content; that the very rhythm (in poetry), or narrative temporalities (in the novel), needed re-examining in order that the new emphasis upon interiority, or the relativism of perception, might find its full and developed expression.

5.1   Friedrich Nietzsche, *Thus Spake Zarathustra* (1883–5; translation by Alexander Tille, 1896)

Nietzsche (1844–1900) remained the most discussed and celebrated philosopher of the first decades of the twentieth century. His work was broadly available in English, often in the form of popular selected 'sayings' or excerpts – which is probably how several of the modernist writers first came across him. Nietzsche was a classical philologist who responded positively to the discovery of evolution, and whose thinking also reflected the influence of Schopenhauer. He sustained a fraught friendship and intellectual engage-

ment with the composer Richard Wagner. Nietzsche's core belief that traditional value-systems, including Christianity, were of no significance to modern humankind, and his emphasis upon the potentiality in the individual, brought him many followers after 1900. His belief was that the individual most true to himself, and most controlled within, might attain the insight and power of an 'overman'. From this state might emerge a new morality and a new poetry, which would not be blind to the suffering or uncertainties of humanity, but which would subsume them within a new vision. Nietzsche felt that contemporary civilization offered a situation of enslavement. To this extent, his work offered a goad, a call to its readers to reconsider their own values and their own place in the world. Thus Spake Zarathustra sees Nietzsche voicing, through his poetic alter ego, his dissatisfaction with many contemporary ideas and modes of being. Zarathustra's speeches on a range of topics present a critique and a parable (this last captured in the biblical manner adopted by the contemporary translation). In the chapter 'Of Self-Surmounting', Nietzsche introduces another of his key concepts: the notion that in each individual there operates a 'will to power'; such a will is not merely power over others, but a call for everyone to attain that originality and creativity of which they are capable.

'Will to truth' call ye that, ye wisest, that inspireth and inflameth you?

'Will to the conceivableness of all being' – thus call *I* your will!

All being ye seek now to *make* conceivable: for ye do right to doubt if it yet be conceivable.[1]

But it shall submit itself and bow before you! Thus your will willeth. Smooth it shall become and subject to the mind, as its mirror and reflected image.

That is your whole will, ye wisest – a will to power – even when ye speak of good and of evil and of the setting-up of values.

Ye will to create the world before which ye may kneel: therefore it is your final hope and ecstasy.

The unwise, indeed, the people – they are like to a river upon which a boat glideth: and in the boat are seated estimates of values, in solemn masquerade.

Your wills and your values have ye set afloat upon the river of becoming; in that in which the people believe as good and evil I discern an ancient will to power.

You it was, ye wisest, that set such guests in the boat and endowed them with pomp and proud names – you and your dominating will!

Now the river beareth onwards your boat; it *must* bear it onwards. Little matter that the breaking wave foameth and angrily resisteth the keel!

It is not the river that is your peril and the end of your good and evil, ye wisest: it is the will itself, the will to power – the unspent, procreative life-will.

---

1 Nietzsche consistently claimed that his ideal individual or mode of life was in the process of becoming; that his was a transitional philosophy in a transitional age.

But that ye may understand my word of good and evil, I will give you also my word of life and of the nature of all things living.

I followed after the living thing, I went upon the broadest and the narrowest paths that I might know its nature.

In an hundredfold mirror I caught its glances when its lips were dumb, that its eye might speak to me. And its eye spake unto me.

But wheresoever I found the living thing, there also I heard speak of obedience. All living is an obedience.

And this is the second thing that I heard: he is commanded that cannot obey his own self. Such is the nature of the living thing.

But the third thing that I heard is this: to command is harder than to obey. And not alone in that he that commandeth beareth the burden of all that obey, and that this burden may perchance crush him: –

But I perceived that there is experiment and jeopardy in all commanding; and ever, in commanding, the living thing ventureth itself thereon.

Yea, even when it commandeth itself: even then it must pay the price of its command. It must become judge and avenger and victim of its own law.

How is this? I asked myself. What persuadeth the living thing that it obeyeth and commandeth and obeyeth even in commanding?

Now hearken to my word ye wisest! Prove well whether I have not crept into the very heart of life, and to the very roots of its heart!

Wheresoever I found living things I found the will to power; and even in the will of them that serve, I found the will to be master.

To serve the stronger the weaker is persuaded by its own will that desireth to be master over that which is weaker yet: this joy alone it will not forgo.

And as the lesser giveth itself to the greater, that it may have joy of and power over the least: so even the greatest giveth itself, and for the sake of power staketh – life.

This is the devotion of the greatest, that it dareth danger and death on the cast of a dice.

And wheresoever there is sacrifice and service and appearance of love: there too is the will to be master. There creepeth the weaker by secret ways into the citadel and into the very heart of the more powerful – and there stealeth it power.

And this secret Life itself told unto me: 'Behold,' it said, 'I am that *which must ever surmount itself.*

Ye call it, indeed, will to procreation, impulse to the end, to the higher, to the more remote, to the more manifold: but all this is one thing and one secret.

Rather would I perish than renounce that one thing; and, verily, wheresoever there is decay and the fall of the leaf, lo, there life sacrificeth itself – for the sake of power!

War must I be, and becoming and end and conflict of ends; ah, he that divineth my will, divineth also, I doubt not, by what *crooked* ways he *must* walk!

Whatsoever I create and howsoever I love it – soon must I become its adversary and the adversary to my love: thus my will willeth it.

And even thou, thou that hast understanding, art but path and footsteps to my will. Verily, my power goeth upon the feet of thy will to truth!

Verily he missed the truth that aimed thereat the word 'will to being': such a will is not!

For that which is not cannot will; but that which is in being, how should it strive for being?

Only where there is life is there will: not will to life, but – thus do I teach thee – will to power!

Much doth the living value higher than life itself; but in the very act of valuing speaketh – the will to power!'

Thus hath Life taught me: and by this, ye wisest, I read you the riddle of your hearts.

Verily, I say unto you: intransient good and evil – they do not exist! By their nature they must ever and again surmount themselves.

With your values and your words of good and evil ye exercise power, ye that establish values; and herein is your secret love, the shining, the trembling, the overflowing of your souls.

But a stronger power groweth out of your values, and a new surmounting: it breaketh both egg and egg-shell.

And he that must be a creator in good and evil – verily, he must first be a destroyer and break values in pieces.

Thus pertaineth the highest evil to the highest good: and this is creativeness.

Let us *speak* thereof, ye wisest, even if it be evil. To be silent is worse; all unuttered truths grow poisonous.

And whatsoever can be broken upon our truths, let it break! Many an house is yet to build!

Thus spake Zarathustra.

5.2 Max Nordau, *Degeneration* (1895; 'Popular edition' in English, 1913)

Nordau (1849–1923) was a physician and early Jewish nationalist, who acted as vice-president to several international Zionist congresses. He settled in Paris in 1880, and immediately began developing his ideas attacking the bases of contemporary social institutional structures and experimental avant-garde artistic ideas. His earlier work, The Conventional Lies of Our Civilization, *went through an incredible 73 editions, proving the immense popularity of this kind of argument at the time. His fin-de-siècle vision of the threatening decadence associated with literature and art was still very much debated during the modernist period. Translated into English immediately,* Degeneration *was responsible for introducing a range of European artists and writers to a broader English-speaking public, but succeeded in doing so in a concertedly, obsessively, negative light. Here, for instance, we find the English Pre-Raphaelite poets and*

*painters attacked alongside the French Symbolist poets (who were to be so important to
W. B. Yeats and T. S. Eliot), Tolstoy and Richard Wagner as 'mystical degenerates'.
Here we find Charles Baudelaire lined up alongside Oscar Wilde, the playwright Henrik
Ibsen and the German philosopher Friedrich Nietzsche as 'ego-maniacs'. Figures who,
therefore, in the early years of the twentieth century, were to be seen as interlocutors and
examples for the emerging generation of writers, had already garnered a lurid and
dangerous reputation amongst the literary circles of London through Nordau's study.
Nordau dedicated his book to the Italian criminologist Caesar Lombroso. Lombroso had
argued that criminals and 'lunatics' could be identified through hereditary and physical features (the size of their skulls, for example); Nordau, as he writes in his dedica-
tory preface, was seeking to achieve a similar identification amongst his authors, who
displayed the same 'mental characteristics', in his view, as Lombroso's criminals. To
that degree, he saw his work as the first attempt at 'a really scientific criticism', which
is not overwhelmed by an emotional reaction to literature, but which seeks out the
'psycho-physiological elements' from which it springs. Nordau saw as the causal etiol-
ogy of contemporary degeneracy a range of modern features: too much alcohol or
tobacco or other drugs; poor diet; the growth in size of towns; excess speed of modern
communications through newspapers and the postal service; primarily the fatigue
which plagued modernity through rapid travel and stress at work. These symptoms he
felt were manifest in the high rate of heart attacks and 'nerve' disease, but also caused
that instability and lack of perspective which he saw in contemporary literature, art,
and music. The extracts here include an initial comment on the 'Fin-De-Siècle', then
concentrate upon Nordau's vision of the approaching 'Twentieth Century'.*

One epoch of history is unmistakably in its decline, and another is announcing
its approach. There is a sound of rending in every tradition, and it is as though
the morrow would not link itself with to-day. Things as they are totter and
plunge, and they are suffered to reel and fall, because man is weary, and there is
no faith that it is worth an effort to uphold them. Views that have hitherto
governed minds are dead or driven hence like disenthroned kings, and for their
inheritance they that hold the titles and they that would usurp are locked in
struggle . . . men look with longing for whatever new things are at hand, without presage whence they will come or what they will be. They have hope that in
the chaos of thought, art may yield revelations of the order that is to follow on
this tangled web. The poet, the musician, is to announce, or divine, or at least
suggest in what forms civilization will further be evolved.

In this book we have observed the various embodiments which degeneration
and hysteria have assumed in the art, poetry, and philosophy of our times. We
have seen the mental disorder affecting modern society manifesting itself chiefly
in the following forms: mysticism, which is the expression of the inaptitiude for
attention, for clear thought and control of the emotions, and had for its cause
the weakness of the higher cerebral centres; Ego-mania, which is an effect of

faulty transmission by the sensory nerves, of obtuseness in the centres of perception, of aberration of the instincts from a craving for sufficiently strong impressions, and of the great predominance of organic sensations over representative consciousness; and false Realism, which proceeds from confused aesthetic theories, and characterizes itself by pessimism and the irresistible tendency to licentious ideas, and the most vulgar and unclean modes of expression. In all three tendencies we detect the same ultimate elements, viz., a brain incapable of normal working, thence feebleness of will, inattention, predominance of emotion, lack of knowledge, absence of sympathy or interest in the world and humanity, atrophy of the notion of duty and morality. From a clinical point of view somewhat unlike each other, these pathological pictures are nevertheless only different manifestations of a single and unique fundamental condition, to wit, exhaustion, and they must be ranked by the alienist in the genus melancholia, which is the psychiatrical symptom of an exhausted central nervous system.

Degenerates must succumb. . . . They can neither adapt themselves to the conditions of nature and civilization, nor maintain themselves in the struggle for existence against the healthy. But the latter – and the vast masses of the people still include unnumbered millions of them – will rapidly and easily adapt themselves to the conditions which new inventions have created in humanity. Those who, by marked deficiency of organization, are unable to do so, among the generation taken unawares by those inventions, fall out of the ranks. . . . The end of the twentieth century, therefore, will probably see a generation to whom it will not be injurious to read a dozen square yards of newspapers daily, to be constantly called to the telephone, to be thinking simultaneously of the five continents of the world, to live half their time in a railway carriage or in a flying machine, and to satisfy the demands of a circle of ten thousand acquaintances, associates, and friends. It will know how to find its ease in the midst of a city inhabited by millions, and will be able, with nerves of gigantic vigour, to respond without haste or agitation to the almost innumerable claims of existence.

In all countries aesthetic theorists and critics repeat the phrase that the forms hitherto employed by art are henceforth effete and useless, and that it is preparing something perfectly new, absolutely different from all that is yet known. Richard Wagner first spoke of 'the art-work of the future', and hundreds of incapable imitators lisp the term after him. . . .

New forms! Are not the ancient forms flexible and ductile enough to lend expression to every sentiment and every thought? Has a true poet ever found any difficulty in pouring into known and standard forms that which surged within him, and demanded an issue? Has form, for that matter, the dividing, predetermining, and delimitating importance which dreamers and simpletons attribute to it? . . . The most important thing is the having something to say. Whether it be said under a lyric, dramatic, or epic form is of no essential consequence, and the author will not easily feel the necessity of leaving these forms in order to invent some dazzling novelty in which to clothe his ideas.

It is not unusual at present to meet this sentence: 'The art and poetry of the future will be scientific!' Those who say this assume extraordinarily conceited attitudes, and consider themselves unmistakably as extremely progressive and 'modern'. I ask myself in vain what these words could mean. . . . In the past a confusion between art and science was possible; in the future it is unimaginable. The mental activity of man is too highly developed for such an amalgamation. Art and poetry have emotion for their object, science has knowledge. The former are subjective, the latter objective. . . . One thing only is correct: the images issuing from the old anthropomorphic conception, the allusions to obsolete states of things and ideas – all this will disappear from art.

I can now sum up in a few words my prognosis. The hysteria of the present day will not last. People will recover from their present fatigue. The feeble, the degenerate, will perish; the strong will adapt themselves to the acquisitions of civilizations, or will subordinate them to their own organic capacity. The aberrations of art have no future. They will disappear when civilized humanity shall have triumphed over its exhausted condition. The art of the twentieth century will connect itself at every point with the past, but it will have a new task to accomplish – that of introducing a stimulating variety into the uniformity of civilized life, an influence which probably science alone will be able to exert, many centuries later, over the great majority of mankind.

5.3   William James, *Pragmatism: A New Name for Some Old Ways of Thinking* (1907)

James (1842–1910) was a psychologist and philosopher who, after years studying medicine and physiology – and after an exploration of Brazil alongside the naturalist Louis Agassiz – taught for a quarter-century at Harvard. James took forward the ideas of the American logician C. S. Peirce, who had developed a 'pragmatics', or sense that all human understanding must be founded upon the world as we have it, and not upon abstract ideas. Peirce primarily applied this pragmatism to work in the physical sciences. James saw the validity of Peirce's methodology for discovering useful concepts in a range of areas relating to the human psyche, from psychological functionalism to religious experience (an extract from his work in this area is included in Section 4). More closely related to Peirce's own methods was his assertion that psychology needed to become a distinct practice, separated from the branches of philosophy with which it had normally been connected, and that it also be treated in a scientific manner through experimentation in laboratories. This aspect of his work was then carried on by later American philosophers, most notably John Dewey (see Section 2). Like all these mens' work, James's version of pragmatism derives its vigour from its attack on any meta-

physical system, be it religious or philosophical, or rationalist and Platonic; that is to say, any system which presumes that there is a pattern or meaning to existence which exists outside or prior to experience. For James, ideas are both derived from actions in the world and (properly) lead to further actions. They are not able to resolve unknowable and abstract questions about the nature of Being. James's personal embodiment of his philosophy through his Harvard connection was something that several later writers found themselves grappling with positively or negatively: Gertrude Stein, who was taught by James, shows the impact of his ideas in her writings across her career; T. S. Eliot, who was not taught by James, but who was at Harvard when Pragmatism *appeared, rejected his human-centred philosophy. Later writers seeking a distinctive American voice and identity in their work, including John Dos Passos, Marianne Moore and William Carlos Williams, showed the strong impact of James's ideas in achieving a founding native philosophy. The extracts here come from a collection of James's later thoughts on his key concerns, and show his (political) attention to lived details as the basis for his meditations.*

'We are aware of the presence of God in His world,' says a writer in a recent English Review. . . . . 'The Absolute is the richer for every discord, and for all diversity which it embraces,' says F. H. Bradley (*Appearance and Reality*, 204).[2] He means that these slain men make the universe richer, and that is Philosophy. But while a whole host of guileless thoroughfed thinkers are unveiling Reality and the Absolute and explaining away evil and pain, this is the condition of the only beings known to us anywhere in the universe with a developed consciousness of what the universe is. What these people experience *is* Reality. It gives us an absolute phase of the universe. It is the personal experience of those most qualified in all our circle of knowledge to *have* experience, to tell us *what is*. Now, what does *thinking about* the experience of these persons come to compared with directly, personally feeling it, as they feel it? The philosophers are dealing in shades, while those who live and feel know truth. And the mind of mankind – not yet the mind of philosophers and of the proprietary class – but of the great mass of the silently thinking and feeling men, is coming to this view. They are judging the universe as they have heretofore permitted the hierophants of religion and learning to judge *them*.

The pragmatic method is primarily a method of settling metaphysical disputes that otherwise might be interminable. Is the world one or many? – fated or free? – material or spiritual? – here are notions either of which may or may not hold good of the world; and disputes over such notions are unending. The pragmatic method in such cases is to try to interpret each notion by tracing its respective

---

2 Bradley was an Oxford-based idealist philosopher; his work formed the subject of T. S. Eliot's doctoral thesis.

practical consequences. What difference would it practically make to anyone if this notion rather than that notion were true? If no practical difference whatever can be traced, then the alternatives mean practically the same thing, and all dispute is idle. Whenever a dispute is serious, we ought to be able to show some practical difference that must follow from one side or the other's being right.

A glance at the history of the idea will show you better what pragmatism means. The term is derived from the same Greek word *pragma*, meaning action, from which our words 'practice' and 'practical' come. It was first introduced into philosophy by Mr. Charles Peirce in 1878. In an article entitled 'How to Make Our Ideas Clear' in the 'Popular Science Monthly' for January of that year Mr. Peirce, after pointing out that our beliefs are really rules for action, said that, to develop a thought's meaning, we need only determine what conduct it is fitted to produce: that conduct is for us its sole significance. And the tangible fact at the root of all our thought-distinctions, however subtle, is that there is no one of them so fine as to consist in anything but a possible difference of practice. To attain perfect clearness in our thoughts of an object, then, we need only consider what conceivable effects of a practical kind the object may involve – what sensations we are to expect from it, and what reactions we must prepare. Our conception of these effects, whether immediate or remote, is then for us the whole of our conception of the object, so far as that conception has positive significance at all.

Metaphysics has usually followed a very primitive kind of quest. You know how men have always hankered after unlawful magic, and you know what a great part, in magic, *words* have always played. If you have his name, or the formula of incantation that binds him, you can control the spirit, genie, afrite, or whatever the power may be. Solomon knew the names of all the spirits, and having their names, he held them subject to his will. So the universe has always appeared to the natural mind as a kind of enigma, of which the key must be sought in the shape of some illuminating or power-bringing word or name. That word names the universe's *principle*, and to possess it is, after a fashion, to possess the universe itself. 'God,' Matter,' 'Reason,' 'the Absolute,' 'Energy', are so many solving names. You can rest when you have them. You are at the end of your metaphysical quest.

But if you follow the pragmatic method, you cannot look on any such words as closing your quest. You must bring out of each word its practical cash-value, set it at work within the stream of your experience. It appears less as a solution, then, than as a program for more work, and more particularly as an indication of the ways in which existing realities may be *changed*.

Theories thus become instruments, not answers to enigmas, in which we can rest. We don't lie back upon them, we move forward, and, on occasion, make nature over again by their aid. Pragmatism unstiffens all our theories, limbers them up and sets each one at work. Being nothing essentially new, it harmonizes with many ancient philosophical tendencies. It agrees with nominalism, for instance, in always appealing to particulars; with utilitarianism in emphasizing practical aspects; with positivism in its disdain for verbal solutions, useless questions, and metaphysical abstractions.

All these, you see, are *anti-intellectualist* tendencies. Against rationalism as a pretension and a method, pragmatism is fully armed and militant. But, at the outset, at least, it stands for no particular results. It has no dogmas, and no doctrines save its method. As the young Italian pragmatist Papini[3] has well said, it lies in the midst of our theories, like a corridor in a hotel. Innumerable chambers open out of it. In one you may find a man writing an atheistic volume; in the next someone on his knees praying for faith and strength; in a third a chemist investigating a body's properties. In a fourth a system of idealistic metaphysics is being excogitated; in a fifth the impossibility of metaphysics is being shown. But they all own the corridor, and all must pass through it if they want a practicable way of getting into or out of their respective rooms.

No particular results, then, so far, but only an attitude of orientation, is what the pragmatic method means. *The attitude of looking away from first things, principles, 'categories', supposed necessities; and of looking towards last things, fruits, consequences, facts.*

Even to-day science and philosophy are still laboriously trying to part fancies from realities in our experience; and in primitive times they made only the most incipient distinctions in this line. Men believed whatever they thought with any liveliness, and they mixed their dreams with their realities inextricably. The categories of 'thought' and 'things' are indispensable here – instead of being realities we now call certain experiences only 'thoughts'. There is not a category, among those enumerated, of which we may not imagine the use to have thus originated historically and only gradually spread.

That one Time which we all believe in and in which each event has its definite date, that one Space in which each thing has its position, these abstract notions unify the world incomparably; but in their finished shape as concepts how different they are from the loose unordered time-and-space experiences of natural men! Everything that happens to us brings its own duration and extension, and both are vaguely surrounded by a marginal 'more' that runs into the duration and extension of the next thing that comes. But we soon lose all our definite bearings, and not only do our children make no distinction between yesterday and the day before yesterday, the whole past being churned up together, but we adults still do so whenever the times are large. It is the same with spaces. On a map I can see distinctly the relation of London, Constantinople, and Pekin to the place where I am; in reality I utterly fail to *feel* the facts which the map symbolizes. The directions and distances are vague, confused and mixed. Cosmic space and cosmic time, so far from being the intuitions that Kant said they were, are constructions as patently artificial as any science can show. . . .

---

3 Giovanni Papini was a poet and novelist, and a leading figure in the Italian Futurist movement.

Permanent 'things' again; the 'same' thing and its various 'appearances' and 'alterations'; the different 'kinds' of thing; with the 'kind' used finally as a predicate, of which the thing remains the 'subject' – what a straightening of the tangle of our experience's immediate flux and sensible variety does this list of terms suggest! And it is only the smallest part of his experience's flux that anyone actually does straighten out by applying to it these conceptual instruments. Out of them all our lowest ancestors probably used only, and then most vaguely and inaccurately, the notion of 'the same again.' But even if you had asked them whether the same were a 'thing' that had endured throughout the unseen interval, they would probably have been at a loss, and would have said that they had never asked that question, or considered matters in that light.

What shall we call a *thing* anyhow? It seems quite arbitrary, for we carve out everything, just as we carve out constellations, to suit our human purposes. . . . We break the flux of sensible reality into things at our will. We create the subjects of our true as well as of our false propositions.

We create the predicates also. Many of the predicates of things express only the relations of the things to us and to our feelings. Such predicates of course are human additions. Caesar crossed the Rubicon, and was a menace to Rome's freedom. He is also an American school-room pest, made into one by the reaction of our schoolboys on his writings. The added predicate is as true of him as the earlier ones.

You see how naturally one comes to the humanistic principle: you can't weed out the human contribution. Our nouns and adjectives are all humanized heirlooms, and in the theories we build them into, the inner order and arrangement is wholly dictated by human considerations, intellectual consistency being one of them. Mathematics and logic themselves are fermenting with human rearrangements; physics, astronomy and biology follow massive cues of preference. We plunge forward into the field of fresh experience with the beliefs our ancestors and we have made already; these determine what we notice; what we notice determines what we do; what we do again determines what we experience; so from one thing to another, although the stubborn fact remains that there *is* a sensible flux, what is *true of it* seems from first to last to be largely a matter of our own creation.

We build the flux out inevitably.

5.4   Henri Bergson, *Creative Evolution* (authorized translation by Arthur Mitchell, 1911; published in France, 1907)

Alongside Nietzsche, Bergson (1859–1941) was probably the major philosophical influence upon the writing of the first thirty years of the twentieth century. During his time as Professor of Philosophy at the Collège de France, from 1900 to 1921, Bergson's dynamic lecturing style made him a major 'draw' for writers and artists living in, or visiting, Paris. T. E. Hulme, himself an important transmitter of Bergson's ideas to the artistic community in London, and T. S. Eliot, who lived in Paris as a student in 1910–11, were amongst the many to attend a course of Bergson lectures, and to have been, however temporarily, influenced by what they heard. Hulme's translation of Bergson's Introduction to Metaphysics *appeared in 1912. The title of Bergson's doctoral dissertation,* Time and Free Will *(published 1889; translated into English 1910), gives a firm suggestion of the focus of his philosophy. The relation between 'mechanical' time, hours, minutes, seconds, 'duration' (a key term), memory, and those visionary or mystical moments in which the individual seems to exist free and separate from time, was to occupy much of his thinking and written work. In* Creative Evolution, *however, we find Bergson shifting his ground from the kinds of opposition outlined in his doctoral work. In* Time and Free Will, *Bergson had held that the succession of time's passing required a perceiving consciousness in order to be understood. In* Creative Evolution, *as in the earlier* Matter and Memory, *Bergson came to argue that duration and succession happened independently of any individual's interaction with them. Such issues of temporality, and of the human experience of it, might be taken as a formative preoccupation of modernist writing, from Woolf, to the Eliot of* Four Quartets, *to Samuel Beckett. In the work extracted here, Bergson furthers his arguments to explicate his notion that scientific conceptions of evolution, as the mere survival of the fittest, or as adaptation to circumstance, were inadequate to explain the force (or* élan vital) *of creation which drives all life forward. In the latter phase of this book, he outlines his idea of a 'cinematographical' mechanism of thought, which takes his former discussions of time into a visual medium. The extracts come from Bergson's Introduction, which outlines the general case; Chapter 1 on 'Duration'; and Chapter IV on 'The Cinematographical Mechanism of Thought and the Mechanistic Illusion'.*

The line of evolution that ends in man is not the only one. On other paths, divergent from it, other forms of consciousness have been developed, which have not been able to free themselves from external constraints or to regain control over themselves, as the human intellect has done, but which, none the less, also express something that is immanent and essential in the evolutionary movement. Suppose these other forms of consciousness brought together and amalgamated with intellect: would not the result be a consciousness as wide as life? And such a consciousness, turning around suddenly against the push of life which it feels behind, would have a vision of life complete – would it not? – even though the vision were fleeting.

It will be said that, even so, we do not transcend our intellect, for it is still with our intellect, and through our intellect, that we see the other forms of consciousness. And this would be right if we were pure intellects, if there did not remain, around our conceptual and logical thought, a vague nebulosity, made of the very substance out of which has been formed the luminous nucleus that we call the intellect. Therein reside certain powers that are complementary to the understanding, powers of which we have only an indistinct feeling when we remain shut up in ourselves, but which will become clear and distinct when they perceive themselves at work, so to speak, in the evolution of nature. They will thus learn what sort of effort they must make to be intensified and expanded in the very direction of life.

This amounts to saying that *theory of knowledge* and *theory of life* seem to us inseparable.

Our duration is not merely one instant replacing another; if it were, there would never be anything but the present – no prolonging of the past into the actual, no evolution, no concrete duration. Duration is the continuous progress of the past which grows into the future and which swells as it advances. And as the past grows without ceasing, so also there is no limit to its preservation. . . . The cerebral mechanism is arranged just so as to drive back into the unconscious almost the whole of this past, and to admit beyond the threshold only that which can cast light on the present situation or further the action now being prepared – in short, only that which can give *useful* work.[4] At the most, a few superfluous recollections may succeed in smuggling themselves through the half-open door. These memories, messengers from the unconscious, remind us of what we are dragging behind us unawares. But, even though we may have no distinct idea of it, we feel vaguely that our past remains present to us. What are we, in fact, what is our *character*, if not the condensation of the history that we have lived from our birth – nay, even before our birth, since we bring with us prenatal dispositions? Doubtless we think with only a small part of our past, but it is with our entire past, including the original bent of our soul, that we desire, will and act. Our past, then, as a whole, is made manifest to us in its impulse; it is felt in the form of tendency, although a small part of it only is known in the form of idea.

From this survival of the past it follows that consciousness cannot go through the same state twice. The circumstances may still be the same, but they will act no longer on the same person, since they find him at a new moment of his history. Our personality, which is being built up each instant with its accumulated experience, changes without ceasing. By changing, it prevents any state, although superficially identical with another, from ever repeating it in its depth. That is why our duration is irreversible. We could not live once again a single moment, for we should have to begin by effacing the memory of all that had followed. Even could we erase this memory from our intellect, we could not from our will.

Thus our personality shoots, grows and ripens without ceasing. Each of its moments is something new added to what was before. We may go further: it is not only something new, but something unforeseeable. Doubtless, my present

---

4 The closeness of Bergson's ideas to that pragmatist strain of American philosophy, as represented in this anthology by extracts from William James (with whom Bergson carried on a mutually-admiring correspondence) and John Dewey, is evidenced in such phrases.

state is explained by what was in me and by what was acting on me a moment ago. In analysing it I should find no other elements. But even a superhuman intelligence would not have been able to foresee the simple indivisible form which gives to these purely abstract elements their concrete organization.

It is then right to say that what we do depends on what we are; but it is necessary to add also that we are, to a certain extent, what we do, and that we are creating ourselves continually. This creation of self by self is the more complete, the more one reasons on what one does. For reason does not proceed in such matters as in geometry, where impersonal premises are given once for all, and an impersonal conclusion must perforce be drawn. Here, on the contrary, the same reasons may dictate to different persons, or to the same person at different moments, acts profoundly different, although equally reasonable. The truth is that they are not quite the same reasons, since they are not those of the same person, nor of the same moment. That is why we cannot deal with them in the abstract, from the outside, as in geometry, nor solve for another the problems by which he is faced in life. Each must solve them from within, on his own account.

Succession is an undeniable fact, even in the material world. Though our reasoning on isolated systems may imply that their history, past, present, and future, may be instantaneously unfurled like a fan, this history, in point of fact, unfolds itself gradually, as if it occupied a duration like our own. If I want to mix a glass of sugar and water, I must, willy-nilly, wait until the sugar melts. This little fact is big with meaning. For here the time I have to wait is not that mathematical time which would apply equally well to the entire history of the material world, even if that history were spread out instantaneously in space. It coincides with my impatience, that is to say, with a certain portion of my own duration, which I cannot protract or contract as I like. It is no longer something *thought*, it is something *lived*. It is no longer a relation, it is an absolute. What else can this mean than that the glass of water, the sugar, and the process of the sugar's melting in the water are abstractions, and that the Whole within which they have been cut out by my senses and understanding progresses, it may be in the manner of a consciousness?

Certainly, the operation by which science isolates and closes a system is not altogether artificial. If it had no objective foundation, we could not explain why it is clearly indicated in some cases and impossible in others. We shall see that matter has a tendency to constitute *isolable* systems, that can be treated geometrically. In fact, we shall define matter by just this tendency. Matter does not go on to the end, and the isolation is never complete. If science does go to the end and isolate completely, it is for the convenience of study; it is understood that the so-called isolated system remains subject to certain external influences.

Matter or mind, reality has appeared to us as a perpetual becoming. It makes itself or it unmakes itself, but it is never something made. Such is the intuition that we have of mind when we draw aside the veil which is interposed between our consciousness and ourselves. This, also, is what our intellect and senses themselves would show us of matter, if they could obtain a direct and disinterested idea of it. But, preoccupied before everything with the necessities of action, the intellect, like the senses, is limited to taking, at intervals, views that are instantaneous and by that very fact immobile of the becoming of matter. Consciousness, being in its turn formed on the intellect, sees clearly of the inner life what is already made, and only feels confusedly the making. Thus, we pluck out of duration those moments that interest us, and that we have gathered along its course. These alone we retain. And we are right in so doing, while action only is in question. But when, in *speculating* on the *nature* of the real, we go on regarding it as our practical interest requires us to regard it, we become unable to perceive the true evolution, the radical becoming. Of becoming we perceive only states, of duration only instants, and even when we speak of duration and of becoming, it is of another thing that we are thinking.

Suppose we wish to portray on a screen a living picture, such as a marching past of a regiment. There is one way in which it might first occur to us to do it. That would be to cut out jointed figures representing the soldiers, to give to each of them the movement of marching, a movement varying from individual to individual although common to the human species, and to throw the whole on the screen. We should need to spend on this little game an enormous amount of work, and even then we should obtain a very poor result: how could it, at its best, reproduce the suppleness and variety of life? Now, there is another way of proceeding, more easy and at the same time more effective. It is to take a series of snapshots of the passing regiment and to throw these instantaneous views on the screen, so that they replace each other very rapidly. This is what the cinematograph does. With photographs, each of which represents the regiment in a fixed attitude, it reconstitutes the mobility of the regiment marching. It is true that if we had to do with photographs alone, however much we might look at them, we should never see them animated: with immobility set beside immobility, even endlessly, we could never make movement. In order that the pictures may be animated, there must be movement somewhere. The movement does indeed exist here; it is in the apparatus. It is because the film of the cinematograph unrolls, bringing in turn the different photographs of the scene to continue each other, that each actor of the scene recovers his mobility; he strings all his successive attitudes as the invisible movement of the film. The process then consists in extracting from all the movements peculiar to all the figures an impersonal movement abstract and simple, *movement in general*, so to speak: we put this into the apparatus, and we reconstitute the individuality of each particular movement, by combining this nameless movement with personal attitudes. Such is the contrivance of the cinematograph. And such is also that of our knowledge. Instead of attaching ourselves to the inner becoming of things, we place ourselves outside them in order to recompose their becoming artificially. We take snapshots, as it were, of the passing reality, we have only to string them on a becoming, abstract, uniform and invisible, situated at the back of the apparatus of knowledge, in order to imitate what there is that is characteristic in this becoming itself. Perception, intellection, language so proceed in general. Whether we should think becoming, or express it, or even perceive it, we hardly do anything else than set going a kind of cinematograph inside us. We may therefore sum up what we have been saying in the conclusion that the *mechanism of our ordinary knowledge is of a cinematographical kind.*

5.5 T. E. Hulme, 'Romanticism and Classicism' (lecture written 1911 or 1912)

Hulme (1883–1917) was a significant figure in London literary circles in the years before the First World War, and in the development of what became modernist poetry and poetics. Having been sent down from his course at Cambridge through misbehaviour, Hulme began an itinerant existence, travelling to Canada, Belgium, France and Germany with periods in between spent back in London. In 1908 he joined a group of amateur poets called 'The Poet's Club' (the American poet Ezra Pound was to join shortly after, on his arrival in England). Through lectures and discussions at the club, Hulme began developing a series of ideas about the nature of aesthetics in the modern world. These ideas were initially influenced by Hulme's knowledge of Bergson's work, which he had become familiar with in 1907; but, over the next few years, that interest was mediated through an interest in the thinking of the reactionary French configuration of writers and politicians which went by the name Action Française. Contributors to this eclectic group included the right-wing politician, Charles Maurras, but they also embraced the syndicalism of Georges Sorel, for example (see extract in Section 2). The conservative political implications of his interest are carried in passages from this lecture that I have not had space to extract. Hulme's central thinking, that the modern age was one which had moved beyond the Romanticism of the nineteenth century, and which was no longer focused upon the individual's sentiment or emotional response, was crucial for the development of Imagism as orchestrated by Pound, and, later, to the development of T. S. Eliot's ideas on poetry and religion. Pound in fact published Hulme's five 'Complete Poetical Works' at the end of his own gathering of shorter poems, Personae *(1952). Hulme's association just before the war with the group of writers and artists going under the banner of Vorticism showed him bringing forward the inherently dynamic nature of his vision of 'Classicism', as explained in this extracted lecture from the early 1910s. On the advent of the war, Hulme immediately enlisted, was wounded in 1915, but continued writing articles on his key ideas from the Front. He was killed by shelling in September 1917.*

I want to maintain that after a hundred years of romanticism, we are in for a classical revival, and that the particular weapon of this new classical spirit, when it works in verse, will be fancy. And in this I imply the superiority of fancy – not superior generally or absolutely, for that would be obvious nonsense, but superior in the sense that we use the word good in empirical ethics – good for something, superior for something. I shall have to prove then two things, first that a classical revival is coming, and secondly, for its particular purposes, fancy will be superior to imagination. . . .

I know that in using the words 'classic' and 'romantic' I am doing a dangerous thing. They represent five or six different kinds of antitheses, and while I may be using them in one sense you may be interpreting them in another. In the present connection I am using them in a perfectly precise and limited sense.

The thing which created enthusiasm, which made the [French Revolution] practically a new religion [amongst people], was . . . a positive ferment about liberty. There must have been some idea which enabled them to think that something positive could come out of so essentially negative a thing. There was, and here I get my definition of romanticism. They had been taught by Rousseau[5] that man was by nature good, that it was only bad laws and customs that had suppressed him. This is what made them think that something positive could come out of disorder, that this is what created the religious enthusiasm. Here is the root of all romanticism: that man, the individual, is an infinite reservoir of possibilities; and if you can so rearrange society by the destruction of oppressive order then these possibilities will have a chance and you will get Progress.

One can define the classical quite clearly as the exact opposite to this. Man is an extraordinarily fixed and limited animal whose nature is absolutely constant. It is only by tradition and organisation that anything decent can be got out of him. . . .

Put shortly, these are the two views, then. One, that man is intrinsically good, spoilt by circumstance; and the other that he is intrinsically limited, but disciplined by order and tradition to something fairly decent. To the one party man's nature is like a well, to the other like a bucket. The view which regards man as a well, a reservoir full of possibilities, I call the romantic; the one which regards him as a very finite and fixed creature, I call the classical.

One may note here that the Church has always taken the classical view since the defeat of the Pelagian heresy[6] and the adoption of the sane classical dogma of original sin.

It would be a mistake to identify the classical view with that of materialism. On the contrary it is absolutely identical with the normal religious attitude. I

---

5 Jean-Jacques Rousseau (1712–78), who believed in equality and a *Social Contract* between individuals existing originally in an innocent and free state, was one of the key philosophers behind European and British Romanticism.

6 Pelagius was a Romano-British monk of the late third and early fourth century AD, who promulgated a heresy which argued that human free will was essential to human perfection. He minimized the role of divine redemption and – immediately pertinent to Hulme's case – felt that humanity had been little damaged by the Fall from grace in Eden.

should put it in this way: That part of the fixed nature of man is the belief in the Deity. This should be as fixed and true for every man as belief in the existence of matter and in the objective world. It is parallel to appetite, the instinct of sex, and all the other fixed qualities.

I must now shirk the difficulty of saying exactly what I mean by romantic and classical in verse. I can only say that it means the result of these two attitudes towards the cosmos, towards man, in so far as it gets reflected in verse. The romantic, because he thinks man infinite, must always be talking about the infinite; and as there is always the bitter contrast between what you think you ought to be able to do and what man actually can, it always tends, in its later stages at any rate, to be gloomy. I can't really go any further than to say it is the reflection of these two temperaments, and point out examples of the different spirits. On the one hand I would take such diverse people as Horace, most of the Elizabethans, and the writers of the Augustan age, and on the other side Lamartine, Hugo, parts of Keats, Coleridge, Byron, Shelley and Swinburne. . . .

What I mean by classical in verse, then, is this. That even in the most imaginative flights there is always a holding back, a reservation. The classical poet never forgets this finiteness, this limit of man. He remembers always that he is mixed up with earth. He may jump, but he always returns back; he never flies away into the circumambient gas.

You might say if you wished that the whole of the romantic attitude seems to crystallize in verse round metaphors of flight. . . . The word infinite in every other line.

In the classical attitude you never seem to swing right along to the infinite nothing. If you say an extravagant thing which does not exceed the limits inside which you know man to be fastened, yet there is always conveyed in some way at the end an impression of yourself standing outside it, and not quite believing it, or conspicuously putting it forward as a flourish. Yet never go blindly into an atmosphere more than the truth, an atmosphere too rarefied for man to breathe for long. You are always faithful to the conception of a limit. It is a question of pitch; in romantic verse you move at a certain pitch of rhetoric which you know, man being what he is, to be a little high-falutin. . . . In the coming classical reaction that will feel just wrong. For an example of the opposite thing, a verse written in the proper classical spirit, I can take the song of *Cymbeline* beginning 'Fear no more the heat of the sun.' I am just using this as a parable. I don't quite mean what I say here. Take the first two lines:

> 'Golden lads and girls all must,
> Like chimney sweepers come to dust.'[7]

---

7 Hulme slightly misquotes Shakespeare's lines from Act IV, sc. 2, 263. The second line should read 'As chimney-sweepers, come to dust.'

Now, no romantic would ever have written that. Indeed, so ingrained is romanticism, so objectionable is this to it, that people have asserted that these were not
part of the original song.

Apart from the pun, the thing that I think quite classical is the word lad. Your
modern romantic could never write that. He would have to write golden youth,
and take up the thing at least a couple of notes in pitch.

I want now to give the reasons which make me think that we are nearing the
end of the romantic movement.

The first lies in the nature of any convention or tradition in art. A particular
convention or attitude in art has a strict analogy to the phenomena of organic
life. It grows old and decays. It has a definite period of life and must die. All the
possible tunes get played on it and then it is exhausted; moreover its best period
is its youngest. Take the case of the extraordinary efflorescence of verse in the
Elizabethan period. All kinds of reasons have been given for this – the discovery
of the new world and all the rest of it. There is a much simpler one. A new
medium had been given them to play with – namely, blank verse. It was new and
so it was easy to play new tunes on it.

The great aim [of classical verse] is accurate, precise and definite description.[8]
The first thing is to recognise how extraordinarily difficult this is. It is no mere
matter of carefulness; you have to use language, and language is by its very
nature a communal thing; that is, it expresses never the exact thing but a
compromise – that which is common to you, me and everybody. But each man
sees a little differently, and to get out clearly and exactly what he does see, he
must have a terrific struggle with language, whether it be with words or the technique of other arts. Language has its own special nature, its own conventions
and communal ideas. It is only by a concentrated effort of the mind that you can
hold it fixed to your own purpose. I always think that the fundamental process
at the back of all the arts might be represented by the following metaphor. You
know what I call architect's curves – flat pieces of wood with all different kinds
of curvature. By a suitable selection from these you can draw approximately any
curve you like. The artist I take to be the man who simply can't bear the idea of
that 'approximately'. He will get the exact curve of what he sees whether it be
an object or an idea in the mind. I shall here have to change my metaphor a
little to get the process in his mind. Suppose that instead of your curved pieces
of wood you have a springy piece of steel of the same types of curvature as the
wood. Now the state of tension or concentration of the mind, if he is doing
anything really good in this struggle against the ingrained habit of the technique, may be represented by a man employing all his fingers to bend the steel

---

8 Compare this statement with the first two 'principles' of Imagism, which, Pound declared in 'How to
Read', had been decided upon by himself, H.D., and Richard Aldington in the summer of 1912 –
probably not long after this lecture by Hulme: direct treatment of the 'thing'; and 'to use absolutely
no word which does not contribute to the presentation' (see Introduction to the Sourcebook).

out of its own curve and into the exact curve which you want. Something different to what it would assume naturally.

There are then two things to distinguish, first the particular faculty of mind to see things as they really are, and apart from the conventional ways in which you have been trained to see them. Second, the concentrated state of mind, the grip over oneself which is necessary in the actual expression of what one sees. To prevent one falling into conventional curves of ingrained technique, to hold on through infinite detail and trouble to the exact curve you want. Wherever you get this sincerity, you get the fundamental quality of good art without dragging in infinite or serious.

I can now get at that positive fundamental quality of verse which constitutes excellence, which has nothing to do with infinity, with mystery or with emotions.

This is the point I aim at, then, in my argument. I prophesy that a period of dry, hard, classical verse is coming. I have met the preliminary objection founded on the bad romantic aesthetic that in such verse, from which the infinite is excluded, you cannot have the essence of poetry at all.

5.6   Oswald Spengler, *The Decline of the West* (1918; 1922 revised edition; authorized translation by Charles Francis Atkinson, 1926)

Spengler (1880–1936) was a German philosopher with a broad academic knowledge and interest, which included mathematics and science alongside the major humanities disciplines. The Decline of the West was Spengler's sole significant work, but it caused phenomenal discussion across Europe even before its translation into a variety of other languages. Appearing as it did in the immediate aftermath of the First World War, the book was read as a commentary upon the destruction of civilization which had taken place in the past four years. The book's argument that Europe had entered a last phase of rapid growth and technological development before the advent of a new age, was to become a familiar one for much post-war literature in Britain, America and Europe. It was a view shared by many, including D. H. Lawrence, and W. B. Yeats, whose prophetic work A Vision shares Spengler's cyclical version of historical change, the movement and turn between historical phases. Yet Spengler adamantly claimed that the central argument of his book had been settled upon before 1914, and that it had been worked through in its complete version by the start of the war; it was redrafted across the years down to 1917. Spengler concluded that his work should been seen, therefore, as a pre-war reading of history rather than a post-war one – although he did not comment on how that reading might be changed by the scene on the Western Front. The Decline of the West's two volumes form a compendious work, pulling in the whole range of Spengler's interests in the arts and sciences. As he said in his Preface to the 1922 revised edition, the method of the book is 'intuitive and depictive', abundant in narrative and commentary, rather than abstract and 'offering an army of ranked concepts'. The work throughout displays the impact of its proclaimed influences: the

German writer Goethe, and the philosopher Nietzsche. Spengler, however, ultimately distrusts Culture, and in an extraordinary paean early in the work, celebrates imperialism as the high-point of civilization – imperialism as embodied in the form of the British colonialist Cecil John Rhodes, who had died in 1902. The extracts offered here all relate to the discussion of the book's methodology in comparative – what he calls 'historically relative' – history. The final paragraphs extracted provide an indication of the reasons for Spengler's belief in the contemporary decline of Culture (always, for him, in this authorized translation, carrying a capital 'c').

In this book is attempted for the first time the venture of predetermining history, of following the still untravelled stages in the destiny of a Culture, and specifically of the only Culture of our time and on our planet which is actually in the phase of fulfilment – the West – European – American.

Hitherto the possibility of solving a problem so far-reaching has evidently never been envisaged, and even if it had been so, the means of dealing with it were either altogether unsuspected or, at best, inadequately used.

Is there a logic of history? Is there, beyond all the casual and incalculable elements of the separate events, something that we may call a metaphysical structure of historic humanity, something that is essentially independent of the outward forms – social, spiritual and political – which we see so clearly? Are not these actualities indeed secondary or derived from that something? Does world-history present to the seeing eye certain grand traits, again and again, with sufficient constancy to justify certain conclusions? And if so, what are the limits to which reasoning from such premises may be pushed?

Is it possible to find in life itself – for human history is the sum of mighty life-courses which have already had to be endowed with ego and personality, in customary thought and expression, by predicating entities of a higher order like 'the Classical' or 'the Chinese Culture', 'Modern Civilization' – a series of stages which must be traversed, and traversed moreover in an ordered and obligatory sequence? For everything organic the notions of birth, death, youth, age, life-time are fundamentals – may not these notions, in this sphere also, possess a rigorous meaning which no one has yet extracted? In short, is all history founded upon general biographic archetypes?

The decline of the West, which at first sight may appear, like the corresponding decline of the Classical Culture, a phenomenon limited in time and space, we now perceive to be a philosophical problem that, when comprehended in all its gravity, includes within itself every great question of Being.

What concerns us is not what the historical facts which appear at this or that time *are*, per se, but what they signify, what they point to, *by appearing*. Present-day historians think they are doing a work of supererogation in bringing in religious and social, or still more art-history, details to 'illustrate' the political sense of an epoch. But the decisive factor – decisive, that is, in so far as visible history is the expression, sign and embodiment of soul – they forget. I have not hitherto found one who has carefully considered the *morphological relationship*[9] that inwardly binds together the expression-forms of *all* branches of a Culture. . . . Who realizes that between the Differential Calculus and the dynastic principle of politics in the age of Louis XIV, between the Classical city-state and the Euclidean geometry, between the space-perspective of Western oil-painting and the conquest of space by railroad, telephone and long-range weapon, between contrapuntal music and credit economics, there are deep uniformities? Yet, viewed from this morphological standpoint, even the humdrum facts of politics assume a symbolic and even a metaphysical character, and – what has perhaps been impossible hitherto – things . . . can, as symbols, be made *uniformly* understandable and appreciable. . . .

That there is, besides a necessity of cause and effect – which I may call the *logic of space* – another necessity, an organic necessity in life, that of Destiny – the *logic of time* – is a fact of the deepest inward certainty, a fact which suffuses the whole of mythological religious and artistic thought and constitutes the essence and kernel of all history (in contradistinction to nature) but is unapproachable through the cognition forms which the 'Critique of Pure Reason'[10] investigates.

This, then, is our task. We men of the Western Culture are, with our historical sense, an exception and not a rule. World-history is *our* world picture and not all mankind's. Indian and Classical man formed no image of a world in progress, and perhaps when in due course the Civilization of the West is extinguished, there will never again be a Culture and a human type in which 'world-history' is so potent a form of the waking-consciousness.

What, then, *is* world-history? Certainly, an ordered presentation of the past, an inner postulate, the expression of a capacity for feeling form. But a feeling for form, however definite, is not the same as form itself. No doubt we would feel world-history, experience it, and believe that it is to be read just as a map is read. But, even to-day, it is only forms of it that we know and not *the* form of it, which is the mirror-image of *our own* inner life.

Everyone, of course, if asked, would say that he saw the inward form of History quite clearly and definitely. The illusion subsists because no one has seriously reflected on it, still less conceived doubts as to his own knowledge, for no one uses the slightest notion how wide a field for doubt there is. In fact, the *layout* of world-history is an unproved and subjective notion that has been handed

---

9 Spengler's sense that the relationship is *morphological* skilfully carries forward both sides of his argument about Being or life and Culture: morphology relates both to the study of form in plants *and* to the study of the development of forms of language and communication.

10 Spengler here marks his resistance to the idea in Immanuel Kant's *Critique of Pure Reason* (1781) that the world is fundamentally unknowable through the reason, and that in Kant's view the world offers instead only material from which sensations are developed.

down from generation to generation (not only of laymen but of professional historians) and stands badly in need of a little of that scepticism which from Galileo onward has regulated and deepened our unborn ideas of nature.

Thanks to the subdivision of history into 'Ancient', 'Medieval', and 'Modern' – an incredibly jejeune and *meaningless* scheme, which has, however, entirely dominated our historical thinking – we have failed to perceive the true position in the general history of higher mankind, of the little part world which has developed on West-European soil from the time of the German-Roman Empire, to judge of its relative importance and above all to estimate its direction. The Cultures that are to come will find it difficult to believe that the validity of such a scheme with its rectilinear progression and its meaningless proportions, becoming more and more preposterous with each century, incapable of bringing into itself the new fields of history as they successively come into the light of our knowledge, was, in spite of all, never whole-heartedly attacked.

The ground of West-Europe is treated as a steady pole, a unique patch chosen on the surface of the sphere for no better reason, it seems, than because we live on it – and great histories of millennial duration and mighty far-away Cultures are made to revolve around this pole in all modesty. . . .

We know quite well that the slowness with which a high cloud or a railway train in the distance seems to move is only apparent, yet believe that the *tempo* of all early Indian, Babylonian, or Egyptian history was really slower than that of our recent past. And we think of them as less substantial, more damped-down, more diluted, because we have not learned to make the allowance for (inward and outward) distances.

It is self-evident that for Cultures of the West the existence of Athens, Florence or Paris is more important than that of Lo-Yang or Pataliputra. But is it permissible to found a scheme of world-history on estimates of such a sort?

I see, in place of that empty figment of *one* linear history which can only be kept up by shutting one's eyes to the overwhelming multitude of the facts, the drama of a *number* of mighty Cultures, each springing with primitive strength from the soil of a mother-region to which it remains firmly bound throughout its whole life-cycle; each stamping its material, its mankind, in *its own* image; each having *its own* idea, *its own* passions, *its own* life, will and feeling, *its own death*. Here indeed are colours, lights, movements, that no intellectual eye has yet discovered. Here the Cultures, peoples, languages, truths, gods, landscapes bloom and age as the oaks and the stone-pines, the blossoms, twigs and leaves – but there is no aging 'mankind'. Each culture has its own new possibilities of self-expression which arise, ripen, decay, and never return. There is not *one* sculpture, *one* painting, *one* mathematics, *one* physics, but many, each in its deepest essence different from the others, each limited in duration and self-contained, just as each species of plant has its peculiar blossom or fruit, its special type of growth and decline.

World-city and province – the two basic ideas of every civilization – bring up a wholly new form-problem of History, the very problem that we are living through to-day with hardly the remotest conception of its immensity. In place of a world, there is *a city, a point*, in which the whole life of broad regions is collecting while the rest dries up. In place of a type-true people, born of and grown on the soil, there is a new sort of nomad, cohering unstably in fluid masses, the parasitical city dweller, traditionless, utterly matter-of-fact, religionless, clever, unfruitful, deeply contemptuous of the countryman and especially that highest form of countryman, the country gentleman. This is a very great stride towards the inorganic, towards the end –what does it signify? France and England have already taken the step and Germany is beginning to do so. After Syracuse, Athens, and Alexandria comes Rome. After Madrid, Paris, London come Berlin and New York. It is the destiny of whole regions that lie outside the radiation-circle of one of these cities to become 'provinces'.

. . . To the world-city belongs not a folk but a mass. Its uncomprehending hostility to all the traditions representative of the Culture (nobility, church, privileges, dynasties, convention in art and limits of knowledge in science), the keen and cold intelligence that confounds the wisdom of the peasant, the new-fashioned naturalism that in relation to all matters of sex and society goes back beyond Rousseau and Socrates to quite primitive instincts and conditions,[11] the reappearance of the *panem et circenses*[12] in the form of wage-disputes and football-grounds – all these things betoken the definite closing-down of the Culture and the opening of a quite new phase of human existence – anti-provincial, late, futureless, but quite inevitable.

This is what has to be *viewed*, and viewed not with the eyes of the partisan, the ideologue, the up-to-date novelist, not from this or that 'standpoint', but in a high, time-free perspective embracing whole millenniums of historical world-forms, if we are really to comprehend the great crisis of the present.

---

11 Spengler's attack – like those most famously from T. E. Hulme and his followers, including T. S. Eliot, in the English-speaking world – is upon a Romantic tradition which favours the freedom of the individual's will over some predetermined (and harsh or fallen) destiny, and which sees 'nobleness' in even the most early cultures.

12 'Bread and circuses' – or a pandering to the profane and ill-informed desires and pastimes of the populace.

6
'High' Culture

Introduction

Developments in the non-literary arts in the latter part of the nineteenth century were as important as those in the content of the novel and poetry which established the impetus towards the revolution in Anglo-American writing in the early 1910s. The interrogation of visual representation, which began in French painting from the early 1860s, introduced a challenging of traditional perspective, and also heralded an introduction of contemporary, and oddly-juxtapositioned, content. This painting very much looks forward to later representations (both painterly and literary) that deliberately jumble up standard perception, and reposition the centre of consciousness of the artwork. Think of Éduoard Manet's huge rendition, in very flat colours, of the strangely elongated limbs of the naked prostitute in his *Olympia* of 1863, or the disorientatingly-foregrounded figure of the woman in the pool of his *Déjeuner sur l'Herbe* of the same year. In both cases, the viewer is challenged to reconsider her or his own sense of perspective and the nature of perception, as well as her or his understanding of the 'proper' content of 'high' art and of the ordering of social hierarchies. Such pictures are calculated in their affront. The challenge presented by Manet is then carried forward in visual art by the Impressionist painters, with their urgency to capture sights in the instant of time, however that instant might violate the formal framing of the picture; and thence, as we see below, to the further challenge of the post-impressionist artists, who take this logic one step further and abandon 'natural' use of colour, or use of perspective within the picture at all.

Similarly, listening to Romantic music of the late nineteenth century, we find a stretching, and sometimes a breaking, of the traditional formal conventions. In the late works of the Austrian composers Anton Bruckner and (more especially) Gustav Mahler, we find repetition of melodic motifs and use of tonalities which can sound difficult and alien to the ear – which, again, challenge our understanding of what the medium is, and of its function and proper achievement. In Mahler also we find a strong use of parody, a sudden breaking into the music of a recognized form such as a waltz or a military march, which grates against our sense of musical development, and which renders the waltz or march themselves hollow and empty. These passages are included in the score deliberately, as a kind of meaningless performance which no longer sustains any fris-son or meaning for us. In French classical music, from such as Claude Debussy or Maurice Ravel, we find also a determination to challenge our sense of formal expectation. Debussy's impressionistic sound-pictures, which capture everything from the sounds in the night in the Spanish city of Granada to the sea in a storm, defy any pattern or formal conclusion; they are to be enjoyed for their sensuousness in performance and for the images and ideas they conjure in the auditor's mind, rather than for their re-expression of the classical sense of form.

Modernist writing in English, as in Europe, is everywhere infected by an awareness of the innovations achieved in the other arts. Some writers, including Pound, Woolf and Lawrence, wrote critical essays on music or on painting (Lawrence himself painted; Pound wrote operas). Others, ranging broadly from such as Gertrude Stein, to Wallace Stevens, to Katherine Mansfield, not only included, but advertised, pictorial techniques in their work. Meanwhile, new techniques of representation, such as film and photography, were making possi-ble further innovations and questionings of the everyday and traditional means of understanding and structuring the formal representation of the world around.

The extracts in this section accumulate around a variety of artistic media, and historical 'moments' which have become part of the narrative surrounding modernism in all genres. The pieces relating to the London Post-Impressionist Exhibition, the New York Armory Show, as well as the early performances of music by Stravinsky and Schoenberg, give us early reactions to events which we know the key modernist writers themselves attended. These events were surrounded by a massive and unprecedented publicity and media response; the writers hastened to attend them as did thousands upon thousands of others, and were affected in their thinking about their own work by what they saw or heard. The pieces represented here give critical responses from the time both for and against the new painting or music, to offer a better sense of what modernist artists were reacting against in contemporary expectation, and also of the cross-media background to the kinds of positive appreciation they were achieving. The last two extracts here relate to the relatively new artistic medium of photogra-phy, and to innovation in theatre – innovation which, as in all of the writing included, demonstrates how, in the early years of the twentieth century, in the words of Walter Pater's highly influential *The Renaissance* (1873), 'all art constantly aspires towards the condition of music'.

6.1 Marinetti in London, 1912 and 1913

Filippo Tommaso Marinetti (1876–1944) was the founder and leading spokesperson of the movement Futurism (see Introduction to the Sourcebook). The movement's determi-nation to cast away the seeming self-indulgence of Romanticism, and to re-cast the subject-matter of poetry and the visual arts so that they were attuned to the modern world, marked a radical and aggressive model of what modern art might achieve.

Futurism was viewed interestedly by the Imagists, the Vorticists, and by a range of less obviously susceptible writers: D. H. Lawrence's conception of his new work towards The Rainbow *and* Women in Love *came in part, as his letters of the time attest, from a thinking through of Futurist ideas. Marinetti's glorification of machines, cars and planes, and his flamboyant personality, drew him much attention in both the popular and the highbrow press, and his performances of his work on his visits to European capitals drew sometimes riotous response. The two pieces here – contemporary reports given in full – relate to several of these performances in London.*

'"Futurist" Leader in London. Makes an Attack on the English Nation', Daily Chronicle, 20 March 1912

At the Bechstein Hall last night, Signor Marinetti, pioneer, poet, and philosopher, of the 'Futurists', gave a lecture to a select audience of those curious people who find an immense interest in every new form of crankism and intellectual conceit.

There have been many meetings in Italy and France when Signor Marinetti has been assailed with rotten eggs and other missiles, and when the audiences have fought with each other until police intervened. The poet and philosopher is also a martyr to his faith, having been sentenced to a term of imprisonment for a Futurist novel which went far beyond the bounds of merely modern frankness.

But last night, at the Bechstein Hall, the long-haired gentlemen in the stalls and the ladies with Rossetti eyes and lips,[1] rewarded him with their laughter and applause. Yet he did not moderate the very violence of language which is the very spirit of Futurist eloquence. He began by praising England for its material progress, for its brutality and arrogance, but after these few words of courtesy launched into a denunciation of this country as a nation of sycophants and snobs, enslaved by old worm-eaten traditions, social conventions, and romanticism.

Romanticism is the Scarlet Woman of the Futurists, and Signor Marinetti flung his arms about and spoke with passionate rapidity when he expounded his hatred of that spirit which fosters old buildings, old shrines, and old 'rubbish' such as one finds in Rome, Florence, and Venice, beloved of the tourists of the world. He would pull all these things down.

Better to a Futurist is the grim ugliness of a factory belching smoke from its chimneys than the beauty of an ancient cathedral. The Futurists are the poets, the painters and philosophers of the mechanical force. They sing songs of electricity and rise to rapture on a monoplane, and put upon their canvas the speed,

---

1 The writer of the article interestingly seeks to defuse the radical modernity of Marinetti's work by suggesting that its appeal is to those still posing themselves as aligned to the nineteenth-century 'brotherhood' of Pre-Raphaelite poets and artists.

the movement, the tremendous power of the modern spirit carried forward by Futurist ideals.

Signor Marinetti as the orator of his school is an exponent of brutality. He admires violence and vital energy in all its forms, and that man fills the Futurist code who, with a strong, relentless purpose, achieves all his natural and animal and intellectual instincts regardless of the suffering they cause to others, and the old laws violated by his actions. A pretty philosophy for ladies and gentlemen in the Bechstein Hall!

'Futurism in Poetry: Signor Marinetti on the New Movement', The Times, 18 November 1913

Signor F. T. Marinetti gave an address at a dinner of the Poets' Club[2] last night on 'Futurism in Poetry' – a movement of which he is founder and leader.

Signor Marinetti, who spoke in French, said the Futurist movement in Italy aimed at renovating and reawakening the Italian race, which for long had been under the domination of the cult of the past. Precisely because it had a splendid past Italy was to-day in some sort disinherited. The cult of the past was upheld among them by a world of interested people, and the Futurist movement in its creative effort was hampered not only by such economic hindrances but by the mental cowardice of the people. In art you must continually advance; those who stop are already dead, or candidates for death. The Romanticism of artists like Baudelaire and Wagner and Flaubert was inspired by two or three principles which were today worn out. *Salammbo*[3] was the type romance of that old sensibility. In a certain sense such Romanticism was the identification of the idea of beauty with the idea of woman. We were at the end of that period. Women as the centre, the obsession, had absolutely gone out of poetry. As a *leit-motif* it no longer had the same force; other problems had taken its place. According to the Futurist view, poetry was nothing but a more intense, a more exalted life – and that was why they combated in art the obsession of adultery, which was in a sense the essence of the French novel[4] and which had been its ruin.

The Futurists were to be found everywhere; in England they were represented by Mr. H. G. Wells. They realized the need to be more rapid, more intense, more essential: and though their method of expression had been stigmatised as 'telegraphic lyricism', he took no exception to that, for he preferred *lyrisme télégraphique* to *lyrisme diligence*.[5] Rhyme had no longer any *raison d'être*, and the

---

2 This was a group of amateur poets which included T. E. Hulme and Ezra Pound; the group which was originating, and disseminating in various forms at this time, the ideas behind Imagism.

3 This is a short historical novel (1863) by Gustave Flaubert, set in ancient Carthage.

4 This was notoriously the theme of Flaubert's 1857 novel *Madame Bovary*, which landed its author in court for his supposed immorality.

5 Telegraphic lyricism to over-careful lyricism.

formal mould of the Alexandrine[6] was remote from the manner in which an individual would seek to express himself to-day. Art was not a religion; it was the best part of our strength, of our physiological being. It was in consequence absurd to consider it as a system, as something to worship with joined hands; it should express all the intensity of life – its beauty, greatness, its fire, its brutality, its sordidness. And Futurism in poetry represented a realism profound, rapid, intense – the very complex of our life to-day.

6.2   The Ballets Russes

The Russian Ballet, or Ballets Russes, was founded in 1909 by the Paris-based impresario Sergei Diaghilev and the choreographer Michel Fokine – the ballet remained in its original form until Diaghilev's death in 1929. Its most famous dancers were Vaslav Nijinsky, Lydia Lopokova, and Anna Pavlova. The company was centred upon Fokine's vision of twentieth-century ballet as integrating various of the other arts: music, dance, obviously, but also drama and painting. The stage designs for the various ballets were created in collaboration with some of the most innovative artists of the day, including the painters Pablo Picasso and Georges Braque, Henri Matisse, and the poet–artist Jean Cocteau. Diaghilev commissioned music from leading modern composers, Igor Stravinsky, Darius Milhaud, Erik Satie, Maurice Ravel and Manuel de Falla. After its first successful seasons in Paris, the company began touring its work abroad, coming to London, and undertaking a successful tour of America in 1916. Wherever they played, their impact was immense and controversial. This was true not just with the notorious premières of Stravinsky's Le Sacre du Printemps *(The Rite of Spring) in 1913 (in Paris, May; London, July), where the cat-calls and punch-ups in the audience were so noisy that the dancers could not hear the orchestra. Later work, like the Satie-scored and Picasso-designed* Parade *(1917), also met with a baffled and hostile reception. The performances by the Ballets Russes attracted many writers and artists, themselves seeking to discover distinctly modern techniques, often drawing upon a unification of various arts, in their own work. The extracts on the Ballet here relate to the 1913 and the 1919 London seasons. The first is from a review of the first English performances of* Le Sacre *by H. C. Colles; the second is a general reflection on ballet in the light of the Russian company's performances, written by Arthur Symons, the mediator of French Symbolist poetics to English-speaking audiences.*

H. C. Colles, ' "Le Sacre du Printemps" at Drury Lane', The Times, 26 July 1913

London takes both its pleasures and its pains more quietly than Paris. When *Le*

---

6 This is a twelve-syllable poetic line of six iambic feet.

Sacre du Printemps, the latest joint production by MM. Nijinsky and Stravinsky, was produced for the first time in England last night at Drury Lane, the applause was measured, but so were the cries of disapproval. Mr. Evans, it is true, was obliged to cut short his preliminary remarks before the curtain, and a certain amount of whistling and half-suppressed laughter was heard during the performance. . . .

Le Sacre du Printemps is on quite different lines from either of Stravinsky's former ballets and marks a fresh stage in his development. *L'Oiseau de Feu* dealt with the world of spirits and magicians, and was written in an idiom that was unlike any one else's, but was logically developed from Borodin and Ravel. *Pétroushka* dealt with the world of puppets, half toys half human, and was couched in language that was a little further removed from that of contemporary writers, but was still perfectly clear and entirely consistent. In *Le Sacre du Printemps* we go back to the beginning of the world, when men were just ceasing to be animals and were coming into their heritage as human beings, while the music, at any rate on the harmonic side, though again perfectly consistent, has moved so far ahead even of *Pétroushka* that it parts company with anything coming even from Paris that one has heard before. . . . . In its relation to the stage as well as in its own inherent nature, the music of *Le Sacre du Printemps* is on new lines, for it does not condition the action of the stage as the music conditions the action of the dances in *Prince Igor*[7] . . . It sounds, in fact, as though it had been written as absolute music conceived in varieties of a single mood rather than as programme music, and as though the incidents on the stage had been roughly fitted together and made to synchronise with the music because they happened to illustrate ideas conceived in a similar mood.[8] This similarity of mood between action and music as once differentiates this music [from the *Ballets'* earlier productions] in neither of which does the music seem to have any particular relation to what is taking place on stage.

The incidents in *Le Sacre du Printemps*, such as they are, cannot be called dramatic, for they follow each other without much feeling for rational sequence or climax. When the curtain goes up a stretch of wild hilly country stretches before us . . . and on the grass is visible, by the light of a night in spring, a troupe of young men, who first take lessons in sympathetic magic from an old sorceress – more than 300 years old the programme assured us – and then join in dances and games with a group of young women. They are very properly followed by their parents and seniors, the oldest of whom goes through the rite of blessing the earth, presumably on the precautionary principles employed by savages. All this part of the ballet, indeed, looks like an illustration of one of the

---

7 The dances from Alexsandr Borodin's unfinished opera were performed at the end of the same performance as Stravinsky's new ballet.

8 Colles's judgement on this proved prophetic; Stravinsky's *Rite* soon received a concert performance in April 1914, in Paris, which, unlike the ballet performance, was rapturously applauded, as it was subsequently in London and in its first American hearing, in Philadelphia, March 1922.

many picturesque examples of primitive magic to be found in *The Golden Bough*.[9] The scene now changes to the crest of the hill, hanging between heaven and earth . . . on which a religious dance takes place, one of the dancing girls . . . going into a trance and thus settling the question as to which of the number is to be sacrificed to the spring. She is not sacrificed alive, for her trance turns into a frenzy, at the height of which she suddenly reels and falls dead. The curtain falls as she is carried out on the shoulders of her friends.

The gestures of the new ballet, which, like the scenario, have been designed by M. Nijinsky, are more consistent than those in [the earlier ballets]. Some of them undoubtedly do express emotion in a primitive way – fear, for instance, and joy and religious ecstasy – and the general impression is often the one given of children at play. . . . But most of the time one seems to be looking at marionettes rather than children or savages, and many of the movements seem to be the result of some stern and invisible hand moving the puppets by an inexorable decree, the purport of which is known to the owner of the hand, but has only at certain moments been declared to others.

The music, as we have said, is unlike anything that has been given us either by the Russians or by anyone else, though one can trace its origin in much that Stravinsky has already written in *Pétroushka*. Harmonically it is extraordinarily rough and strident: in one place a theme fully harmonised in D minor grates uncompromisingly on a countersubject in D major over an accompaniment played fortissimo in A major on the top of chords of C major with an augmented fourth; in another, chords of the dominant seventh in the key of A flat are hurled against full chords of E major, while another subject is given out 'marcato e sempre mf' in E flat major, and so on. There is much that is hideously and cruelly harsh, even to ears accustomed to modern music, and much, too, that is exceedingly monotonous. Where the players are at rest or are moving slowly the music is almost consistently dull, but in moments of excitement the composer, with his extraordinary gift for driving home rhythm, carries everything before him. It is this rhythmical energy, in fact, which gives the music its vitality, and that alone, so that when it flags the music flags too and sounds merely empty and pretentious. It will be interesting to see what M. Stravinsky's next work will be like. Of one thing, at any rate, one can be fairly certain, and that is that it can hardly make severer demands than *Le Sacre du Printemps*.

Arthur Symons, 'The Russian Ballets', *Fortnightly Review*, *111 (January 1919)*

The dance is life, animal life, having its own way passionately. Part of that natural madness which men were once wise enough to include in religion, it began with the worship of the disturbing deities, the gods of ecstasy, for whom

---

9 The anthropologist Sir James G. Frazer's monumental work (1890–1915) is excerpted in Section 4.

wantonness and wine, and all things in which energy passes into evident excess, were sacred. From the first it has mimed the instincts; but we lose ourselves in the boundless bewilderments of its contradictions.

As the dancers dance, under the changing lights, so human, so remote, so desirable, so evasive, coming and going to the sound of a thin, heady music which marks the rhythm of their movements like a kind of clinging drapery, they seem to sum up in themselves the appeal of everything in the world that is passing and coloured and to be enjoyed. Realising all humanity to be but a masque of shadows, and this solid world an impromptu stage as temporary as they, it is with a pathetic desire of some last illusion, which shall deceive even themselves, that we are consumed with this hunger to create, to make something for ourselves, if at least the same shadowy reality as that about us. The art of the ballet awaits us, with its shadowy and real life, its power of letting humanity drift into a rhythm so much of its own, and with ornament so much more generous than its wont. And, as all this is symbolical, a series of living symbols, it can but reach the brain through the eyes, in the visual and imaginative way; so that the ballet concentrates in itself a good deal of the modern ideal in matters of artistic impression.

I am avid of impressions and sensations; and in the Russian Ballet at the Coliseum, certainly, there is a new impression of something not easily to be seen elsewhere. I need not repeat that, in art, rhythm means everything. And there can be a kind of rhythm even in scenery, such as one sees on the stage. Convention, even here, as in all plastic art, is founded on natural truth very closely studied. The rose is first learned, in every wrinkle of its petals, petal by petal, before that reality is elaborately departed from, in order that a new, abstract beauty may be formed out of these outlines, all but those outlines being left out.

So, in these Russian Ballets, so many of which are founded on ancient legends, those who dance and mime and gesticulate have at once all that is humanity and more than is humanity. And their place there permits them, without disturbing our critical sense of the probability of things, to seem to assume a super-human passion; for, in the Art of the Ballet, reality must fade into illusion, and then illusion must return into a kind of unreal reality.

The primitive and myth-making imagination of the Russians shows a tendency to regard metaphors as real and to share these tendencies with the savage, that is to say with the savagery that is in them, dependent as they are on rudimentary emotions.[10] Other races, too long civilised, have accustomed themselves to the soul, the mystery. Russia, with centuries of savagery behind it, still

---

10 The first original ballet commissioned by Diaghilev, Stravinsky's *The Firebird* (1910), as well as his later *The Rite of Spring*, drew upon these 'primitive' folk-tales – or variants of them from the composer's imagination; the 1912 production *L'après-midi d'un faune*, to music by the French composer Claude Debussy, which was the first to be choreographed by Nijinsky, shocked audiences through its eroticism.

feels the earth about its roots, and the thirst in it of the primitive animal. It has lost none of its instincts, and it has just discovered the soul. So, in these enigmatical dancers, the men and the women, who emerge before us, across the flaming gulf of the footlight . . . one finds the irresponsibility, the gaiety, the sombreness, of creatures who exist on the stage for their own pleasure and for the pleasure of pleasing us, and in them something large and lyrical, as if the obscure forces of the earth half-awakened had begun to speak. And these live, perhaps, an exasperated life – the life of the spirit and of the senses – as no others do; a life to most people inconceivable; to me, who have travelled in Russia, conceivable.

Lydia Lopokova is certainly a perfect artist, whose dancing is a delight to the eyes, as her miming appeals to the senses. She has passion, and of an excitable kind; in a word, Russian passion. She can be delicious, malicious, abrupt in certain movements when she walks; she has daintiness and gaiety; her poses and poises are exquisite; there is an amazing certainty in everything she does. A creature of sensitive nerves, in whom the desire of perfection is the same as her desire for fame, she is on the stage and off the stage essentially the same; and, in her conversations with me I find imagination, an unerring instinct, an intense thirst for life and for her own art; she has *la joie de vivre.*

Her technique, of course, is perfect; and, as in the case of every artist, it is the result of tireless patience. Technique and the artist: that is a question of interest to the student in any art. The rope-dancer or the acrobat must be perfect in technique before he appears on the stage at all; in his case, a lapse from perfection brings its own penalty, death perhaps; his art begins when his technique is already perfect. Artists who deal in materials less fragile than human life should have no less deviating a sense of responsibility to themselves and to art.

The English theatre with its unreal realism and its unimaginative pretences towards poetry left me untouched and unconvinced. I found the beauty, the poetry, that I wanted only in two theatres, the Alhambra and the Empire. The ballet seemed to me the subtlest of the visual arts, and dancing a more significant speech than words. I could have said as Verlaine said to me,[11] in jest, coming away from the Alhambra: 'J'aime Shakespeare, mais – j'aime mieux le ballet.' A ballet is simply a picture in movement. It is a picture where the imitation of nature is given by nature itself; where the figures of the composition are real, and yet, by a very paradox of travesty, have a delightful, deliberate air of unreality. It is a picture where the colours change, re-combine, before one's eyes; where the outlines melt into one another, emerge, and are again lost in the mazes of the dancing.

---

11 The French symbolist poet Paul Verlaine lived in England for several periods in the 1870s, and
   visited subsequently.

The most magical glimpse I ever caught of a ballet was from the road in front, from the other side of the road, one night when two doors were suddenly thrown open as I was passing. In the moment's interval before the doors closed again I saw, in that odd, unexpected way, over the heads of the audience, far off in a sort of blue mist, the whole stage, its brilliant crowd drawn up in the last pose, just as the curtain was beginning to go down.

I liked to see a ballet from the wings, a spectator, but in the midst of the magic. To see a ballet from the wings is to lose all sense of proportion, all knowledge of the piece as a whole, but, in return, it is fruitful in happy accidents, in momentary points of view, in chance felicities of light and movement and shade. It is almost to be in the performance oneself, and yet passive, with the leisure to look about one. . . .

And there is charm, not wholly imaginary, in that form of illusion known as make-up. To a face really charming it gives a new kind of exciting savour; and it has, to the remnant of the Puritan conscience that is the heritage of us all, a certain sense of dangerous wickedness, the delight of forbidden fruit. . . .

The art of the ballet counts for much in the evolution of many favourite effects of contemporary drawing, and not merely because Degas – who meant to me everything when I was writing on the ballets, standing in the wings, writing verses in which I was conscious of transgressing no law of art in taking that scarcely touched material for new uses – has drawn dancers, with his reserved, essentially classical mastery of form. By its rapidity of flight within bounds, by its bird-like and flower-like caprices of colour and motion, by that appeal to the imagination which comes from its silence (to which music is but like an accompanying shadow, so closely, so discreetly does it follow the feet of the dancers), by its appeal to the eyes and to the senses, its adorable artificiality, the ballet has tempted almost every draughtsman, as the interiors of music-halls have also been singularly tempting, with their extraordinary tricks of light, their suddenness of gesture, their fantastic humanity.

6.3   Classical Music

Igor Stravinsky (1882–1971), who became one of the principal composers for the Ballets Russes, and Arnold Schoenberg (1874–1951) were perhaps the most challenging and innovative composers of the age. The Russian Stravinsky, who eventually settled in Paris in 1920, famously noted in his 1935 Autobiography *that 'music expresses nothing', and that the performer of his scores must give an objective performance, one unsullied by any urge to 'interpretation', or to 'self-expression'. By this time, however, he was deep into his neo-classical phase, creating ironic and parodic work in the manner of the seventeenth and eighteenth centuries. His earlier scores for the ballet, and for various combinations of strings, wind and percussion, had displayed a strong interest in Russian folk rhythms and melodies, and had deployed large orchestras to create new and sometimes harsh and powerfully repetitive sound-worlds. Schoenberg, an Austrian composer, was also a painter of note, and both composed and exhibited his art for a period alongside that of the Russian painter Wassily Kandinsky. Perhaps his most influential composition* Pierre Lunaire *(1912; but not performed in England and America until 1923) belongs to this period. Schoenberg's dissatisfaction with traditional musical harmony and tonal relationships led him progressively to explore his own system, the twelve-tone system, which he developed between 1908 and 1923. Instead of being around a common key signature, as had been done by Western composers hitherto, the twelve-tone system proposes a seemingly rigid sequence, in which the twelve notes of the chromatic scale are arranged in an initial order, and thence a composition constructed which uses each tone again in that order. Tones may be used in chords with preceding or succeeding ones, and may be pitched at a higher or lower point in the scale than when they appeared originally. But once the music has gone through its twelve-note sequence, whatever it be, it must start again building its course from the first note in the scale. This system sounds extremely mathematical and constraining, but in fact it can emerge as music of emotional and expressionistic intensity. Schoenberg's refusal to compromise with the audience, attuned and expectant to a certain kind of tonality and progressive structure in what they heard, made him an extremely controversial figure at the time, and his early works, like those of Stravinsky, caused several riots at their first performances. The extracts here are taken from an early review of Schoenberg, which interestingly sees his innovations as being akin to modern sculpture, and a review of the 1919 London offering of the Ballets Russes, in which the reviewer, now that Stravinsky's work had become more familiar, finds time to reflect upon its motivating principles.*

Huntly Carter, 'Schoenberg, Epstein, Chesterton, and Mass-Rhythm', The Egoist, 16 February 1914

I notice that certain dull or obtuse persons are talking a great deal of nonsense about the *new direction of art*. . . . Of course, what these dull and obtuse persons mean is that painters, sculptors, musicians and a playwright or two are seeking a direction. The direction they seek is one most likely to bring them within easy distance of, if not into actual contact with Art itself. For many generations professed artists (i.e. artists by repute) have been separated by culture, superstition and idolatry, from the spring and source and have been trying to experience humanity and its manifestations through the intellect and thereafter to fit them into the rhythm of life (or what they conceived to be the rhythm). In recent years it however occurred to some inquiring minds that these efforts were misdirected and instead of fitting something into something else they were engaged in the act of circumscribing and detaching. In consequence of this conviction they repudiated the intellect, removed the dunghill of materialism it had erected before their working-places and recovered human sensibility. On top of this came the return to nerves and individual temperament. And now it seems to me that a healthy sensitiveness prompts them to remove those vile checks to the flow of rhythm which the folly of the ancients devised and the advanced stupidity of the moderns elaborated. Consciously or unconsciously, they seek to *feel* this rhythm and to create or devise a framework for the eternal flow into which the eternal spirit in human beings is to be drawn. Thus their works form symbols of a force which humanity possesses and through which it may renew itself.

It is not difficult to name some of those who are engaged in the good work of replacing great thought by great feeling, having the simplicity and intensity which distinguishes the manifestations of the unconscious (wrongly called the sub-conscious) vision. In music there is Arnold Schoenberg, whose *Five Orchestral Pieces* were recently given, amid opposition, at the Queen's Hall.[12] Schoenberg's aim in these pieces is to loosen the great unending stream of emotion by removing the checks (in the form of motives) which modern technique has devised. Apparently he believes that motives are the sluice gates which the mind forms by reflecting on the emotions and the ideas and thoughts which spring from these, that they impede and weaken the flowing power of Art, and that they are to be removed by impulse through which alone the Art temperament works. In any case he has made a break from the form of Strauss,[13] who stops to find a motive for every physical thing. Thus Strauss is concerned with weaving an intricate motive pattern which appeals strongly to the intellect, while Schoenberg expresses the big floating movement (I call it mass-rhythm) of the universal element which appeals to the soul in man. I suppose the reason why the critics do not appreciate Schoenberg's recent work is because it is not logical enough to be understood by the intellect. A friend of mine, Mr. Ernest Gerrard, who is anxious to have Schoenberg's music applied to his music-dramas, reminds me that this music resembles Picasso's pictures. . . . Of course he means that Picasso's work is full of mass-music. It is the work of a sensible being and not of a logician or a metaphysician.

The same element of mass-rhythm (or mass-music) appears in the sculpture by Jacob Epstein,[14] especially that exhibited at the Twenty-One Gallery. Epstein's work is not merely an experiment in the elimination of motives. It exhibits a great flowing power, begins and ends nowhere, and defies logical analysis. I would say that it does reveal a sincere intention to take us into the cosmic rhythm. To me it has the same feeling as those very elemental things which express the universal flow and draw us into it. Perhaps only very elemental things can do this. I have a number of stones which I have gathered on the

---

12 Schoenberg's opus 16, of 1909, represents an early experiment with writing that wholly abandons traditional formal composition, and operates a 'free atonality' with a large orchestra to create its expressionism.

13 The German composer Richard Strauss, who was heavily influenced by the Romantic tradition in music, at this time was known as a composer of symphonic poems and operas.

14 Epstein was a Russian-Polish sculptor who had taken up residency in England in 1910. Initially influenced by Rodin, his work became more interested in destructiveness and machinery in the years before the war. His violent sculpture *Rock Drill* (1913–16) provided Ezra Pound with a title and metaphor for a section of the *Cantos*.

sea shore. They have been moulded by the universal flow and express a variety of vital forms and colours. One represents the head of an Assyrian warrior. It is a calm, dignified and compelling piece of work. It might have been carved by a highly sensitive primitive. It is not fascinating in the Greek sense; it is fascinating in a truthful sense. It is without law yet full of universal law. It draws the human soul into it and sets it expanding in harmony with the rhythm of the universe. The reincarnated Greek would repudiate it as a work of art simply because he would be searching for something 'created' by the faculty of understanding in that which is created by the strength, simplicity, and intensity of feeling. Epstein's work carries us into the universal flow by its power, simplicity, and intensity of feeling.

Leigh Henry, 'The Russian Ballets', The Egoist, July 1919

After the morbid grovelling among musical mausoleums which has characterised the past musical season, and which reaches its apotheosis of monotony and boredom with the Henry J. Wood 'Parsifal'[15] concerts, and the Robert Newman Beethoven Festival Concerts, it is pleasant to have fresh air let in upon musical functions with the advent of the Daghailief Russian Ballet Season at the Alhambra. . . .

If Daghailief had done nothing more than revive the two Stravinsky ballets, 'PETROUSHKA'[16] and 'THE FIRE BIRD', we would have been greatly in his debt. For not only is STRAVINSKY, as Granville Bantock says, 'the outstanding figure in Russian music to-day'; he is, as a creative force, something of an entirely new musical order. With the advent of Stravinsky, music attains not only a development in the commonly-accepted sense, but a new direction evincing entirely new creative possibilities.

Stravinsky is the first great creative musician to recognise, employ, and postulate consistently, a direct objective treatment of sound, apart from all intellectual promise, or abstract theory. He is never lured into abstract speculation or prejudiced dogma, but uses his acute mentality to investigate and co-ordinate the musical facts made apparent by his ever-active and subtle sensibility and his tireless experiments with the *aural* qualities of sound. He, in fact, does what the direct treaters of media do in painting. In all creative directions he maintains his reason free from prejudice, 'feeling-bias', and sterile habit, and works by direct scientific experiment and verification alone.

As a natural result of his objective treatment of sound, it follows that Stravinsky has no artificial technical limitations or conventions. The restrictions of model melody and harmony – themselves entirely arbitrary – which are

---

15 Richard Wagner, the nineteenth-century opera composer who had previously sought to create a
     new kind of art, produced this, his last work, in 1882.
16 This had first been produced in Paris in 1911.

apparent in the diatonically-writing Classics, the tono-central chromaticism of the Romantics, and of composers of the immediately pre-contemporary stage of musical development, such as Strauss, Elgar, d'Indy, and others, or the more particularised whole-tone specialisations of Debussy, and the scale-chord formula of Scriabine, have all equally no part in his work. Still further does he stand from the mathematical theoretical methods of the academically-dominant Teutonic system which persists, through Wagner, Strauss, Pfitzner, Mahler, and Bruckner, to Schoenberg. . . . Stravinsky is naturally too objective to set his face prejudicedly against such devices, but he is never obsessed by them, and only utilises them particularisedly, and for occasional purposes, after experiment which shows them to be the most exact means for the expression of that which he desires in a given instance to convey. He deals with music in substance, not according to mode; his compositions are written to be heard, not to be measured pedantically on paper with a German music-carpenter's foot-rule. Stravinsky is practical, not theoretical; he has methods, but no pre-fixed system. His musical values are intrinsically those of sound; utilised as a 'thing-in-itself'. By its means he seeks to convey, not abstract, philosophical, literary, or symbolic, meanings, but to invoke what JACQUES COPEAU has indicated as the primary essential of art-comprehension, 'un état de sensibilité,'[17] in which his conceptions may be directly, sensitively apprehended and comprehended.

With this mental objectivity it is only natural that Stravinsky should turn to the ballet as an appealing medium of expression. For choreography, in its most developed forms, is more concrete, more consistently tangible in substance, and more direct in appeal, than any type of drama wedded to words. Even the most subtle literary drama is liable to have its significance obscured by the mental linguistic associations and subjective habits of an audience. The art of choreography, directly dependent upon tangible visual presentation and appeal, is free from the intermediary modifying factors which dilute the mood-essence of the literary drama. The purpose of a choreographic poem is concentrated in concrete action, sensorily enhanced by music and imaginatively pointed colour and light. Hence, by reason of the plasticity of its component factors, it has an immense fluidity, and therefore a capacity for conveying extremely minute and subtle transitions and inflections of moods, impossible to convey through the measured terms of logical speech. Words cannot obtain the synthetic force obtainable by means of gestures, steps, and facial expression, which have a capacity for more rapid alternation, succession, and simultaneous combination and therefore for more manifold and condensed significance. In short, choreography affects the whole physique by a quickening of kinaesthetic ideas, after the manner of idea-motor action. . . . Hence it follows that choreography is more

---

17 Copeau was a French actor and director of the day, who presented poetic and stylized productions in which he argued that the staging of a play must be subservient to the text, so that the text of the play might be directly mediated to the audience.

capable of stimulating that 'state of being' which places the observer in a position to gain a new aspect of consciousness, to give him a new experience – one of the primary motives of all art – than any other type of established drama.

Stravinsky himself says 'I want neither to suggest situations or emotions, but merely to manifest, to express them. Though I find it extremely hard to do so, I always aim at straightforward expression in its simplest form. I have no use for working out in dramatic or lyric music. The one essential is to feel, and to express one's feelings.'

Hence he employs the choreographic form as objectively as he utilises the aural possibilities of sound. . . . Stravinsky negated set numbers of the old 'ballerina' type in the choreographic poem; in his creations the music and action flow in consistent, interactive, and subtly-developed streams of movement and sound . . .

Always he is as concise and condensed as possible. Hence the dramatic force of his works; hence their clarity, brilliancy, and their wit. His emotion is always intense, never diffused; his work evinces first-class intelligence. . . . The music he writes for his choreographic poems never distracts from the dramatic theme. . . . The crowd music in his 'Petroushka' is no thing of melodic refrains and set harmonic cadencies; it is an inter-active fusion of kaleidoscopic images exactly equivalent to the shifting impressions from which the exhilarating atmosphere of crowded scenes is built up.

As an orchestral composer Stravinsky's objectivity maintains itself, and contributes greatly to his synthetic dramatic methods. He negates the old conventional formula of instrumental group-divisions, and treats each instrument particularisedly as an individual contributory factor to the general effect, writing for each with experimental verification of its particular qualities and characteristics of timbre. By this means he obtains a diversity and multiplicity of tonal colour quite unprecedented, which gives to his orchestration a rarity of atmosphere and a subtlety of tonal nuance which at times seems to embody moods hovering on the farthest verge of sense.

To his orchestral effects his objective treatment of rhythm also contributes greatly. For Stravinsky's rhythmic expression is a unifying factor in his music which operates far more effectively than the ordinary formal musical structural divisions, and 'chopped-off' musical periods. Negating the detailed arithmetical sectioning of classic forms, he utilises his rhythmic movement of sound as a delineative factor, co-ordinating by its means all the constituent thematic and harmonic subtleties of which his music is made up, and grading his orchestral dynamics with extraordinary subtlety. The effect approximates to that produced by certain painters, such as Cézanne, who in a similar manner co-ordinate the component colours and images of actuality in broad planes of colour design. By this means his music has a unity more consistently intrinsic to music than any mathematical formula of construction can produce.

6.4   Fine Art

(a) The Post-Impressionist Exhibitions in London, 1910–11 and 1912

Perhaps the most significant public event in the British art world across these years came with the first exhibition of recent art at the Grafton Galleries, London, which closed in January 1911. 'Manet and the Post-Impressionists' allowed the work of Paul Cézanne, Paul Gauguin, Vincent Van Gogh, Henri Matisse and Pablo Picasso, amongst others, to be viewed together for the first time in the English-speaking world. The impact was immediate, and also seemed retrospectively to mark a decisive shift from the old world to the new. The exhibition prompted Virginia Woolf to declare in a lecture that eventually became her polemical essay 'Mr Bennett and Mrs Brown' that, 'in or about December 1910, human character changed'. Both exhibitions were curated by Woolf's friend and fellow member of the so-called Bloomsbury set, Roger Fry, of whom she later wrote a biography. The defining feature of the Post-Impressionist painters was their not feeling constrained to present their subjects realistically or naturalistically. Through a vivid use of colour, or through a free treatment of form and space, they went beyond their Impressionist precursors, who had sought to render a moment of time in as full and realized a way as possible. With the Post-Impressionists, perspective becomes fore-shortened or annulled, certain parts of the composition loom disproportionately from the canvas. Woolf's sense that 'human character' was changed in this particular month of the first exhibition derives from her and others' resultant feeling, upon seeing these pictures, that the need to represent fully the external features or characteristics of a subject had been superseded. They were focused now by the possibility of an art which explored both the interior form and structure of a subject, and also the interior response of the individual artist in surveying the subject. The externality of much representation of the human character hitherto – in other words, the categorization of individuals according to their social or class function – was now removed, for painters, but also for writers and artists. As Fry's catalogue note to the second, 1912, Post-Impressionist exhibition put it, these artists no longer aim to 'offer a pale reflex of actual appearance, but to arouse the conviction of a new and definite reality. They do not seek to imitate form, but to create form; not to imitate life, but to find an equivalent to life.' Both the extracts selected here relate to the first exhibition, in order to capture the bewilderment which it aroused in some, and the excitement and new understanding in others.

Unsigned review, 'Manet and the Post-Impressionists', The Athenaeum, 12 November 1910

When the visitor to the Grafton Galleries is attempting a verdict on the work at present exhibited there, he may well hesitate between the alternatives of bless-ing and banning which alone seem open to him. His decision one way or another will give on this occasion no measure of his critical capacity; that will be supplied rather by his reasons, and to give reasons for either opinion is to risk leaving the firm ground suited to the argument.

. . . Many generations of sustained thought on long-established premises have given a certain concrete reality to standards of truth, morals, and aesthetics. Of these we may speak with ever-increasing clearness, and, though doubtless we must examine our structure as we proceed, there must in practice be a limit to the mere anarchism which questions every cornerstone of creed, and postulates its opposite. Many feel that too much groping in the elemental is, as Samuel Butler put it, 'stirring mud' – that, for good or ill, the time for such questioning has passed, the development of mankind as a whole having sealed the decision.

We are by no means implying that all points raised by this band of revolutionary painters are of a like unpractical nature. Our analysis of its highly composite elements will aim at eliminating and ignoring what is merely destructive. It is patent, however, that to many critics what is most attractive about these painters is that their acceptance would seem to imply a wiping-out of our whole system of aesthetics – a cleaning of the slate and a fresh start. Their enthusiastic reception on such grounds is not a healthy sign, for to undervalue what we possess is one of the most vulgar of errors.

The (on the whole) well-written introduction to the Catalogue does not carry us very far towards defining the aims of the Post-Impressionists. Of almost every decent painter of the later generation we might say that he 'aims at synthesis in design – that is to say, he is prepared to subordinate consciously his power of representing the parts of his picture, as plausibly as possible, to the expressiveness of the whole design.' To that extent we are most of us Post-Impressionists, but we might object that the imperfection of the parts, rather than the expressiveness of the whole, seems to have been the object of some of the painters gathered here under that title.

It is a conveniently vague title which does not characterize, but merely dates, and beneath the same banner we find men of widely different aims. In the first place we have the painting which is not (as is rightly stated to be the typical attitude of the newer men) *reactionary* against Impressionism, but an *exaggeration* of Impressionism, and of such work as *Anvers* by Othon Frietz, as an excellent example. This repellent orgy of colour attempts not merely to match the brilliance of nature in a rabid mood, but stridently to outblaze it. Not only is the scheme transposed to a range of colours such as one never sees in nature, but the sequence of tones is also distorted so as to envenom contrasts; but it is distorted consistently, so that just as a face seen in a convex mirror retains its essential relations in perverted form, so this picture remains astonishingly true to nature. Matisse himself is often little more 'advanced' than this beyond the Impressionist position.

Gauguin was a greater – potentially an infinitely greater – artist. . . . He represented the reaction against the science of the Impressionists, and here there can be no doubt the impulse was valid. Long before a child has mastered the idea of its mother as a material object in three dimensions, it learns to distinguish between her frown and smile, and difficult as it is to disentangle them, doubt-less spiritual expression must take precedence of material presentment. Gauguin's instinct for the human figure was very imperfect, and, alas! The soul must largely be presented by means of the body. Nevertheless, he is on the whole the most impressive figure of the group as they are displayed here. He also refused the disintegrated touch of the Impressionists, and loved large tranquil silhouettes, disposed in his case with considerable decorative sense. . . . His colour is almost always agreeable – dependent not a little upon taste, so long an exile from the esteem of modern French painters. Gauguin painted South Sea islanders, and made decorations not unsuitable for our own houses. His confr-eres painted European subjects in a manner only fit for the huts of savages.

The last criticism is not meant as a gibe. There is much of this Post-Impressionist work which seems deliberately intended to outrage every canon of accepted aesthetics, and yet has a certain intrinsic logic. Cézanne's *Portrait d'Homme, Cravate Bleue* is a fine example. Many of Van Gogh's works are less favourable instances. The typical classical design of all times has generally the aspect of being based on a starting-point of firm line. The artist seeks to define in what degree forms depart from the straight line; he compares their variations of angle from the perpendicular and horizontal, tending, perhaps uncon-sciously, to minimize the number and degree of such variations. It is by virtue of such comparison that painting falls into relation with architecture, and becomes tolerable as decoration. What makes much of Van Gogh's painting so terribly out of place in any architecture is that *formlessness* seems to be the norm from which he registers but a few departures in varying degree. Cézanne's portrait already cited is finely related within itself, but its first aspect is distress-ing. Not a line holds firmly in place – the whole face is a mere wriggle. But if we can bring ourselves to accept the transposition of a linear composition from our own standard of form to another in which everything writhes unsteadily, then we must admit that such transposition has been successfully accomplished with-out any disturbance of relative values, and that the head is powerfully charac-terized and eloquent.

More than that – we may admit that the thing gains thereby a certain symbolic power, as of kinship with the restlessness of nature, in which all is in a state of flux, and nothing keeps still. It looks a monstrosity within the square walls of our cold room, but if it were set in a native hut of which the walls were of plaited grass and the pillars of pliant osier, where every object gibbers in the rarefied air, and vivid dreams meet vague realities in the stupor of the siesta, then a severer art might seem stilted beside this – lacking in blood and sap, fail-ing to confess the brutish bond of the earth. With Van Gogh the churned-up paint moves more spasmodically: beside the well-controlled stroke of the great masters this is the twitch of a paralytic. The faces grimace not without an odd reality – more convincing, perhaps, to the barbarous vision than others more subtly constructed. This, if any, is the unifying direction which these painters have in common – they aim at coarser sensation, but are themselves obviously moved. When they are thus sincere, they may usefully serve to remind the proud of intellect that art is not always effective in proportion as it is intellectual, or even in proportion as it is grammatical. On the other hand, to people greedy of novelty they will probably be rather a corrupting influence.

A. Clutton-Brock, 'The Post-Impressionists', Burlington Magazine, January 1911

The art of painting nowadays is as confused and uncertain in its aims as the art of poetry was in the eighteenth century. We have learned that the proper end of poetry is the expression of emotion, to which all reasoning and statement of fact should be subsidiary; but we have not learned that painting should have the same end, using representation only as a means to that end, and representing only those facts of reality which have emotional associations for the painter. In primitive pictures, it is true, we look for the expression of emotion rather than the illusion, and that is the reason why so many people get a real pleasure from primitive art. They judge it by the right standard, and ask of it what it offers to them. But from modern pictures they demand illusions – that is to say, the kind of representation they are used to; and when they do not get it they accuse the artist of incompetence. There is a prevalent notion, based upon the history of art in the fourteenth and fifteenth centuries, that painting must always advance in fullness of representation, that when it does not it is deliberately retrograde. But that notion is refuted by the facts of the modern history of painting. . . . The Impressionists themselves, though they represented some new facts, discarded many old ones. Their very name is a token of their refusal to be bound by any laws of representation. But their aesthetics were confused by their scientific interest in the new facts which they chose to represent. Their advocates often talk as if the whole business of a painter were to produce the illusion of sunlight, as if sunlight were the essential fact without which no picture could be a work of art. Thus they ignored one set of facts for the sake of another set, not for the sake of expression. They did not give the artist freedom, but imposed a new bondage on him. They never arrived at the truth that to painting, as to poetry, no facts are essential, that all are subsidiary to expression, and therefore may be represented or ignored as the artist chooses. This is the truth upon which the art of Post-Impressionism is based; and to distinguish them from the Impressionists we might, perhaps, call them Expressionists. . . .

So the failures of the Post-Impressionists are obvious because they do not attempt to conceal them with irrelevant feats of representation. Their only end is expression, and when they do not accomplish that they accomplish nothing. If Cézanne, Gauguin, and Van Gogh were charlatans, they were like no other charlatans that ever lived. If their aim was notoriety, it is strange that they should have spent solitary lives in penury and toil. If they were incompetents, they were curiously intent upon the most difficult problems of their art. The kind of simplification which they attempted is not easy, nor, if accomplished, does it make a picture look better than it is. The better their pictures are, the more they look as if anyone could have painted them who had had the luck to conceive them. . . . Like the great Chinese artists, they have tried to know thoroughly what they paint before they begin to paint it, and out of the fullness of their knowledge to choose only what has an emotional interest for them. Their representations have the brevity and concentrated force of the poet's descriptions. He does not go out into the country with a note-book and then versify all that he has observed. His descriptions are often empty of fact, just because he only tells us what is of emotional interest to himself and relevant to the subject of his poem; and they are justified, not by the information they convey, but by the emotion they communicate through the rhythm and sound of words. The Post-Impressionists try to represent as the poet describes. They try to give to every picture an emotional subject matter and to make all representation relevant to it. Hence the formal or decorative qualities of their pictures, which, like the formal qualities of poetry, are the result of expression.

Not that the emotional experience of our time, as it is expressed in literature and art, is not rich or full or confident or joyous. The artist nowadays, partly because he is bewildered by the multitude of new ideas and increase of new knowledge, partly because he is not at ease in our modern society, suffers from a great insecurity of emotion. Intellectual scepticism and exasperation produce in him emotional scepticism and exasperation. In a painter this state of mind is very unfavourable to fullness of representation. The sincere artist finds himself hating almost as many things as he loves for their emotional associations, and he finds that many things in the mechanical bustle of modern life have no emotional association for him whatever. Thus even the finest art of our time is inferior in richness, in serenity, and in accomplishment to the finest art of the past. But it has at least this merit, without which art is only a shadow of itself, that it does express the artist's own emotional experience of life.

Cézanne, Gauguin and Van Gogh were men of very different minds; but they were alike in this, that they all attempted to subordinate representation to expression, and were all determined to express only their own emotional experience. Cézanne, a friend of the Impressionists and of Zola, could not content himself with Impressionist triumphs of representation. Above all, he revolted from the Impressionist insistence on the momentary aspects of reality. He was, so to speak, a kind of Plato among the artists of his time, believing that in reality there is a permanent order, a design which reveals itself to the eye and mind of the artist, and which it is his business to expose in his work. But this design he was determined to discover in reality itself, not in the works of other artists. His task was enormously difficult because he would take

Marcel Duchamp, *Nude Descending a Staircase, No. 2*

nothing whatever at second hand. Nature must tell him all her own secrets, and he would not listen even to her when she told him commonplaces. He was not interested, so to speak, in her caprices, in her chance effects of beauty that anyone can see. He painted landscape as Titian and Rembrandt painted portraits; searching always for the permanent character of the place, for that which, independent of weather or time distinguished it from other places. This permanent element he found in structure and mass; but, like Titian and Rembrandt, he would not abstract these from colour. For him, as for these masters, structure and mass revealed themselves in colour, and all three must be verified by incessant observation. He felt that there was a proper colour belonging to every representation of structure and mass, with the same kind of permanence based upon its relation to the permanent character of the scene represented; and in his pictures we can see the result of these convictions. There is no brilliant illusion in them, nor is there any sacrifice of colour to form. They do not represent some ideal state of being which he desires, nor do they express lyrically some passing emotion of his mind. He is a classical painter by nature and not because he admires the classics. Without help from the past he tries, by a classical balance of representation, to express his own permanent relation to reality by insisting upon its permanent elements. In his landscapes, although the colour has an independent force and freshness like the colour of the Impressionists, yet it never confuses the design, and that is always based upon structure and mass. He represents a world in which heavy things have not lost their weight, for that seems to him an essential part of their character. For him, a hill is not a screen for the play of light; it is built up of earth and rocks. Nor is a tree a mere rippling surface, but a living thing with the structure of its growth. Everywhere he looks for character; yet he subordinates the character of the details to the character of the whole. And the character of the whole means for him its permanent character, which he expresses in a design not imposed upon it but discovered in it, as Michelangelo discovered the statue in the block of marble. It is the perfect balance of Cézanne's art that makes it difficult.

(b) The 'Armory Show', New York, 17 February to 15 March 1913

The show of Post-Impressionist work organized by the Association of American Painters and Sculptors in an armory building of New York – where the floor space was divided into 15 separate galleries – created the same effect as the shows at the Grafton Galleries in London had in previous years. The Armory Show was recognized partly for its being one of the most major art exhibitions ever organized in America; native artists were included, although in small numbers, alongside the major European works. It was noted by several commentators, however, that only the conservative and established American artists were on display, and this only served to exaggerate the 'shock value' of the international work. The show, and particularly its centrepiece, Marcel Duchamp's[18] *'Nude Descending a Staircase, No. 2', created a huge scandal for its violation of popular taste and established aesthetic beliefs: predictably, the attendance by the public was huge, with over 250,000 people paying to visit.*

Unsigned review, 'History of Modern Art at the International Exhibition', The New York Times Magazine Section, 23 February 1913

It cannot be denied that the Post Impressionists and the Cubists predominate at the Armory Exhibition. Their numbers may not be greater than the combined numbers of the older and more familiar schools, but aggressiveness is of the very essence of their quality, and the size of their separate contributions and the force of their often violent and always powerful color in the same exhibition with the tender shimmer of Monet and Corot gives an impression of an equal number of bass drums and violins playing at the same moment. The exhibition makes . . . a great deal of noise.

In studying it from the simple point of view of a person 'who wants to know', however, it offers an unusual opportunity. We can see, if we care to take the trouble, how the art of painting developed from Ingres down to Seurat, and we can observe the sudden backward jump toward savage art in the work of Matisse and the Cubists. Luckily for the critic, there is no such thing as taking sides. In the presence of such a polyhedron as modern art he would be in trouble enough.

Here, side by side with Monet and Seurat, we find these Post-Impressionists, who are in love with science but not with objective reality, and who have added to the science of color, which they employ in a different way from that of the Impressionists, the element of symbolism. . . . In Matisse we have Post-Impressionism, the expression of movement, the expression of mass, denuded of all that has given joy to past generations in the relations of one form to another and one color to another. We enter a stark region of abstractions that are hideous to our unaccustomed eyes, whatever they may become to the vision of the future. Here and there we see a decorative placing of a great shape of color with another great shape, and see something that would please us in a piece of Indian weaving. But it seems to us to be written in art that a man cannot successfully combine crudity with sophistication. M. Matisse gets back some of the force, some of the decorative value of the work done by savage races, but he presents it with a sophistication that mitigates its effect. He will neither cut loose

---

18 Duchamp was a French-born artist who was to settle in New York in 1915. He was, after the Armory Show, to change his art, and to present everyday objects as sculpture. The most notorious example of this development being 'Fountain', a urinal signed by 'R. Mutt', in 1917. Duchamp's immigration to America brought with it the introduction into America of European ideas about art generally, including those underlying the contemporary European movements of Cubism and Dada.

from nature nor from convention, but his convention is not conventional enough and his nature is not natural enough to reconcile us to his method. What he has added to the art of the present, however, is force of color. It will be long before we can again work with a weak palette.

Matisse has been freely called a charlatan, which implies wilful eccentricity in pursuit of sensation, but our business is not with his motives. We have not even anything to do with his avowed intentions. All that concerns us is what he has done that is different from the work of his predecessors and that is at the same time worthy of consideration. We may as well say in the first place that his pictures are ugly, that they are coarse, that they are narrow, that to us they are revolting in their inhumanity. His simplifications are so extreme that the lines at which he finally stops as expressing the essential contours are to the ordinary observer no more suggestive of the human face and figure than the paintings of animals in the palaeolithic age are suggestive of the originals. Nevertheless he has found in the human structure the basic lines, which he throws so brutally upon his canvas. They are not created out of nothing, and it is here that we feel their defect most strongly.

Humanity grows richer and more interesting in its complexity as civilization advances. To throw over that complexity, which a great artist like Cézanne synthesizes into a significant and intense simplicity, in order to return to the primary simplicity empty of spiritual interest which satisfied the savage, seems to us to subtract from the resources of art instead of adding to them. . . . Matisse, up to the point of our present familiarity with him, seems to have thrown psychology, the artist's last great opportunity, quite over, or else to have reduced it to a purely animal significance. This seems to us the real reason why his paintings are repellent to us and to many others, the turning of humanity back to its brutish beginnings. The task, as he has performed it, is not an easy one. He has shown great skill and power, but we do not see before him a goal worth striving for. We repeat, however, that he has made it possible for the younger school of artists to revitalize their color and achieve combinations even of pale tints that have force.

Frank H. Mather, 'Old and New Art', The Nation, 6 March 1913

Feeling as I do that Post-Impressionism is mostly ignorant splurge, and Cubism merely occult and curious pedantry, I feel also that the Association has done valuable service in bringing over a full representation of this latest eccentric work. It was reaching us piecemeal in unimportant examples, or, worse, at second hand, in the deceptions of programmes and the sophistries of critical special pleading. Now we have the pictures and sculpture and may test ourselves by them. . . .

The platform of Post-Impressionism is a simple one – complete spontaneity independent of all images of outer nature; swift, succinct, and powerful execution of symbolic color – these are the chief tenets of the movement. Certain of William Blake's maxims prefigure this tendency: 'Mere enthusiasm is the all in all,' or, again, 'Knowledge of ideal beauty is not to be acquired. It is born in us. The man who says we have no innate ideas must be a fool or a knave.' At some risk, then, of falling into an undesirable category, I must approach the spontaneity of Matisse. . . . Matisse is an original and powerful draughtsman. One has only to see his crayon drawings form the nude to be convinced of that. They are of quite extraordinary potency and simplicity. His pictorial ideas, innate ones perhaps, we may grant, are either trivial, monstrous, or totally lacking. The Portrait in Madras Red illustrates his power. The torso is swung in with a quite magnificent gesture that ignores all details; for the rest, a coarse emphasis of the intentness of the face, raw color, mean surfaces – a prodigal expenditure of violent means to achieve a passing and negligible effect.

For this anti-realistic movement, of which so much is said, is merely the tardy coming into art of a tendency that has long since spent its literary force, namely, neurotic symbolism. The present revolutionaries are no more going to make art over than Mallarmé . . . made all things new in letters. And even as a revolt, Post-Impressionism has the fatal defect of misunderstanding its foe. Ostensibly, it is an escape into the imagination from the appalling dullness of recent painting, and this dullness is laid to a too servile following of nature. Now, nature is perhaps the most ambiguous word in all language; and right here it may be asked if it is possible for the art of painting to sin from too much naturalness. It seems to me not. Since the pigment scale is far shorter than that of light, and since a plane surface must be made to give the sense of depth, any painting, however good or bad it is, is highly symbolic. It is no record of a thing seen, but a token of intelligence. Moreover, no painting can possibly give seriously what is seen at a particular moment, just that and nothing more. . . . And nature, in any accurate sense, can merely mean what is seen at a particular instant. As soon as memory comes in, and more or less it does inevitably, nature is becoming, not an external fact, but a composite and shifting personal creation. All painters are symbolists; some dull, some sublime, some mediocre. Such symbolism may be conducted along lines of relative inhibition of the artist's personal and emotional attitude; such men we loosely call realists; or along lines of enhancement of the artist's emotional attitude, and such with almost equal looseness we call romanticists, Post-Impressionists, or Expressionists, or what not. . . .

Post-Impressionism, then, is the feeblest imaginative reform for real artistic evils deeply based in the hesitancy of the present social order. Whenever, out of the clash of democracy with socialism and anarchy, a central social tradition is attained, the artist will readily find his place. Especially the minor artist will then cease to be a dullard or a pretender, and will find a useful and respectable function in devotedly sustaining the central tradition. . . . Because the minor artist of the present is urged to cultivate that originality which is only the prerogative of the great, he is often a woeful apparition. And so far as Post-Impressionism is setting hundreds of young painters to coddling their sacred impulses, so far as it accentuates an already exaggerated cult of the individual, it will work nothing but harm.

Upon the Cubist work of Picasso, Picabia, and Marcel Duchamp I cannot dwell. We seem to have to do either with a clever hoax or a negligible pedantry. I am told that these experimenters are working at the problem of mass, weight, and spatiality. Finding that these third-dimensional qualities are most vividly conveyed by the simpler geometric solids, they adopt these as units of expression. Picasso conceives a head as so many facets, leaving the junctures sharp. . . . Picasso shows a bronze bust in conical forms. It has a sinister impressiveness, and looks like a badly carved Gothic thing. Picasso's early painting had much grim power and decorative balance; only a portrait represents him in this phase; his latest work, in which geometry dominates, is singularly dreary in color and morbid in expression. Both Picasso and Picabia mineralize their world and present it in terms of crystallography. The transposition is often ingenious; both men are evidently accomplished mechanical draughtsmen, but none of their work reveals to an eye that has honestly weighted either spatial quality, mass, or handsome decorative effect. Marcel Duchamp, whose units of expression are slabs and shavings, is said to have out-geometrized the Cubists themselves. His pictures are monochromes in brown, with the general look of an elevation of a volcanic cliff. In the stratifications we are told by the catalogue to look for nudes, faces, and groups; but I advise no one to make the attempt. If any images there be, these are mental and symbolic. These paintings, so far as genuine, are merely expressions of anti-naturalism reduced to the absurd along ratiocinative lines, just as Post-Impressionism is merely the emotional reduction to the absurd of the same anti-naturalist fallacy. . . .

And here the question of taste comes in. The trouble with the newest art and its critical champions is that fundamentally they have no real breadth of taste. These people are devoted to fanaticisms, catchwords, all manner of taking themselves too seriously. Where something like taste exists, the new brusque procedures are readily assimilated.

6.5 Photography

From the early years of the twentieth century, photography had played an important part in the development of notions of modern art. In Europe in the 1920s, surreal art would find some of its most compelling expression in the work of photographers like the American Man Ray and the Hungarian László Moholy-Nagy. But in earlier years up to the First World War, the driving force in this area was probably Alfred Stieglitz, who along with Edward Steichen founded the Photo-Secession movement in New York in

1902. This movement was concerned to foster an understanding of new art movements. Stieglitz's own work of this time includes many shots taken out in the city streets, seemingly realistic and of-the-moment. Later, through the journal Camera Work, *and through his gallery '291', at 291 Fifth Avenue, Stieglitz began promoting innovative American work, including that of Edward Weston, Ansel Adams, and Imogen Cunningham. Before the war, Stieglitz's own work was soft-focus and dreamy, like that of some contemporary painting, including that of his idol, J. M. Whistler. Later, in the 1920s, however, he, along with Paul Strand and Weston, adopted more abstract natural forms, in an attempt to free photography from its proximity to painting. As this extract, a contemporary hymn to the multitudinousness of Stieglitz's art, reveals, it was the sense that everything in the modern world offered itself as a basis for art that enabled the medium to move beyond its posed nineteenth-century origins.*

Paul Rosenfeld, 'Stieglitz', Dial, vol. 70, no. 4 (April 1921)

Alfred Stieglitz is of the company of the great affirmers of life. His photographs bear witness to the presence in him of a sense of the significance of animate and inanimate things as catholic as any which man has ever possessed. . . . For the man who out of the black box and the bath of chemicals produced these cool dynamic prints, there seems scarcely to be anything, any object, in all the world without high import, scarcely anything that is not in some fashion related to himself. The humblest objects appear to be, for him, instinct with marvellous life. The dirt of an unwashed window pane, a brick wall, a piece of tattered matting, the worn shawls of immigrant women, horses steaming in the smudged snow of a New York thoroughfare, feet bruised and deformed by long encasement in bad modern shoes, seem, for this man who has shoved the nozzle of his camera so close to them, as wonderful, as germane to his spirit, as the visage of a glorious woman, the regard of ineffable love out of lucent unfathomable eyes, the gesture of chaste and impassioned surrender. . . . Indeed, Stieglitz' rich shadowed prints, his black and platinum planes and segments of planes, are built up by means of the forms of objects most often humdrum, banal, common. He has found universal, found forming a related design, the wheelrims and the sides of carts, sign-painted walls, the storm-light of a feverish August afternoon in New York, rippling lake-water and rain-drops, typewriters and paper packages and pipes stuffed with burning tobacco, all sorts of common materials, all sorts of rough clothing.

How clearly all of these things sing for him, how chock-full of life they are for him, how naturally they compose themselves for him into a rounded work of art, that the quality of his prints attests. There have never before been such photographs. Never before have such completely organized surfaces, such robustly living and functioning bodies, been born of the photographic process. Out of the forms and textures of the myriad humdrum objects, the myriad

Alfred Stieglitz, *The Steerage, 1907*

confused objects attacked by the lens, there has been made an expression ideal as is music; an order as pure, as complete, as that of Cézanne or of any of the greater masters of the aesthetic pictural organization. Some of the prints, no doubt, deserve to rank with some of the work of the great masters of poly-phonic music. Clothes-lines and hands, white shirts and leafing trees, gutter and gallery of 291 set daintily with Brancusi[19] sculptures, have all been taken into the photographer and issued again, suffused utterly with his own law and revelatory of it. There is no vagueness, no indecision in them. Every particle of them is active. The entire chaos and pell-mell that rolls all the time before our eyes, is issued out of Stieglitz defined, related, form; and expressive of the high significance of which he has caught sight within them. Indeed, the prints of Stieglitz are among the very sensitive records of human experience. So vivid and delicate are they that one wants to touch them. So highly sensitized is the medium, so drenched with a personality, that one feels present in the work the very natural forces which have created man, and which he, in turn, is striving fitfully to make part of his body. The prints are like the Chinese concerted pieces in which one hears sing not only the human being, but the animal kingdom and the mineral kingdom as well. Workers in other media, it is possible, have produced objects greater in amount, in volume, in passion. But it remains doubtful whether any one has approached the dark wet quick of man more nearly than Stieglitz. Neither the pigment of the Chinese nor the water-colour of Cézanne, neither the orchestra of Debussy nor the dialogue of Schnitzler, records more subtly, more delicately, the quality of the life in a man, the movement always in progress within him. Before Stieglitz' work we are made to think perforce of the writing of a needle sensitive to the minute vibrations of the crust of the earth. These forms recall not so much the picture-making of other times, as they do highly complex mathematical and chemical formulae.

But the photographs of Stieglitz affirm life not only because they declare the wonder and significance of myriad objects never before felt to be lovely. They affirm it because they declare each of them the majesty of the moment, the augustness of the here, the now. They attest in clearest tones that life is present fully in every instant of time; that the present contains both the past and the future; that there is no instant of time not fully bound and related to every other.[20] For they themselves are but the record of moments. The camera can record nothing else. It is able to 'take' nothing but the objects before it. For it, nothing exists save what is before the lens, no movement save the movement when its shutter is opened to the light. But each of the instants fixed by Stieglitz and his machine have the weight of a sum of life. Stieglitz has caught many moments, some apparently the most fugitive, some apparently the most trivial. He has caught fleeting facial expressions, sudden twitching smiles, momentary flashes of anger and pain. He has arrested apparently insignificant motions of the hands, motions of hands sewing, gestures of hands poised fitfully on the

---

19 Constantin Brancusi (1876–1957) was a Romanian sculptor who had settled in Paris, whose abstract and often ovoid forms of birds and animals were much discussed at the time, by the poets Pound and Mina Loy amongst others.

20 Note the similarity here between Rosenfeld's remarks on the achievements of the photograph and Henri Bergson's ideas of temporality (see Section 5).

breast, motions of hands peeling apples. And in each of them, he has found a symbol of himself. For he himself, so his works attest, has always been willing to live every moment as though it were the last of his life, the last left him to expend his precious vitality. He himself has always been willing, in order to fix the instant, the object before him, and to record all that lay between him and it, to pour out his energy with gusto, with abandon. His life always appears to be present at the surface of his body.

6.6   Theatre

Edward Gordon Craig, 'The First Dialogue' (1905)

Craig's important essay on his ideals for modern theatre first appeared as a pamphlet, but was then included in his On the Art of Theatre *(1911; revised four times before 1924, and translated into French, Russian, Japanese and Italian). Craig (1872–1966) was an actor, designer and director who was very well integrated into contemporary literary circles, having collaborated with the Anglo-Irish poet W. B. Yeats in the early 1900s (Yeats's Symbolist drama in later life also owed much to Craig's example). Craig worked extensively in Europe and Russia, and influenced generations of directors and designers, from Stanislavsky (with whom he co-produced his most famous performances, those of* Hamlet *at the Moscow Art Theatre in 1912) down to our contemporary Peter Brook. Craig saw all aspects of direction and design as being impelled by the need to strip the stage of its representative qualities, and to reduce scenery down to a minimum. He wrote attacking the contemporary theatre movements of Naturalism and Realism, which held sway in the work – popular at that time amongst intellectual English audiences – of the Norwegian Henrik Ibsen. Craig favoured movement in the theatre over all other traits, and resented anything which distracted the eye (including even spoken dialogue) from this essential quality. At one extreme, following the arguments of the earlier German writer Heinrich von Kleist, Craig favoured the use of puppets in the theatre to tell stories, thus superseding the egoism, and the irritating urge to interpret their roles, displayed by human actors. The extracts given here come from the opening of Craig's piece, which is cast in the dialogue form of the ancient Greek philosophy of Plato, displaying his contention that it is the origins of drama which display its real essence. In his attempt to revive these ancient forms, Craig's arguments echo those of many modernist writers and artists such as Stravinsky, with their concentration upon classical and even earlier sources, as a means to revivify modern writing.*

An expert and a playgoer are conversing.

STAGE DIRECTOR: You have been over the theatre with me, and have seen its general construction, together with the stage, the machinery for manipulating scenes, the apparatus for lighting, and the hundred other things, and have also heard what I have had to say of the theatre as a machine; let us rest here in the auditorium, and talk a while of the theatre and of its art. Tell me, do you know what is the Art of the Theatre?

PLAYGOER: To me it seems that acting is the Art of the Theatre.

STAGE DIRECTOR: Is a part, then, equal to a whole?

PLAYGOER: No, of course not. Do you, then, mean that the play is the Art of the Theatre?

STAGE DIRECTOR: A play is a work of literature, is it not? Tell me, then, how one art can possibly be another?

PLAYGOER: Well, then, if you tell me that the Art of Theatre is neither the acting nor the play, then I must come to the conclusion that it is the scenery and the dancing. Yet I cannot think you will tell me this is so.

STAGE DIRECTOR: No; the Art of Theatre is neither acting nor the play, it is not scene nor dance, but it consists of all the elements of which these things are composed: action, which is the very spirit of acting; words, which are the body of the play; line and colour, which are the very heart of the scene; rhythm, which is the very essence of dance.

PLAYGOER: Action, words, line, colour, rhythm! And which of these is all-important to art?

STAGE DIRECTOR: One is no more important than the other, no more than one colour is more important to a painter than another, or one note more important than another to a musician. In one respect, perhaps, action, is the most valuable part. Action bears the same relation to the Art of Theatre as drawing does to painting, and melody does to music. The Art of Theatre has sprung from action – movement – dance.

PLAYGOER: I always was led to suppose that it had sprung from speech, and that the poet was the father of the theatre.

STAGE DIRECTOR: This is the common belief, but consider it for a moment. The poet's imagination finds voice in words, beautifully chosen; he then either recites or sings these words to us, and all is done. That poetry, sung or recited, is for our ears, and, through them, for our imagination. It will not help the matter if the poet shall add gesture to his recitation or to his song; in fact, it will spoil all.

PLAYGOER: Yes, that is clear to me. I quite understand that the addition of gesture to a perfect lyric poem can but produce an inharmonious result.

STAGE DIRECTOR: . . . Do you know who was the father of the dramatist?

PLAYGOER: No, I do not know, but I suppose he was the dramatic poet.

STAGE DIRECTOR: You are wrong. The father of the dramatist was the dancer. And now tell me from what material the dramatist made his first piece?

PLAYGOER: I suppose he used words in the same way as the lyric poet.

STAGE DIRECTOR: Again you are wrong, and that is what everyone else supposes who has not learnt the nature of dramatic art. No; the dramatist made his first piece by using action, words, line, colour, and rhythm, and making his appeal to our eyes and ears by a dextrous use of these five factors.

PLAYGOER: And what is the difference between this work of the first dramatists and that of the modern dramatists?

STAGE DIRECTOR: The first dramatists were children of the theatre. The modern dramatists are not. The first dramatist understood what the modern dramatist does not yet understand. He knew that when he and his fellows appeared in front of them the audience would be more eager to *see* what he would *do* than to *hear* what he might say. He knew that the eye is more swiftly and powerfully appealed to than any other sense; that it is without question the keenest sense of the body of man. The first thing which he encountered on appearing before them was many pairs of eyes, eager and hungry. Even the men and women sitting so far from him that they would not always be able to hear what he might say, seemed quite close to him by reason of the piercing keenness of their questioning eyes. To these, and all, he spoke in poetry or prose, but always in action: in poetic action which is dance, or in prose action which is gesture. . . . My point is this, that the people still flock to *see*, not to hear, plays. But what does that prove? Only that audiences have not altered. They are there with their thousands of pairs of eyes, just the same as of old. And this is all the more extraordinary because the playwrights and the plays have altered. No longer is a play a balance of actions, words, dance, and scene, but it is either all words or all scene. Shakespeare's plays, for instance, are a very different thing to the less modern miracle and mystery plays, which were made entirely for the theatre.[21] *Hamlet* has not the nature of a stage representation. *Hamlet* and the other plays of Shakespeare have so vast and so complete a form when read, that they can but lose heavily when presented to us after having undergone stage treatment. . . . The reason why you are not given a work of art on the stage is not because the public does not want it, not because there are not excellent craftsmen in the theatre who could prepare it for you, but because the theatre lacks the artist – the artist of the theatre, mind you, not the painter, poet, musician. The many excellent craftsmen . . . are, all of them, more or less helpless to change the situation. They are forced to supply what the managers of the theatre demand, but they do so most willingly. The advent of the artist in the theatre world will change all this. He will slowly but surely gather around him these better craftsmen of whom I speak, and together they will give new life to the art of the theatre . . . [i]f these same men once realised that they were craftsmen, and would train as such – I do not speak only of the stage-carpenters, electricians, wigmakers, costumiers, scene-painters, and actors (indeed, these are in many ways the best and most willing craftsmen) – I speak chiefly of the stage director. If the stage director was to technically train himself for his task of interpreting the plays of the dramatist

---

21 Craig's point here is, presumably, that the medieval religious play cycles, such as the York or Coventry mysteries, which used to be performed in the open air, were, because they were simply renditions of familiar biblical stories, more theatrical and less dependent upon a written text than even a Renaissance drama.

– in time, and by a gradual development he would again recover the ground lost to the theatre, and finally would restore the Art of Theatre to its home by means of his own creative genius.

PLAYGOER: Then you place the stage director before the actors?

STAGE DIRECTOR: Yes; the relation of the stage director to the actor is precisely the same as that of the conductor to his orchestra, or of the publisher to his printer.

PLAYGOER: And you consider that the stage director is a craftsman and not an artist?[22]

STAGE DIRECTOR: When he interprets the plays of the dramatist by means of his actors, his scene-painters, and his other craftsmen, then he is a craftsman – a master craftsman; when he will have mastered the uses of actions, words, line, colour, and rhythm, then he may become an artist. Then we shall no longer need the assistance of the playwright – for our art will then be self-reliant.

---

22 Note Craig's dependence for his conception of the means towards his 'new' art of the theatre upon nineteenth-century ideals of the craftsman as creator, promulgated by theorists such as William Morris and John Ruskin (see the 'Society, Politics and Class' section of this Sourcebook).

7

'Popular' Culture

Introduction

In an influential study, *After the Great Divide* (1986), Andreas Huyssen argued that modernist art was radicalized and defined by its resistance to 'mass culture', the kinds of popular art being enjoyed by the vast majority of the population in this era. Much subsequent criticism, both that on individual authors, and that surveying the modernist literary period more broadly, have, however, placed their emphasis upon the fact that there is no such thing as a 'great divide' at this point. Writers, like many others, were after all eager to be present at, and were often influenced by, popular song, dance, movies, vaudeville and Music Hall. To take but one example – one of the most seemingly austere of the modernists, T. S. Eliot, attended tea dances in London with his first wife; he enjoyed the latest movies, but more particularly the vaudeville entertainments with which he was familiar in his youth, and their British equivalent, the Music Halls. He wrote an elegiac piece on one of the most famous of the music-hall performers, 'Marie Lloyd' (1923). He read detective fiction, and knew the Sherlock Holmes stories by Arthur Conan Doyle well enough to be able to quote from them at length at parties. His own work shows the influence of vaudeville 'turns', especially the unfinished experimental drama *Sweeney Agonistes* (1927). But the first section of *The Waste Land* is punctuated by several popular songs of the time, adding to its uncertain and wildly unstable tonality.

This Section covers commentary on three of the most popular forms of entertainment at the time; film, jazz, and vaudeville. Movies had gained commercial popularity in the United States from the time of the 1903 *The Great Train Robbery*, and by the time of D. W. Griffith's most famous productions, *The Birth of the Nation* (1915) and *Intolerance* (1916), were capable of producing epic works fronted by glamorous stars. The industry was by then in the process of moving to the hospitable climate of Hollywood. In Britain and Europe, from the early 1900s there had been an exponential growth in the number of new silent cinemas, geared to showing the latest American products, but also local work. In Britain, especially, during these early years, there was an emphasis upon cinema as an educational medium, and many of the silent films shown were also on religious and biblical themes. By the time of the First World War, Britain had over 3,000 cinemas, and film was deployed strategically in the drive for recruits to the

Front. The Department of Information in the British Government became adept
at producing patriotic representations of the battles in France to encourage
others to join the struggle: the first Battle of the Somme began on 1 July, 1916
(see Section 1); by 21 August, the film bearing that title was showing in over
1,000 cinemas. Movies brought a major change in conceptions of representation
and performance, but it is interesting to note that the terms used to describe the
greatest international star, Charlie Chaplin, for instance, are loaded with the
kinds of rhetoric that we are used to seeing deployed to describe the action of
modernist texts (see extract 7.1).

Jazz, which has its origins in the music of America's black population, moved
north in the country, with the migration of many workers to the urban centres
of Chicago and New York, in the early years of the twentieth century. It, along
with spirituals, and the strains of ragtime and the blues, which became incorpo-
rated into jazz in those early years, soon became a mark of definition for the
emerging black confidence and consciousness in the 1910s and 1920s. But the
rhythms of jazz soon became appropriated by white musicians, painters, and
writers. In classical music, Igor Stravinsky wrote jazz-influenced pieces, as did the
French composers Darius Milhaud and Erik Satie. Henri Matisse painted jazz
pictures. In literature, jazz formed not just a part of the ambience, as in the short
stories of the Fitzgeralds, but became a metaphor for the racy and multi-linguis-
tic language of the city streets: as the poet Mina Loy put it, 'on the baser avenues
of Manhattan, every human voice swings'.

7.1 ' "I Am Here To-day": Charlie Chaplin'. Gilbert Seldes, *The Seven Lively Arts* (1924)

*The Seven Lively Arts is the classic defence of popular culture in the early part of the
century. Containing revised versions of essays originally contributed to journals including* Vanity Fair *and* The Dial *(of which he was managing editor), Seldes's book seeks
to dispel the distinction between 'high' and 'low' culture, proposing instead a different
category, the lively arts. His proposal was that 'Except in a period when the major arts
flourish . . . the lively arts are likely to be the most intelligent phenomena of their day.
That the lively arts as they exist in America to-day are entertaining, interesting, and
important. That with few exceptions these same arts are more interesting to the adult
cultivated intelligence than most of the things which pass for art in cultured society.'
Seldes (1893–1970) studied literature at Harvard, and was a friend of the modernists
e.e. cummings and John Dos Passos. He had been a drama critic on* The Dial *before
going to Europe in order to write this book; later he was the first Director of Programmes
at CBS. The first of the selections from Seldes's book covers the iconic tramp Charlie
Chaplin, arguably the first actor to be more-or-less recognizable across the world, and,
to that extent, a universal symbol at the time. Seldes's Chaplin is a modernist artist,
keyed to rhythm and 'line', the progress he makes across the screen, but also self-
contained and remote from the world to which all of his work seemingly refers.*

For most of us the grotesque effigy dangling from the electric sign or propped against the side of the ticket-booth must remain our first memory of Charlie Chaplin. The splay feet, the moustache, the derby hat, the rattan walking-stick, composed at one the image which was ten years later to become the universal symbol of laughter. '*I am here to-day*' was his legend, and like everything else associated with his name it is faintly ironic and exactly right. The man who, of all the men of our time, seems most assured of immortality, chose that particularly transient announcement of his presence, 'I am here to-day,' with its emotional overtone of 'gone tomorrow,' and there is always something in Charlie that slips away. 'He does things,' said John S. Sargent once, 'and you're lucky if you see them.' Incredibly lucky to live when we have the chance to see them.

Like every great artist in whatever medium, Charlie has created the mask of himself – many masks, in fact – and the first of these, the wanderer, came in the Keystone comedies. It was there that he first detached himself from life and began to live in another world, with a specific rhythm of his own, as if the pulse-beat in him changed and was twice or half as fast as that of those who surrounded him. He created then that trajectory across the screen which is absolutely his own line of movement. No matter what the actual facts are, the curve he plots is always the same. It is of one who seems to enter from a corner of the screen, becomes entangled or involved in a force greater than himself as he advances upward and to the centre; there he spins like a marionette in a whirlpool, is flung from side to side, always in a parabola which seems centripetal until the madness of the action hurls him to refuge or compels him to flight at the opposite end of the screen. He wanders in, a stranger, an imposter, an anarchist; and passes again, buffeted, but unchanged.

The Keystone[1] was the time of his wildest grotesquerie . . . as if he needed, for a beginning, sharply to contrast his rhythm, his gait, his gesture, *mode*, with the actual world outside. . . . [i]n *His Night Out* the effect is perfect, and is intensified by the alternating coincidence and syncopation of rhythm in which Ben Turpin worked with him. Charlie's drunken line of march down a stairway was first followed in parallel and then in not-quite-parallel by Turpin; the degree of drunkenness was the same, then varied, then returned to identity; and the two, together, were always entirely apart from the actuality of hotels and bars and fountains and policemen which were properties in their existence.

The Kid[2] was undoubtedly a beginning in 'literature' for Charlie. I realize that in admitting this I am giving the whole case away, for in the opinion of certain critics the beginning of literature is the end of creative art. This attitude is not so

1 Chaplin began his career with the Keystone Film Company, for which he made more than 70 films.
2 This was a movie Chaplin completed in 1921, soon after he founded the United Artists Corporation, when he gained the freedom to write, direct, produce and compose the music for his own products.

familiar in America, but in France you hear the Charlot[3] of *The Kid* spoken of as 'theatre', as one who has ceased to be of the film entirely. I doubt if this is just. Like the other great artist in America (George Herriman,[4] with whom he is eminently in sympathy), Charlie has always had the Dickens touch, a thing which in its purity we do not otherwise discover in our art. Dickens himself is mixed; only a part of him is literature, and that not the best, nor is that part essentially the one which Charlie has imported to the screen. *The Kid* had some bad things in it: the story, the halo round the head of the unmarried mother, the quarrel with the authorities; it had an unnecessary amount of realism and its tempo was uncertain, for it was neither serious film nor Keystone. Yet it possessed moments of unbelievable intensity and touches of high imagination. The scenes in and outside the doss-house were excellent and were old Charlie; the glazier's assistant was inventive and the training of Coogan to look like his foster-father was beautiful. Far above them stood the beginning of the film: Charlot, in his usual polite rags, strolling down to his club after his breakfast (it would have been grilled bone) and, avoiding slops as Villon[5] did, twirling his cane, taking off his fingerless gloves to reach for his cigarette case (a sardine box), and selecting from the butts one of quality, *tamping it* to shake down the excess tobacco at the tip – all of this, as Mr Herriman pointed out to me, was the creation of a society gentleman, the courageous refusal to be undermined by slums and poverty and rags. At the end of the film there was the vision of heaven: apotheosis of the long suffering of Charlot at the hands of the police, not only in *The Kid* – in a hundred films where he stood always against the authorities, always for his small independent freedom. The world in which the policemen have wings shatters too; but something remains. The invincible Charlot, dazed by his dream, looking for wings on the actual policeman who is apparently taking him to jail, will not down. For as they start, a post comes between them, and Charlot, without the slightest effort to break away, too submissive to fight, still dodges back to walk round the post and so avoid bad luck. A moment later comes one of the highest points of Charlie's career. He is ushered into a limousine instead of a petrol wagon – it is the beginning of the happy ending. And as the motor starts he flashes at the spectators of his felicity a look of indescribable poignancy. It is frightened, it is hopeful, bewildered; it lasts a fraction of a second and is blurred by the plate glass of the car. I cannot hope to set down the quality of it, how it becomes a moment of unbearable intensity, and how one is breathless with suspense – and with adoration.

For, make no mistake, it is adoration, not less, that he deserves and has from us. He corresponds to our secret desires because he alone has passed beyond our categories, at one bound placing himself outside space and time. His escape from

---

3 A French pet name for Charlie.
4 Herriman was one of the most famous comic strip artists of the time, creator of the surreal 'Krazy Kat' cartoons (1911–44).
5 François Villon, a medieval French poet, and notorious jail resident.

the world is complete and extraordinarily rapid, and what makes him more than a figure of romance is his immediate creation of another world. He has the vital energy, the composing and functioning brain. This is what makes him aesthetically interesting, what will make him for ever a school not only of acting, but of the whole creative process. The flow of his line always corresponds to the character and the tempo; there is a definite relation between the melody and the orchestration he gives it. Beyond his technique – the style of his pieces – he has composition, because he creates anything but chaos in his separate world. 'You might,' wrote Mr Stark Young . . . 'really create in terms of the moving picture as you have already created in terms of character.'

7.2 'Toujours Jazz'

This second selection from Seldes's book relates to the black American musical form which famously migrated across colour and national divides in the late 1910s and early 1920s. In his article 'Jazz at Home' in The New Negro *(an anthology excerpted in Section 9), J. A. Rogers puts the case that jazz is the modern artform, a 'marvel of paradox'. 'It is too fundamentally human, at least as modern humanity goes, to be typically racial, too international to be characteristically national, too much abroad in the world to have a special home.' But Rogers claims that jazz has an ambiguous image, since it amounts to 'transplanted exoticism' rather than to a truly international phenomenon. Therefore the jazz to be heard outside of its true home in Harlem is 'mundane', since it does not have the true 'Negro rhythm' of the lower-class black performer. Seldes's exposition has been selected since it is a mark of the 'internationalizing' tendency towards jazz at the time, and the way that it retained a contentious status amongst white intellectuals. Seldes's 'take' on jazz is extremely racist, ultimately, seeing it as a more primitive form which does not seem to have developed fully. But his elucidation of the distinctive qualities of jazz is extremely lucid, and usefully ties it in to the work of white European artists. The article was originally published in* The Dial *in August 1923, as a riposte to the rebuttal of the medium by the English critic associated with the Bloomsbury set, Clive Bell.*

The word jazz is already so complicated that it ought not to be subjected to any new definitions, and the thing itself so familiar that it is useless to read new meanings into it. Jazz is a type of music grown out of ragtime and still ragtime in essence; it is also a method of production and as such an orchestral development; and finally it is the symbol, or the byword, for a great many elements in the spirit of our time – as far as America is concerned it is actually our characteristic expression. This is recognized by Europeans; with a shudder by the English and with real joy by the French, who cannot, however, play it.

The fact that jazz is our current mode of expression, has reference to our time and the way we think and talk, is interesting; but if jazz music weren't itself good the subject would be more suitable for the sociologist than for an admirer of the gay arts. Fortunately, the music and the way it is played are both of great interest, both have qualities which cannot be despised; and the cry that jazz is the enthusiastic disorganization of music is as extravagant as the prophecy that if we do not stop 'jazzing' we will go down, as a nation, into ruin. I am quite ready to uphold the contrary. If – before we have produced something better – we give up jazz we shall be sacrificing nearly all there is of gaiety and liveliness and rhythmic power in our lives. Jazz, for us, isn't a last feverish excitement, a spasm of energy before death. It is the normal development of our resources, the expected, and wonderful, arrival of America at a point of creative intensity.

Strictly speaking, jazz music is a new development – something of the last two years, arriving long after jazz had begun to be played. . . . In jazz ragtime the accent can occur anywhere in the bar and is attractively unpredictable. Rhythmically – essentially – jazz is ragtime, since it is based on syncopation, and even without jazz orchestration we should have had the full employment of precise and continuous syncopation which we find in jazz now. It is syncopation, too, which has so liberated jazz from normal polyphony, from perfect chords. . . . The reason why syncopation lies behind all this is that it is fundamentally an anticipation or a suspension in one instrument (or in the bass) of what is going to happen in another (the treble); and the moment in which a note occurs prematurely or in retard is, frequently, a moment of discord on the strong beat. A dissonance sets in which may or may not be resolved later.

The title of this essay is provoked by that of the best and bitterest attack launched against the ragtime age – Clive Bell's *Plus de Jazz*. 'No more jazz,' said Mr Bell in 1921, and 'Jazz is dying.' Recalling that Mr Bell is at some pains to dissociate from the movement the greatest of living painters, Picasso; that he concedes to it a great composer, Stravinsky, and T. S. Eliot, whom he calls 'about the best of our living poets,' James Joyce whom he woefully underestimates, Virginia Woolf . . .

   . . . if he is jazz, then Mr Joyce's sense of form, his tremendous intellectual grasp of his aesthetic problem, and his solution of that problem, are far more proof than is required of the case for jazz. Similarly for Mr Eliot. It is not exactly horror of the noble that underlies Mr Joyce's travesty of English prose style, nor is it to Mr Eliot that the reproach about irony and wit is to be made.[6] In music it is not of course impudence, but emphasis (distortion or transposition of emphasis) which finds its technical equivalent in syncopation, for syncopation is a method of rendering an emotion, not an emotion in itself. (Listen to Stravinsky) Surprise, yes . . . Nobility – no. But under what compulsion are we always to be noble? The cocktail drinkers may have been told a lot of nonsense about their position as arbiters of the arts; precisely the same nonsense is taught

6 In a passage from Bell's article, quoted by Seldes, he says that 'Irony and wit are for the grown-ups. Jazz dislikes them as much as it dislikes nobility and beauty.'

in our schools and preached by belated aesthetes to people whose claims are not a wit better – since it doesn't matter what their admirers think of themselves – it is what jazz and . . . Michelangelo are in themselves that matters. I have used the word art throughout this book in connexion with jazz and jazzy things; if anyone imagines that the word is belittled thereby and can no longer be adequate to the dignity of Leonardo or Shakespeare, I am sorry. I do not think I have given encouragement to 'fatuous ignorance' by praising simple and unpretentious things at the expense of the fake and the *faux bon*. I have suggested that people do what they please about the gay arts, about jazz; that they do it with discrimination and without worrying whether it is noble or not, or good form or intellectually right. I am fairly certain that if they are ever actually to see Picasso it will be because they have acquired the habit of seeing . . . because they will know what the pleasure is that a work of art can give, even if it be jazz art.

7.3   Music Hall

The history of Music Hall dates back as far as the seventeenth century, when, as later, it was associated with decadent and even riotous behaviour. Having acquired church organs, which the Puritans at the time had banished from worship, contemporary tavern-keepers deployed them for the entertainment of customers. From this beginning, Music Hall grew to form the staple business of many British theatres, both in London and in the provinces. The high-point of Music Hall entertainment came at the turn of the nineteenth into the twentieth century, when the stars of the medium, who included Albert Chevalier, Marie Lloyd and Vesta Tilley, enjoyed incredible fame as they toured the country. After Lloyd (1870–1922) died on stage at the Edmonton Empire in October 1922, over one hundred thousand people attended her funeral. T. S. Eliot, who had been an habitué of the Music Halls from the time of his arrival in England, was shocked, as others were, by Lloyd's early death, and was immediately prompted into writing a memorial essay. In it, he regrets not having fully recognized the 'uniqueness' of Lloyd's 'genius'; her success 'in giving expression to the life' of her audience, 'in raising it to a kind of art'. Lloyd, a performer from Lancashire who carried her regional accent onto the stage, was for Eliot 'the expressive figure of the lower classes', who translated the facets of that impoverished life into her act. Eliot's essay then turns on the cultureless (as he perceives them) middle classes in England for their lack of values and morality, their inability to produce performers with the 'moral superiority' of a Lloyd. Finally, he turns against cinema, which was at the time as he acknowledges, superseding Music Hall as the most popular form of entertainment, fantastically (from our point of view) suggesting that it could bring about the end of 'civilization' because of the boredom it induces.[7] Later performers in the Music Halls, including Gracie Fields and the Crazy Gang, became the first stars of the new medium, radio.

---

7 T. S. Eliot, 'Marie Lloyd', *Selected Essays* (London: Faber, 1972), pp. 456–9.

Below are two extracts bringing together thoughts from key promoters of Music Hall as a form of entertainment, the Welshman Arthur Symons and the Italian Futurist poet F. T. Marinetti.[8] Symons was an early aficionado of the medium who, as this extract shows, travelled Europe seeking out different varieties of performance. Symons's many writings on Music Hall were instrumental in suggesting that this 'popular' form could appeal to a sophisticated modern audience, for its spontaneity and for its mixture of the thrilling and the grotesque, a mixture familiar to 1890s writers and also to those modernists including Eliot and Joyce who later shared Symons's enthusiasm. Symons's response to the Music Hall, which involved him recording the glinting impressions made upon him by crowd, performers, and orchestra, furthered that impressionistic style of writing which marked his interest in French painting and writing of the period, and which he importantly mediated to English-speaking writers through his book on the French Symbolists extracted in the 'Religion and Belief' section of this Sourcebook. In Marinetti's article, we find the Music Hall deployed as a typical weapon against the bourgeois conventions of contemporary literary theatre, a Futurist call to arms which shares many of the perceptions of Symons's response nearly twenty years earlier. It seeks to harness the popular theatre to its own revolutionary aims, but at the same time delineates those aspects of the theatre which make it perfect for that possibility.

Arthur Symons, 'A Spanish Music-Hall', Fortnightly Review, 57 (May 1892)

I AM *aficionado*, as a Spaniard would say, of music-halls. They amuse me, and I am always grateful to anyone or anything that amuses me. The drama, if it is to be looked upon as an art at all, is admittedly frivolous – the consecration of the frivolous. The more it approaches the legitimate drama the less characteristic, the less interesting, it is. . . . I come to the music-hall for dancing, for singing, for the human harmonies of the acrobat. And I come for that exquisite sense of the frivolous, that air of Bohemian freedom, that relief from respectability, which one gets here, and no more surely than here. In the music-hall the audience is a part of the performance. The audience in a theatre, besides being in itself less amusing, is on its best behaviour; you do not so easily surprise its 'humours'. Here we have a tragic comedy in the box yonder, a farce in the third row of the stalls, a scene from a ballet in the promenade. The fascination of these private performances is irresistible; and they are constantly changing, so full of surprises, so mysterious and so clear. . . .

At the beginning of last May I spent a few days in Barcelona, and one night I went to the Alcazar Español, the most characteristic place I could find, extremely curious to see what a Spanish music-hall would be like. . . . There was a bar at one end of the room, and a few small tables placed near two embrasures,

---

8 For biographical information on Symons see his selection in the 'Religion and Belief' section; on Marinetti see the opening extracts of the ' "High" Culture' section, above.

through which one saw an inner room. This was the hall. At one end was a little stage; the curtain was down, and the musicians' chairs and desks were vacant. . . . Then a few people came in, and a few more, and the place gradually filled. The audience was not a distinguished one. None of the women wore hats, and few of them assumed an air of too extreme superiority to the waiters. . . . And now the musicians were gathering. The grey-haired leader of the orchestra, smoking a cigar, brought in the score. He sat down at his piano, and handed round the sheets of music. The members of the orchestra brought newspapers with them. The man who played the clarionet was smoking a cigarette fixed in an interminable holder. He did his duty by his instrument in the overture that followed, but he never allowed the cigarette to go out. I thought the performance remarkable.

The band, for a music-hall of no higher pretensions, was extremely good. It had a genuine music-hall swing, and a sympathetic delicacy which I had not expected. The overture sounded very Spanish. It was a *pot-pourri* of some kind, with much variety of airs, a satisfying local colour. After the overture the curtain rose . . . there was a good deal of excited movement, a series of rather disconnected episodes, a good deal of noise. Anna Durmance was best in a scene where she came on as a washerwoman. There were moments when Mlle. Durmance was excellent; certain gestures, a typically Spanish way of walking. But one was not sorry when, in the usual sudden way, all the performers rushed together upon the stage; there were some exclamations, some laughter, some joining of hands, and the curtain was down amid a thunder of applause.

The next performer was really a Frenchwoman. . . . She was a great favourite with the audience, and in the pauses between the stanzas she would smile and nod to her friends here and there. I did not share their enthusiasm, having heard the same songs much better given elsewhere. When, after an interval, she came on the stage again, dressed as a man, I was surprised to see how well she could look. She was to take charge of a Teatro Lilliputien, and she made her bow before disappearing behind a curtain. The Lilliputian Theatre has not, I think, reached England, though it has long been at home in Paris. It is a contrivance after the style of a Punch and Judy show, only, instead of marionettes who do all the action, there is a combination between the operator and his puppets. As in a certain sort of caricature, one sees a large head supported by a tiny body, with finikin arms and legs, which move as they are worked from behind. The head is that of the performer, the rest belongs to the puppets; and it is indeed comic to see the perfect sympathy which exists between the head which sings, the puppet hands which gesticulate, and the puppet legs which dance.[9]

. . . Four women took their places on the stage, facing one another two by two. They raised their arms, the eight pairs of castanets clanged at once, and the

---

9 See the thoughts on marionette theatre as 'high' art by Gordon Craig for comparison, the last extract of the previous Section.

dance began. . . . The swaying movement of the hips became more pronounced; the body moved in a sort of circle upon itself. And then they would cross and recross, accentuating the rhythm with a stamp of the heels. Their arms waved and dipped, curving with the curves of the body. The dance grew more exciting, with a sort of lascivious suggestiveness, a morbid, perverse charm, as the women writhed to and fro, now languishingly, now furiously, together and apart. It ended with a frantic *trémoussement* of the hips, a stamp of the heels, and a last clash of the castanets as the arms grew rigid in the sudden immobility of the body. There were two encores, and two more dances, much the same as the first, and then at last the curtain was allowed to descend, and the women went tranquilly back to the corner where they had been drinking coffee with their friends.

'The Meaning of the Music-Hall. By the Only Intelligible Futurist. F. T. Marinetti', Daily Mail, Friday, 21 November 1913

We Futurists are profoundly disgusted with the contemporary stage because it stupidly fluctuates between historical reconstruction (*pastiche* or plagiarism) and a minute, wearying, photographic reproduction of actuality. We delight in frequenting the music-hall or variety theatre, smoking concert, circus, cabaret, and night-club, which offer to-day the only theatrical entertainment worthy of the true Futurist spirit.

Futurism exalts the variety theatre because, born as it were with us, it fortunately has no tradition, no masters, no dogmas, and subsists on the moment. The variety theatre is absolutely practical because it aims at entertaining and amusing the public by performances either comic or startling to the imagination. The authors, actors, and mechanics of the variety theatre exist and conquer their difficulties only for one purpose, that of everlastingly startling by new inventions. Hence the absolute impossibility of stagnation or repetition, the desperate emulation of brain and muscle to beat all previous records in agility, speed, strength, complexity, and grace.

FUTURISTIC WONDER

The variety theatre offering the most lucrative medium for endless inventive effort most naturally produces what I call the *Futuristic Wonder*, a product of modern mechanism. It presents caricature in its fullest form, foolery of the deepest kind, impalpable and delicious irony, absorbing and decisive symbols, torrents of irrepressible hilarity, profound analogies between human beings and the animal, the vegetable, and the mechanical world; swift revelations of cynicism, a network of spritely wit, puns, and cock-and-bull stories which pleasantly fan the intellect; all the scales of laughter to relax the nerves; all the scales of such fun, foolery, doltishness, absurdity as insensibly urge the soul to the very edge of madness; all the meanings of light, sound, poise, and speech and their mysterious, inexplicable correspondence with the utmost unexplored centres of our sensibility.

The modern variety theatre is the overflowing melting-pot of all those elements which are combining to prepare for our new sensibility. It lends itself to the ironical decomposition of all our worn-out prototypes – the beautiful, the great, the solemn, the religious, the fierce, the seductive, the terrible; and also to the abstract forecasting of those new prototypes which shall succeed them.

The variety theatre is the only kind of theatre where the public does not remain static and stupidly passive, but participates noisily in the action, singing, beating time with the orchestra, giving force to the actor's words by unexpected tags and queer improvised dialogues. . . .

'TO PROVOKE IMMENSE ROWS'

Futurism wants to perfect variety theatre by transforming it into the theatre of wonders and of records. It is absolutely necessary to abolish every vestige of logic in the performances of variety theatre; to exaggerate luxury; multiply contrasts and give the supreme place on the stage to the improbable and the absurd (example: to oblige singers to dye their necks, their arms, and especially their hair, all colours, hitherto unused for the purposes of seduction: green hair, violet arms, blue neck, orange chignons, etc.). . . .

To debauch systematically all classical art, producing, for instance, in one single evening all the Greek, French, and Italian tragedies in abridged form. To enliven the works of Beethoven, Wagner, Bach, Bellini, Chopin by cutting into them with Neapolitan songs. To soap carefully the planks of the stage so that the actors may slip up at the most tragic moments.

7.4 Vaudeville

Whilst in Britain Music Hall entertainment was in decline in the 1910s (T. S. Eliot's obituary piece for the popular entertainer Marie Lloyd (1923) is virtually an elegiac lament for the whole form), the same years saw the tremendous popularity in America of a relatively new style of performance which shared many of its original features with the older Music Hall. Vaudeville had come to mean by the nineteenth century a series of acts or short performances by a range of artists put together to form an evening's entertainment. In the 1880s, vaudeville had taken on a commercial prominence through the creation of chains of theatres which spanned all of the major cities. By 1928, at the end of our era, it has been estimated that 2 million people attended vaudeville theatres in the US every evening, and that there were over a thousand performances being staged at any one time. The evening comprised a range of types of performance including comedy, song, juggling, and animal acts. It combined American artists with European counterparts, including in New York the Scottish comedian and singer Sir Harry Lauder, and the famous French classical actress Sarah Bernhardt. Whilst vaudeville soon went into decline from this peak of popularity, in the face of the combined competition from movies and the radio, it was in its time the place where many of the other American arts – jazz, ragtime – were to be heard by the mass of the people.

Mary Cass Canfield, 'The Great American Art', The New Republic, 22 November 1922

'Say it with music.' So far America, the hoi polloi, if you will (but the hoi polloi[10] is the nation), has not said anything except with music. National restlessness exists in the conflicting rhythm of jazz. In the precise insouciance of ragtime, leap out America's own efficiency and lack of reflection, its good nature, its self-conscious smartness, its childish and oddly pathetic craving for gaiety.

Ragtime is the noise that fills a too empty room, it is the drunkenness of prohibitionists, the longing for movement and color of those who sit on packing cases and look in vain for beauty and rhythm up and down Main Street. It is barbarically fierce in its effort to conquer the vacuum and the horn of the talking machine is its loud mouthed interpreter, generously underscoring the violent cheerfulness of its staccato. Barbaric it is and yet subtle, a medley of strange minor gradations running through the major implication of its tone, like the disquiets, the doubts, the melancholy, distressing the American's determined sense of optimism.

Ragtime is our folk song. It would seem that we have not developed sufficiently to have evolved anything authentic beyond folk song, any distinctive art of our own in the plastic or literary field. Stray geniuses, Whitman and Emerson, have only served to show up the careful orthodoxy of their fellows. Literature, particularly poetry, shows signs of pulling out of the rut of foreign imitation. Robinson and Frost, Masters and Sandburg are building up an art which mirrors America and expresses the national temperament. They are thus founding an American poetry. But their voices, heard by the few, are but thrush chirps in a wilderness; and the great American art, the art of the people, for the people, by the people, remains ragtime.

Perfection is the aim and the sign of great art. Mr Ziegfeld's *Follies*[11] or the Winter Garden, or an afternoon of vaudeville at the Palace are perfect of their kind. It is, therefore, with sincere enthusiasm and without a trace of irony that one recommends these phases of the American drama as the highest example of a national art. Vaudeville is happy; therefore it is both good and beautiful. Laughter preaches fellowship better than sermons; enjoyment throws magic loveliness, a golden glow, over a bare stage where a comedian in a check suit gregariously leans against a backdrop lamp post. What is more, ragtime haunted vaudeville . . . delights us with the unexpected. Irony cannot exist in the face if such vanquishing vitality, such ingenuity of setting and entertainment, such speed, effectiveness, grace and lightness of touch. No song or dance or comic skit is too long; brevity, queen of qualities, smiles triumphantly out at us between

---

10 The ordinary people.
11 Florenz Ziegfeld (1867–1932) was a manager of musical entertainers who, in New York in 1907, staged the first of his spectacular shows, famous for their glamour.

the quick rises and falls of innumerable, fantastically colored curtains. Vaudeville leads us breathless but interested, from acrobats to sentimental songs, from pony ballets to well-played one-act tragedy. Every musician in the orchestra is mentally on his toes, every pulley is supergreased. To concentrate on the stage management of the Follies is like watching a thoroughbred take a series of fences. The revolving stage has a soul, it bounds forward to its task with a swagger, it prides itself on never making a mistake. It is American. One's brain reels at the thought of how many rehearsals have brought this Protean miracle into existence. Elaborate sets succeed each other, great masses of people parade across the stage and are gone, the orchestra melts from one time to another, all with the bewildering ease of mastery. The pulchritude of the performers, the quality of the dancing, of the humor, of the costumes and scenic effects, cause our vaudeville to tower above the vaudeville of any other country. . . .

Closer attuned to the general audience is the humor of such shows. Humor is as much a necessity to us as sweets; and perhaps for the same climatic reason. Nerves strung to top pitch demand both food and relaxation. Nowhere is the strength of our demand for humor better gauged than by the response it found in cabaret and vaudeville dancing. Shimmying, shuffling, eccentric and awkward movements are only answers to the national love of the grotesque. About the grotesque, which is a tragic thing, a negation of beauty, an expression of inhibited or disappointed search for the ideal, one could, had one the space, philosophize at length. The theory that our really characteristic art is a reaction from sensuous starvation and like all reactions, a violent thing, is certainly borne out by such manifestations as Mark Twain's bitter chuckle or the calculated extravagance of our dancing; our dancers are experts in rhythmic dislocation, in accurately timed physical buffoonery. All art is exaggeration. But in the American exaggeration there is always a self-criticism, an undertone of humor, which is an attempt at fire extinguishing that does not reduce but curiously discolors the flame.

Grotesque or not, vaudeville represents a throwing away of self-consciousness, of Plymouth Rock[12] caution, devoutly to be wished for. Here we countenance the extreme, we encourage idiosyncrasy. The dancer or comedian is, sometimes literally, encouraged to develop originality; he is adored, never crucified for difference. Miss Fannie Brice[13] and Sir Harry Lauder are examples of vaudeville performers who have been hailed, joyfully and rightfully, as vessels containing the sacred fire, and who have been encouraged into self-emphasis by their audiences; they are now, as a result of this appreciative stimulus, rare and interesting artists in their field.

---

12 This is the spot where the Pilgrims traditionally first set foot on American soil in 1620, and so it stands here for a kind of founding and perennial Puritanism.

13 A performer known for her moving performance of dramatic songs and humorous Yiddish dialect numbers, her life is commemorated in the movie *Funny Girl*.

8

Literary Production and Reception

Introduction

In the early years of the twentieth century, publishing underwent a technical revolution. The arrival of rotary presses and Linotype machines, together, crucially, with the cheap and ready availability of paper, meant that the cost and the speed of newspaper, journal and book production changed rapidly. This led to the publication of mass-circulation newspapers such as Lord Northcliffe's *Daily Mail* and mass-market magazines such as *Strand* and *Tit-bits* (read on the lavatory by Joyce's protagonist Leopold Bloom in *Ulysses*) in Britain; and the *Ladies Home Journal*, *Cosmopolitan* and *Vanity Fair* in the US. In terms of books, there was a drastic fall in the price of the novel, which led to a broader book-buying readership, able to 'keep up' with the latest bestsellers, and a sudden flood of inexpensive editions of classic literary works from publishing houses such as J. M. Dent (the 'Everyman' and 'Temple Classics' series), and Grant Richards (the 'World's Classics'). The broad allusiveness of modernist writing, its perpetual reference to texts from earlier literary moments, owes a debt in part to the sudden availability, at prices all could afford, of editions, including translations, of classical poetry, drama and fiction, with handy contextualizing introductions by experts in their respective fields, including Ernest Rhys, Arthur Symons, A. C. Swinburne, and others.

The new publishing technologies also enabled, from the early 1910s, the publication of a range of literary, arts and cultural journals – the so-called 'little magazines' – key to the early publication and marketing of modernist works. *The Little Review*, *Dial*, *Poetry*, *Contact*, *Others* and *The Masses* in America; *The Egoist*, *New Age* and *English Review*, as well as, later, *The Criterion*, edited by T. S. Eliot, in Britain, produced a stream of poetry, stories and novels which we now consider as the central texts of modernism. Literary work was printed alongside articles on philosophy and culture, and reviews of arts and entertainment events alongside more considered and expansive essays on the state of the artistic scene. These magazines, all of which had ambitions to become mass-market successes, soon survived on the patronage of wealthy sponsors. The two magazines excerpted here, for instance, had limited audiences: *The Egoist* started with a circulation of 1,500 copies, but by 1915 only 750 were being printed of each number. *The Little Review* peaked at around 3,000 copies per issue, but largely sold around 1,000 less.

Whatever the modernist writers' ambition to change the consciousness of its readers, and literary form itself, therefore, their work was originally seen by a very limited number of people. Even their most 'significant' issues from our perspective, numbers of 'little' magazines like the special 'Imagist' issue of *The Egoist* in May 1915, sold no more than 1,250 copies originally. And, despite the rise of the literary agent in the early years of the century, arranging publication contracts with the more major publishers (Henry James and Joseph Conrad were early beneficiaries of this kind of mediation), such relationships for the modernists were often fraught and unsatisfactory. D. H. Lawrence, as revealed in his letters, for instance, is frequently resisting his agent's demands to cut or alter his texts to make them more 'marketable', and some of his more radically confrontational later work, like the poetry of *Pansies*, and *Lady Chatterley's Lover*, appeared in small editions on the European continent. Lawrence, like Joyce, fell foul of the censorship laws of his day, a fact which hit his own ability to survive without the aid of others.

In practice, therefore, there was a more amateur process of securing publication for some of the more radically-experimental work. In this, the key figure was that of the American poet Ezra Pound, who selflessly harassed a series of magazine editors until they overcame their scepticism, and included work by Joyce or Eliot or others in their next issues.

The difficulty of securing publication in journals was even more serious when it came to the publication of modernist works in book form, with the major publishing houses rejecting immediately many of the modernist masterworks, for fear of obscenity charges, but more for fear of the certain commercial losses entailed. This era therefore saw the establishment of small publishing houses, with low costs, in order to promote the new literature. *The Egoist* evolved into the Egoist Press; Virginia Woolf, together with her husband Leonard, established the Hogarth Press, in order to ensure high-quality publication of Virginia's work, but also to promote work which they thought of value, including that by Eliot and Katherine Mansfield. There was also elsewhere recourse to *de luxe* editions in order to publish several key works, including Joyce's *Ulysses*.

What is most notable now, looking back at the early history of modernist publishing, before the situation eased for those writers still alive in the 1930s, is the predominant part played in it by women. Dora Marsden and then Harriet Shaw Weaver edited the *Egoist*; the couple Margaret Anderson and Jane Heap issued *The Little Review*; Harriet Monroe edited *Poetry*; later, Marianne Moore edited *The Dial* for a period. Sylvia Beach's Shakespeare and Company in Paris produced *Ulysses*. It was women who were prepared to take the commercial and legal risk of seeing into print writing which they felt really did 'make it new', and which brought new philosophical, political and cultural perspectives to a jaded culture within their respective countries.

8.1   Walter Dill Scott, *The Psychology of Advertising* (American edition, 1908; English, 1909)

Across the past ten years, some significant research into the modernist period has focused upon the similarity between the promotional aspects of the literature of the time, and the concurrent rise in commodity advertising. Modernist sloganeering, as represented most notoriously perhaps by the American poet Ezra Pound's 'Make it New!', as a call for modern works to break from the (cloying Victorian) past and to strike out into new territories and ideas, had, as recent critics have claimed, learnt much from the adverts which appeared, often in the same journal in which the modern writ-ers were being published. Margaret Anderson, the editor of the American The Little Review, *even notoriously printed a series of white pages in one issue, with brief state-ments pointing out that local booksellers, or publishers, or even piano-makers, might be advertising in these empty spaces.* The Little Review, *like the other 'little magazines', was largely supported via personal patronage, but also needed the revenue from adver-tisers to sustain itself. These extracts from Dill Scott's founding and several-times reprinted text in the area are striking in a variety of ways; they are an attempt to apply the emerging 'science' of psychology to the promotion of commodities; they show an awareness of literary criticism and its application in this field; and they show an educated awareness of the concurrence of the relation between the thoughts and emotions involved in advertising and their consideration within contemporary American philosophy. Dill Scott frequently and at length cites William James in order to support his insights, and envisages a continuum between his activities in the world of business and those of leaders in contemporary ideas. Like the modernists, in their Romantic distrust of the power of reason, he aims advertising at the emotions, at the suggested rather than at the obvious and articulated. As becomes clear, he feels that the most successful advertisements are those which demand your attention, and the most successful advertising locations are those where people are required to spend time, within the onrush of modern life – locations such as street railways. This spending time in order to achieve effectiveness is something Dill Scott associates with poetry and music. These gists from across Dill Scott's book give a flavour of the areas he involves himself (and which he sees all advertisers as having to involve themselves) in.*

Advertising has as its one function the influencing of human minds. Unless it does this it is useless and destructive to the firms attempting it. As it is the human mind that advertising is dealing with, its only scientific basis is psychol-ogy, which is simply a systematic study of those same minds which the adver-tiser is seeking to influence.

When the question arises – how to construct an advertisement so that the reader cannot forget it, we find that the question is answered by the proper application of the principles enunciated above. The advertisement that is repeated over and over again at frequent intervals gradually becomes fixed in the memory of the reader. It may be a crude and an expensive method, but it seems to be effective.

This method gains added effect by repeating one or more characteristic features, and by changing some of the fixtures at each appearance of the advertisement.

The intensity of the impression which an advertisement makes is dependent upon the response which it secures from the readers. The pedagogue would call this action the 'motor response'. . . . Rhymes and alliterations are rhetorical forms which seem to be of great assistance when we attempt to commit verses, and even when we do not want to remember them the rhythm may make such an impression that we can't forget them. . . . Anything humorous or ridiculous – even a pun – is hard to forget.

The advertiser should present his argument in such a form that it will naturally and easily be associated by the reader with his own former experience. This is best done by appealing to those interests and motives which are the ruling principles of the reader's thinking. Personally, I should forget a recipe for a cake before I had finished reading it, but to a cook it is full of interest, and does not stand out as an isolated fact, but as a modification or addition of something already in his mind.

Man is not pre-eminently logical, but . . . his thinking is influenced by his present state of feelings.

The modern business man does his utmost to minister to the pleasure of the customers in his store. He knows that they will place a larger order if they are feeling happy than if they are feeling otherwise. The American slang expression, 'jolly up', means pleasing by flattery of the one from whom it is desired to obtain favour.

It was once supposed that suggestion was something abnormal and that reason was the common attribute of men. Today we are finding that suggestion is of universal application to all persons, while reason is a process which is exceptional, even among the wisest. We reason rarely, but act under suggestion constantly. . . .

Suggestion and persuasion are not antagonistic; both should be kept in mind. However, in advertising, suggestion should not be subordinated to persuasion but should be supplemented by it. The actual effect of modern advertising is not so much to convince as to suggest. The individual swallowed up by a crowd is not aware of the fact that he is not exercising a normal amount of deliberation. His actions appear to him to be the result of reason, although the idea, as presented, is not criticised at all and no contradictory or inhibiting idea has any possibility of arising in his mind. In the same way we think that we are performing a deliberate act when we purchase an advertised commodity, while in fact we may never have deliberated upon the subject at all. The idea is suggested by the advertisement, and the impulsiveness of human nature enforces the suggested idea, hence the desired result follows in a way unknown to the purchaser.

The habit which the public has formed of reading advertisements so hastily makes it difficult for the advertisement writer to construct his advertisements to meet the emergency of the case; it makes it difficult for the merchant to discover the direct results of his advertising campaign and, on the other hand, it makes the right sort of advertising particularly effective, by making the reader more susceptible to confusion as to the source of his information.

As a result of investigations upon magazine and newspaper advertising the conclusion was reached that on average only ten per cent of the time devoted to newspapers and magazines was spent in looking at the advertisements. . . . As a conclusion deduced from these results it was recommended that advertisements should be so constructed that the gist of each could be comprehended at a glance, for most advertisements in newspapers and magazines receive no more than a glance from the average reader. The ordinary reader of newspapers and magazines *glances* at all of the advertising pages and sees all the *larger and more striking* advertisements.

It has been said that we have learned nothing perfectly until we have forgotten how we learned it. This has a special application to advertising. An advertisement has not accomplished its mission till it has instructed the possible customer concerning the goods and then has caused him to forget where he received his instruction. . . .

This forgetfulness of the source of our information is due to the interval which has elapsed between the first time the advertisement was seen and the present. The more frequently the advertisement is seen, the more rapidly will the memory of the first appearance fade and leave us with the feeling that we have always known the goods advertised.

8.2 Two editorial notes from *The Egoist*

With its change of title from The New Freewoman *to* The Egoist *in 1914, this key 'little magazine' of the period signalled a shift from a politics of engagement with the cause of women's rights and the suffragist cause, to a politics of the individual founded upon the ideas of the German thinker Max Stirner. The shift happened when Harriet Shaw Weaver took over the journal from Dora Marsden, although Marsden stayed on and contributed leading articles outlining her own version of Egoist philosophy to nearly every issue of the reformed magazine. The most important shift in focus for our purposes, however, occurs with Weaver's active sponsorship, aided and abetted often by Ezra Pound, of the most experimental writing and writers of the age. Over the years 1914–19, when it ceased publication,* The Egoist *printed Pound's own work alongside that by D. H. Lawrence, May Sinclair, H.D., Richard Aldington, T. S. Eliot, and William Carlos Williams amongst others, though there was a special 'Imagist number' in 1915. James Joyce's* A Portrait of the Artist as a Young Man, *which had encoun-*

*tered a long-running series of obstacles to its appearing in complete book form, was seri-
alized in these pages in 1914–15; later, Wyndham Lewis's* Tarr *appeared similarly.
Richard Aldington served as Assistant Editor for several years; when he was called up
for service at the Front, H.D. took on the role briefly, before T. S. Eliot took it on until
the final issue. Partly as a response to Joyce's difficulties, the Egoist Press was established – it published in a few years the book of* A Portrait, *Eliot's* Prufrock and Other
Observations, Tarr, *Pound's* Quia Pauper Amavi, *H.D.'s* Iphegenia in Aulis *and
more. These extracts are taken from two issues: the first from Dora Marsden's 'Some
Critics Answered' (vol. II, no. 2, 1 February 1915), in which the ambition of the magazine is outlined; and the second from the final issue's 'Notice to Readers' (vol. VI, no.
5, December 1919), in which the pressures upon such a magazine of this kind at the
period are made clear. These are partly attributed to the danger of prosecution for the
magazine's printers, owing to the potentially obscene nature of some episodes of Joyce's*
Ulysses, *which formed the current serialization in the magazine (*The Little Review *in
America was so prosecuted – see the extract below).*

In short, as far as our activities in THE EGOIST are concerned, we are luxurious
people, gleefully, if laboriously, contributing to our own amusement by attempting to plot out a geography of the human mind.

THE EGOIST is creating a psychology; it is therefore a superlatively Reckless
Indiscretion in addition to being that which should never be owned up to by
solicitors of the people – a luxury. It makes no compromises or accommodations, plays up to no one. It serves no one's 'good', fosters no interest, no
cause. It is always ready to learn – a most profoundly suspicious trick; it means
that it is ready to abandon any prejudice without compunction, to be faithless
to any Idea. It abandons itself to curiosity, to 'finding out', as to some suspiciously pleasurable business. . . . Ordinarily, a powerful intelligence looks, sees
– and says nothing; it may thus exploit its superior knowledge the more
unhamperedly. Here an intelligence looks, sees – and tells. Half its audience it
offends and the other half it puts suspiciously on their guard. Such 'telling' is
like giving way to a vice. To gratify it one must be prepared to waste one's
material substance. How much of this world's spoil might one secure if . . . ?
It is the unfinished calculation which all prodigals and spendthrifts have to
put to themselves.

Curiosity – which is untired wonder – is a gift; the publication of the results
of the activities is to be regarded solely as an expensive luxury. . . . There are, of
course, people who regard their luxuries as necessities; but it is all their own business. In the end it is they who must foot the bill, and they are foolish if they
expect to meet with sympathy – even less with support – from those who are
proud of being content with little, or from those who know to what inconve-
nience indiscretions may lead. So the problem which faces such as are possessed
of a gift whose exercise has an overweening fascination for themselves is the one
with which the ant dumbfounded the grasshopper: 'How can one make one's

vices and master-passions profitable?' Doubtless it can be done. Pavlova[1] to the grasshopper should prove some small encouragement and comfort.

It is possible that such a journal as THE EGOIST would be able, even in Anglo-Saxon countries, to survive if it made its frankness diverting enough to outweigh the effect of its depredations. People are willing to pay for old familiar things whose character they know and which suits them: all good Liberals will readily pay their penny for the *Daily News*. . . . On the other hand they might not. The Pavlova illustration is misleading: her dancing is diverting, but her audience would probably cease to find it so if she demanded as a sort of tribute the offering up of their most prized pieces of china to be shattered by her nimble feet.

At this moment when we propose concentrating our energies upon book production exclusively, we shall be pardoned for going at some length into the motives which have been operating with us throughout our publishing activities. At the outset we undertook such activities solely in order to give existence in book form to Mr. Joyce's novel, *A Portrait of the Artist as a Young Man*, and only after it had been proved impossible to find for that book any other English publisher willing to risk prosecution by the censor. However, from the experience acquired in trying to avoid this particular undertaking, we came to realise how urgent was the need for a publishing concern animated neither on the one hand by desire for financial gain, nor on the other by propagandist aims of a limitedly partisan kind. We realised that in the main, monetary profit was the spirit which dominated publication, though there did exist concerns prepared to publish at financial loss works which supported some specialist propaganda or other. But nowhere was there any appearance of an enterprise prepared to lose money in fostering and satisfying disinterested curiosity in humanity and in the soul and mind of man as a whole. . . . Consideration as to why this should be, led us to conclude that the offenders primarily to be held responsible were the artists and philosophers themselves. The mass of humanity is dead to every general feature of the science of human life, because those who speak for the science speak in the manner they do. They speak in muffled tones out of which their hearers can make nothing. They use worn phrases from which the meaning has gone; confused phrases which never possessed any precise and workable meaning. The question is: Why do those whose business it is to illumine these matters traffic so persistently in the blurred phrase? In our opinion, explanation is to be found in the smallness of the number of persons who know what they mean when they speak of anything save the most obvious and concrete facts of their experience; and to this smallness the multitude of those who call themselves artists and philosophers makes no appreciable difference. . . . So, if art and philosophy, instead of being excrescences, are to give form to the life and ways

---

1 The Russian classical ballerina Anna Pavlova was the most famous dancer in this form of her day, much written about in association with literary ideas because of the poeticism of her movement.

which should be shaping the whole course of human affairs, there must be in the first place, a winnowing movement among the ranks of philosophers and artists themselves. A test must be applied which will separate the genuine from the make-believe. That test in our opinion is clarity. The insight born of genius is neither accidental nor mysterious. . . .

Hence to establish intellectual curiosity in a front place in men's interests, it is necessary in the first instance to get rid of the pseudo-intellectuals and the poseurs. This it seems possible to do by insisting that artists be competent to give a coherent statement of the significance of their work and of the innovations they support. They must be expected to be articulate as to the meaning of their work, and that in the common tongue. Thus, artists would become their own premier critics. Thus, creation, exposition and criticism would and should all spring first hand from the one source. Only, indeed, from craftsmen actually practising their craft would criticism carry its full weight. So artists would be compelled to become philosophic: that is to say, *brains* would become an absolute necessity in an artist, a positively revolutionary thought indeed.

It seemed to us that, in establishing on non-commercial lines an enterprise limiting itself to the production of works either of original matter having a general philosophic bearing or to works of exposition giving the philosophy of new departures in art-works, we should be making operative an influence capable of transforming our entire world of form – thought and action.

8.3   John Gould Fletcher, 'Vers Libre and Advertisements', *The Little Review*, vol. II, no. 2 (April 1915)

This playful extract, from the Kansas poet Fletcher (1886–1950) reveals how alert contemporary writers were to the potential relationship between their work and the commoditization of all products in this era. In a witty parody of the key terms and attitudes of modernist slogans and manifestos, and of the language of the advertisers such as that of Dill Scott, extracted above, Fletcher performs a deft act of literary criticism on banal material to make his point. Vers libre (free verse) had, as the term suggests, originated in France; it was an attempt to free poetry from the straitjacket of traditional metre ('to break the pentameter' as Pound later put it) and form. It was an innovation particularly associated with Imagist writing, and created long-running 'tradition v. modernity' arguments about the 'proper' use of poetic form on both sides of the Atlantic. Fletcher was known himself to write in the Imagist mode, so there is a strong self-irony running through this witty commentary.

In common with all judicious readers of American magazines and newspapers, I have learned to look on the advertising pages for the best of news the journalist can offer. Advertisement writers are the best-paid, least rewarded, and best-trained authors that America possesses. Compared to these, even the income of a Robert Chambers pales into insignificance. Moreover, they understand the public thoroughly and do not attempt to overstrain its attention by overserious-ness, or exhaust its nerves by oversentimentality. That is, the best ones do not. . . .

It never occurred to me, however, that there might be gems of poetic ability hidden away in these tantalizing concoctions – these cocktails of prose. But I must revise my estimate. Without wishing to boom or discourage anyone's prod-ucts I cannot resist quoting some recent advertisements that I and I alone have discovered, seized, and gloated upon. After all, I approach the subject purely from the angle of form. . . .

The following appeared in a well-known monthly. The editor doubtless looks on free verse as the rankest heresy:

> A pipe, a maid,
> A sheet of ice,
> The glow of life –
> And that glow doubled
> By the glow of 'Lady Strike'
> Cuddling warm in the bowl.
> This is the life
> In the good old winter-time!

I do not say this is without faults. With the substance I have, naturally, nothing to do. But as regards form, which of your scribblers of cosmic bathos and 'uplift stuff' could more cunningly weave *pipe*, *ice*, *life*, *strike*, and *time* into a stanza that has half as much swing and verve, as this? Note also the absence of adjectives.[2] In short, here is poetry with a 'punch' to it. . . .

Gentlemen of the poet's profession, be ashamed of yourselves! How can you expect to find readers by lazily sticking to your antiquated formulas, when even the advertisement writers in the very magazines you do your work for, are getting quite up-to-date?

8.4 Jane Heap, 'Art and the Law', *The Little Review*, vol. III, no. 3 (September–December 1920)

One of the most notorious and defining moments of modernist writing came on 14 February 1921. The two editors of The Little Review, *Jane Heap and Margaret Anderson, were found guilty of publishing material which was 'obscene, lewd, lascivi-ous, filthy, indecent and disgusting'. They were fined $100, and had their fingerprints taken for the record. The material in question was an episode from James Joyce's novel* Ulysses. *In the 'Nausicaa' episode, one of Joyce's two protagonists in the book, Leopold*

---

2 The use of 'superfluous' rhetoric, including adjectives, was something which the Imagists and Pound went to war on particularly: see his essay 'A Few Don'ts' (March 1913).

Bloom, masturbates while gazing upon a young girl, Gerty MacDowell, as she looks after her friends' siblings, and reflects upon Bloom's gaze on her, on a beach near Dublin. When the US postal authority learnt of the nature of the writing they were being expected to deliver to subscribers, copies of this issue of the Review *were seized and destroyed. The episodes of the work as they appeared had also caught the attention of the New York Society for the Suppression of Vice, and their secretary, John S. Sumner, swore a complaint against Heap and Anderson for publishing 'obscenity' – the complaint which brought the case to trial. Although ably defended by the lawyer and patron of modernist writers, John Quinn, there was no doubt of the outcome. The case was the latest episode in modernist determination to challenge the values of contemporary bourgeois society. When four episodes from Joyce's novel had appeared in England in* The Egoist *in 1919, they had been expurgated by Ezra Pound, who was seeking to promote the novel on Joyce's behalf – and still there were huge problems in finding a printer willing to risk being fined for printing such material. More specifically, the later American court case destroyed Joyce's lingering hopes of finding a mainstream publisher for* Ulysses *in the US or the UK. The novel eventually appeared in a limited edition from Shakespeare and Company in Paris, run by Sylvia Beach, in 1922 – it would not receive broad circulation until the editions from Random House, New York (1934), and The Bodley Head in London (1936). After Sumner had sworn his complaint, Jane Heap offered a riposte from the magazine.*

The society for which Mr. Sumner is agent, I am told, was founded to protect the public from corruption. When asked *what public?* its defenders spring to the rock on which America was founded: the cream of sentimentality, and answer chivalrously 'Our young girls'. So the mind of the young girl rules this country? In it rests the safety, progress and lustre of a nation. . . .

The present case is rather ironical. We are being prosecuted for printing the thoughts in a young girl's mind. Her thoughts and actions and the meditations which they produced in the mind of the sensitive Mr. Bloom. If the young girl corrupts can she also be corrupted? Mr. Joyce's young girl is an innocent, simple, childish girl who tends children . . . she hasn't had the advantage of the dances, cabarets, motor trips, open to the young girls of this more pure and free country.

If there is anything I really fear it is the mind of the young girl.

I do not understand Obscenity; I have never studied it nor had it, but I know that it must be a terrible and peculiar menace to the United States. I know that there is an expensive department maintained in Washington with a chief and fifty assistants to prevent its spread. . . .

To a mind used to life Mr. Joyce's chapter seems to be a record of the simplest, most unpreventable, most unfocused sex thoughts possible in a rightly-constructed, unashamed human being. Mr. Joyce is not teaching early Egyptian perversions nor inventing new ones. Girls lean back every where showing lace and silk stockings; wear low cut sleeveless gowns, breathless bathing suits; men think thoughts and have emotions about these things everywhere – seldom as delicately and imaginatively as Mr. Bloom – and no one is corrupted. Can merely reading about the thoughts he thinks corrupt a man when his thoughts do not? All power to the artist, but this is not his function.

It was the poet, the artist, who discovered love, created the lover, made sex everything that is beyond a function. It is the Mr. Sumners who have made it an obscenity. It is a little too obvious to discuss the inevitable result of damming up a force as unholy and terrific as the reproductive force with nothing more powerful than silence, black books, and censure. 'Our young girls' grow up conscious of being possessed as by a devil, with some urge which they are told is shameful, dangerous and obscene. They try to be 'pure' with no other incantations than a few 'obstetric mutterings'. . . .

Only in a nation ignorant of the power of Art . . . insensitive and unambitious to the need and appreciation of Art . . . could such a habit of mind obtain. Art is the only thing that produces life, extends life – I am speaking beyond physically and mentally. A people without the experience of the Art influence can bring forth nothing but a humanity that bears the stamp of a loveless race. Facsimile women and stereotyped men – a humanity without distinction or design, indicating no more the creative touch than if they were assembled parts.

There are still those people who are not outraged by the mention of natural facts who will ask 'what is the necessity to discuss them?' But that is not a question to ask about a work of Art. The only question relevant at all to *Ulysses* is – Is it a work of Art? The men best capable of judging have pronounced it a work of the first rank. Anyone with a brain would hesitate to question the necessity in an artist to create, or his ability to choose the right subject matter. Anyone who has read *Exiles*,[3] *The Portrait*, and *Ulysses* from the beginning, could not rush in with talk of obscenity. No man has been more crucified on his sensibilities than James Joyce.

---

3 Joyce's play *Exiles* had been written in 1914, and published without difficulty in 1918.

9

Empire, Race and Postcolonialism

Introduction

The last twenty-five years of the nineteenth century, and the years before the First World War of the twentieth, saw a rapid expansion by the major European powers and by the USA of colonial territorial holdings across the globe. Britain increased its already wide influence by over a further 4 million square miles, mainly in Africa and into Burma; France by over 3.5 million square miles; Germany by over 1 million, and so on. America acquired over 100,000 square miles, largely in Asia. The impulse towards this rampant and often bloody colonization was largely commercial, but also complicatedly political: the need to open new markets for trade, and also the need to obtain more raw materials on the one hand; the need to prevent other nations acquiring potentially valuable goods and resources on the other. Out of this imperial impulse, as several contemporary commentators cited in various parts of this book realized, arose the tangled web of alliances and forces which led to the catastrophic and accelerated breakdown of international relations which brought about the First World War in 1914.

The technological and industrial conditions and consumerism which had developed by the latter part of the nineteenth century made the major nations in many ways dependent upon their colonies. Rubber for mechanical products and tyres came from the Congo and the Amazon basin; tin, essential for metal alloys, came from Asia and southern America. Gold and diamonds impelled the struggle for South Africa. Western tastes were now attuned to 'colonial' products, including tea (India and Ceylon), coffee (the Caribbean and South America), sugar and bananas (the Caribbean).

The greatest export *from* the imperial centres to the colonies was probably people, with a continuing flow of emigrants, particularly from amongst the poorest classes of society, seeking better conditions in the white dependencies, including Canada, Australia and New Zealand. But there was also a significant exchange of peoples, for however limited an amount of time, for educational or economic purposes. Indians, Africans, and whites from the dependencies came into London, for instance, seeking amongst other things political empowerment. The Pan-African Congresses in the British capital in 1900 and 1911 brought together people of African descent from across the globe, including the

Americas, seeking solidarity from which to begin to alleviate the conditions of deprivation under which many blacks lived. Other future national leaders, including Gandhi, also spent periods at the heart of this the largest empire.

Race issues were being foregrounded also in the US, with the influx of blacks from the South seeking better living and employment conditions in the northern cities. New York and Chicago were transformed geographically, politically and culturally, across these years, as an increasingly confident and educated black leadership began questioning the racial divide, and establishing their own perspective upon nationhood.

In many ways modernism bears the stamp of this situation. The national background of those involved in the main discussions about the direction of literature during the period is extraordinarily diverse – Ireland (Yeats, Joyce); America (James, Pound, Eliot, H.D., Stevens, Moore, the immigrant Williams); Poland (Conrad); New Zealand (Mansfield); alongside the English writers. Shared amongst the writers from outside Britain is the sense that their nation of origin offers them little by way of a local literary tradition upon which they might draw for their own work. Shared amongst many of the English writers is a sense that they are operating outside the mainstream in terms of their regional identity, or class, or gender. In all of these ways, modernism is an eclectic phenomenon in terms of the identity that the writers are seeking to establish through their works; but, especially, it resounds with imperial history. This is so even amongst the English writers: think of Woolf's mentions of Anglo-Indian family background in *The Years*, or the return of Peter from India in *Mrs Dalloway*; Forster's *A Passage to India*; Lawrence's stories of travel to Ceylon (Sri Lanka) and his novels from Australia, *Kangaroo* and his collaborative *The Boy in the Bush*. For all of these writers, as for others including Gertrude Stein, the visual art of the day was hugely influential, and that art, from Picasso's deployment of African influence in such seminal work as *Les Demoiselles d'Avignon* (1907) to Paul Gauguin's many pictures from the South Seas, demonstrates in many ways the impact of empire upon form and representation in this period.

The early twentieth century, of course, also saw the beginnings of a destabilization of the imperial order, just as it had extended itself to its greatest limit, and the correlative extension of fears, expressed even in the work of an empire-supporter such as Rudyard Kipling, that Britain in particular had over-reached itself. Following the Boer War over territory and diamond wealth in South Africa, Britain was facing a series of challenges in the 1910s – the rise of a nationalist movement in India; the Imperial Conference in 1911 which sought to rationalize Britain's relations to its white dominions; the formation of the party later to become the nationalist African National Congress in South Africa in 1912; and, finally, the uprising in Britain's own backyard in Dublin, Ireland, at Easter 1916. All of these events look forward to the unstable period between the world wars when Britain, exhausted and drained of resources by 1914–18, found it increasingly difficult to manage the vast extent of an empire inherited from the previous generation.

The extracts in this section seek to cover many of these major issues and tensions, as well as, in the first few documents, striving to give a sense of the instability at the heart of Britain's Empire at the turn of the century, as liberal voices hugely important to the intellectual climate of the time became increasingly strident in their claim that imperialism itself was a misguided project.

9.1   John M. Robertson, *Patriotism and Empire* (1899)

Robertson (1856–1933) was a freethinker, and initially a follower of the ideas of the social reformer Charles Bradlaugh, who advocated individual freedom, democracy, and the rights of women. Robertson later supported the work of another advocate of Bradlaugh's ideas, including that on birth control, Annie Besant (see later in this section). Robertson served in the British Parliament as a Liberal MP, 1906–18. He earned his living mostly, however, from his writing, which covered a large range of topics, from the history of freethought and socialism, to sociology, economics, and work on Shakespeare and English Elizabethan literature (this last was to prove influential in forming the ideas of T. S. Eliot). Robertson's ideas on empire were strongly influenced by another liberal, J. A. Hobson (see next extract), whose preliminary writings on the subject had appeared in 1898. Robertson felt that imperialism was a disease much like its earlier incarnation, patriotism, and that this disease blighted much of the developed world, including the United States: 'To put the case shortly, if nationalism is bad, imperialism is worse.' Unlike Hobson's economic analysis of empire, therefore, Robertson largely saw the currently inflated urge towards imperialism to be of 'the same animal root' as nationalism, patriotism and militarism. Most notably, he recognized that the desire for imperial riches from the upper and middle or business classes in Britain was preventing the possibility of necessary and widespread social reforms at home being addressed and realized. The extracts here come from Robertson's chapter on 'The Theory and Practice of Imperialism', including his reading of the recent political history underlying the imperial drive, and then move on to his broader diagnoses of what he persists in the book in calling the 'malady' of imperialism.

It is when we come to the outstanding political problem of the period – the problem signalized by the word Imperialism – that all our issues come into their clearest light. Patriotism, conventionally defined as love of country, now turns out rather obviously to stand for love of more country; and the militarism urged upon us as a fountain of domestic virtues comes out once for all, in our own case, as a needed instrument of foreign expansion. But a special set of pleadings emerges on the news issue; and in relation to it the others take on new phases.

No change in the drift of British politics since 1870, perhaps, is more marked than that set up in the prevailing tone of allusion to the colonies and dependencies of the State. It is since Mr. Gladstone's death, however, that the tide has flowed highest. In the years of Disraeli's ascendancy, from 1874 to 1880, the 'imperial idea' had indeed been swiftly and successfully grown, to the point even of over-shadowing Gladstonian Liberalism.[1] On a policy of naked aggression, ungilded by any clear appeal to commercial interests, the adroit leader of the Right was able to detach vote after vote in the House from his rival's side; and we know that he at length believed he had thrust Gladstone out of power for twenty years.

Gladstone was an inspirer and commander rather than an educator; he had really no constructive ideal fitted to oust [Disraeli], and he was hardly settled in office when he found himself carried into strictly Disraelian causes. Of each and all of them he duly repented; but his lapse was the expression at once of his practical empiricism and of the real strength of the forces he seemed to conquer. They consisted, roughly speaking, of (1) the 'service' interests, which since his own abolition of purchase tax in 1871 had become knit as never before with the middle class; (2) the specifically capitalist interests, which were directly involved in Egypt, and were reaching out towards South Africa; (3) the general trading interests, which spontaneously leant to 'expansion' as a way of widening the market; (4) the temper of national pride developed in the latter-day commercial aristocracy and rich middle class, as of old in the aristocracies of feudalism, and of the landlord system of last century. The forcing forward of the Home Rule issue by the skill and strength of Parnell in 1885–86, and the energy with which Gladstone fought it up till 1893, kept that issue in the forefront, and called off to it the forces of imperialism, which were now nearly all arrayed on the side of Unionism, and were thus organized on a new tactical basis. But when the defeat of Home Rule was followed by the withdrawal and death of Gladstone, and his lieutenants, for lack of a common ideal, decided to keep no constructive policy whatever before the nation, imperialism inevitably began to carry all before it.

The average citizen who talks of empire is not very clearly conscious that he uses a word which properly means 'rule' – rule over other communities than his own. As applied in the phrase 'our colonial empire', it is already diverted to a merely geographical sense, seeing that the colonies neither pay tribute to, nor receive laws from, the mother-country. Even the Sovereign is 'Empress' only of India, though the convenience of the expression 'the British Empire' has fixed it in use for the whole connections and possessions of the United Kingdom. But it is the more important to remember the historical meaning of empire, seeing that it is at empire, in a slight modification of the historical sense, that imperialism aims.

The significant thing is that, to say nothing of the most ancient known military empires, which grew out of the conquest of city by city, the most expressly 'free' or democratic of the communities of historic Greece coveted empire from the instant it became possible to her.

---

1 The successive British Prime Ministers, the Liberal William Gladstone and the Conservative Benjamin Disraeli, had been instrumental in establishing the competing strands of British imperial policy in the late nineteenth century.

One of the most unpromising symptoms of our case is the uncomprehending way in which the British imperialist always scans the story of ancient Rome. Noting the decadence which is the upshot of the whole, he seems to suppose that somehow Christianity will avail to save later empires from the same fate, though Rome was Christianized during the decline; or that haply the elimination of chattel slavery will avert decay, though Christian Spain was free from chattel slavery at home; or that industrialism will avail, though the Moors and the Florentines were tolerably industrial. Any theory will serve to burke the truth that the special cause of decay is just empire.

Shortly put, the imperialist's case is that expansion of 'the empire' is necessary –

(1) To provide openings for the emigration of our superfluous population; and
(2) To 'open up fresh markets'.

When answered that we need not our own markets, and that trade normally goes on between different States, he answers,

(3) That 'trade follows the flag'.

Incidentally he is apt to point to the benefits bestowed by British rule on the natives of India and Egypt; and he is at times led by the exigencies of argument to affirm that the bestowal of such benefits is his and his nation's master passion; though the previous propositions might be supposed to invalidate it for the intelligence even of the lowest races concerned. . . .

Putting aside the 'pasteboard portico' of the pseudo-Malthusian theory, we come to the real motives: (1) The primary desire of the speculative commercial class for new grounds in which to buy cheap and sell dear; (2) the suffusive instinct of spoliation and dominion which, on the part of the services and the general public, backs them up; and (3) the sinister interest of those industrial sections which thrive on the production of war material. It would be hard to conceive a more mindless system of social evolution than that presupposed by the resort, at this time of day, to the early ideal that trade is best to be pushed by barter with semi-barbarians.

We come back, then, to the vital aspect of imperialism for the mass of the working population. The only interests really furthered by fresh expansion are those of the speculative trading class, the speculative capitalist class, the military and naval services, the industrial class which supplies war material, and generally those who look to an imperial civil service as a means of employment for themselves and their kin. . . .

As against all the sophistries we have passed under review, the central truth falls to be stated thus: imperial expansion is substantially a device on the part of the moneyed class, primarily to further its own chances, secondarily to put off the day of reckoning as between capital and labour. It does not and cannot bring a socially just solution any nearer: it does but secure a possible extension of employment for labour on the old terms. In so far, then, as labour is led by any or all of the sophisms of imperialist patriotism, it is gulled to its own ultimate perdition. While imperialism prospers, there will be no vital social reform; and reactionary Ministers have begun to see that by playing the game of militarist imperialism they can safely push aside the appeal for such reform. One of the first sequelae of the triumph of Omdurman was the definite repudiation of Ministerial promises in the direction of Old Age Pensions.

In fine, wisdom and righteousness for a nation are not vitally different from what we esteem as wisdom and righteousness in individual men. And that nation which thinks to prosper by inverting the principles of stable human relations, by calling rapine righteousness and profligacy prudence, will but illustrate sooner or later the fatality of natural law. On such lines no nation as such can survive. The conclusion is not one of a too ideal ethic: it is the lesson read to us in age after age, in civilization after civilization, by empire after empire that has left only its ruins behind to warn us against the errors by which it perished.

9.2   J. A. Hobson, *Imperialism: A Study* (1902; 1905 revised edition)

John Atkinson Hobson (1858–1940) was born into a privileged background in Derby, in the British Midlands; he studied Classics at Oxford, and, after a period of school-teaching, became a leading figure in the Liberal movement. After 1900, he became the national spokesman for a 'New Liberalism', which included a call for the re-distribution of wealth, and for the provision of welfare services at a national level. Hobson's critique of empire formed his most famous work; his understanding of the economic propulsion behind the enhanced imperial drive on behalf not just of Britain but also of the other European powers, was widely respected for its detail and knowledge at the time. In a 1938 edition of the book, Hobson said that he still stood by his analysis. In another book, the 1911 Economic Interpretation of Investment, *he had seemed to waver, when calling imperialism a part of the progress towards democracy and healthy nationalism which modern nations had embarked upon. The First World War, however, changed his views back to their beginnings, and in* Democracy and the War *(1917), he clearly sets the urge to discover potential new markets at the root of imperialism and thence of the disastrous militarism which had been the driver towards conflict: 'the ever-growing urgency for . . . access to favourable supplies of raw materials and the desire for exclusive areas for lucrative investments and personal spheres of business exploitation – these keen persistent desires of strong well-organised groups of business men within each Western nation will be found everywhere to supply the driving force in foreign and colonial policy and so to operate as a demand for militarism!' The extracts here from* Imperialism *span the book, from Hobson's initial reading of imperialism as a nationalism gone wrong, through his diagnosis of the truth*

behind the imperial situation, whatever the official propaganda, to his critique of the
supposedly benevolent and progressive doctrines of the imperialists themselves.

Turning from the territorial and dynastic nationalism [of the earlier nineteenth century] to the spirit of racial, linguistic, and economic solidarity which has been the underlying motive, we find a still more remarkable movement. Local particularism on the one hand, vague cosmopolitanism upon the other, yielded to a ferment of nationalist sentiment, manifesting itself among the weaker peoples not merely in a sturdy and heroic resistance against political absorption or territorial nationalism, but in a passionate revival of decaying customs, language, literature, and art. . . .
    It is a debasement of this genuine nationalism, by attempts to overflow its natural banks and absorb the near or distant territory of reluctant and unassimilable peoples, that marks the passage from nationalism to a spurious colonialism on the one hand, Imperialism on the other.

Officially, British 'colonial possessions' fall into three classes – (1) 'Crown colonies, in which the Crown has the entire control of legislation, while the administration is carried on by public officers under the control of the Home Government; (2) colonies possessing representative institutions, but not responsible government, in which the Crown has no more than a veto on legislation, but the Home Government retains the control of public affairs; (3) colonies possessing representative institutions and responsible government, in which the Crown has only a veto on legislation, and the Home Government has no control over any officer except the Governor.'
    Now, of the thirty-nine separate areas which have been annexed by Great Britain since 1870 as colonies or protectorates, not a single one ranks in class 3 and the Transvaal alone in class 2.
    The new Imperialism has established no single British colony endowed with responsible self-government. Nor, with the single exception of the three new States in South Africa,[2] where white settlers live in some numbers, is it seriously pretended that any of these annexed territories is being prepared and educated for representative, responsible self-government; and even in these South African States there is no serious intention, either on the part of the Home Government or of the colonists, that the majority of the inhabitants shall control the government.

Seeing that the Imperialism of the last three decades is clearly condemned as a business policy, in that at enormous expense it has procured a small, bad, unsafe increase of markets, and has jeopardised the entire wealth of the nation in rousing

---

2 Under the treaty signed at the end of the Boer War in 1902, the territories of Transvaal and the Orange Free State became British Crown Colonies.

the strong resentment of other nations, we may ask 'How is the British nation induced to embark upon such unsound business?' The only possible answer is that the business interests of the nation as a whole are subordinated to those of certain sectional interests that usurp control of the national resources and use them for their private gain. . . .

The vast expenditure on armaments, the costly wars, the grave risks and embarrassments of foreign policy, the stoppage of political and social reforms within Great Britain, though fraught with great injury to the nation, have served well the present business interests of certain industries and professions.

In view of the part which the non-economic factors of patriotism, adventure, military enterprise, political ambition, and philanthropy play in imperial expansion, it may appear that to impute to financiers so much power is to take a too narrow economic view of history. And it is true that the motor-power of Imperialism is not chiefly financial: finance is rather the governor of the imperial engine, directing the energy and determining its work: it does not constitute the fuel of the engine, nor does it directly generate the power. Finance manipulates the patriotic forces which politicians, soldiers, philanthropists, and traders generate; the enthusiasm for expansion which issues from these sources, though strong and genuine, is irregular and blind; the financial interest has those qualities of concentration and clear-sighted calculation which are needed to set Imperialism to work. An ambitious statesman, a frontier soldier, an overzealous missionary, a pushing trader, may suggest or even initiate a step of imperial expansion, may assist in educating patriotic public opinion to the urgent need of some fresh advance, but the final determination rests with financial power. The direct influence exercised by great financial houses in 'high politics' is supported by the control which they exercise over the body of public opinion through the Press, which, in every 'civilised' country, is becoming more and more their obedient instrument.

Such is the array of distinctively economic forces making for Imperialism, a large loose group of trades and professions seeking profitable business and lucrative employment from the expansion of military and civil services, and from the expenditure on military operations, the opening up of new tracts of territory and trade with the same, and the provision of new capital which these operations require, all these finding their central guiding and directing force in the power of the general financier.

The play of these forces does not openly appear. They are essentially parasites upon patriotism, and they adapt themselves to its protecting colours. In the mouths of their representatives are noble phrases, expressive of their desire to extend the area of civilization, to establish good government, promote Christianity, extirpate slavery, and elevate the lower races. Some of the business men who hold such language may entertain a genuine, though usually a vague, desire to accomplish these ends, but they are primarily engaged in business, and they are not unaware of the utility of the more unselfish forces in furthering their ends.

The present condition of the government under which the vast majority of our fellow-subjects in the Empire live is eminently un-British in that it is based, not on the consent of the governed, but upon the will of imperial officials; it does indeed betray a great variety of forms, but they agree in the essential of un-freedom. Nor is it true that any of the more enlightened methods of administration we employ are directed towards undoing this character. Not only in India, but in the West Indies, and wherever there exists a large preponderance of coloured population, the trend, not merely of ignorant, but of enlightened public opinion, is against a genuinely representative government on British lines. It is perceived to be incompatible with the economic and social authority of a superior race.

Though it can hardly be denied that the ambitions of individuals or nations have been the chief conscious motives in Imperialism, it is possible to maintain that here, as in other departments of human history, certain larger hidden forces operate towards the progress of humanity. The powerful hold which biological conceptions have obtained over the pioneers in the science of sociology is easily intelligible. It is only natural that the laws of individual and specific progress so clearly discerned in other parts of the animal kingdom should be rigorously applied to man; it is not unnatural that the deflections or reversals of the laws of lower life by certain other laws, which only attain importance in the higher psychical reaches of the *genus homo*, should be underrated, misinterpreted, or ignored. . . .

Others, taking the wider cosmic standpoint, insist that the progress of humanity itself requires the maintenance of a selective and destructive struggle between races which embody different powers and capacities, different types of civilization. It is desirable that the earth should be peopled, governed, and developed, as far as possible, by the races which can do this work best, i.e. by the races of highest 'social efficiency'; these races must assert their right by conquering, ousting, subjugating, or extinguishing races of lower social efficiency. . . .

This genuine and confidant conviction about 'social efficiency' must be taken for the chief moral support of Imperialism. . . . So easily we glide from natural history to ethics, and find in utility a moral sanction for the race struggle. Now, Imperialism is nothing but this natural history doctrine regarded from the standpoint of one's own nation. We represent the socially efficient nation, we have conquered and acquired dominion and territory in the past: we must go on, it is our destiny, one which is serviceable to ourselves and to the world, our duty.

Thus, emerging from natural history, the doctrine soon takes on a large complexity of ethical and religious finery, and we are wafted into an elevated atmosphere of 'imperial Christianity', a 'mission of civilization', in which we are to teach 'the arts of good government' and 'the dignity of labour.'

9.3   W. E. B. Du Bois, *The Souls of Black Folk* (1903)

William Edward Burghardt Du Bois (1868–1963) grew up in the US South, and became the first black person to receive a PhD from Harvard, where he studied under (amongst others) William James and George Santayana. Du Bois was an historian and a sociologist, a Professor of Economics and History at Atlanta University for many years, and was responsible for conducting the first researches into the black experience in America. Soon after he left Harvard, Du Bois's voice was increasingly raised against the most respected advocate of black civil rights of the time, Booker T. Washington. Du Bois disagreed strongly with Washington's compromising line with whites over education and constitutional reform, feeling that the two races remained separate. These views prevailed throughout Du Bois's life. When the National Association for the Advancement of Colored People – a pressure group containing both blacks and whites – was founded in 1910, Du Bois was elected as one of its founding officers. Twenty-four years later, however, he was forced to resign from the Association since he still advocated a non-integrationist policy, arguing that blacks should found their own businesses and industries in order to advance their economic status. Du Bois had first indicated his notion that the black experience in the US implied a double-consciousness in the late 1890s; The Souls of Black Folk, however, gave the notion its most expansive elucidation in the early years. Souls is notable for its eclectic form – the book is a mixture of history, politics, cultural reflection and autobiography. This eclecticism was to form a notable feature of black writing in the early years of the twentieth century, including that in the New Negro Anthology *(see extracts below) and other work from the Harlem Renaissance group of artists. In 'The Forethought' to* Souls, *Du Bois declared that 'Herein lie buried many things which if read with patience may show the strange meaning of being black in the dawning of the Twentieth Century. This meaning is not without interest to you, Gentle Reader; for the problem of the Twentieth Century is the problem of the color-line.' These extracts come from the beginning of the book, where he lays out his understanding both of this line, and of his most famous concept, double-consciousness.*

Between me and the other world there is ever an unanswered question: unasked by some through feelings of delicacy; by others through the difficulty of rightly framing it. All, nevertheless, flutter around it. They approach me in a half-hesitant sort of way, eye me curiously or compassionately, and then, instead of saying directly, How does it feel to be a problem? they say, I know an excellent colored man in my town; or, I fought at Mechanicsville;[3] or, Do not these Southern outrages make your blood boil? At these I smile, or am interested, or reduce the boiling to a simmer, as the occasion may require. To the real question, How does it feel to be a problem? I answer seldom a word.

And yet, being a problem is a strange experience, – peculiar even for one who

---

3 A Civil War battle, near Richmond, Virginia.

has never been anything else, save perhaps in babyhood in Europe. It is in the early days of rollicking boyhood that the revelation first bursts upon one, all in a day, as it were. I was a little thing, away up in the hills of New England. . . . In a wee wooden schoolhouse, something put it into the boys' and girls' heads to buy gorgeous visiting-cards – ten cents a package – and exchange. The exchange was merry, till one girl, a tall newcomer, refused my card, – refused it peremptorily, with a glance. Then it dawned upon me with a certain suddenness that I was different from the others; or like, mayhap, in heart and life and longing, but shut out from their world by a vast veil. I had thereafter no desire to tear down that veil, to creep through; I held all beyond it in common contempt, and lived above it in a region of blue sky and great wandering shadows. That sky was bluest when I could beat my mates at examination-time, or beat them at a foot-race, or even beat their stringy heads. Alas, with the years all this fine contempt began to fade; for the worlds I longed for, and all their dazzling opportunities, were theirs, not mine. But they should not keep these prizes, I said; some, all, I would wrest from them. . . .

After the Egyptian and Indian, the Greek and Roman, the Teuton and Mongolian, the Negro is a sort of seventh son, born with a veil, and gifted with second-sight in this American world,[4] – a world which yields him no true self-consciousness, but only lets him see himself through the revelation of the other world. It is a peculiar sensation, this double-consciousness, this sense of always looking at one's self through the eyes of others, of measuring one's soul by the tape of a world that looks on in an amused contempt and pity. One ever feels his two-ness, – an American, a Negro; two souls, two thoughts, two unreconciled strivings; two warring ideals in one dark body, whose dogged strength alone keeps it from being torn asunder.

The history of the American Negro is the history of this strife, – this longing to attain self-conscious manhood, to merge his double self into a better and truer self. In this merging he wishes neither of the older selves to be lost. He would not Africanize America, for America has too much to teach the world and Africa. He would not bleach his Negro soul in a flood of white Americanism, for he knows that Negro blood has a message in the world. He simply wishes to make it possible for a man to be both a Negro and an American, without being cursed and spit upon by his fellows, without having the doors of Opportunity closed roughly in his face.

This, then, is the end of his striving: to be a co-worker in the kingdom of culture, to escape both death and isolation, to husband and use his best powers and his latent genius. These powers of body and mind have in the past been strangely wasted, dispersed, or forgotten. The shadow of a mighty Negro past flits through the tale of Ethiopia the Shadowy and of Egypt the Sphinx.

---

4 Like other races, including the Celtic, African Americans traditionally felt that all of these qualities made for special, prophetic, abilities.

Throughout history, the powers of single black men flash here and there like falling stars, and die sometimes before the world has rightly gauged their brightness. Here in America, in the few days since Emancipation,[5] the black man's turning hither and thither in hesitant and doubtful striving has often made his very strength to lose effectiveness, to seem like absence of power, like weakness. And yet it is not weakness, – it is the contradiction of double aims. The double-aimed struggle of the black artisan – on the one hand to escape white contempt for a nation of mere hewers of wood and drawers of water, and on the other hand to plough and nail and dig for a poverty-stricken horde – could only result in making him a poor craftsman, for he had but half a heart for either cause. By the poverty and ignorance of his people, the Negro minister or doctor was tempted toward quackery and demagogy; and by the criticism of the other world, toward ideals that made him ashamed of his lowly tasks. The would-be black *savant* was confronted by the paradox that the knowledge his people needed was a twice-told tale[6] to his white neighbors, while the knowledge which would teach the white world was Greek to his own flesh and blood. The innate love of harmony and beauty that set the ruder souls of his people a-dancing and a-singing raised but confusion and doubt in the soul of the black artist; for the beauty revealed to him was the soul-beauty of a race which his larger audience despised,[7] and he could not articulate the message of another people. This waste of double aims, this seeking to satisfy two unreconciled ideals, has wrought sad havoc with the courage and faith and deeds of ten thousand thousand people, – has sent them often wooing false gods and invoking false means of salvation, and at times has even seemed about to make them ashamed of themselves.

9.4   A. G. Crafter, ' "England's Day of Reckoning" ', *The New Age*, 22 and 29 May 1913

The years leading up to the First World War saw serious questions asked about the nature of the relationship between various of the colonized countries in the British Empire and the 'mother country'. This, in turn, raised questions about the nature and identity of the country itself. After years of argument, Australia had eventually become a Commonwealth member with its own governing parliament in 1901. In Canada, the request for support and troops for Britain to help fight the Boer War (1899–1902) met with a lukewarm response; in 1910 pressure to contribute to the expanding British Navy was met with rebuff and the Canadian government instead built a small navy of its

---

5 Abraham Lincoln's Emancipation Proclamation of 1862 freed all slaves held by rebellious Southerners as of the 1st January the next year.

6 Du Bois is playing upon the title of a short-story collection by the American writer Nathaniel Hawthorne (1837).

7 Like later writers, Du Bois throughout this book identifies black separateness specifically through Negro spirituals and other music.

own. A pre-war trade treaty with the United States seemed further to distance the Canadian Confederation from Britain. In India, strength of support for the nationalist cause grew in the wake of the Russo-Japanese war of 1904–5, which showed a smaller nation challenging a colonizing aggressor; the movement for national unification drove the ideals of the Muslim League, founded in 1906, and was partially met by the 1909 India Councils Act, which allowed for very limited self-government. Meanwhile bombings and assassinations continued in the nationalist cause, particularly in Bengal. In Ireland, a third Home Rule Bill was introduced in 1912, following on from the failed attempts to cede a large amount of self-rule to the country in 1883 and 1896. Yet again, the issue became caught up in the parliamentary process; but the supporters of the largely Protestant Unionist cause, who wished to retain the connection with Britain unaltered, were perturbed by the crisis, and half a million, largely from the north-east of the island, signed the Ulster Covenant drawn up by Sir Edward Carson in 1912. A paramilitary volunteer army was also mobilized, numbering 100,000 by 1913. The First World War altered many of these quarrels between Britain and her colonies, perhaps for the reasons signalled by Crafter in this article; many troops from all of these countries died in the Allied cause. But the tensions, and questions about national identity, set out here (Crafter was Canadian), were increasingly to come to the fore in the debilitated years of the peace after 1918.

Are any of us consciously predominantly 'English' or 'British'? Is the crown Canadian or British? Is an Australian a Briton? What is nationality? What is patriotism? Somewhere, in the greatest empire, is a Sovereign Power. What is it? Is an Imperial nationality – that is, a British empire nationality, including, as it must, white citizens and coloured subjects of the Crown in the following rough proportions, e.g., 325 million East Indians, 35 million Negroes, 30 million 'British' and about 30 million 'English' – a possibility? This, by the way, is the 'ideal' of Imperialism. But is it desirable; would it be stable? Or, on the other hand, would a National Federation of the one people and five Parliaments of what in reality is now the Sovereign Power – the British race – be preferable? This, in turn, is Nationalism, not Imperialism.

It is conceivable, and is here seriously suggested, that the Nation is greater than its Empire – the brain greater than its body. I do not agree that mere bulk is either Glory or anything more than mere bulk. I do not agree that this civilisation, of British national and historical development, should, or can, amalgamate with, among themselves, the antagonistic castes, races, creeds, and other civilisations of the British subject and tropical empire, to all of which, be it noted, the two words 'nationality' and 'patriotism' are foreign and incomprehensible idioms. But this, as I have said, is the ideal and aspiration of the leaders of the Imperialist movement, if, that is, we assume that that movement (with its dominating subscribers) is at least as sincere as it is unintelligible.

Is not Imperialism, for all this people of the sovereign race are Britons, with,

among other essentials of nationality, a common Crown, and a common patriotism – a patriotism based on their common history? Among these, it does not
matter whether they are Canadians, Welsh, or English, their patriotism is British.
Each of these five environmental sections of the race, may, shall, and should, be
loyal to their own Government, love their own country; but the patriotism of all
– a greater and another matter – is inseparable from their united identity.

But this un-English, non-party, broader attitude does not yet find favour with
the Imperialistic sentiments of a host of Englishmen, who, carried away by local
partisan phrases, have never had time to analyse, or to understand, what these
things mean, or whither they – their tribe or nation – drift. National security,
and national well-being, are less to-day than a local self-styled 'statesman's' local
and personal stake in a minor and local Bill. . . .

The following from the pen of Mr Arnold White, in a recent number of the
'Referee', is typical of a certain section of society and its mind. Speaking of
English, Scotch, and Welsh 'nationalities', he says: 'Let all Englishmen use the
word English when writing or speaking of a thing which is English. The navy is
English; the army is predominantly English; India has never heard of the United
Kingdom' (or, presumably, of the *British* Crown, or *British* nation. It may be
remembered that 'the Princes and people of India' sent a congratulatory message
last year to 'the Great *English* people', through the Viceroy, a British official).
England she knows.

. . . But fortunately this prolific Imperialist and publicist has nothing at this
time to say of the Irish 'nation', or, is it, of Irish nationalities? To Mr Redmond
the people of Ireland are a 'nation'.[8] Yet the leader of the opposition told his
Blenheim audience:[9] 'There are two nations in Ireland.' Whereas this, again, was
denied by Sir Edward Carson, who instructed the House that the Irish were not
a nation at all.

On the same phase of the same subject in the current 'British Review' Mr.
Cecil Chesterton says, 'I am convinced that our difficulties in Ireland are due
almost wholly to our refusal to recognise the sentiment of Irish nationality.'
Now with the profoundest respect for this scribe's splendid and more than
English journalism, to my mind, he is here expressing a transitory sentiment,

8 John Redmond was leader of the Irish Nationalist Party (1900–18), which held the balance of power
   in the British Parliament after 1910, when the two main parties, the Conservative and Unionists on
   the one hand and the Liberals on the other, were evenly split. In return for his support of the Liberal
   Government, the third Home Rule Bill was eventually passed through the Parliament in May 1914,
   but its chances of being enacted were destroyed by the advent of world war and the threat of a civil
   war in Ireland itself.

9 Andrew Bonar Law, the leader of the Conservative and Unionist opposition in the British Parliament,
   the House of Commons, had made a speech on Ireland at Blenheim Palace, Oxfordshire, in July 1912,
   in which he showed strong support for the notion that the predominantly Protestant and Unionist
   north-east of the island might be split away from the rest – effectively deserting those Unionists who
   lived in the south, now the Republic of Ireland.

and a sentiment only, of uninformed, or misinformed, local public opinion. The Irish, because of mis-government and distrust (in which they are not alone), express their revolt against the 'English' only, in the disintegrating threat or suggestion of this 'national' claim. Patriotism will always, and can only, follow nationality.

A serious error in Britain's domestic policy might easily shatter the whole national structure as well as the Empire, with the consequence of forthwith precipitating the transfer of Anglo-Saxon dominion from the Atlantic and Britain to the three great continental English-speaking States of that coming world's centre, under the headship of the United States. The alternative, a simple matter of historical and terminological accuracy, is for the English to subordinate their mere tribal and only domestic aspirations to the true national title and national spirit, which is not English, but which is, and can only continue, British.

The nation is greater than its Empire, will fight for its Empire, but the subject Empire will never fight for the nation. 'Loyalty to the Empire,' on the part of Britons, is loyalty to their common responsibilities in connection with the races and countries which are outside their patriotism, but which are subject to their Sovereign nation. . . . As a matter of fact, no one has ever yet produced a feasible and acceptable scheme of Imperial Unity, and no one ever will. On the other hand, a war threatening these shores would immediately evolve a national union. . . . That, or the end of the Empire, and the end of the British power.

9.5   Benjamin Brawley, *A Social History of the American Negro: Being a History of the Negro Problem in the United States* (1921)

Brawley (1882–1939) studied, inter alia, at the universities of Chicago and Harvard. He was a clergyman and black historian who was also a Professor of English (his New Survey of English Literature *appeared in 1925).* A Social History of the American Negro *is a striking book, in that it takes the debate about race in America forward from pioneering work like that of W. E. B. Du Bois. Self-consciously an assessment of the ironically called race 'problem' in the light of a world war in which the United States had come to new prominence in the world order, Brawley's work seizes the moment to review the new situation from the point of view of the continuingly oppressed black population. The war had seen a significant migration from the states in the South to the northern cities, as the demand for labour could no longer be met through immigration from Europe. Brawley uses this factor, as the extracts from later in his book reveal, to seek to understand the race issue in America in the broader context of both international and national questions. Later, Brawley became saddened by the fact, as he saw it, that many writers associated with the Harlem Renaissance represented blacks either as comic figures, or as having lower natures than whites: he expressed these views forcefully in* The Negro Genius *(1937).*

There are two fundamental assumptions upon which all so-called Western civilization is based – that of racial and that of religious superiority. Sight has been lost of the fact that there is really no such thing as a superior race, that only individuals are superior to one another, and a popular English poet has sung of 'the white man's burden' and 'of lesser breeds without the law'.[10] These two assumptions have accounted for all of the misunderstanding that has arisen between the West and East, for China and Japan, India and Egypt can not see by what divine right men from the West suppose that they have the only correct ancestry or by what conceit they presume to have the only true faith. Let them but be accepted, however, let a nation be led by them as guiding-stars, and England becomes justified in forcing her system upon India, she finds it necessary to send missionaries to Japan, and the lion's paw pounces upon the very islands of the sea.

The whole world, however, is now rising as never before against any semblance of selfishness on the part of great powers, and it is more than ever clear that before there can be any genuine progress toward the brotherhood of man, or toward comity among nations, one man will have to give some consideration to the other man's point of view. One people will have to respect another people's tradition. The Russo-Japanese War gave men a new vision.[11] The whole world gazed upon a new power in the East – one that could be dealt with only upon equal terms. Meanwhile there was unrest in India, and in Africa there were insurrections of increasing bitterness and fierceness.[12] Africa especially had been misrepresented. The people were all said to be savages and cannibals, almost hopelessly degraded. The traders and the politicians knew better. They knew that there were tribes and tribes in Africa, that many of the chiefs were upright and wise and proud of their tradition, and that the land could not be seized any too quickly. Hence they made haste to get into the game.

It is increasingly evident also that the real leadership of the world is not a matter of race, not even of professed religion, but of principle. Within the last hundred years, as science has flourished and colonization grown, we have been led astray by materialism. The worship of the dollar has become a fetish, and the man or the nation that had the money felt that it was ordained of God to rule

---

10 The 'popular poet' is Rudyard Kipling. The first phrase comes from an 1899 poem of that title, containing the injunction ('take up the white man's burden'), addressed to 'The United States'. By a treaty ending the Spanish–American war of 1898–9, the States had had the Philippines ceded to it; the second phrase comes from Kipling's 1897 poem 'Recessional', which reviews imperial progress.

11 The war was fought 1904–5. Russia had been trying to extend its influence into East Asia and had leased Port Arthur from China; this conflicted with Japanese attempts to gain a foothold in Asia. The Japanese launched a surprise attack, despite being the weaker power by far, and blockaded Port Arthur. They won a succession of unlikely victories, and caused huge damage to the Russian military, but were eventually exhausted, and accepted mediation from the US President Theodore Roosevelt.

12 There had been a Zulu rising in Natal in 1906; the 1919 Amritsar massacre, in which British troops killed 400 political demonstrators, drew world attention to unrest in India.

the universe. Germany was led astray by this belief, but it is England, not Germany, that has most thoroughly mastered the *Art of Colonization*. Crown colonies are to be operated in the interest of the owners. Jingoism is king. It matters not that the people in India and Africa, in Hayti and the Philippines, object to our benevolence; *we* know what is good for them and therefore they should be satisfied. . . .

It is not strange that the worship of industrialism, with its attendant competition, finally brought about the most disastrous war in history and such a breakdown of all principles of morality as made the whole world stand aghast. Womanhood was no longer sacred; old ideas of ethics vanished; Christ himself was crucified again – everything holy and lovely was given to the grasping demon of Wealth.

Here rises the question of our own country. To the United States at last has come that moral leadership – that obligation to do the right thing – that opportunity to exhibit the highest honor in all affairs foreign and domestic – that is the ultimate test of greatness. Is America to view this great problem in Africa[13] sympathetically and find some place for the groping for freedom of millions of human beings, or is she simply a pawn in the game of English colonization? Is she to abide by the principles that guided in 1776, or simply seize her share of the booty? . . . In such a country the law can know no difference of race or class or creed, provided all are devoted to general welfare. Such is the obligation resting upon the United States – such the challenge of social, economic, and moral questions such as have never before faced the children of men.

Just what is the Negro race worth as a constructive factor in American civilization? Is it finally to be an agency for the upbuilding of the nation, or simply one of the forces that retard? What is its real promise in American life?

In reply to this it might be worth while to consider first of all the country's industrial life. The South, and very largely the whole country, depends upon Negro men and women as the stable labor supply in such occupations as farming, saw-milling, mining, cooking, and washing. All of this is hard work and necessary work. In 1910, of 3,178,554 Negro men at work, 981,922 were listed as farm laborers and 798,509 as farmers. That is to say, 56 per cent of the whole number were engaged in raising farm products either on their own account or by way of assisting someone else, and the great staples of course were the cotton and corn of the Southern states. If along with the farmers we take those engaged in the occupations employing the next greatest numbers of men – those of the building and hand trades, saw and planing mills, as well as those of railway firemen and porters, draymen, teamsters, and coal mine operatives – we shall find

---

13 Brawley has drawn attention in previous paragraphs to torture in the Congo and the racially exclusive Land Acts in South Africa.

a total of 71.2 per cent engaged in such work as represents the very foundation of American industry. Of the women at work, 1,047,146, or 52 per cent, were either farm laborers or farmers, and 28 per cent more were either cooks or wash-erwomen. In other words, a total of exactly 80 per cent were engaged in some of the hardest and at the same time some of the most vital labor in our home and industrial life. The new emphasis on the Negro as an industrial factor in the course of the recent war is well known. When immigration ceased, upon his shoulders very largely fell the task of keeping the country and the army alive. Since the war closed he has been on the defensive in the North; but a country that wishes to consider all of the factors that enter into the gravest social prob-lem could never forget his valiant service in 1918. . . .

Very soon after the Civil War, when conditions were chaotic and ignorance was rampant, the ideals constantly held before the race were those of white people. Some leaders indeed measured success primarily by the extent to which they became merged in the white man's life. At the time this was very natural. A struggling people wished to show that it could be judged by the standards of the highest civilization within sight, and it did so. To-day the tide has changed. The race now numbers a few millionaires. In almost every city there are beauti-ful homes owned by Negroes. Some men have reached high attainment in schol-arship, and the promise grows greater and greater in art and science. Accordingly the Negro now loves his own, cherishes his own, teaches his boys about black heroes, and honors and glorifies his own black women. Schools and churches and all sorts of co-operative enterprises testify to the new racial self-respect, while a genuine Negro drama has begun to flourish. A whole people has been reborn; a whole race has found its soul.

9.6 Annie Besant, *Theosophy and World-Problems* (1922)

Besant (1847–1933) was associated with freethinking and women's rights movements in the UK; she worked with the socialist Fabian Society and advocated birth-control. She joined the Theosophical Society in 1887, and was its President from 1907 until her death. The Society had been founded by Madame Blavatsky in New York in 1875, and proclaimed the infinitude and unknowability of a God who disseminated all matter and spirit. Blavatsky's ideals leant heavily upon Oriental religious beliefs. Shortly after joining the Society, Besant travelled to India and became leader of a series of nationalist move-ments; she became President of the Indian Home Rule League in 1916, of the Indian National Congress in 1917, and General Secretary of the National Convention of India in 1923. In these extracts from a lecture to a Theosophical convention, we find Besant uniting her religious ideals with her political vision for the rise of a new and free India.

Man is essentially divine. Looking on man as naturally evil poisons the very roots of action, founding it on a falsehood, and leading to base motives. The sinfulness of our progenitor comes down like a hereditary disease to every father and mother; they hand it on to their children, whom they brought into the world. One result was the using as motive the appeal to the selfishness in man, and not the appeal to the self-sacrifice. . . . Every public speaker knows that a crowd rises to an appeal to heroism and sacrifice, that miners spring forward to risk their lives to save a comrade, just because the appeal is to the 'Hidden God', and He responds.

Now all that is a necessary stage. The mind had to be evolved, because the next great stage in human evolution, the appearance of Buddhi, the unifying force, could not be reached until the strong individual was evolved. Nature, it is often said, makes no leaps. She must go from rung to rung up the great ladder of evolution. So we have this combative civilisation, this struggling of one against the other, the weakest continually going down as the wheel turns, until they are seething in a poverty more terrible than the world has ever known before, amid wealth so great in the hands of the few, that they cannot find ways of using it. . . . We cannot continue as we are. It is too intolerable to be borne. Some people want to go backward. They say all this modern civilisation is really a curse.

So they say: 'Let us go back to the simple life. Let us wear as little cloth as possible, and feed on as simple food as possible. Let us live like villagers, like peasants, let us get rid of all the things that this concrete mind has been discovering for these hundreds of years.' This is what I may call the physical side of Mr. Gandhi's ideals. You can read it in that interesting book of his called *Indian Home Rule*.[14] He wants to get rid of all machinery, to go back to the simple action of a spinning-wheel and hand-loom. He wants to confine people to hand-made goods and to have no machine-goods at all, because he regards machinery as devilish. He wants to have no government, because all government is satanic. He does not want any modern science, nor any doctors, for hospitals are also the work of the devil, and the drugs given by doctors are more mischievous than useful. . . . He wishes that we all should go back to the pastoral stage of long-ago civilisation, the simple village life which was a stage in the growth of mankind. Everything else was to be swept away. . . . I know it sounds absurd, when you put it sentence after sentence in this way, but it is moving great masses of people who do not in the least understand what it means, but who know that they are suffering, and have a blind faith in his imagined 'supernatural powers' of which he has given no sign. But the question for us is what is the ideal towards which we should move, and his ideal is the going back to a very simple state of human life . . . . Well, many of us do not wish to go back. We do not wish to force the cultured to the level of the illiterate, but to raise the illiterate to the many-aspected life of the cultured.

---

14 A strong strain within Gandhi's *swaraj* (or 'self-rule') independence movement was the boycotting of British goods, and the resistance to long-running British industrial and commercial exploitation of Indian villages by a return to an ethos in cottage industry.

We do not wish to make the rich poor, but to lift the poor so that they may share the comforts and refinements of the life of the highest class. . . .

Now what must going forward mean? It must mean starting from an entirely different basis as regards the conception of man. It means the lifting up of a new Ideal, the declaration that man is fundamentally divine and not devilish.

On industry I want to put to you one point. You know how you sometimes call the creation of the whole world the Lila of Ishvara, His play, His amusement, and every one of you takes pleasure in a thing you can do well. You like to create a thing that you can create well. It is a joy to you, not a toil. We have had many examples both here and in England. In the old Guild system, whether in India or in England it does not matter, the work of the craftsman was done admirably for the sake of, and for the joy in, his work. He would shape a thing well, work it out regularly. He must do well what he did, and his joy and pride was in the perfection of the article that he created. . . . You may say: 'Yes, that is all true, but are you sure, if they started that system again, they would succeed?' I say, yes. They have started that system again as an experiment in a small way. There are Building Guilds in England.[15] . . . I believe this feeling and system will spread over here also, because it is much more in consonance with the Indian spirit than the spirit of competition, which has been imported here in labour questions. That is the work I want some people to take up here, who can really work it on sound business lines.

9.7   Two documents relating to Ireland, Easter 1916

The extracts here are the complete texts of two central documents relating to the Rebellion in Ireland (see, for details, the head note to the extracts relating to this in Section 1). The 'Proclamation' issued from the General Post Office, in O'Connell Street, Dublin, which the rebels had seized on Easter Monday, is notable both for its claim of responsibility and for its claim of foreign support for the Rebellion. The Irish Volunteers were a reduced force, somewhere between 3,000 and 10,000 thousand strong, by this point (estimates of their numbers vary vastly). They were formed initially in response to the gathering of a defence force in the north of the island to defend the Protestant interest (see extract 9.4 above), but had split over the question of whether Irishmen should fight with the British in the war. There is little evidence, however, that they knew of the involvement of the Irish Republican Brotherhood (IRB) in planning the Rebellion. Founded in 1858, the IRB had gone through various transformations, but represented throughout a radical and violent form of nationalism; by this stage, they

---

15 Despite her distrust of Gandhi's ideals, Besant shows here a reliance upon nineteenth-century English political beliefs, promulgated by Ruskin (a key influence upon Gandhi himself), Morris and many others, that the ills brought about by modern industry could best be countered by a return to a medieval guild method of communal working.

probably numbered only 2,000, however. The Irish Citizen Army was a private army formed during a workers' lock-out in 1913, and numbered only 200. So the rebels were a small group, with different interests, suddenly proclaimed to be a united force. The supporting 'gallant allies in Europe' was of course Germany, from whom the rebels had sought support for several years, and who had eventually promised to deliver 20,000 guns to the rebels for Easter 1916. Their delivery proved a fiasco, with leaked information, and misunderstandings, ending in the scuttling of the arms ship and the arrest of the go-between, Sir Roger Casement. But both documents stand as testimony to the determination, and determination in self-sacrifice, of the rebels led by Patrick Henry Pearse (1879–1916). The documents are notable for their literary nature; Pearse, a committed teacher of Gaelic, was a poet and songwriter who shared platforms as a speaker and reader with W. B. Yeats.

Proclamation of the Republic, Easter Monday, 24 April 1916

POBLACHT NA H EIREANN.
THE PROVISIONAL GOVERNMENT
OF THE
IRISH REPUBLIC
TO THE PEOPLE OF IRELAND

IRISH MEN AND IRISHWOMEN: In the name of God and of the dead generations from which she receives her old tradition of nationhood, Ireland, through us, summons her children to her flag and strikes her freedom.

Having organised and trained her manhood through her secret revolutionary organisation the Irish Republican Brotherhood, and through her open military organisations, the Irish Volunteers and the Irish Citizen Army, having patiently perfected her discipline, having resolutely waited for her right moment to reveal herself, she now seizes that moment, and, supported by her exiled children in America and by gallant allies in Europe, but relying in the first on her own strength, she strikes in full confidence of victory.

We declare the right of the people of Ireland to the ownership of Ireland, and to the unfettered control of Irish destinies, to be sovereign and indefeasible. The long usurpation of that right by a foreign people and government has not extinguished the right, nor can it ever be extinguished except by the destruction of the Irish people. In every generation the Irish people have asserted their right to national freedom and sovereignty; six times during the past three hundred years they have asserted it in arms. Standing on that fundamental right and again asserting it in arms in the face of the world, we hereby proclaim the Irish Republic as a Sovereign Independent State, and we pledge our lives and the lives of our comrade-in-arms to the cause of its freedom, of its welfare, and of its exaltation among nations.

The Irish Republic is entitled to, and hereby claims, the allegiance of every

Irishman and Irishwoman. The Republic guarantees religious and civil liberty, equal rights and equal opportunities to all its citizens, and declares its resolve to pursue the happiness and prosperity of the whole nation and of all its parts, cherishing all the children of the nation equally, and oblivious of the differences carefully fostered by an alien government, which have divided a minority from a majority in the past.

Until our arms have brought the opportune moment for the establishment of a permanent National Government, representative of the whole people of Ireland and elected by the suffrages of all her men and women, the Provisional Government, hereby constituted, will administer the civil and military affairs of the Republic in trust for the people.

We place the cause of the Irish Republic under the protection of the Most High God, Whose blessing we invoke upon our arms, and we pray that no one who serves that cause will dishonour it by cowardice, inhumanity, or rapine. In this supreme hour the Irish nation must, by its valour and discipline and by the readiness of its children to sacrifice themselves for the common good, prove worthy of the august destiny to which it is called.

Signed on behalf of the Provisional Government,
THOMAS J. CLARKE
SEAN MACDIARMADA   THOMAS MACDONAGH
P. H. PEARSE   EAMONN CEANNT
JAMES CONNOLLY   JOSPEH PLUNKETT

Notice issued on Tuesday, 25 April, by the Volunteers

The Provisional Government
TO THE
CITIZENS OF DUBLIN
The Provisional Government of the Irish Republic salutes the CITIZENS OF DUBLIN on the momentous occasion of the proclamation of a
Sovereign Independent Irish State
now in the course of being established by Irishmen in Arms.

The Republican forces hold the lines taken up at Twelve noon on Easter Monday, and nowhere, despite fierce and almost continuous attacks of the British troops, have the lines been broken through. The country is rising in answer to Dublin's call, and the final achievement of Ireland's freedom is now, with God's help, only a matter of days. The valour, self-sacrifice, and discipline of Irish men and women are about to win for our country a glorious place among nations.

Ireland's honour has already been redeemed; it remains to vindicate her wisdom and her self-control.

All citizens of Dublin who believe in the right of their Country to be free will give their allegiance and their loyal help to the Irish Republic. There is work for everyone: for the men in the fighting line, and for the women in the provision of food and first aid. Every Irishman and Irishwoman worthy of the name will come forward to help their common country in her supreme hour.

Able bodied citizens can help by building barricades in the streets to oppose the advance of the British troops. The British troops have been firing on our women and on our Red Cross. On the other hand, Irish Regiments in the British Army have refused to act against their fellow countrymen.

The Provisional Government hopes that its supporters – which means the vast bulk of the people of Dublin – will preserve order and self-restraint. Such looting as has already occurred has been done by hangers-on of the British Army. Ireland must keep her new honour unsmirched.

We have lived to see an Irish Republic proclaimed. May we live to establish it firmly, and may our children and our children's children enjoy the happiness and prosperity which freedom will bring.

Signed on behalf of the Provisional Government,

P. H. Pearse

Commanding in Chief the Forces of the Irish Republic,

and President of the Provisional Government.

9.8 Alain Locke, Preface to *The New Negro: An Interpretation* (1925)

Alain LeRoy Locke (1886–1954) produced this anthology in the mid-1920s, but it had been gestating in his mind since a six-month tour he took in the American South in 1911. His shock at the conditions there led him to believe that it was time for blacks to assert their rights and define their political and cultural identity. Out of his research following this experience came the 1916 book Race Contacts and Inter-Race Relations. *Locke was one of the new class of black intellectuals envisioned by Brawley; he held degrees from Harvard, in the footsteps of Du Bois, and from Oxford. He was for many years Professor of Philosophy at Howard University. But it is the seminal work that* The New Negro *achieved which resonates across the literature and art of this period. The anthology, with its title of Locke's own coinage, was a foundational text for the Harlem Renaissance group, bringing together as it did work by painters and illustrators, creative writers including Jean Toomer, Langston Hughes and Claude McKay, essays on jazz, on Harlem itself by James Weldon Johnson, literary criticism and social commentary by such as Du Bois himself. The Harlem district of New York had been a particular area of settlement for the blacks coming into the northern cities during the First World War, and had soon established its own distinctive rhythm and identity separate from white culture or white appropriations of some black art forms (African art, jazz itself), at the time. Johnson, indeed, calls it in his contribution to the anthology 'The Cultural Capital' of America at that moment. The extracts here are taken from Locke's first paragraphs to the book, in which he explains his ideas when conceiving it.*

In the last decade something beyond the watch and guard of statistics has happened in the life of the American Negro and the three norns[16] who have traditionally presided over the Negro problem have a changeling in their laps. The Sociologist, the Philanthropist, the Race-leader are not unaware of the New Negro, but they are at a loss to account for him. He simply cannot be swathed in their formulae. For the younger generation is vibrant with a new psychology; the new spirit is awake in the masses, and under the very eyes of the professional observers is transforming what has been a perennial problem into the progressive phases of contemporary Negro life.

Could such a metamorphosis have taken place as suddenly as it has appeared to? The answer is no; not because the New Negro is not here, but because the Old Negro had long become more of a myth than a man. The Old Negro, we must remember, was a creature of moral debate and historical controversy. He has been a stock figure perpetuated as an historical fiction partly in innocent sentimentalism, partly in deliberate reactionism. The Negro himself has contributed his share to this through a sort of protective social mimicry forced upon him by the adverse circumstances of dependence. So for generations in the mind of America, the Negro has been more of a formula than a human being – a something to be argued about, condemned or defended, to be 'kept down', or 'in his place', or 'helped up', to be worried with or worried over, harassed or patronized, a social bogey or a social burden. The thinking Negro even has been induced to share this same general attitude, to focus his attention on controversial issues, to see himself in the distorted perspective of a social problem. His shadow, so to speak, has been more real to him than his personality. Through having had to appeal from the unjust stereotypes of his oppressors and traducers to those of his liberators, friends and benefactors he has had to subscribe to the traditional positions from which his case has been viewed. Little true social or self-understanding has or could come from such a situation.

But while the minds of most of us, black and white, have thus burrowed in the trenches of the Civil War and Reconstruction, the actual march of development has simply flanked these positions, necessitating a sudden reorientation of view. We have not been watching in the right direction. . . .

Recall how suddenly the Negro spirituals revealed themselves; suppressed for generations under the stereotypes of Wesleyan hymn harmony, secretive, half-ashamed, until the courage of being natural brought them out – and behold, there was folk-music. Similarly the mind of the Negro seems suddenly to have slipped from under the tyranny of social intimidation and to be shaking off the psychology of imitation and implied inferiority. By shedding the old chrysalis of the Negro problem we are achieving something like a spiritual emancipation. Until recently, lacking self-understanding, we have been almost as much of a problem to ourselves as we still are to others. But the decade that found us with

---

16 The female Fates in Scandinavian mythology.

a problem has left us only with a task. The multitude perhaps feels as yet only a strange relief and a new vague urge, but the thinking few know that in the reaction the vital inner grip of prejudice has been broken.

With this renewed self-respect and self-dependence, the life of the Negro community is bound to enter a new dynamic phase, the buoyancy from within compensating for whatever there may be of conditions from without. The migrant masses, shifting from countryside to city, hurdle several generations of experience at a leap, but more important, the same thing happens spiritually in the life-attitudes and self-expression of the young Negro, in his poetry, his art, his education and his new outlook, with the additional advantage, of course, of the poise and greater certainty of knowing what it is all about. . . . The day of 'aunties', 'uncles' and 'mammies' is gone. Uncle Tom and Sambo have passed on.

First we must observe some of the changes which since the traditional lines of opinion were drawn have rendered these quite obsolete. A main change has been, of course, that shifting of the Negro population which has made the Negro problem no longer exclusively or even predominantly Southern. Why should our minds remain secularized, when the problem itself no longer is? Then the trend of migration has not only been toward the North and the Central Midwest, but city-ward and to the great centers of industry – the problems of adjustment are new, practical, local and not peculiarly racial. Rather they are an integral part of the large industrial and social problems of our present-day democracy.

With each successive wave of it, the movement of the Negro becomes more and more a mass movement toward the larger and more democratic chance – in the Negro's case a deliberate flight not only from countryside to city, but from medieval America to modern.

Take Harlem as an instance of this. Here in Manhattan is not only the largest Negro community in the world, but the first concentration in history of so many diverse elements of Negro life. It has attracted the African, the West Indian, the Negro American; has brought together the Negro of the North and the Negro of the South; the man from the city and the man from the town and village; the peasant, the student, the business man, the professional man, artist, poet, musician, adventurer and worker, preacher and criminal, exploiter and social outcast. Each group has come with its own separate motives and for its own special ends, but their greatest experience has been the finding of one another. Proscription and prejudice have thrown these dissimilar elements into a common area of contact and interaction. Within this area, racial sympathy and unity have determined a further fusing of sentiment and experience. So what began in terms of segregation becomes more and more, as its elements mix and react, the laboratory of a great race-welding.

There is a growing realization that in social effort the co-operative basis must supplant long-distance philanthropy, and that the only safeguard for mass relations in the future must be provided in the carefully maintained contacts of the enlightened minorities of both race groups. In the intellectual realm a renewed and keen curiosity is replacing the recent apathy; the Negro is being carefully studied, not just talked about and discussed. In art and letters, instead of being wholly caricatured, he is being seriously portrayed and painted.

To all of this the New Negro is keenly responsive as an augury of a new democracy in American culture. He is contributing his share to a new social understanding. But the desire to be understood would never in itself have been sufficient to have opened so completely the protectively closed portals of the thinking Negro's mind. There is still too much possibility of being snubbed or patronized for that. It was rather the necessity for fuller, truer self-expression, the realization of the unwisdom of allowing social discrimination to segregate him mentally, and a counter-attitude to cramp and fetter his own living – and so the 'spite-wall' that the intellectuals built over the 'color-line' has happily been taken down. Much of this reopening of intellectual contacts has centered in New York and has been richly fruitful not merely in the enlarging of personal experience, but in the definite enrichment of American arts and letters and in the clarifying of our common vision of the social tasks ahead.

10

Science and Technology

Introduction

The years 1880–1920 saw major breakthroughs in several areas of scientific inquiry, which had an immediate effect, once fully realized, on various aspects of humans' perception and their sense of their relation to the world. Just as in other areas of inquiry included in this book, such as philosophy, or concepts of society, these breakthroughs in themselves did much to question long-held presumptions about the laws and systems which govern life.

A major metaphor across this book has been that provided by the 'organic', which in our period we have found applied to ideal social structures, to modes of thought, to ancient communities, and, most appropriately, to the 'whole' which the individual work of art is envisaged as forming, an integrated unit in which every part is connected with every other in balance and harmony. That metaphor had only been available since 1828, when organic chemistry was defined as research into carbons and carbon compounds wherever they were to be found, therefore breaking down former barriers between supposed living and inert matter. In the early twentieth century, also, that sense of the 'organic' is frequently supplemented by the evolutionary, the sense after Darwin that living matter is constantly developing, and (ideally) progressing. Such ideas received a further aspect early in the century with the serious application of theories of genetic inheritance (see extract 10.3 below), which began a strand of research into how that development actually takes place, a strand which has lain behind the genome project in our own time.

Perhaps it is in physics that the most important, and destabilizing, aspects of inquiry were being carried out at the time, however; 1900 had seen the arrival of Quantum Theory, through the German scientist Max Planck's discovery that, contrary to former ideas, energy can only be transmitted from, or absorbed into, matter in small units, called 'quanta'. Planck's theory challenged previous assumptions that light was emitted in waves, by claiming instead that it was the quanta which radiated energy. Quanta are subject to (albeit very small) random movement; therefore there entered into the notion of physics a so-called 'uncertainty' principle. The established laws of the universe came into question, and an element of doubt about formerly perceived 'certainties' had entered.

Soon afterwards, in another field of physics, Albert Einstein began his radical questioning of the Newtonian laws about the relationship between matter, space and time, arguing that rather than being measurable in terms of its place in space and time, matter had to be measured according to a third element, space-time (see several extracts below), which introduced the principle of relativity into all relationships between inert entities.

There were several claims made in our period that the kinds of insight which literature might bring in the 1910s to 1920s is equivalent to that of science, or that, by analogy, the writer performs a scientific function, as when Eliot, in 'Tradition and the Individual Talent' (1919), describes the poet as a 'catalyst'. The turn of the century saw science itself brought to a similar cross-over point between writing and a dynamic but objective insight, in the classic study of the conscious and unconscious mind which was being developed through the psychoanalysis of Sigmund Freud. It is with this very literary and essayistic version of what science had become at the start of the twentieth century that the extracts begin, and later texts pick up on the developments in this theory which were brought about by the historical and personal tragedy of the First World War.

10.1 Sigmund Freud, *The Interpretation of Dreams* (1900, authorised translation of the 3rd edition by A. A. Brill, 1913; publisher's note on cover: 'The sale of this book is limited to Members of the Medical, Scholastic, Legal, and Clerical professions.')

Freud (1856–1939) trained in Vienna, where he lived most of his adult life. Before he set up a private practice in 1886 in order to treat patients with nervous disorders, he had spent three years working in psychiatry and dermatology at the General Hospital in Vienna, then a brief time as a lecturer in neuropathology at the University there. While a lecturer, Freud was awarded a grant to study for 19 weeks under the French neurologist Jean Charcot. Charcot was at this time treating nervous diseases using hypnosis, and was particularly interested in the condition of hysteria. Seeing Charcot at work greatly influenced Freud, and focused his own ideas derived from what he had seen at the Vienna Hospital. Freud collaborated on research into hysteria, which formed a book on the subject in 1893, with Josef Bauer. Applying Charcot's use of hypnotism to patients, the authors argued that hysterics displayed signs of strong and unresolved emotional trauma, usually associated with events that the patients were unable to recall when normally conscious. This work on hysteria, in other words, was the beginning for Freud of his interest in the repression which the unconscious mind enacts in order to prevent the conscious mind realizing traumatic experience. Increasingly, he felt that trauma was associated with infantile sexuality, and that his analysis of dreams proved there to be recurring patterns of neurosis in this area. The Interpretation of Dreams is seen by many as Freud's most important work. The Introductory Remarks to the volume, however, reveal Freud's own traumas in producing this work. His ambition, after a review of the literature relating to dreams and their interpretation, was to describe a method through which they might be 'read'. But, as the introduction shows, he found the use of such seemingly insubstantial material as dreams in itself difficult, especially when using dream materials from both patients and himself. Moreover, the book veered inappropriately away from science and toward autobiography, since 'inseparably connected with my own dreams was the circumstance that I was obliged to expose more of the intimacies of my psychic life than I should like and than generally falls to the task of an author who is not a poet but an investigator of nature'. Lastly, Freud says that the book was affected by the self-analysis brought on him by the death of his father, 'the most significant event, the deepest loss, in the life of a man'. The introduction signals something of the borderline upon which the whole text operates, since it holds that creative writers are those best able to 'withdraw' the 'watchers from the gate' of their intelligence, which interrupts the flow of creative ideas. In this sense poems are analogous to the ideal recounting of dreams, which is destroyed by any 'critique'. The extracts outline Freud's method, and offer an early rendition of his notion of the Oedipus complex.

With the hypothesis that dreams are interpretable, I at once come into contradiction with the prevailing dream science . . . for to 'interpret a dream' means to declare its meaning, to replace it by something which takes its place in the concatenation of our psychic activities as a link of full importance and value. But, as we have learnt, the scientific theories of the dream leave no room for a problem of dream interpretation, for, in the first place, according to these, the dream is no psychic action, but a somatic process which makes itself known to the psychic apparatus by means of signs. The opinion of the masses has always been quite different. It asserts its privilege of proceeding illogically, and although it admits the dream to be incomprehensible and absurd, it cannot summon the resolution to deny the dream all significance. Led by a dim intuition, it seems rather to assume that the dream has a meaning, albeit a hidden one; that it is intended as a substitute for some other thought process, and that it is only a question of revealing this substitute correctly in order to reach the hidden signification of the dream.

The laity has, therefore, always endeavoured to 'interpret' the dream, and in doing so has tried two essentially different methods. The first of these procedures regards the dream content as a whole and seeks to replace it by another content which is intelligible and in certain respects analogous. This is symbolic dream interpretation; it naturally goes to pieces at the outset in the case of those dreams which appear not only unintelligible but confused. . . . Most of the artificial dreams contrived by poets are intended for such symbolic interpretation, for they reproduce the thought conceived by the poet in a disguise found to be in accordance with the characteristics of our dreaming, as we know these from experience. The idea that the dream concerns itself chiefly with future events whose course it surmises in advance – a relic of the prophetic significance with which dreams were once credited – now becomes the motive for transplanting the meaning of the dream, found by means of symbolic interpretation, into the future by means of an 'it shall.' . . .

The other of the two popular methods of dream interpretation entirely abandons such claims. It might be designated as the 'cipher method', since it treats the dream as a kind of secret code, in which every sign is translated into another sign of known meaning, according to an established key. For example, I have dreamt of a letter, and also of a funeral or the like; I consult a 'dream book', and find that 'letter' is to be translated by 'vexation,' and 'funeral' by 'marriage, engagement'. It now remains to establish a connection, which I again am to assume pertains to the future, by means of the rigmarole which I have deciphered. . . .

The worthlessness of both these popular interpretation procedures for the scientific treatment of the subject cannot be questioned for a moment. The symbolic method is limited in its application and is of no general demonstration. In the cipher method everything depends upon whether the key, the dream book, is reliable, and for that all guarantees are lacking. One might be tempted to grant the contention of the philosophers and psychiatrists and to dismiss the problem of dream interpretation as a fanciful one.

I have come, however, to think differently. I have been forced to admit that here once more we have one of those not infrequent cases where an ancient and stubbornly retained popular belief seems to have come nearer to the truth of the matter than the judgement of the science which prevails to-day. I must insist that the dream actually has significance, and that a scientific procedure in dream interpretation is possible. . . .

In the course of [my] psychoanalytical studies, I happened upon dream interpretation. My patients, after I had obliged them to inform me of all the ideas and thoughts which came to them in connection with the given theme, related their dreams, and thus taught me that a dream may be linked into the psychic concatenation which must be followed backwards into the memory from the pathological idea as a starting-point. The next step was to treat the dream as a symptom, and to apply to it the method of interpretation which had been worked out for such symptoms.

For this a certain psychic preparation of the patient is necessary. The double effort is made with him, to stimulate his attention for his psychic perceptions and to eliminate the critique with which he is ordinarily in the habit of viewing the thoughts which come to the surface in him. For the purpose of self-observation with concentrated attention, it is advantageous that the patient occupy a restful position and close his eyes; he must be explicitly commanded to resign the critique of the thought-formations which he perceives. He must be told further that the success of the psychoanalysis depends upon his noticing and telling everything that passes through his mind, and that he must not allow himself to suppress one idea because it seems to him unimportant or irrelevant to the subject, or another because it seems nonsensical. He must maintain impartiality towards his ideas; for it would be owing to just this critique if he were unsuccessful in finding the desired solution of the dream, the obsession, or the like.

The first step in the application of this procedure now teaches us that not the dream as a whole, but only the parts of its contents separately, may be made the object of our attention. If I ask a patient who is as yet unpractised: 'What occurs to you in connection with this dream?' as a rule he is unable to fix upon anything in his psychic field of vision. I must present the dream to him piece by piece, then for every fragment he gives me a series of notions, which may be designated as the 'background thoughts' of this part of the dream. In this first and important condition, then, the method of dream interpretation which I employ avoids the popular, traditional method of interpretation by symbolism famous in the legends, and approaches the second, the 'cipher method'. Like this one it is an interpretation in detail, not *en masse*; like this it treats the dream from the beginning as something put together – as a conglomeration of psychic images.

Dreams of the death of parents predominantly refer to that member of the parental couple which shares the sex of the dreamer, so that the man mostly dreams of the death of his father, the woman of the death of her mother. I cannot claim that this happens regularly, but the predominating occurrence of this dream in the manner indicated is so evident that it must be explained through some factor that is universally operative. To express the matter boldly, it is as though a sexual preference becomes active at an early period, as though the boy regards his father as a rival in love, and as though the girl takes the same attitude toward her mother – a rival by getting rid of whom she cannot but profit.

Before rejecting this idea as monstrous, let the reader consider the actual relations between parents and children. What the requirements of culture and piety demand of this relation must be distinguished from what daily observation shows us to be the fact. More than one cause for hostile feeling is concealed within the relations between parents and children; the conditions necessary for the actuation of wishes which cannot exist in the presence of the censor are most abundantly provided. Let us dwell first on the relation between father and son. I believe that the sanctity which we have ascribed to the injunction of the Decalogue dulls our perception of reality. Perhaps we hardly dare notice that the greater part of humanity neglects to obey the fifth commandment. In the lowest as well as the highest strata of human society, piety towards parents is in the habit of receding before other interests. The obscure reports which have come to us in mythology and legend from the primeval ages of human society give us an unpleasant idea of the power of the father and the ruthlessness with which it is used. . . . The more despotically the father ruled in the ancient family, the more must the son have taken the position of an enemy, and the greater must have been his impatience, as designated successor, to obtain mastery himself after his father's death. Even in our own middle-class family the father is accustomed to aid the development of the germ of hatred which naturally belongs to the paternal relation by refusing the son the disposal of his own destiny, or the means necessary for this. . . . The causes of conflict between mother and daughter arise when the daughter grows up and finds a guardian in her mother, while she desires sexual freedom, and when, on the other hand, the mother has been warned by the budding beauty of her daughter that the time has come for her to renounce sexual claims.

If the *Oedipus Tyrannus* is capable of moving modern men no less than it moved the contemporary Greeks, the explanation of this fact cannot lie merely in the assumption that the effect of the Greek tragedy is based upon the opposition between fate and human will, but is to be sought in the peculiar nature of the material by which the opposition is shown. There must be a voice within us which is prepared to recognize the compelling power of fate in *Oedipus* . . . and there must be a factor corresponding to this inner voice in King Oedipus. His fate moves us only for the reason that it might have been ours, for the oracle has put the same curse upon us before our birth as upon him. Perhaps we are all destined to direct our first sexual impulses towards our mothers, and our first hatred and violent wishes towards our fathers; our dreams convince us of it. King Oedipus, who has struck his father Laius dead and has married his mother Jocasta, is nothing but the realized wish of our childhood. But more fortunate than he, we have succeeded, unless we have become psychoneurotics, in withdrawing our sexual impulses from our mothers and in forgetting our jealousy of our fathers. We recoil from the person for whom this primitive wish has been fulfilled with all the force of the repression which these wishes have suffered within us. By his analysis, showing us the guilt of Oedipus, the poet urges us to recognise our own inner self, in which these impulses, even if suppressed, are still present.

I shall now undertake a résumé of this extended discussion of dream activity. We were confronted by the question whether the mind exerts all its capabilities to the fullest development in dream formation, or only a fragment of its capabilities, and those restricted in their activity. Our investigation leads us to reject such a formulation of the question as inadequate to our circumstances. But if we are to remain on the same ground when we answer as that on which the question is urged upon us, we must acquiesce in two conceptions which are apparently opposed and mutually exclusive. The psychic activity in dream formation resolves itself into two functions – the provision of the dream thoughts and the transformation of these into the dream content. The dream thoughts are entirely correct, and are formed with all the psychic expenditure of which we are capable; they belong to our thoughts which have not become conscious, from which our thoughts which have become conscious also result by means of a certain transposition. Much as there may be about them which is worth knowing and mysterious, these problems have no particular relation to the dream, and have no claim to be treated in connection with dream problems. On the other hand, there is that second portion of the activity which changes the unconscious thoughts into the dream content, an activity peculiar to dream life and characteristic of it. Now, this peculiar dream-work is much further removed from the model of waking thought than even the most decided depreciators of psychic activity in dream formation have thought. . . . It is something qualitatively different from waking thought, and therefore not in any way comparable to it. It does not in general think, calculate, or judge at all, but limits itself to transforming. It can be exhaustively described if the conditions which must be satisfied at its creation are kept in mind. This product, the dream, must at any cost be withdrawn from the censor, and for this purpose the dream activity makes use of the *displacement of psychic intensities* up to the transvaluation of all psychic values; thoughts must exclusively or predominatingly be reproduced in the material of visual or acoustic traces of memory, and this requirement secures for the dream-work the *regard for presentibility*, which meets the requirement by furnishing new displacements.

10.2   Alfred North Whitehead, *An Introduction to Mathematics* (1911)

Whitehead (1861–1947) was a mathematician and metaphysician who made a lasting contribution to early twentieth-century philosophy. He taught at the universities of London, Cambridge, and Harvard. Perhaps his most famous work was the three-volume Principia Mathematica *(1910–13), on which he collaborated with his pupil at Cambridge, the philosopher Bertrand Russell. This mammoth work contains the essence of Whitehead's method across his career, in that it endeavours to discover and explain the principles within mathematics as equivalent to those in symbolic logic, such as class and membership of a class. He felt that, with sufficient exploration, the abstract mathematical patterns underlying all phenomena could be realized, even those within mathematics itself. He believed absolutely in the truth of perception, both of single objects and of their relation to other objects. He resisted, therefore, as the first part of these extracts demonstrates, the scientists' propensity to over-complicate those perceptions and relations. The later extracts here offer his attempt to discover the basic rules regulating space and time.*

There is not one world of things for my sensations and another for yours, but one world in which we both exist. . . . Also we hear and we touch the same world as we see.

It is easy, therefore, to understand that we want to describe the connections between these external things in some way which does not depend on any particular sensations, nor even on all the particular sensations of any particular person. The laws satisfied by the course of events in the world of external things are to be described, if possible, in a neutral universal fashion, the same for blind men as for deaf men, and the same for beings with faculties beyond our ken as for normal human beings.

But when we have put aside our immediate sensations, the most serviceable part – from its clearness, definiteness, and universality – of what is left is composed of our general ideas of the abstract formal properties of things. . . . Thus it comes about that, step by step, and not realizing the full meaning of the process, mankind has been led to search for a mathematical description of the properties of the universe, because in this way only can a general idea of the course of events be formed, freed from reference to particular persons or to particular types of sensation. For example, it might be asked at dinner: 'What was it which underlay my sensation of sight, yours of touch, and his of taste and smell?' the answer being 'an apple.' But in its final analysis, science seeks to describe an apple in terms of the positions and motions of molecules, a description which ignores me and you and him, and also ignores sight and touch and taste and smell. Thus mathematical ideas, because they are abstract, supply just what is wanted for a scientific description of the course of events.

This point has usually been misunderstood, from being thought of in too narrow a way. Pythagoras had a glimpse of it when he proclaimed that number was the source of all things. In modern times the belief that the ultimate explanation of all things was to be found in Newtonian mechanics was an adumbration of the truth that all science as it grows towards perfection becomes mathematical in its ideas.

Our perception of the flow of time and of the succession of events is a chief example of the application of . . . ideas of quantity. We measure time . . . by the repetition of similar events – the burning of successive inches of a uniform candle, the rotation of the earth relatively to the fixed stars, the rotation of the hands of a clock are all examples of such repetitions. Events of these types take the place of the foot-rule in relation to lengths. It is not necessary to assume that events of any one of these types are exactly equal in duration at each recurrence. What is necessary is that a rule should be known which will enable us to express the relative durations of, say, two examples of some type. For example, we may if we like suppose that the rate of the earth's rotation is decreasing, so that each day is longer than the preceding by some minute fraction of a second. Such a rule enables us to compare the length of any day with that of any other day. But what is essential is that one series of repetitions, such as successive days, should be taken as the standard series; and, if the various events of that series are not taken as of equal duration, that a rule should be stated which regulates the duration to be assigned to each day in terms of the duration of any other day.

What then are the requisites which such a rule ought to have? In the first place it should lead to the assignment of nearly equal durations to events which common sense judges to possess equal durations. A rule which made days of violently different lengths, and which made the speeds of apparently similar operations vary utterly out of proportion to the apparent minuteness of their differences, would never do. Hence the first requisite is the general agreement with common sense. But this is not sufficient absolutely to determine the rule, for common sense is a rough observer and very easily satisfied. The next requisite is that minute adjustments of the rule should be made so as to allow of the simplest possible statements of the laws of nature. For example, astronomers tell us that the earth's rotation is slowing down, so that each day gains in length by some inconceivably minute fraction of a second. Their only reason for their assertion . . . is that without it they would have to abandon the Newtonian laws of motion. In order to keep the laws of motion simple, they alter the measure of time. This is a perfectly legitimate procedure so long as it is thoroughly understood.

What has been said above about the abstract nature of the mathematical properties of space applies with appropriate verbal changes to the mathematical properties of time. A sense of the flux of time accompanies all our sensations and perceptions, and practically all that interests us in regard to time can be paralleled by the abstract mathematical properties which we ascribe to it. Conversely what has been said about the two requisites for the rule by which we determine the length of the day, also applies to the rule for determining the length of a yard measure – namely, the yard measure appears to retain the same length as it moves about. Accordingly, any rule must bring out that, apart from minute changes, it does remain of invariable length. Again, the second requisite is this, a definite rule for minute changes shall be stated which allows of the simplest expressions of the laws of nature. For example, in accordance with the second requisite the yard measures are supposed to expand and contract with changes of temperature according to the substances which they are made of.

Apart from the facts that our sensations are accompanied with perceptions of locality and of duration, and that lines, areas, volumes, and durations, are each in their way quantities, the theory of numbers would be of very subordinate use in the exploration of the laws of the Universe. As it is, physical science reposes on the main ideas of number, quantity, space, and time. The mathematical sciences associated with them do not form the whole of mathematics, but they are the substratum of mathematical physics as at present existing.

10.3 Raymond Pearl, *Modes of Research in Genetics* (1915)

Genetics was a relatively new science in the early years of the twentieth century, and only received its name from the British biologist William Bateson in 1906. The study arose when several biologists independently rediscovered the work of an Austrian monk, Gregor Mendel, which had been published in 1866. Mendel's study of the hereditary characteristics of garden peas led him to understand that each parent has a pair of 'units', or kinds of characteristic, which they in turn have inherited from their parents. But they only pass on one of those 'units' to their own offspring. Modern biologists, whose science had developed rapidly in the intervening years since Mendel published his results, saw immediate similarities between the splitting of the paired 'units' he described and cell division, in which paired chromosomes are separated. They soon gave Mendel's 'units' the name 'genes' – and much modern biology continues to derive its importance from this kind of study. Genetics is important in the period covered by this Sourcebook, since it added further aspects to the interest coming out of the nineteenth century in eugenics, the hope that it might be possible to eradicate the degenerative aspects of the human race through the introduction of controlled breeding techniques. This was an interest displayed (and sometimes critiqued) by, amongst others, H. G. Wells, D. H. Lawrence, T. S. Eliot, W. B. Yeats and Virginia Woolf at various moments in their careers, often as an exasperated reaction to a perceived intractability in the awfulness of contemporary conditions. The extracts here come from an American geneticist, Raymond Pearl, because he lays out lucidly the state of study in inheritance at the time of the First World War. As the extracts demonstrate, Pearl saw genetics operating a choice between two possible methods of study: the statistical (biometric and Mendelian – with the latter still very prominent) and the more modern and flexible biological approach.

The problem of heredity can easily be defined in a *general* way in terms which are perfectly objective. It is a matter of common observation that there is a greater or less degree of resemblance in respect of all sorts of traits or characteristics between relatives, and in particular between parent and offspring. By heredity is meant the complex of causes, not now further specified or defined, which, taken together, determines this likeness or resemblance between individuals genetically related to each other. From a purely logical standpoint the problem of heredity is the problem of the analysis of this complex.

The difficulties of the problem, both methodological and technical, arise from certain reasonably obvious relationships between genetically connected individuals. In order to see what these are let us attempt to list in strictly objective terms, and into broad categories, what is actually known about the relationship of two individuals standing in the genetic series as parent and offspring. For the purpose of the present analysis it is desirable that the categories in such a list shall be broad ones.

The phenomena of heredity may be divided in three essential categories:

A.   Resemblance between adult individuals.
This resemblance is the central observed fact of heredity. Every individual organism is different in some degree from every other, but any particular individual is more like the individuals genetically closely related to it, than it is like other individuals. This resemblance marks the end stage of heredity regarded as a process. . . .

B.   Gametogenesis. The intervention of a relatively undifferentiated stage (the germ cell) in the cycle of reproduction of the individual.
In higher organisms ordinarily each time an individual reproduces itself it does

so by means of a single cell, which separates completely from the other cells which together make the individual. After separation this cell may for a time derive its nourishment from the individual which produced it, but morphologically and physiologically the completely formed gamete is essentially a separate and independent entity, with certain limitations as to the possibility of its continued independent existence. . . .

C. Somatogenesis. (Development and differentiation.)
The adult offspring, in whose adult characters we perceive a resemblance to the parents, is the result of a long and complicated process of development and growth from a single cell. This cell is itself a composite structure produced by the fusion of two cells, one derived from each of the parents. From the standpoint of heredity the most striking thing about the fertilized germ cell is that it carries the potentiality of producing a higher degree of differentiation in the individual which develops from it, than it exhibits in its own structure. The existence of such potentiality is demonstrated by the *specificity* of the developmental behavior of the fertilized egg. Under no circumstances does a hen's egg ever develop into a turkey. . . .

Of much greater significance from the standpoint of heredity than the potentiality for development, though this of course in itself constitutes one of the fundamental problems of biology, is the specificity of the process, at once unique and manifold. Not only does any particular hen's egg produce always a hen, but it is also a particular kind of hen which is produced, the particularity extending to the most minute details. . . .

D. From these observed facts two definite inferences are not only plain, but indeed inescapable. They are:

1. That germinal substance is innately possessed of a definite and particular *specificity*, which reaches, in degree, to the order of the individual, and which finds its most obvious objective expression in the specificity of somatogenesis; and
2. That the processes of reproduction are of such a sort as to tend to maintain this specificity from generation to generation.

In the light of this summary analysis of elementary facts it seems clear that *the critical problem of inheritance is the problem of the cause; the material basis; and the maintenance of the somatogenic specificity of germinal substance.*

Certain definite nuclear components, the chromosomes, are distributed during gamete formation in a manner which parallels the distribution of hereditary characters as observed in Mendelian segregation. In other words, the chromosomes behave on gametogenesis as any structures which were the bearers of the causative agents of the inherited characters would be expected *a priori* to behave.

This discovery is clearly one of first-class importance. It is justly to be regarded as one of the greatest achievements of modern biology. It furnishes strong grounds in favor of the basic conclusion that the determination of hereditary specificity is resident in the chromosomes. The familiar and widely accepted doctrine that the chromosomes are the exclusive 'bearers' of heredity is a crude form of this conclusion.

All [previous statistical and biological] methods are valuable, and each has contributed to our present knowledge of heredity. No one of the methods alone can, however, solve the problem. They all have at least one fundamental limitation in common. This is that they offer no means of *directly* getting at any definite information regarding the origin, cause, or real nature of that specificity of living material which is the very foundation of the phenomenon of heredity. . . .

It is plain, I think, what must be the mode of attack on this outstanding problem of genetics. In the present state of knowledge it is beyond dispute that the basis of the specificity of living substances lies in its chemistry. This plain fact has long been recognized by biologists. . . . The obvious complexity of the chemical processes going on in living material has made any direct investigation of the problem from this side seem hopeless to the biologist. But this period of despairing wonderment is passing, and that rapidly. The remarkable development of bio-chemistry in the last twenty years has put at the disposal of the geneticist a new technical equipment with which he may directly attack problems which formerly seemed impossible of approach.

10.4   Anthony Frieling, 'Loss of Personality from "Shell Shock"', *The Lancet*, 10 July 1915

This and the following extract, from a lecture by W. H. R. Rivers, relate to the issue of the psychoanalytical response to one of the major new crises caused at the Western Front in the First World War, that of the multiple mental traumas brought on by the constant bombardment of heavy artillery. Almost as soon as the War was begun, and certainly once the prolonged trench warfare took hold in late 1914, there was a technological and industrial race between the opposing nations to develop the most devastating heavy weaponry possible, with the ambition to smash the enemy defences and break through the stalemate. At the start of the conflict, the shells used on all sides were relatively primitive, often containing an explosive charge and shrapnel. By July 1915, the combatants had developed sophisticated high-explosive shells, which exploded on impact. The effect of this on the soldiers trapped in the small space of the trenches – those, that is, not killed or severely physically wounded – could often be to create a range of mental disorder and associated behavioural symptoms. The newly developed science of psychoanalysis was brought into play at the various war hospitals to try and cope with the vast influx of traumatized men. As a result, the science itself changed fundamentally: partly as a result of observing war neuroses, Sigmund Freud redrew his earlier map of the human mind and its repressive drives founded upon the primal traumas of infantile sexuality. Whilst he continued to see these as crucial, from his 1920 Beyond the Pleasure Principle *onwards, he saw humanity as driven by two opposing drives, Eros and Thanatos, the drive towards love and desire, and the drive toward death. During the war itself, the leading British medical journal* The Lancet *published many articles relating to the treatment of the mental effects of the war upon soldiers. Several literary texts of the time – perhaps most notably Virginia Woolf's* Mrs Dalloway *and Rebecca West's* The Return of the Soldier *– portray men suffering from shell shock, of course. The poets Wilfred Owen and Siegfried Sassoon both experienced shell shock, and depicted shell-shocked victims in their poems. But these medical articles also raise questions about the nature of personality and individuality which we find crucially in numerous other texts of the time.*

The present campaign in Flanders has made such unexampled demands on the nervous system of the soldier that we are not surprised to meet with many cases of neurasthenia, hysteria, and various disturbances of the special sense organs. Numerous cases of blindness, deafness, dumbness, and loss of memory have already been reported, as well as the more common cases of functional paralysis of a limb or limbs, and all have aroused considerable interest and discussion as to their nature and appropriate treatment. The majority of cases of loss of memory hitherto recorded have been generally of a more or less transitory nature; moreover, the period of time covered by the amnesia has been, as a rule, only that just before, during, and immediately following the trauma, whether such were physical or mental, or both.

The case which I wish to record here is one of exceptional interest. It amounts, in fact to a complete dissociation[1] or obliteration of personality. The term 'double personality' is hardly applicable, as will appear from subsequent remarks. It may be regarded as a case of loss of memory or amnesia of such a degree that all conscious memories of the patient's life, as well as the countless memories forming his knowledge of letters, objects, and life in general were completely suppressed. In order to follow the case more clearly and the better to appreciate the interesting problem presented by the patient it will perhaps be best to take the case exactly as it appeared to my observation.

The patient, aged 24, a bandsman in the 2nd Battalion Wiltshire Regiment, was admitted to the Hospital for Epilepsy and Paralysis, Maida Vale, on Jan. 21st, 1915. . . . From information supplied it would appear that the history was as follows. On an uncertain date – some time at the end of October, 1914 – the patient was buried in a trench near Ypres. He was rescued and eventually trans-

---

1 This word was shortly to gain a famous literary currency in the wake of the War. 'Dissociation of sensibility' is the phrase that T. S. Eliot deployed to describe the historical rift which entered English literary history in another war, the English Civil War, in his 1921 essay 'The Metaphysical Poets'. See also the next extract.

ferred to the 2nd Western General Hospital, Manchester. Major Wilson has kindly supplied me with the following note of his condition at that time – 'He speaks quite sensibly, understands, and remembers anything which took place since he was buried, but as regards matter previous to that his mind was blank. He was admitted to this hospital on Oct. 31st, 1914. He did not know his own father or relatives. He was quite able to speak while here, but was slightly deaf. This defect disappeared.'

On physical examination he appeared perfectly healthy. The only abnormality observed was a certain nervous twitching of the eyelids and facial muscles. When questioned he gave the following peculiar account of himself. 'I came to myself in a strange place which I was told was Manchester. I could not remember anything at all. I think I could speak all right.' Attention was good; he was polite, and seemed to try to answer before saying 'I can't remember.' . . .

No sign of any organic disease of the nervous system was found. On all subjects relevant to his life in hospital and his experiences since he came to himself in Manchester his statements were perfectly coherent and straightforward. He stated that he did not know his parents, but took them on trust, having been told that they were his parents. He had been at home at Winterslow for some time since leaving the hospital at Manchester, but did not recollect that he had ever seen the place before.

As he seemed to make no progress towards recovery, it was decided to try the effect of hypnotism. . . . In this state he answered all the questions put to him, and volunteered many details of incidents occurring in his past life and in his experiences on active service in Flanders. . . . Towards the end of October, 1914, his regiment was ordered abroad.

At this time he took part in the first battle at Ypres, and for about ten days experienced very severe trench fighting. Finally, on a certain day, the exact date of which is unknown, the trench in which he was fighting was blown in by a high-explosive shell and he was buried in a mass of mud and debris. He stated that he remained thus buried for about 12 hours when he was dug out at night. His father added the information that he was unconscious for 24 hours and deaf and dumb for three days. From the ruined trench he was transferred to a clearing hospital and thence to another hospital. Eventually, he was taken to the hospital at Manchester where, as we have seen, he 'came to himself'. . . . The most interesting fact which came to light in the course of our conversations was that when hypnotised he returned completely to the personality which possessed him immediately previous to the moment of awakening in Manchester. Thus on first seeing me (when he was first commanded to open his eyes under hypnosis) he declared that he had never seen me before, and in this state he never knew my name, although in his ordinary state he knew me well and would always address me by name. He maintained that he was then in Manchester, was completely puzzled as to his surroundings in the hospital at Maida Vale. . . . There was always a complete ignorance of what had taken place during hypnosis. He said that he thought he had been asleep. If he were left for some time before being waked he would experience dreams obviously of a disturbing character. The hands clenched and the arms thrown across the body in an attitude of defence, with the lips drawn back in a snarling expression. Words and short sentences were muttered, such as 'Give it them,' or 'Got him.' and other similar expressions. The whole attitude illustrated quite obviously some re-enacted drama of fighting.

The case is obviously one of a more than mere ordinary amnesia, and yet it seems to me that the title of double personality is hardly justified. For the second personality (really in point of time the first) was only called out by hypnosis, and unless this or some other similar means had been employed would probably never have been brought to light. . . . In the present case there appeared to be absolutely no connexion between the two personalities. . . . Any profound psychic trauma is frequently able to produce an amnesia more or less extensive. There is no particular reason why this should be so complete as to constitute a loss of personality.

10.5   W. H. R. Rivers, 'An Address on the Repression of War Experience', *The Lancet*, 2 February 1918

Rivers (1864–1922) is now probably best known as the Medical Officer at Craiglockhart War Hospital in Scotland, where he had amongst his patients the war poets Siegfried Sassoon and Wilfred Owen. But, by this point, he had been working in the field of physiological psychology for nearly two decades; in 1897 he had been made director of the first experimental psychology laboratory at the University of London. Before the war and afterwards, he worked extensively in the area of anthropology and early religion, drawing upon his earlier field researches in Melanesia and Polynesia. His work with war victims led him to doubt some of the tenets of Freudian psychology, particularly the claim that traumas might be traced back to some incident in burgeoning infantile sexuality which was subsequently suppressed through the repressive drives of the unconscious mind. Instead Rivers concluded that humans were driven by a set of instincts – territorial, mating, fear – that we share with animals, instincts which are most obviously on display amongst primitive peoples. Here, his anthropological researches and his psychoanalytic work meet. He felt that the current First World War was bringing to the surface another of these instincts, the instinct for survival. As part of this, he sought to describe in this paper another kind of repression than that of Freud's concept of the unconscious; in this case the conscious and voluntary suppression of the experience the soldier had suffered at the Front. Rivers sees this kind of repression as 'a necessary element in education and in all social progress', but feels that there are kinds of repression brought about which fail in their aim to re-adapt the patient to his environment, and which therefore lead to continuing trauma. It is the kinds of repression brought about in the unknown circumstances of the current war which Rivers writes of, and he sees the alleviation of this false kind of repression – one which relieves the patient of the pain of memory but which fails to adapt him to his environment – as his task.

It is natural to thrust aside painful memories just as it is natural to avoid danger-ous or horrible scenes in actuality, and this natural tendency to banish the distressing or the horrible is especially pronounced in those whose powers of resistance have been lowered by the long-continued strains of trench-life, the shock of shell-explosion or other catastrophes of warfare. Even if patients were left to themselves most would naturally strive to forget distressing memories and thoughts. They are, however, very far from being left to themselves, the natural tendency to repress being in my experience almost universally fostered by their relatives and friends, as well as by their medical advisors. Even when patients have themselves realised the impossibility of forgetting their war experiences and have recognised the hopeless and enervating character of the treatment by repression, they are often induced to attempt the task in obedience to medical orders.

RECORDS OF ILLUSTRATIVE CASES

In some cases there can be little question that the most distressing symptoms were being produced or kept in activity by reason of repression. The cessation of the repression was followed by a disappearance of the most distressing symp-toms and great improvement in the general health, It is not always, however, that the line of treatment adopted in these case is so successful. Sometimes the experience which a patient is striving to forget is so utterly horrible or disgust-ing, so wholly free from any redeeming feature which can be used as a means of readjusting the attention, that it is difficult or impossible to find an aspect which will make its contemplation endurable.

Such a case is that of a young officer who was flung down by the explosion of a shell so that his face struck the distended abdomen of a German several days dead, the impact of his fall rupturing the swollen corpse. Before he lost consciousness the patient had clearly realised his situation and knew the substance which filled his mouth and produced the most horrible sensations of taste and smell was derived from the decomposed entrails of an enemy. When he came to himself he vomited profusely and was much shaken, but carried on for several days, vomiting frequently and haunted by persistent images of taste and smell.

When he came under my care several months later, suffering from horrible dreams in which the events I have narrated were faithfully reproduced, he was striving by every means in his power to keep the disgusting and painful memory from his mind. His only period of relief had occurred when he had gone into the country far from all that could remind him of the war, and his experience, combined with the utterly horrible nature of his memory and images, not only made it difficult for him to discontinue the repression, but also made me hesitate to advise this measure with any confidence. The dream became less frequent and less terrible, but it still recurred, and it was thought best that he should leave the Army and seek the conditions which had previously given him relief. . . .

DISSOCIATION

In the cases I have just narrated there was no evidence that the process of repression had produced the state of suppression or dissociation. The memories or other painful experience were at hand ready to be recalled or even to obtrude themselves upon consciousness at any moment. A state in which repressed elements of the mental content find their expression in dreams may perhaps be regarded as the first step towards suppression or dissociation, but, if so, it forms a very early stage of the process.

There is no question that some people are more liable to become the subjects of dissociation or splitting of consciousness than others. In some persons there is probably an innate tendency in this direction; in others the liability arises through some shock or illness; while other persons become especially susceptible as the result of having been hypnotised.

Not only do shock and illness produce a liability to dissociation, but these factors may also act as its immediate precursors and exciting causes. How far the process of voluntary repression can produce this state is doubtful. . . . The great frequency of the process of voluntary repression in cases of war neurosis might be expected to provide us with definite evidence on this head, and there is little doubt that such evidence is present.

As an example I will cite the case of a young officer who had done well in France until he had been deprived of consciousness by a shell explosion. The next thing he remembered was being conducted by his servant towards the base, thoroughly broken down. On admission into hospital he suffered from fearful headaches and had hardly any sleep, and when he slept he had terrifying dreams of warfare. When he came under my care two months later his chief complaint was that, whereas ordinarily he felt cheerful and keen on life, there would come upon him at times, with absolute suddenness, the most terrible depression, a state of a kind absolutely different from an ordinary fit of the blues, having a quality which he could only describe as 'something quite on its own.'

For some time he had no attack and seemed as if he had not a care in the world. Ten days after admission he came to me one evening pale and with a tense anxious expression which wholly altered his appearance. A few minutes earlier he had been writing a letter in his usual mood when there descended upon him a state of deep depression and despair which seemed to have no reason. He had had a pleasant and not too tiring afternoon on some neighbouring hills, and there was nothing in the letter he was writing which could be supposed to have suggested anything painful or depressing. As we talked the depression cleared off and in about ten minutes he was nearly himself again.

He had no further attack of depression for nine days, and then one afternoon, as he was standing idly looking from a window, there suddenly descended upon him the state of horrible dread. I happened to be away from the hospital and he had to fight it out alone. It was so severe that he believed he would have shot himself if his revolver had been accessible. On my return to the hospital some hours after the onset of the attack he was better, but still looked pale and anxious. . . .

The gusts of depression to which this patient was subject were of the kind which I was then inclined to ascribe to the hidden working of some forgotten yet active experience, and it seemed natural at first to think of some incident during the time which elapsed between the shell explosion which deprived him of consciousness and the moment when he came to himself walking back from the trenches. I considered whether this was not a case in which the lost memory might be recovered by means of hypnotism, but in the presence of the definite tendency to dissociation I did not like to employ this means of diagnosis, and less drastic methods of recovering any forgotten incident were without avail. . . .

He became less cheerful generally and his state acquired more closely the usual characters of anxiety neurosis, and this was so persistent that he was finally passed by a medical board as unfit for military service.

Catharsis

The disappearance or improvement of symptoms on the cessation of voluntary repression may be regarded as due to the action of one form of the principle of catharsis. This term is generally used for the agency which is operative when a suppressed or dissociated body of experience is brought to the surface so that it again becomes re-integrated with the ordinary personality. It is no great step from this to the mode of action recorded in this paper, in which experience on its way towards suppression has undergone a similar, though necessarily less extensive, process of re-integration.

There is, however, another form of catharsis which may have been operative in some of the cases I have described. It often happens in cases of war neurosis in general, that the sufferers do not repress their painful thoughts, but brood over them constantly until their experience assumes vastly exaggerated and often distorted importance and significance. In such cases the greatest relief is afforded by the mere communication of these troubles to another. This form of catharsis may have been operative in relation to certain kinds of experience in some of my cases, and this complicates our estimation of the therapeutic value of the cessation of repression.

10.6 A. S. Eddington, *Space, Time and Gravitation: An Outline of the General Relativity Theory* (1920)

Sir Arthur Stanley Eddington (1882–1944) was Chief Assistant at the Royal Observatory at Greenwich from 1906 to 1913, and thereafter Professor of Astronomy at Cambridge University. He did important work in elucidating Einstein's discoveries about relativity (see head note to extract below), and in relating them to his own particular interests in astronomy. Through this work he made significant mathematical additions to Einstein's basic ideas. Eddington was also a promoter of difficult new scientific concepts to a broader public; it is from one of these books that our extracts are taken.

Although there is an absolute past and future, there is between them an extended neutral zone; and simultaneity of events at different places has no absolute meaning. . . . The denial of absolute simultaneity is a natural complement to the denial of absolute motion. The latter asserts that we cannot find out what is the same place at two different times; the former that we cannot find out what is the same time at two different places. It is curious that the philosophical denial of absolute motion is readily accepted, whilst the denial of absolute simultaneity appears to many people revolutionary.

The division into past and future (a feature of time-order which has no analogy in space-order) is closely associated with our ideas of causation and free-will. In a perfectly determinate scheme the past and future may be regarded as lying mapped out – as much available to present exploration as the distant parts of space. Events do not happen; they are just there, and we come across them. 'The formality of taking place' is merely the indication that the observer has on his voyage of exploration passed into the absolute future of the event in question; and it has no important significance. We can be aware of an eclipse in the year 1919, very much as we are aware of an unseen companion to Algol. Our knowledge of things *where* we are not, and of things *when* we are not, is essentially the same – an inference (sometimes a mistaken inference) from brain impressions, including memory, *here* and *now*.

So, if events are determinate, there is nothing to prevent a person from being *aware* of an event before it happens; and an event may cause other events previous to it. Thus the eclipse of the Sun in May 1919 caused observers to embark in March. It may be said that it was not the eclipse, but the calculations of the eclipse, which caused the embarkation; but I do not think any such distinction is possible, having regard to the indirect character of our acquaintance with all events except those at the precise point of space where we stand. A detached observer contemplating our world would see some events apparently causing events in their future, others apparently causing events in their past – the truth being that all are linked by determinate laws, the so-called causal events being merely conspicuous foci from which the links radiate.

However successful the theory of a four-dimensional world may be, it is difficult to ignore a voice inside us which whispers 'At the back of your mind, you know that a fourth dimension is all nonsense.' I fancy that voice must often have had a busy time in the past history of physics. What nonsense to say that this solid table on which I am writing is a collection of electrons moving with prodigious speeds in empty spaces, which relatively to electronic dimensions are as wide as the spaces between the planets in the solar system! What nonsense to say that the thin air is trying to crush my body with a load of 14lbs to the square inch! What nonsense that the star-cluster, which I see through the telescope obviously there *now*, is a glimpse into a past age 50,000 years ago! Let us not be beguiled by this voice. It is discredited.

But the statement that time is a fourth dimension may suggest unnecessary difficulties which a more precise definition avoids. It is in the external world that the four dimensions are united – not in the relations of the external world to the individual which constitute his direct acquaintance with space and time. Just in that process of relation to an individual, the order falls apart into the distinct manifestations of space and time. An individual is a four-dimensional object of greatly elongated form; in ordinary language we say that he has considerable extension in time and insignificant extension in space. Practically he is represented by a line – his track through the world. When the world is related to such an individual, his own asymmetry is introduced into the relation; and that order of events which is parallel with his track, that is to say with *himself*, appears in his experience to be differentiated from all other orders of events.

10.7   Albert Einstein, *The Meaning of Relativity: Four Lectures Delivered at Princeton University*, May 1921 (translated by Edwin Plimpton Adams, 1922)

The German-born physicist Einstein (1879–1955) was actually working in a patents office in Switzerland when he made the discoveries which have revolutionized our understanding of mechanics, space, and time. Something of a self-taught thinker, Einstein published in 1905 a paper 'On the Electrodynamics of Moving Bodies', which contained his so-called 'Special Theory of Relativity'. Einstein had realized that the Newtonian laws of physics, which had been accepted as 'true' for hundreds of years, suffered from fundamental flaws. These laws, as they affect space and time, presume that two distant events occur simultaneously. But this is only so, as Einstein pointed out, because our understanding of distance is derived from the limited measurements we can make on our own planet. If we think in terms of vastly greater distances, then that notion of simultaneity undergoes odd changes. Light leaving a distant star at this moment, for instance, will only reach earth in fifty or so years' time. Einstein's 'Special Theory', therefore, seeks to account for the fact that both time and space are needed to understand the relation between a fixed point of view, and a rapidly moving object. In fact, it is no longer possible to speak of 'time' and 'space' as distinct entities – we need now to think in terms, as the Eddington extract above suggests, of a fourth dimension, or 'space-time'. From 1907, still at the patents office, Einstein began to problematize his own solution in the 'Special Theory', and to think about what happens if both objects involved in a measurement are moving rapidly and randomly. The way of obtaining this measurement, which was called 'The General Theory of Relativity', was published in 1916, by which time Einstein was well established on his academic (and widely travelled) career. The Princeton lectures excerpted here are helpful in that they give, in part, Einstein's own account of his progress towards his final discoveries in this field.

['Space and Time in Pre-Relativity Physics'] The theory of relativity is intimately connected with the theory of space and time. I shall therefore begin with a brief investigation of the origin of our ideas of space and time, although in doing so I know that I introduce a controversial subject. The object of all science, whether natural science or psychology, is to co-ordinate our experiences and to bring them into a logical system. How are our customary ideas of space and time related to the character of our experiences?

The experiences of an individual appear to us arranged in a series of events; in this series the single events which we remember appear to be ordered according to the criterion of 'earlier' and 'later', which cannot be analysed further. There exists, therefore, for the individual, an I-time, or subjective time. This in itself is not measurable. I can, indeed, associate numbers with the events, in such a way that a greater number is associated with the later event than with an earlier one; but the nature of this association might be quite arbitrary. This association I can define by means of a clock by comparing the order of events furnished by the clock with the order of the given series of events. We understand by a clock something which provides a series of events which can be counted, and which has other properties of which we shall speak later.

By the aid of speech different individuals can, to a certain extent, compare their experiences. In this way it is shown that certain sense perceptions of different individuals correspond to each other, while for other sense perceptions no such correspondence can be established. We are accustomed to regard as real those sense perceptions which are common to different individuals, and which therefore are, in a measure, impersonal. The natural sciences, and in particular, the most fundamental of them, physics, deal with such sense perceptions. The conception of physical bodies, in particular of rigid bodies, is a relatively constant complex of such sense perceptions. A clock is also a body, or a system, in the same sense, with the additional property that the series of events which it counts is formed of elements all of which can be regarded as equal.

The only justification for our concepts and system of concepts is that they serve to represent the complex of our experiences; beyond this they have no legitimacy. I am convinced that the philosophers have had a harmful effect upon the progress of scientific thinking in removing certain fundamental concepts from the domain of empiricism, where they are under our control, to the intangible heights of *a priori*. For even if it should appear that the universe of ideas cannot be deduced from experience by logical means, but is, in a sense, a creation of the human mind, without which no science is possible, nevertheless this universe of ideas is just as little independent of the nature of our experiences as clothes are of the form of the human body. This is particularly true of our concepts of time and space, which physicists have been obliged by the facts to bring down from the Olympus of the *a priori* in order to adjust them and put them in a serviceable condition. . . .

The earth's crust plays such a dominant role in our daily life in judging the relative positions of bodies that it has led to an abstract conception of space which certainly cannot be defended. In order to free ourselves from this fatal error we shall speak only of 'bodies of reference', or 'space of reference'. It is only through the theory of general relativity that refinement of these concepts became necessary, as we shall see later.

It is assumed in pre-relativity physics that the laws of the orientation of ideal rigid bodies are consistent with Euclidean geometry. . . . Involved in this assumption there are some which are rather less special, to which we must call attention on account of their fundamental significance. In the first place, it is assumed that one can move an ideal rigid body in an arbitrary manner. In the second place, it is assumed that the behaviour of ideal rigid bodies towards orientation is independent of the material of the bodies and their changes of position, in the sense that if two intervals can once be brought into coincidence, they can always and everywhere be brought into coincidence. Both of these assumptions, which are of fundamental importance for geometry and especially for physical measurements, naturally arise from experience; in the theory of general relativity their validity needs to be assumed only for bodies and spaces of reference which are infinitely small compared to astronomical dimensions.

['The Theory of Special Relativity']   The previous considerations concerning the configuration of rigid bodies have been founded, irrespective of the assumption as to the validity of the Euclidean geometry, upon the hypothesis that all directions in space, or all configurations of Cartesian systems of co-ordinates, are physically equivalent. We may express this as the 'principle of relativity with respect to direction,' and it has been shown how equations (laws of nature) may be found, in accord with this principle. . . . We now inquire whether there is a relativity with respect to the state of motion of the space of reference; in other words, whether there are spaces of reference in motion relatively to each other which are physically equivalent. From the standpoint of mechanics it appears that equivalent spaces of reference do exist. For experiments upon the earth tell us nothing of the fact that we are moving about the sun with a velocity of approximately 30 kilometres a second. On the other hand, this physical equivalence does not seem to hold for spaces of reference in arbitrary motion; for mechanical effects do not seem to be subject to the same laws in a jolting railway train as in one moving with uniform velocity; the rotation of the earth must be considered in writing down the equations of motion relatively to the earth. It appears, therefore, as if there were Cartesian systems of co-ordinates, the so-called inertial systems, with reference to which the laws of mechanics (more generally the laws of physics) are expressed in the simplest form. We may infer the validity of the following theorem: if K is an inertial system, then every other system K^1 which moves uniformly and without rotation relatively to K, is also an inertial system; the laws of nature are in concordance with all inertial systems. This statement we shall call the 'principle of special relativity'.

. . . It follows from what has gone before, that co-ordinates with respect to an inertial system are physically defined by means of measurements and constructions with the aid of rigid bodies. In order to measure time, we have supposed a clock . . . present somewhere, at rest relatively to K. But we cannot fix the time, by means of this clock, of an event whose distance from the clock is not negligible; for there are no 'instantaneous signals' that we can use in order to compare the time of the event with that of the clock. . . . The assumption which was made in pre-relativity physics of the absolute character of time (i.e. the independence of time of the choice of the inertial system) does not follow at all from this definition.

['The General Theory of Relativity'] All of the previous considerations have been based upon the assumption that all inertial systems are equivalent for the description of physical phenomena, but that they are preferred, for the formulation of the laws of nature, to spaces of reference in a different state of motion. We can think of no cause for this preference for definite states of motion to all others, according to our previous considerations, either in the perceptible bodies or in the concept of motion; on the contrary, it must be regarded as an independent property of the space-time continuum. The principle of inertia, in particular, seems to compel us to ascribe physically objective properties to the space-time continuum. Just as it was necessary from the Newtonian standpoint to make both statements, *tempus est absolutum, spatium est absolutum*,[2] so from the standpoint of the special theory of relativity we must say, *continuum spatii et temporis est absolutum*.[3] In the latter statement *absolutum* means not only 'physically real', but also 'independent in its physical properties, having a physical effect, but not itself influenced by physical conditions.'

As long as the principle of inertia is regarded as the keystone of physics, this standpoint is certainly the only one which is justified.

What justifies us in dispensing with the preference for inertial systems over all other co-ordinate systems, a preference that seems so securely established by experience based upon the principle of inertia? The weakness of the principle of inertia lies in this, that it involves an argument in a circle: a mass moves without acceleration if it is sufficiently far from other bodies only by the fact that it moves without acceleration. Are there, in general, any inertial systems for very

---

2 Time is absolute, space is absolute.
3 The continuum of space and time is absolute.

extended portions of the space-time continuum, or, indeed, for the whole universe? We may look upon the principle of inertia as established, to a high degree of approximation, for the space of our planetary system, provided that we neglect the perturbations due to the sun and planets. Stated more exactly, there are finite regions, where, with respect to a suitably chosen space of reference, material particles move freely without acceleration, and in which laws of the special theory of relativity . . . hold with remarkable accuracy. Such regions we shall call 'Galilean regions'. . . .

The principle of equivalence demands that in dealing with Galilean regions we may equally well make use of non-inertial systems, that is, such co-ordinate systems as, relatively to inertial systems, are not free from acceleration and rotation. If, further, we are going to do away completely with the difficult question as to the objective reason for the preference of certain systems of co-ordinates, then we must allow the use of arbitrarily moving systems of co-ordinates. As soon as we make this attempt seriously we come into conflict with that physical interpretation of space and time to which we were led by the special theory of relativity.

10.8   Bertrand Russell, *ABC of Relativity* (1925)

Russell (1872–1970) was a philosopher with a social conscience. A Fellow at Cambridge from the 1890s, he was imprisoned and dismissed from his Fellowship during the First World War because of his strong objection to the conflict. He became a migrant teacher until 1944, when he was given back his Fellowship at Trinity. Himself a collaborator with his tutor, A. N. Whitehead, he later himself worked to support his own student, Ludwig Wittgenstein. A friend and patron of T. S. Eliot during the years of the first war (he had been impressed by Eliot when he met him on a visit to Harvard where the young poet was a student), Russell himself eventually won the Nobel Prize for Literature. During the years of his exile from Cambridge, he wrote several popular works on philosophy and science, where his lucid style enabled him to convey complex materials compellingly. These extracts help us further understand various aspects of Einstein's theories and their relevance in the everyday.

The question of time in different places is perhaps, for the imagination, the most difficult aspect of the theory of relativity. We are accustomed to the idea that everything can be dated. Historians make use of the fact that there was an eclipse of the sun visible in China on August 29th, in the year 776BC. No doubt astronomers could tell the exact hour and minute when the eclipse began to be total at any given spot in North China. And it seems obvious that we can speak of the positions of the planets at a given instant. The Newtonian theory enables us to calculate the distance between the earth and (say) Jupiter at a given time by the Greenwich clocks; this enables us to know how long light takes at that time to travel from Jupiter to the earth – say half an hour; this enables us to infer that half an hour ago Jupiter was where we see it now. All this seems obvious. But in fact it only works in practice because the relative velocities of the planets are very small compared with the velocity of light. When you judge that an event on the earth and an event on Jupiter have happened at the same time – for example that Jupiter eclipsed one of its moons when the Greenwich clocks showed twelve midnight – a person moving rapidly relatively to the earth would judge differently, assuming that both had made the proper allowance for the velocity of light. And naturally the disagreement about simultaneity involves a disagreement about periods of time. If we judged that events on Jupiter were separated by twenty-four hours, another person, moving rapidly relatively to Jupiter and the earth, might judge that they were separated by a longer time.

The universal cosmic time which used to be taken for granted is thus no longer admissible. For each body, there is a definite time-order for the events in its neighbourhood; this may be called the 'proper' time for that body. Our own experience is governed by the proper time of our own body. As we all remain very nearly stationary on the earth, the proper times of different human beings agree, and can be lumped together as terrestrial time. But this is only the time appropriate to *large* bodies on the earth. For electrons in laboratories, quite different times would be wanted; it is because we insist upon using our own time that these particles seem to increase in mass with rapid motion. From our own point of view, their mass remains constant, and it is we who suddenly grow thin or corpulent. The history of a physicist as observed by an electron would resemble Gulliver's travels.

The question now arises: what really is measured by a clock? When we speak of a clock in the theory of relativity, we do not mean only clocks made by human hands: we mean everything which goes through some regular periodic performance. The earth is a clock, because it rotates once in every twenty-three hours and fifty-six minutes. An atom is a clock, because it emits light-waves of very definite frequencies; these are visible as bright lines in the spectrum of the atom. The world is full of periodic occurrences, and fundamental mechanisms, such as atoms, show an extraordinary similarity in different parts of the universe. Any one of these periodic occurrences may be used for measuring time; the only advantage of humanly manufactured clocks is that they are specially easy to observe. However, some of the others are more accurate. Nowadays the standard of time is based on the frequency of a particular oscillation of caesium atoms, which is much more uniform than one based on the earth's rotation. But the question remains: If cosmic time is abandoned, what is really measured by a clock in the wide sense that we have just given of the term?

Each clock gives a correct measure of its own 'proper' time, which . . . is an important physical quantity. But it does not give an accurate measure of any physical quantity connected with events on bodies that are moving rapidly in relation to it. It gives one datum towards the discovery of a physical quantity connected with such events, but another datum is required, and this has to be derived from measurement of distances in space. Distances in space, like periods of time, are in general not objective physical facts, but partly dependent upon the observer.

. . . we have to think of the distance between two events, not between two bodies. This follows at once from what we have found as regards time. If two bodies are moving relatively to each other – and this is really always the case – the distance between them will be continually changing, so that we can only speak of the distance between them at a given time.

The old separation of space and time rested upon the belief that there was no ambiguity in saying that two events in distant places happened at the same time; consequently it was thought that we could describe the topography of the universe at a given instant in purely spatial terms. But now that simultaneity has become relative to a particular observer, this is no longer possible. What is, for one observer, a description of the state of the world at a given instant is, for another observer, a series of events at various different times, whose relations are not merely spatial but also temporal. For the same reason, we are concerned with *events*, rather than with *bodies*. In the old theory, it was possible to consider a number of bodies all at the same instant, and since the time was the same for all of them it could be ignored. But now we cannot do that if we are to obtain an objective account of physical occurrences. We must mention the date at which a body is to be considered, and thus we arrive at an 'event', that is to say, something which happens at a given time. When we know the time and place of an event in one observer's system of reckoning, we can calculate its time and place according to another observer. But we must know the time as well as the place, because we can no longer ask what is its place for the new observer at the 'same' time as for the old observer.

Bibliography and Further Reading

Useful Websites

historyguide.org/Europe/modernism.html
www.iwm.org.uk
www.modjourn.brown.edu
nationalarchives.gov.uk
http://thecriticalpoet.tripodcom/modernism

General Studies of Modernism

Ardis, Ann L., *Modernism and Cultural Conflict, 1880–1922* (Cambridge: Cambridge University Press, 2002).

Berman, Marshall, *All That is Solid Melts into Air: The Experience of Modernity* (New York: Simon & Schuster, 1982).

Bradbury, Malcolm and McFarlane, James (eds), *Modernism, 1890–1930* (Harmondsworth: Penguin, 1976).

Bradshaw, David (ed.), *A Concise Companion to Modernism* (Oxford: Blackwell, 2003).

—— and Dettmar, Kevin J. H. (eds), *A Companion to Modernist Literature and Culture* (Oxford: Blackwell, 2006).

Burger, Peter, *Theory of the Avant-Garde* (Minneapolis: University of Minnesota Press, 1986).

Burwick, Frederick and Douglass, Paul (eds), *The Crisis of Modernism* (Cambridge: Cambridge University Press, 1992).

Chiari, Joseph, *The Aesthetics of Modernism* (London: Vision, 1970).

Clarke, T. J., *Farewell to an Idea: Episodes from a History of Modernism* (New Haven, CT: Yale University Press, 1999).

Ellmann, Richard and Fiedelson, Charles (eds), *The Modern Tradition: Backgrounds of Modern Literature* (London: Oxford University Press, 1965).

Goldman, Jane, *Modernism, 1910–1945: Image to Apocalypse* (Basingstoke: Palgrave Macmillan, 2004).

Kenner, Hugh, *The Pound Era* ((Berkeley: University of California Press, 1971).

—— *A Homemade World: The American Modernist Writer* (New York: Alfred A. Knopf, 1988).

Levenson, Michael, *A Genealogy of Modernism: A Study of English Literary Doctrine* (Cambridge: Cambridge University Press, 1984).

—— (ed.), *The Cambridge Companion to Modernism* (Cambridge: Cambridge University Press, 1999).

Longenbach, James, *Stone Cottage: Pound, Yeats and Modernism* (Oxford: Oxford University Press, 1988).

Matthews, Steven, *Modernism: Contexts in Literature* (London: Edward Arnold, 2004).

Nicholls, Peter, *Modernisms: A Literary Guide* (Basingstoke: Macmillan, 1995).

Perloff, Marjorie, *The Poetics of Indeterminacy: Rimbaud to Cage* (Princeton, NJ: Princeton University Press, 1981).

Quinones, Ricardo, *Mapping Literary Modernism* (Princeton, NJ: Princeton University Press, 1985).

Stead, C. K., *Pound, Yeats, Eliot and the Modernist Movement* (Basingstoke: Macmillan, 1986).

Historical Events

Adams, R. J. Q. and Poirier, Philip P., *The Conscription Controversy in Great Britain, 1900–1918* (Basingstoke: Macmillan, 1987).

Atkin, Jonathan, *A War of Individuals: Bloomsbury Attitudes to the Great War* (Manchester: Manchester University Press, 2002).

Bergonzi, Bernard, *Heroes' Twilight: A Study of the Literature of the Great War* (London: Constable, 1965).

Booth, Allyson, *Postcards from the Trenches: Negotiating the Space between Modernism and the First World War* (New York: Oxford University Press, 1996).

Buitenhuis, Peter, *The Great War of Words: Literature as Propaganda, 1914–18 and After* (London: Batsford, 1989).

Cecil, Hugh, *The Flower of Battle: British Fiction Writers of the First World War* (London: Secker & Warburg, 1995).

Cole, Sarah, *Modernism, Male Friendship, and the First World War* (Cambridge: Cambridge University Press, 2003).

Coogan, Tim Pat, *1916: The Easter Rising* (London: Cassell, 2001).

Costello, Francis J., *The Irish Revolution and its Aftermath* (Dublin: Irish Academic Press, 2003).

Degroot, Gerard, *Blighty: British Society in the Era of the Great War* (Harlow: Longman, 1996).

Delany, Paul, *D. H. Lawrence's Nightmare: The Writer and his Circle in the Years of the Great War* (Hassocks: Harvester, 1979).

Eksteins, Modris, *Rites of Spring: The Great War and the Birth of the Modern Age* (London: Bantam Press, 1989).

Fishbein, Leslie, *Rebels in Bohemia: The Radicals of the Masses, 1911–1917* (Chapel Hill: University of North Carolina Press, 1982).

Foy, Michael and Barton, Brian, *The Easter Rising* (Stroud: Sutton, 1999).

Fussell, Paul, *The Great War and Modern Memory* (Oxford: Oxford University Press, 1975).

Goldman, Dorothy, *Women and World War I: The Written Response* (Basingstoke: Macmillan, 1993).

Hynes, Samuel, *A War Imagined: The First World War and English Culture* (London: Bodley Head, 1990).

Jones, Margaret C., *Heretics and Hellraisers: Women Contributors to 'The Masses', 1911–1917* (Austin: University of Texas Press, 1993).

Levenback, Karen L., *Virginia Woolf and the Great War* (Syracuse, NY: Syracuse University Press, 1999).

Mac Lochlainn, Piaras F., *Last Words: Letters and Statements of the Leaders Executed after the Rising at Easter 1916* (Dublin: Stationery Office, 1990).

Marwick, Arthur, *The Deluge: British Society and the First World War* (Basingstoke: Macmillan, 1991).

O Dubhghaill, M., *Insurrection Fires at Eastertide: A Golden Jubilee Anthology of the Easter Rising* (Cork: Mercier Press, 1966).

Ouditt, Sharon, *Fighting Forces, Writing Women: Identity and Ideology in the First World War* (London: Routledge, 1994).

Parfitt, George, *Fiction of the First World War* (London: Faber & Faber, 1988).

Quinn, Patrick and Trout, Steven, *The Literature of the Great War Reconsidered: Beyond Modern Memory* (Basingstoke: Palgrave Macmillan, 2001).

Raitt, Suzanne and Tate, Trudi, *Women's Fiction and the Great War* (Oxford: Clarendon Press, 1997).

Sherry, Vincent B., *The Great War and the Language of Modernism* (Oxford: Oxford University Press, 2003).

Strachan, Hew, *The First World War: The Call to Arms* (Oxford: Oxford University Press, 2000).

Tate, Trudi, *Modernism, History, and the First World War* (Manchester: Manchester University Press, 1998).

Winter, J. M., *The Great War and the British People* (Basingstoke: Macmillan, 1986)

Society, Politics and Class

Berman, J. S., *Modernist Fiction, Cosmopolitanism, and the Politics of Community* (Cambridge: Cambridge University Press, 2001).

Collini, Stefan, *Liberalism and Sociology: L. T. Hobhouse and Political Argument in England, 1880–1914* (Cambridge: Cambridge University Press, 1979).

Davis, John, *A History of Britain, 1885–1939* (Basingstoke: Macmillan, 1999).

Ferrall, Charles, *Modernist Writing and Reactionary Politics* (Cambridge: Cambridge University Press, 2001).

Foster, Roy, *Modern Ireland, 1600–1972* (Harmondsworth: Penguin, 1989).

Harris, Jose, *Private Lives, Public Spirit: Britain, 1870–1914* (Harmondsworth: Penguin, 1994).

Stevenson, John, *British Society, 1914–1945* (Harmondsworth: Penguin, 1994).

Tratner, Michael, *Modernism and Mass Politics: Joyce, Woolf, Eliot, Yeats* (Standford, CA: Standford University Press, 1995).

Williams, Louise Blakeney, *Modernism and the Ideology of History: Literature, Politics, and the Past* (Cambridge: Cambridge University Press, 2002).

Williams, Raymond, *Culture and Society, 1780–1950* (New York: Columbia University Press, 1958).

——, *The Politics of Modernism: Against the New Conformists* (London: Verso, 1989).

Gender and Sexuality

Alberti, Johanna, *Beyond Suffrage: Feminists in War and Peace* (Basingstoke: Macmillan, 1989).

Atkinson, Diane, *Votes for Women* (Cambridge: Cambridge University Press, 1988).

Baker, Jean H., *Votes for Women: The Struggle for Suffrage Revisited*, Viewpoints on American Culture (Oxford: Oxford University Press, 2002).

Benstock, Shari, *Women of the Left Bank, Paris, 1900–1940* (Austin: University of Texas Press, 1986).

Bland, Lucy, *Banishing the Beast: English Feminism and Sexual Morality, 1885–1914* (London: Penguin, 1995).

Boone, Joseph Allen, *Libidinal Currents: Sexuality and the Shaping of Modernism* (Chicago: University of Chicago Press, 1998).

Burdett, Carolyn, *Olive Schreiner and the Progress of Feminism: Evolution, Gender, Empire* (Basingstoke: Macmillan, 2001).

Carpenter, Edward, *The Intermediate Sex: A Study of Some Transitional Types of Men and Women* (Manchester: S. Clarke, 1909).

DeKoven, Marianne, *Rich and Strange: Gender, History, Modenism* (Princeton: Princeton University Press, 1991).

Felski, Rita, *The Gender of Modernity* (Cambridge, MA: Harvard University Press, 1996).

Gilbert, Sandra and Gubar, Susan, *No Man's Land,* volumes I–III (New Haven, CT: Yale University Press, 1988–1994).

Hall, Lesley A., *Hidden Anxieties: Male Sexuality, 1900–1950* (London: Polity Press, 1991).

Marcus, Jane, *Suffrage and the Pankhursts* (London: Routledge, 1987).

Miller, Jane Eldridge, *Rebel Women: Feminism, Modernism, and the Edwardian Novel* (London: Virago, 1994).

Pankhurst, E. Sylvia, *The Suffrage Movement: An Intimate Account of Persons and Ideals* (London: Longmans, Green, 1931).

Rowbotham, S., *A World of New Women: Stella Brown, Socialist Feminist* (London: Pluto Press, 1977).

Sanger, Margaret, *An Autobiography* (London: Victor Gollancz, 1939).

Scott, Bonnie Kime (ed.), *The Gender of Modernism: A Critical Anthology* (Bloomington: Indiana University Press, 1990).

——, *Refiguring Modernism*, 2 vols (Bloomington: Indiana University Press, 1995).

Showalter, Elaine, *Sexual Anarchy: Gender and Culture at the Fin de Siècle* (London: Virago, 1990).

Souhami, Diana, *The Trials of Radclyffe Hall* (London: Virago, 1999).

Stevens, Hugh and Howlett, Caroline (eds), *Modernist Sexualities* (Manchester: Manchester University Press, 2000).

Thormahlen, Marianne (ed), *Rethinking Modernism* (Basingstoke: Palgrave Macmillan, 2003).

Religion and Belief

Bell, Michael, *Primitivism* (London: Methuen, 1972).

——, *Literature, Modernism, and Myth* (Cambridge: Cambridge University Press, 1997).

Crawford, Robert, *The Savage and the City in the Work of T. S. Eliot* (Oxford: Clarendon Press, 1987).

Fraser, Robert (ed.), *Sir James Frazer and the Literary Imagination* (London: Macmillan, 1990).

Manganaro, Marc (ed.), *Modernist Anthropology: From Fieldwork to Text* (Princeton, NJ: Princeton University Press, 1990).

Vickery, John B., *The Literary Impact of the 'Golden Bough'* (Princeton, NJ: Princeton University Press, 1972).

Wright, T.R., *D.H. Lawrence and the Bible* (Cambridge: Cambridge University Press, 2000).

Philosophy and Ideas

Antliff, Mark, *Inventing Bergson* (Princeton, NJ: Princeton University Press, 1993).

Deleuze, Gilles, *Bergsonism* (New York: Zone Books, 1988).

Foster, John Burt, *Heirs to Dionysus* (Princeton, NJ: Princeton University Press, 1981).

Gilles, Mary Ann, *Henri Bergson and British Modernism* (Montreal: McGill-Queen's University Press, 1996).

Lindberg, Katherine V., *Reading Pound Reading: Modernism after Nietzsche* (Oxford: Oxford University Press, 1987).

Milton, Colin, *Lawrence and Nietzsche* (Aberdeen: Aberdeen University Press, 1987).

Pippin, Robert B., *Modernism as a Philosophical Problem* (Oxford: Blackwell, 1991).

Putz, Manfred (ed.), *Nietzsche in American Literature and Thought* (Columbia, MO: Camden House, 1995).

Quirk, Tom, *Bergson and American Culture* (Chapel Hill: University of South Carolina Press, 1990).

Schwartz, Sanford, *The Matrix of Modernism: Pound, Eliot, and Early Twentieth-Century Thought* (Princeton, NJ: Princeton University Press, 1985).

'High' Culture

Agee, William C., Morrin, Peter and Zilczer, Judith, *The Advent of Modernism: Post-Impressionism and North American Art, 1900–1918* (Atlanta, GA: High Museum of Art, 1986).

Albright, Daniel, *Untwisting the Serpent: Modernism in Music, Literature, and Other Arts* (Chicago: University of Chicago Press, 2004).

Altshuler, Bruce, *The Avant-Garde in Exhibition: New Art in the 20th Century* (Berkeley: University of California Press, 1994).

Auner, Joseph, *A Schoenberg Reader: Documents of a Life* (New Haven, CT: Yale University Press, 2003).

Ballantyne, Andrew, *Architectures: Modernism and After* (Oxford: Blackwell, 2004).

Bochner, Jay and Edwards, Justin D., *American Modernism Across the Arts* (New York: Peter Lang, 1999).

Brody, Elaine, *Paris: The Musical Kaleidoscope, 1870–1925* (London: Robson, 1988).

Brown, Milton W., *American Painting from the Armory Show to the Depression* (Princeton, NJ: Princeton University Press, 1995).

——, *The Story of the Armory Show* (New York: Abbeville, 1988).

Butler, Christopher, *Early Modernism: Literature, Music and Painting in Europe, 1900–1916* (Oxford: Clarendon Press, 1994).

Chipp, Herschel B., *Theories of Modern Art: A Source Book by Artists and Critics* (Berkeley: University of California Press, 1969).

Cross, Jonathan, *The Cambridge Companion to Stravinsky* (Cambridge: Cambridge University Press, 2003).

Crunden, Robert Morse, *Body and Soul: The Making of American Modernism* (New York: Basic Books, 2000).

Dahlhaus, Carl, *Schoenberg and the New Music* (Cambridge: Cambridge University Press, 1987).

Dijkstra, Bram, *Cubism, Stieglitz, and the Early Poetry of William Carlos Williams* (Princeton, NJ: Princeton University Press, 1969).

Garafola, Lynn, *Diaghilev's Ballets Russes* (Oxford: Oxford University Press, 1989).

Green, Martin Burgess, *New York 1913: The Armory Show and the Paterson Strike Pageant* (New York: Charles Scribner's, 1988).

Griffiths, Paul, *Stravinsky* (London: Dent, 1992).

Grigoriev, S. L., *The Diaghilev Ballet, 1909–1929* (London: Constable, 1953).

Kiefer, Geraldine W., *Alfred Stieglitz: Scientist, Photographer, and Avatar of Modernism, 1880–1913* (New York: Garland, 1991).

Prince, Sue Ann, *The Old Guard and the Avant-Garde: Modernism in Chicago, 1910–1940* (Chicago: Chicago University Press, 1990).

Rainey, Lawrence, *Institutions of Modernism: Literary Elites and Public Culture* (New Haven, CT: Yale University Press, 1998).

Sheppard, Richard, *Modernism–Dada–Postmodernism* (Evanston, IL: Northwestern University Press, 2000).

Wright, Frank Lloyd, *Collected Writings* (New York: Rizzoli, 1992).

'Popular' Culture

Bailey, Peter, *Music Hall: The Business of Pleasure* (Milton Keynes: Open University Press, 1986).

Baker, Claude and Chase, Chris, *Josephine: The Hungry Heart* (New York: Random House, 1993).

Baker, Richard Anthony, *Marie Lloyd: Queen of the Music Halls* (London: R. Hale, 1990).

Barkan, Elazar and Bush, Ronald, *Prehistories of the Future: The Primitivist Project and the Culture of Modernism* (Stanford, CA: Stanford University Press, 1995).

Bloom, Clive, *Literature and Culture in Modern Britain*, Volume One: *1900–1929* (London: Longman, 1993).

Bordman, Gerald, *American Musical Theatre: A Chronicle* (Oxford: Oxford University Press, 2001).

Bratlinger, Patrick, *Bread and Circuses: Theories of Mass Culture as Social Decay* (Ithaca: Cornell University Press, 1983).

Cantor, Norman F. and Werthman, Michael S., *The History of Popular Culture* (New York: Macmillan, 1968).

Charney, Leo and Schwartz, Vanessa R., *Cinema and the Invention of Modern Life* (Berkeley: University of California Press, 1995).

Coyle, Michael, *Ezra Pound, Popular Genres, and the Discourse of Culture* (University Park: Pennsylvania University Press, 1995).

Hall, Carolyn, *The Twenties in Vogue* (London: Octopus Books, 1983).

Huyssen, Andreas, *After the Great Divide: Modernism, Mass Culture, Postmodernism* (Basingstoke: Macmillan, 1986).

Kammen, Michael, *The Lively Arts: Gilbert Seldes and the Transformation of Cultural Criticism* (New York: Oxford University Press, 1996).

Leonard, Neil, *Jazz and the White Americans: The Acceptance of a New Art Form* (Chicago: Chicago University Press, 1962).

Levine, Lawrence W., *Highbrow/Lowbrow: The Emergence of Cultural Hierarchy in America* (Cambridge, MA: Harvard University Press, 1988).

May, Lary, *Screening Out the Past: The Birth of Mass Culture and the Motion Picture Industry* (Oxford: Oxford University Press, 1980).

North, Michael, *The Dialect of Modernism: Race, Language and Twentieth-Century Literature* (Oxford: University Press, 1994).

——, *Reading 1922: A Return to the Scene of the Modern* (Oxford: Oxford University Press, 1999).

Pease, Allison, *Modernism, Mass Culture, and the Aesthetics of Obscenity* (Cambridge: Cambridge University Press, 2000).

Strychacz, Thomas, *Modernism, Mass Culture, and Professionalism* (Cambridge: Cambridge University Press, 1993).

Literary Production and Reception

Bornstein, George, *Material Modernism: The Politics of the Page* (Cambridge: Cambridge University Press, 2001).

Carey, John, *The Intellectuals and the Masses* (London: Faber, 1992).

Caws, Mary Ann, *Reading Frames in Modern Fiction* (Princeton, NJ: Princeton University Press, 1985).

Dettmar, Kevin J. H. (ed.), *Rereading the New: A Backward Glance at Modernism* (Ann Arbor: University of Michigan Press, 1992).

—— and Watts, Stephen (eds), *Marketing Modernisms: Self-Promotion, Canonization, Rereading* (Ann Arbor: University of Michigan Press, 1996).

Marek, Jayne, *Women Editing Modernism: 'Little' Magazines and Literary History* (Lexington: University of Kentucky Press, 1995).

McAleer, Joseph, *Popular Reading and Publishing in Britain, 1914–1950* (Oxford: Clarendon Press, 1992).

McDonald, Peter D., *British Literary Culture and Publishing Practice, 1880–1914* (Cambridge: Cambridge University Press, 1997).

Parkes, Adam, *Modernism and the Theater of Censorship* (New York: Oxford University Press, 1996).

Travis, Molly Abel, *Reading Cultures: The Construction of Readers in the Twentieth Century* (Carbondale: Southern Illinois University Press, 1998).

Empire, Race and Postcolonialism

Baker, Houston A. Jr., *Modernism and the Harlem Renaissance* (Chicago: Chicago University Press, 1987).

Boehmer, Elleke, *Colonial and Postcolonial Literature* (Oxford: Oxford University Press, 1995).

——, *Empire, the National, and the Postcolonial, 1890–1920* (Oxford: Oxford University Press, 2002).

Booth, Howard J. and Rigby, Nigel (eds), *Modernism and Empire* (Manchester: Manchester University Press, 2000).

Cairns, David and Richards, Shaun, *Writing Ireland: Colonialism, Nationalism, and Culture* (Manchester: Manchester University Press, 1988).

Castle, Gregory, *Modernism and the Celtic Revival* (Cambridge: Cambridge University Press, 2001).

Chaudhuri, Amit, *D. H. Lawrence and 'Difference'* (Oxford: Oxford University Press, 2002).

Cullingford, Elizabeth, *Yeats, Ireland and Fascism* (Basingstoke: Macmillan, 1984).

De Jongh, James, *Vicious Modernism: Black Harlem and the Literary Imagination* (New York: Cambridge University Press, 1990).

Douglas, Ann, *Terrible Honesty: Mongrel Manhattan in the 1920s* (New York: Farrar, Straus and Giroux, 1995).

Gikandi, Simon, *Writing in Limbo* (Ithaca, NY: Cornell University Press, 1992).

Gurr, Andrew, *Writers in Exile: The Identity of Home in Modern Literature* (Brighton: Harvester, 1981).

Heyward, Michael, *The Ern Malley Affair* (London: Faber, 1993).

Hobsbaum, Eric, *The Age of Empire, 1875–1914* (London: Weidenfeld and Nicolson, 1987).

Michaels, Walter Benn, *Our America: Nativism, Modernism, and Pluralism* (Durham, NC: Duke University Press, 1995).

Parry, Benita, *Conrad and Imperialism* (Basingstoke: Macmillan, 1983).

Science and Technology

Armstrong, Tim, *Modernism, Technology and the Body: A Cultural Study* (Cambridge: Cambridge University Press, 1998).

Bell, Ian F. A., *Critic as Scientist: The Modernist Poetics of Ezra Pound* (London: Metheun, 1981).

Childs, Donald J., *Modernism and Eugenics: Woolf, Eliot, Yeats and the Culture of Degeneration* (Cambridge: Cambridge University Press, 2001).

Daly, Nicholas, *Literature, Technology, and Modernity, 1860–2000* (Cambridge: Cambridge University Press, 2004).

Danius, Sarah, *The Senses of Modernism: Technology, Perception, and Aesthetics* (Ithaca, NY: Cornell University Press, 2002).

Greenslade, William, *Degeneration, Culture, and the Novel, 1880–1940* (Cambridge: Cambridge University Press, 1994).

Kern, Stephen, *The Culture of Time and Space, 1880–1918* (Cambridge, MA: Harvard University Press, 1983).

Ross, Dorothy (ed.), *Modernism: Impulses in the Human Sciences, 1870–1930* (Baltimore, MD: Johns Hopkins University Press, 1994).

Ryan, Judith, *The Vanishing Subject: Early Psychology and Literary Modernism* (Chicago: Chicago University Press, 1991).

Steinman, Lisa, *Made in America: Science, Technology, and American Modernist Poetics* (New Haven, CT: Yale University Press, 1987).

Vargish, Thomas and Mook, Delo E., *Inside Modernism: Relativity Theory, Cubism, Narrative* (New Haven, CT: Yale University Press, 1999).

Whitworth, Michael H., *Einstein's Wake: Relativity, Metaphor, and Modernist Literature* (Oxford: Oxford University Press, 2001).

Index